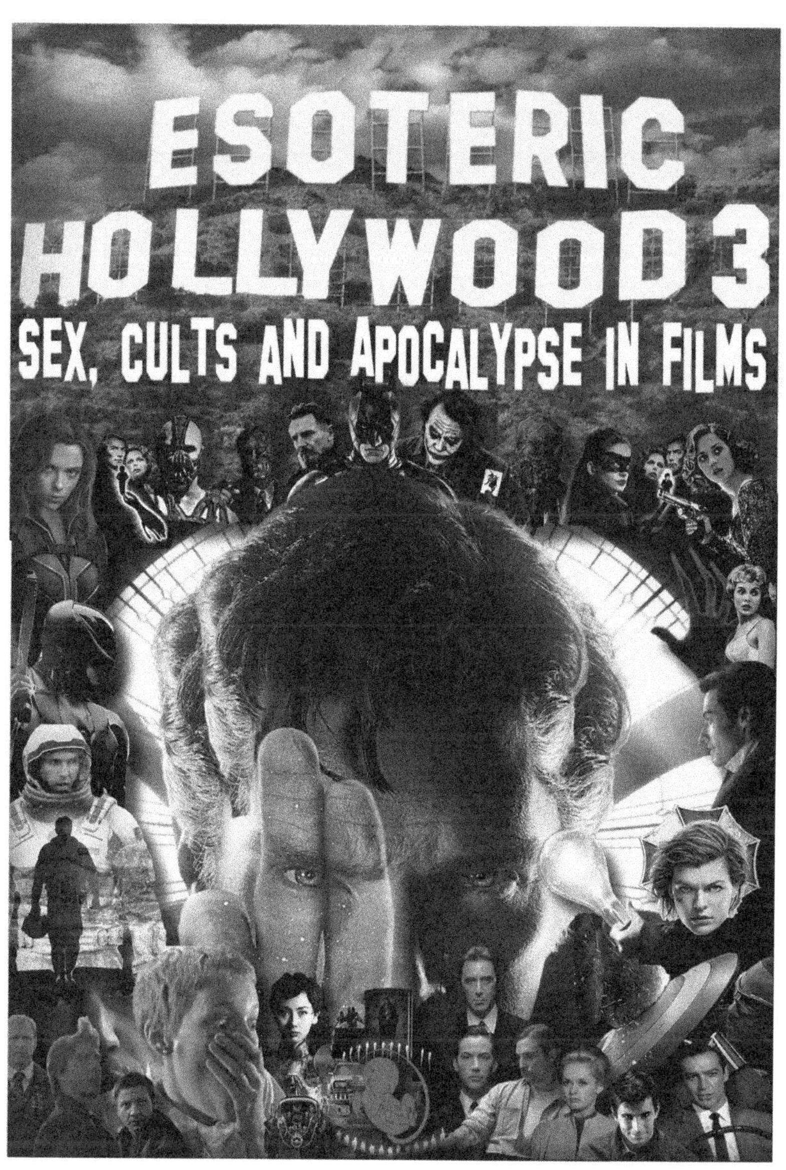

ESOTERIC
HOLLYWOOD 3
SEX, CULTS AND APOCALYPSE IN FILMS
Jay Dyer

Esoteric Hollywood 3: Sex, Cults and Apocalypse in Films
Copyright © 2025 Jay Dyer All Rights Reserved
Published by:
Trine Day LLC
PO Box 577
Walterville, OR 97489
1-800-556-2012
www.TrineDay.com
publisher@TrineDay.net

Library of Congress Control Number: 2025934838

Dyer, Jay
 — 1st ed.
p. cm.
Includes references
Epub (ISBN-13) 978-1-63424-516-6
Print (ISBN-13) 978-1-63424-515-9
1. Motion picture industry -- California -- Los Angeles. 2. Occultism
-- Political aspects -- United States. 3. Subliminal projection -- United
States. I. Dyer, Jay. II. Title

First Edition
10 9 8 7 6 5 4 3 2 1

Printed in the USA
Distribution to the Trade by:
Independent Publishers Group (IPG)
814 North Franklin Street
Chicago, Illinois 60610
312.337.0747
www.ipgbook.com

Publisher's Foreword

You've always had the power, my dear. You've had it all along.
—Glinda, *The Wizard of Oz*

Of all the gin joints, in all the towns, in all the world, she walks into mine.
—Rick Blaine, *Casablanca*

I am big. It's the pictures that got small.
— Norma Desmond, *Sunset Boulevard*

Dreams are windows into the lives of our multiversal selves.
—Dr. Strange, *Multiverse of Madness*

You're waiting for a train, a train that will take you far away. You know where you hope this train will take you, but you don't know for sure. But it doesn't matter.
—Dominick Cobb, *Inception*

Red Donkey: *You know.… Colonel shoot apes when wall's done.*
Caesar: *His wall is … madness. It will not save him, anymore than it will save you.*
Red Donkey: *I save myself.*
Caesar: *Is there anything left of you to save?*
—*War for the Planet of the Apes*

Time continues to flow, the world keeps turning, beckoning us to follow our noses if not muses. Growing up in the 1950s and coming of age in the 1960s was quite the "trip." We were the first fully televisioned generation. *That "box" has always tbeen here.*

We were entertained by Howdy Doody and his friends Flub-a-Dub, Phineas T. Bluster, Dilly Dally, Clarabell and Princess Summerfall Winterspring. By "Jingles" shouting, "Plunk your magic twange, Froggy," Midnight the cat mouthing "Nice." And so many cartoons: crazy classics and a new crop made especially for this up-and-coming medium.

Then there were the comic books. Boy, did I like comic books. They were frowned upon, but it was cheap entertainment. A dime was all that was needed. Once I had a paper route and my own money I ran headlong into the DC and then later the Marvel Universes. To a kid/teen the outside world was something grown-ups worried about, and rarely infected *our* world. That started crashing down in the Sixties. Our WWII parents who had endured the depression imbibed within us a deep patriotic zeal, which surfaced in interesting ways. We had became aware under grandfatherly Ike, burdened by a festering wound from the public murder of Jack Kennedy and then the ensuing obscenities of the Vietnam "Police Action." The corruption was just begining … something was afoot.

With my paper route came the job of knocking on doors asking for money once a month. A tedious, not-enjoyed part of the job, but it did give me an excuse to get out of the house and go watch movies. There were two theaters a block apart changing shows weekly. *I did a lot of collecting!*

Jay does an excellent job exploring the deeper zeitgeist of film-making, delinating the dark dream-weaving shadows of occult philosophy and rituals within. Is it simply strange art? Sinister science? Sordid sorcery? Sponsored by whom? This third volume in Jay's amazing Esoteric Hollywood series *Esoteric Hollywood 3: Sex, Cults and Apocalypse in Films* goes deeper into his understandings and outlooks into what drives our cinema.

Whilst I grew up with the "boob" tube, Jay, his generation and younger folks have become more and more immersed. There are narratives galore as screen time increasingly takes over more of life's activity: video games, Netflix and all the streaming platforms, computers,tablets and the ubiquitous"smart" phone. Adults now spend almost a third of their time consuming content. It is said you are what you eat. Jay helps us to become aware of what's on the menu.

> *Wait a minute, wait a minute, you ain't heard nothin' yet! Wait a minute, I tell ya! You ain't heard nothin'! You wanna hear "Toot, Toot, Tootsie"? All right, hold on, hold on...*
> — Jack Robin, *The Jazz Singer*

Onward to the Utmost of Futures,
Peace,
R.A. "Kris" Millegan
Publisher
TrineDay
April 16, 2024

CONTENTS

SECTION 3: OBSCURE, INDEPENDENT & B MOVIES WITH A MESSAGE!

SPACE VAMPIRES USING SEX MAGICK & OTHER CROWLEYAN FILMS

DAVID CRONENBERG

MIND CONTROLLED BARRYMORE?

SECTION 4: HOLLYWOOD ALCHEMY & HORROR TRAUMA

HOLLYWOOD AS MAGUS

Given the large amount of analyses written over the last ten years, many of the best were unable to be included in the first two installments. Thankfully, as is usually the case, divine providence worked out for the best as some of the new and redone analyses in this volume are immensely improved due to new information I've uncovered in recent years.

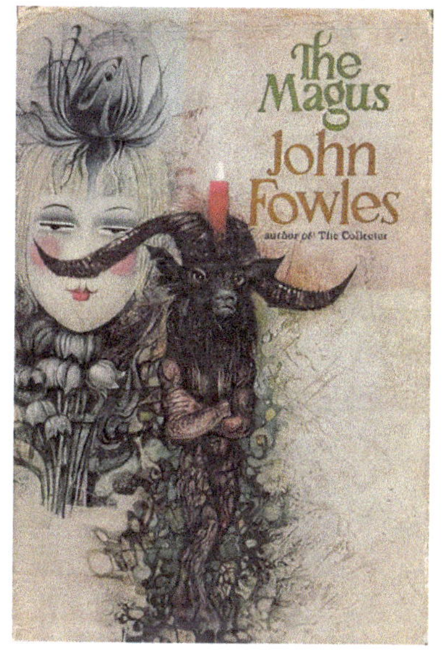

While the classic studio structure of Hollywood has been on a steady course of collapse in recent years, Hollywood mind control and ultimately Hollywood alchemy lives on in the new instantiations of streaming services and the coming metaverse/gaming world. Indeed, the rise of virtual reality and the metaverse were themselves predicted in many Hollywood sci-fi and dystopian productions far earlier than the *Matrix* trilogy analyzed in *Esoteric Hollywood 2*. This completion of the trilogy culminates in an analysis of Hollywood's "Great Work," the alchemical processing of the modern psyche to prepare it for the apocalypse: the end of the era or aeon of how things have been, what we call "normal."

The alchemical apocalypse is about the end of man – and the rise of a new thing: the new man, who is post-human. Thus, many of the analyses in this volume will focus on transformation themes – the comic book takeover and Marvel engineering, highlighting esoteric themes in recent Marvel and D.C. blockbusters, as well as analyzing perhaps today's most famed director, Christoper Nolan's works. These deep dives are followed by a section titled Dystopia Now, where we analyze the most relevant dystopian films often overlooked that contain at times profoundly deep philosophical messages.

Next, we lighten things up a bit with a unique look at obscure and forgotten B movies with a message: they may be low-budget and often campy, but these films will surprise and astound viewers when they watch these with new eyes. Hollywood Horror Trauma is our next section, where films with occult and satanic themes collide with narratives focusing on dissociation and fractured psyches: each of these films will function as microcosm images of what has happened to the culture on the macrocosm level: while Hollywood has not produced many creative positive films of late, they have been busy producing some of the darkest occult films of all time.

Given there are so many insightful organized crime films and television series we have yet to analyze, another section aptly titled Organized Intelligence Crime was necessary to illustrate even more astounding connections between the mafia, intelligence agencies and organized crime. Although I previously covered some Scorsese, it was only scratching the surface. I had overlooked the amazing insights in *Casino*, as well as other Scorcese and Nolan works, it was also necessary to do a deep dive on one of the greatest series of all time, *The Sopranos*!

We conclude this trilogy with an appropriately titled final act: Hollywood Antichrist Apocalypse, where I decode some of the most bizarre, dark and demonic films ever made, with an emphasis on how Hollywood as Babylon has culminated in an synchromystic self-fulfilling prophecy: Hollywood has predicted the end of the world as we know it, as well as participating in that alchemical ritual working.

It seems more and more as if we are living in a bad B movie, replete with cheesy set pieces and a Casio keyboard score – and the reason for that is because we are. We have focused on Hollywood and propaganda often at JaysAnalysis, but we have not looked at the music industry, aside from brief mentions and a few shows. When it comes to the score for that B movie we all live in, the best analysis I've read in a good while is none other than recently deceased Dave McGowan's excellent work, *Weird Scenes Inside the Canyon: Laurel Canyon, Covert Ops & the Dark Heart of the Hippie Dream*. I get emails on a daily basis requesting book recommendations (which is much harder to choose than you'd expect), so I think for the spirit of my site, no better book could be suggested for a reading list than *Weird Scenes* (aside from my own book, of course).

McGowan's thesis is simple: The 1960s counterculture movement was not what it appeared to be. In a purple haze of pot smoke, free love, booze and LSD tabs, the fog of the 60s is believed by most baby-boomers to be a genuine (monstrous for *faux* conservatives) reaction against the system. From student protests to politically active musicians, the anti-war, anti-establishment ethos of the 60s was, so the story goes, a natural, organic reaction to a hawkish, greedy corporate demon, embodied in "the man," opposed by all those revolutionaries who love freedom, expressing themselves in the "arts." After reading McGowan's analysis (a self-confessed fan of this era), it would appear the mainstream view is only slightly correct – some artists were political and genuinely anti-establishment, but the big names, and the movements as a whole, were promoted and directed by design, for large-scale social engineering.

McGowan begins his argument by pointing to Jim Morrison's father, Navy Admiral George Stephen Morrison, who played a central role in the Gulf of Tonkin's false flag event. Morrison, curiously, avoided this association, stating his parents were dead, adding fuel to his mythical narrative of having no musical training and supposedly becoming a musical shaman following ghostly encounters and hallucinogenic trips. While some of that may have been the case (such as the trips and witchcraft initiation, for example, as shown in Oliver Stone's *The Doors*), the real story is likely much closer to McGowan's analysis – Morrison was promoted and made into an icon by the system because of these high level connections. However, being well-connected was not the only explanation – the establishment had a specific motive of derailing any legitimate anti-war activism or artwork, as well as moving the culture into a more degenerate state for social engineering.

Indeed, were the artists and activists of the 60s who became icons of anti-corporatism and fighting the man legitimate, would they have been given major record deals, airtime, major gigs, and expensive advertisements in mainstream magazines? The mainstream narrative of the hippie movement breaks down, once one considers this angle, and McGowan ups the ante even further by noting the hippie movement did not begin at the popularly conceived Haight Ashbury District, but *earlier in Laurel Canyon*. It's the dark underground of Laurel Canyon where the nexus of Hollywood, the occult, the mob and the music industry collide in an orgiastic psychedelia, producing big acts like The Byrds, The Mammas and the Pappas, Zappa, The Doors, and many more.

Further, Jim Morrison was not the only character with a high level military intelligence family, Frank Zappa's father worked for the military in biological warfare, and as I've discussed in relation to John Marks' *The CIA and Mind Control*, LSD was directly associated with Fort Detrick and biological warfare programs.[1] "Managers" and "agents" like Herb Cohen were not merely industry fat cats, but mobsters (connected to Mickey Cohen), while players like John Phillips appear to have been part of CIA covert operations in Cuba. The instances of these infamous details mount up in McGowan's work, and eventually call into question the entire Laurel Canyon scene, replete with underground facilities and a massive, secret film production studio.

After noting Harry Houdini's connection to Laurel Canyon and his role as a spy for Scotland Yard, McGowan reveals one of the best insights missed in most research – Laurel Canyon was home to one of the largest film production studios of its day – run by the Air Force. If that is hard to swallow, the pill becomes much bigger. What would become known as Lookout Mountain Laboratory was originally envisioned as an air defense center.

> "Built in 1941 and nestled in two-and-a-half secluded acres off what is now Wonderland Park Avenue, the installation was hidden from view and surrounded by an electrified fence. By 1947, the facility featured a fully operational movie studio. In fact, it is claimed that it was perhaps the world's only completely self-contained movie studio. With 100,000 square feet of floor space, the covert studio included sound stages, screening rooms, film processing labs, editing facilities, an animation department, and seventeen climate-controlled film vaults. It also had underground parking, a helicopter pad and a bomb shelter:

> "Over its lifetime, the studio produced some 19,000 classified motion pictures – more than all the Hollywood studios combined (which I guess makes Laurel Canyon the real 'motion picture capital of the world'). Officially, the facility was run by the U.S. Air Force and did nothing more nefarious than process AEC footage of atomic and nuclear bomb tests. The studio, however, was clearly equipped to do far more than just process film. There are indications that Lookout Mountain Laboratory had an advanced research and development department that was on the cutting edge of new film technologies. Such technological advances as 3-D effects were apparently first developed at the Laurel Canyon site. And Hollywood luminaries like John Ford, Jimmy Stewart, Howard Hawks, Ronald Reagan, Bing Crosby, Walt Disney and Marilyn Monroe were given clearance to work at the facility on undisclosed projects. There is no indication that any of them ever spoke of their work at the clandestine studio."[2]

The facility retained as many as 250 producers, directors, technicians, editors, animators, etc., both civilian and military, all with top security clearances – and all reporting to work in a secluded corner of Laurel Canyon. Accounts vary as to when the facility ceased operations. Some claim it was in 1969, while others say the installation remained in operation longer. In any event, by all accounts the secret bunker had been up and running for more than twenty years before Laurel Canyon's rebellious teen years, and it remained operational for the most turbulent of those years.

The existence of the facility remained unknown to the general public until the early 1990s, though it had long been rumored that the CIA operated a secret movie studio somewhere in or near Hollywood. Filmmaker Peter Kuran was the first to learn of its existence, through classified documents he obtained while researching his 1995 documentary, *Trinity and Beyond*. And yet even today, some 15 years after its public disclosure, one would have trouble finding even a single mention of this secret military/ intelligence facility anywhere in the 'conspiracy' literature."

Was this where the atomic bomb footage was filmed, and the so-called "moon landings"? McGowan seems to think so, and when combined with his unpublished book *Wagging the Moondoggie,* he makes a convincing case. The big names and players involved in this studio and its productions are astounding and cannot be overlooked, but what it demonstrates is a massive piece of the puzzle I've tried to highlight in my essays and articles – we do live in a giant B movie and books like McGowan's and my own *Hollywood Decoded* TV Show elucidate the mechanics of how this hoodoo goes down.

As I wrote previously, the parallel between the interplay of the deep state and the movie makers is like flip sides of 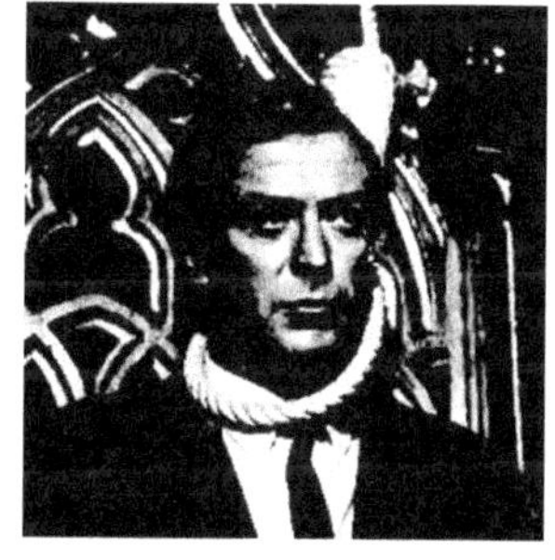 the same coin: *The Magus* is a perfect analogy for how the Hollywood hoodoo works, and while the novel is certainly superior to the film presentation, re-viewing the film version starring Michael Caine and Anthony Quinn although derided by critics, it displays a profound insight into how the elite manipulate the world:

> *The Magus* by John Fowles is a peculiar novel. It is not like anything I'd read previously – a kind of mix between the TV show *Lost* and the Michael Douglas' movie, *The Game,* with a bit of *Eyes Wide Shut* thrown in for good measure: Imagine Aristotle Onassis with a penchant for psychological warfare. Its protagonist is a young Oxford graduate named Nicholas Urfe who, having become bored

of philandering and partying, undergoes an existential crisis and embarks for a teaching position on the Greek island of Phraxos. Before leaving England, however, Nicholas breaks the heart of a beautiful Australian girl named Alison, as he quickly adopts an atheistic, nihilist worldview. As he arrives, he finds that the island is not exactly what it appears to be. Nicholas wanders into the company of a wealthy Greek billionaire named Maurice Conchis who seems to toy with Nicholas at every turn, befriending him, yet in a distant, disingenuous way. Nicholas begins to experience strange events that even make him question his own anti-supernatural presuppositions.

He sees what he thinks are Greek gods, as well as playlets that seem to match up to the Marquis de Sade. Nicholas realizes that these masques become increasingly real, encompassing his entire existence on the island. Eventually, having partaken of a hallucinogenic drug, and falling in love with one of a pair of twins that appears to be in the employ of Maurice, Nicholas experiences another kind of breakdown, resulting in an initiation of sorts similar to the process one sees in *Eyes Wide Shut*, as I argued. The novel is thus not a story of mere intrigue, but of induction into the mysteries. However, this novel presents the mysteries in a different fashion. In Fowles' mind, the initiation is not one wherein Nicholas' world status changes, adjoining him to the elite, but rather operates as a kind of grand "fuck you," where Nicholas is forced to come to grips with the fact that there is an entire strata of individuals for whom generations of enormous wealth has occasioned a godlike status on earth. As such, in Flowles' construal, the world becomes a kind of grand, global masque and stage. In fact, the novel is quite explicit that the controllers are the Illuminati.

They are an Illuminati who are guided solely by science, reason and pragmatism – not some ethereal magickal mysticism. In fact, the magickal, mystery tour which Nicholas is enveloped in is merely part of the journey. While at first Nicholas is led to believe that Conchis and his associates think they have experienced metempsychosis and are reincarnated, eventually these facts become irrelevant. Nicholas is led into a massive psychological game, where it is he who is the subject of all the events. In this, Jungian psychoanalysis comes to the fore, as well as Sartrean elements of existential crisis. Meanwhile, Conchis, and his round table of occult gods and deities have engineered all the events of Nicholas' life after Oxford, including the time spent with Alison, to bring him to the island as the test subject.

The book is spiced throughout with references to Tarot cards, Greek deities, Baphomet, gnosticism, ritual initiation, the Eleutherian mysteries, etc. Conchis eventually reveals to Nicholas, when he's drugged, captured and placed in the judgment role that the real secret is science. While Nicholas is supposed to "judge" the rest of the Illuminists present under the sign of the Pentagram and Baphomet, Nicholas ends up confounded as the group of doctors and PhDs present dissect his entire life with psychoanalysis. Nicholas is then forced to watch a pornographic film with the girl he loves that has been intertwined with his own time spent on the island, recorded by numerous secret cameras. Here Bentham/Foucault-style Panopticism emerges, as the prisoner is subjected to the all-pervading gaze of the eye of the elite. Nicholas not only cannot escape their influence and power, he is also held captive to the narrative they may construct about himself and his life. In short, he is helpless, though he thinks he is "free" in his atheism and nihilism.

Maurice, then, turns out to be a combination of the trickster/magus, as well as the prince/ruler, with his unlimited wealth. He can hire any actors, recreate any scenes, arrange any events he so desires. No matter where Nicholas goes, or what he does, he cannot escape Maurice's designs. Every time Nicholas tries to construct a "mask" or excuse or identity for himself, he is reminded of the existential dictum that he is "condemned to be free." He continues to operate in Sartrean "bad faith" and "inauthenticity" to the end, until he appears to concede that he is helpless.

Overall, the book is worth reading, and ends on an open note, where the reader is invited to interpret Nicholas' final interaction with Alison as he or she wants. This fits well with the meta-narrative theme of the work, where the reader is also in a sense, playing a game, as well as part of the grand masque that is reality. Fowles wants the reader to realize that his or her reality is also part of this play that we call reality, that includes a heavy dose of fiction. And that fiction is largely manipulated by the Illuminati – namely, those billionaires and world-controllers who have an entirely different code of ethics. A code whereby the manipulation of reality and world events is not seen as something inherently evil, but instead a kind of game or labyrinth. As such, the novel becomes one of the top "Illuminist" novels ever written, akin to *Atlas Shrugged*.

Just as Dave McGowan's *Weird Scenes* functions as a perfect window into the deep connection between the government and Hollywood and their status as cultural Fowles-like Magi, so also McGowan's *Programmed to Kill* work explains the notion of human sacrifice on the part of degenerate elites. Hollywood insider Joss Whedon brought this idea of a simulation-based society focused on human sacrifice to the big screen in his 2012 film *Cabin in the Woods.*

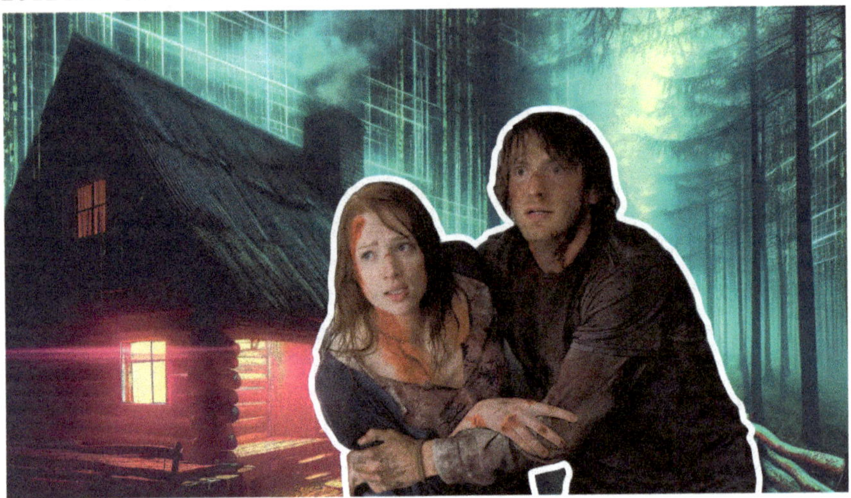

Cabin in the Woods is, on one level, an enjoyable satire of basically every horror movie stereotype and archetype imaginable. The box office hit from 2012 written by Joss Whedon raked in a hefty profit while throwing nods to horror classics like *Friday the 13th, Evil Dead* and *The Shining.* The writing is genuinely funny and the spoofing is spot on, but is there more at work here? Not every film works for JaysAnalysis, but the ones that do work, really work well and *Cabin in the Woods* definitely makes the cut. I had intended to get to the film long ago, but as often happens the timing didn't click as well until now, having recently re-read Dave McGowan's *Programmed to Kill*: its relevance will be seen below.

Our central 5 horror archetypes include the innocent virgin, the foolish pothead, the jock, the dumb blonde and the bookish nerd, as the introductory sequence had shown us government agents in some kind of underground base. The COG ("continuity of government") style agents vaguely match up to intelligence agency operatives, most likely the NSA 'analyst' who probably sits behind a wall of CCTV spy cameras, fulfilling his voyeuristic fantasies. As we begin to suspect, our 5 archetypes have been chosen for their roles, when an earpiece'd agent atop their dorm relays their departure back to headquarters.

This is interesting, and likely wasn't intentional, but the fact the collegians are spotted (and probably coaxed into this trip) in relation to their university career could be significant. We know the MKUltra program and its various sub projects were often connected to dozens of participating universities (as well as psychiatric, military and other institutions), so it's possible this scenario was directly related to a corrupt state university system. Although often overlooked, universities and colleges are suffused with some of the most radical, degenerate, debauched indoctrination practices as you see here that make older MKUltra style projects seem prudish.

Films and shows that display full controlled environments have always fascinated me. We have covered *The Prisoner*, *Maze Runner*, *The Matrix*, *West World* and other "Platonic" themed stories, and they all have their insights. Here, the curious component of ritual human sacrifice becomes intricately bound up with the metaphysics of the controlled environment. Controlled environments generally fall under some supra-governmental shadowy agency and/or some higher level of archon/demiurge that runs "the system."

However, I can't think of any other versions of this narrative that inject the human/blood sacrifice component. This is interesting, because generally the alchemical and Platonic-themed narratives reject the notion of a Creator God precisely on this basis, which is their misunderstanding of believing this Deity needs or is literally placated in some way through blood sacrifice. As we will see, *Cabin in the Woods* is different.

Another interesting element is the scientism/mad scientist element to the process of large-scale engineering the worshippers of the Ancient Ones use, which are ruled over by the higher, demonic sphere. The Ancient Ones are roughly the equivalents of the Titans, who may be the spirits mentioned in the *Book of Enoch*, as cited in St. Jude, and perhaps related to Genesis 6. We read in the *Book of Enoch* that the offspring of the Fallen Ones began the practice of requiring human sacrifice. Amazingly, this seems *more real* today than even a few years ago when the film appeared, now that we've seen the revelations of Spirit Cooking, Jimmy Savile, the Roman Catholic scandals and the numerous Satanic pedophilia networks. Are the mad scientists at the top of the pyramid working for the bankers, or are Satanic bankers at the top, or are the higher levels of the pyramid actually fallen spiritual entities that fool men into believing human sacrifice will grant them power?

As with McGowan's *Programmed to Kill*, the belief in human sacrifice is not as far-off as one might assume. For example, while McGowan mentions well-known cases of serial killers, other cases of human sacrifice cults and even the higher, deep state connections of some of those serial killers come to the fore. Cases like the Matamoros Cult, associated with drug trafficking, or MS-13 and Santa Muerte come to mind, both which include Satanic elements, as well as high-level Italian Satanic networks in the last several decades connected to the "Monster of Florence" cases. Other cases are worth mentioning too, such as self-proclaimed "Emperor of South Africa," Jean-Bodel Bokassa, who had a predilection for eating his enemies when he conquered them (pgs. 353-355).

Many of these individuals and cases seem to have very suspicious high society, deep state connections McGowan mentions that puts a new viewing of *Cabin in the Woods* in a new light. I remember beginning to research these topics ten years ago in books like Craig Heimbichner's *Blood on the Altar* and William Kennedy's *Lucifer's Lodge*, and at that time many of the news stories we know about today in relation to high society deviancy had not come to light. As mentioned, since then we have had a bevy of cases and stories come forward – many in the last year or two – that would have seemed outlandish ten years earlier. With that in mind, is it possible the reality of what has yet emerged is even darker? What if human sacrifice and cannibalism are more prevalent than we are now aware? Some "leaks" and news cases suggest this may be so.

Another interesting insight concerns the deep state controllers using what might roughly be called crisis actors, surveillance and staged scenarios to produce the reactions in the sacrificial lamb characters. The redneck at the gas station is, in fact, a member of the cult and an actor, as well as (in a loose sense) the redneck zombie family that attacks. Although the zombies are not technically actors, they are tools of the Deep State Lovecraftian Cult making them, in a way, actors. Even more surprising is the cult's usage of chemicals in hair care products and aerosol sprays intended to literally dumb down their marks. Also fascinating is the tailored trauma for each character, where it was already known which sounds, symbols and images would trigger each character. The Deep State Cult knows how to tailor trauma and triggers for the purpose of mind control, not just for each character, but also for other cultures, which explains the typical, *Ring*-esque slimy, Japanese ghost scenes.

This, in fact, has a ring of truth, given mass consumer products do have these effects: Only the pothead "fool" archetype is immune due to his previous conspiratorial mindset that presages the entire plot of the film in the early RV sequence. Indeed, if known experiments of MKUltra such as *Operation Midnight Climax* included the clandestine dosing of Johns with hallucinogens were patterns of how the system could mass dose people we can also see these aspects of the film in a new light. In my estimation, BigPharma is really just an extension of MKUltra and the Military Industrial Complex, and shows these arms of the octopus all interconnect.

The worldview of this cult is apparently a kind of primitive paganism whose code is that sacrifice is lawful when the victims "sin" by acquiescing to the temptation. Comically, we discover the real story is the Deep State Cult is underground because they worship the Balrog, basically. Peace and harmony on earth is dependent on these entities accepting the blood and thus not destroying the world, yet here the main characters that survive determine the world ought to go ahead and be destroyed to "cleanse the earth of ignorance." The Fool and the Virgin are the only two that last to the end, yet ultimately capitulate to the dictum of the cult. This was probably done for comic effect, as the cult controls mankind though releasing their "nightmares," which echoes Adam Curtis' documentary of the same name, but in the final analysis the film is a brilliant analogy for how the real world operates that may, in fact, be much more reality than satire. Maybe *blood* and the *power in the blood* has much more significance than the masses are fooled into believing are irrelevant (Lev. 17:11).

SECTION 1

COMIC BOOK ENGINEERING
& CHRISTOPHER NOLAN

BATMAN BEGINS (2005)

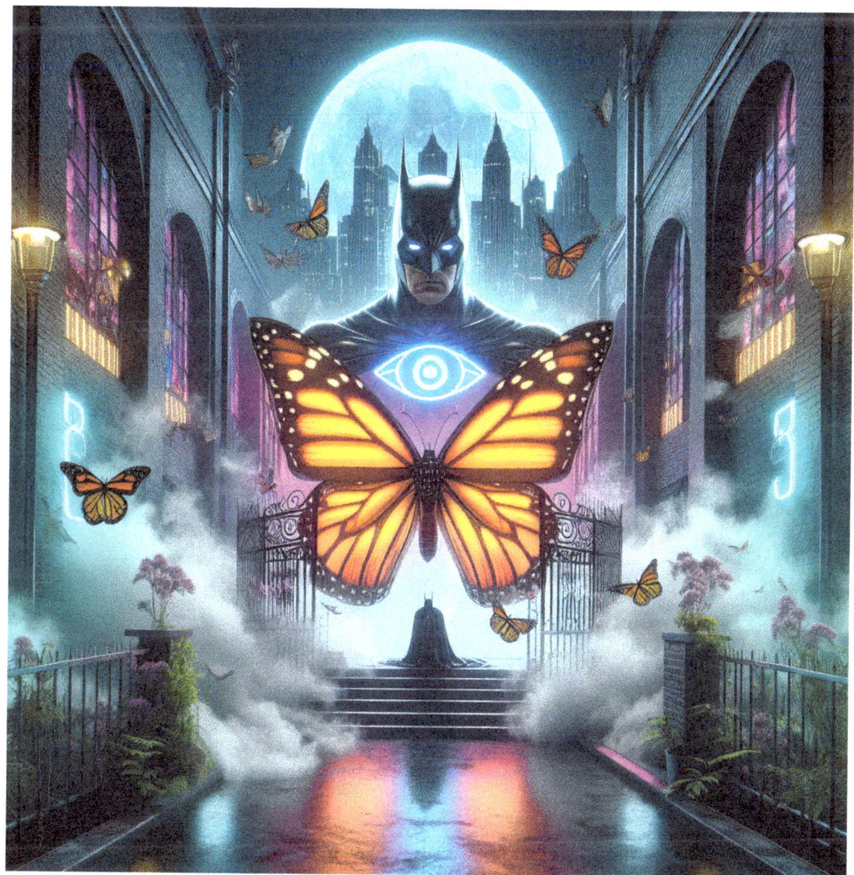

Batman Begins marks a substantive renewal for the popular franchise. Taking the story in a much more serious direction from the 90s version (replete with Prince flopping around, humping the ground), the new version is much more sophisticated. And, along with being much more sophisticated, it also calls for an esoteric analysis. Just as with Christopher Nolan's *Inception* (also analyzed later in this book), so his earlier *Batman Begins* was modeled along the same lines of Jungian psychoanalysis, mixed with occult and gnostic themes, as well as other prevalent popular conspiracy theories and secret societies, as we will see.

The film begins with Bruce Wayne experiencing childhood trauma where he falls down a well, breaks his leg, and is terrified by a sudden battalion of bats. Falling down wells and trips to the underworld are common in Jungian, gnostic and literary exploits. It's an archetypal scheme for both the inner subconscious, as well as the exterior metaphysical realm of the dead. The "underworld" of Homer and Virgil, is also, by association, the subconscious from which our dreams arise, manifesting archetypal patterns. Bruce Wayne's falling down the well is also a window into his unconscious mind, just as are the several layers of dreams in Dominick Cobb's subconscious in *Inception*.

Childhood traumas and fixations are often formed from this stage in development, as both Freud and Jung noted, and this is precisely where Bruce Wayne experiences the defining moment of his future existence – he will eventually become the thing he fears – the dark and the demonic. Now that may sound strange, given that Batman is a good guy, and the Joker and others villains, but once one understands the pagan and gnostic scheme of reality, these words end up purely relative denominators. "Good" as an actual, absolute category is non-existent in this relativistic scheme. This is why Bruce Wayne's journey will be to become his "higher self," the alter ego "Batman." Batman is the embodiment of Bruce Wayne's "shade" or shadow self, his dark-side incarnate.

Batman is not bound by laws, but is instead a Nietzschian vigilante overman, beyond good and evil: *rex lex*. Since the normative social structure of Gotham City is corrupt, Batman is a law unto himself. This is why Bruce is the billionaire capitalist: he is the representation of elite capital, but which also provides Gotham its vast social programs and welfare system, as well as public transportation, etc. This is yet another hint at the actual system that runs the real world – it is controlled by those at the top who are neither capitalist nor socialist. They are elitist, and who (in their minds) transcend dialectics. The Cold War, for example, was a closely steered conflict that allowed a vast intelligence and surveillance grid to be established under the auspices of nuclear threat. Now, our threats are repackaged as environmentalism and the "global war on terror." Bruce Wayne thus embodies the "third way" which is where we are headed – a global corporate financial system that is the synthesis of communism and capitalism, under the guise of world "democracy."

This is also why Bruce Wayne has as his right hand man the sage archetype, "Lucius" (played by Morgan Freeman), who functions as a representation of the vast intelligence/military industrial complex apparatus.

Due to Bruce's billionaire status, he is able to obtain any technology or weapon needed, especially since Wayne Enterprises is who builds it. As with all ages, a culture's art mirrors reality, and modern cinema is far more of a mirror of reality than 99% of the viewing audience realizes, as I (and others) argue at length on my blog.

And, it goes without saying, that "Lucius" brings to mind "Lucifer," the fallen angel from Isaiah 14 who is cast down from heaven, seeking to exalt his throne above God, under the image of the King of Tyre. "Lucifer" also means the light-bearer and morning star, and so it makes sense that the sage archetype would be the character that molds, shapes and grants Batman his technological "powers." Recall, of course, that Batman does not have any superpowers. He is merely a technologically empowered elite, and that is again much closer to the real world system than anything else presented in comic books. Batman, then, is unique in that his "power" is technological wizardry from Lucius/Lucifer.

Let us return to the film: "Ducard" (Liam Neeson) appears early on and represents the criminal underworld and ends up recruiting Wayne in Tibet, who had gone on an extended road trip to find the truth, divesting himself from the upper echelon existence he had been raised with. "Ducard" eventually recruits Wayne for his secret society, the League of Shadows, which appears to have some affiliation with Buddhism, at least exoterically. After learning the arts of the ninja, as well as enduring other feats of physical endurance, Wayne undergoes a hallucinogenic initiation where he "travels inward" and confronts his "bat demon" (his shade), shall we say. Notably, this occurs after he climbs a mountain to obtain a rare blue flower from which the powerful hallucinogen is drawn.

This is interesting, inasmuch as many esoteric secret societies do utilize drugs as a path to obtaining esoteric knowledge. It is also interesting that the League of Shadows seems to be based in the mountains of Tibet, and appears as a composite of a number of actual occult orders. Borrowing from the notorious Helena Blavatsky and her Theosophical sect and it's Tibetan "Great White Brotherhood" of ascended masters (who were likely intelligence handlers),[3] as well as Satanist Aleister Crowley's groups, and possibly even the Nazi esoteric philosophies of those like Himmler, who also obsessed over Tibetan myths. As with Nazi ideology, the focus of the League of Shadow's doctrines is the triumph of will. "Will is everything," Ducard hammers home to Wayne. It also appears to borrow elements of masonic initiation, as Ducard asks Wayne, "What do you seek?" To which the masonic initiate responds, "Light."

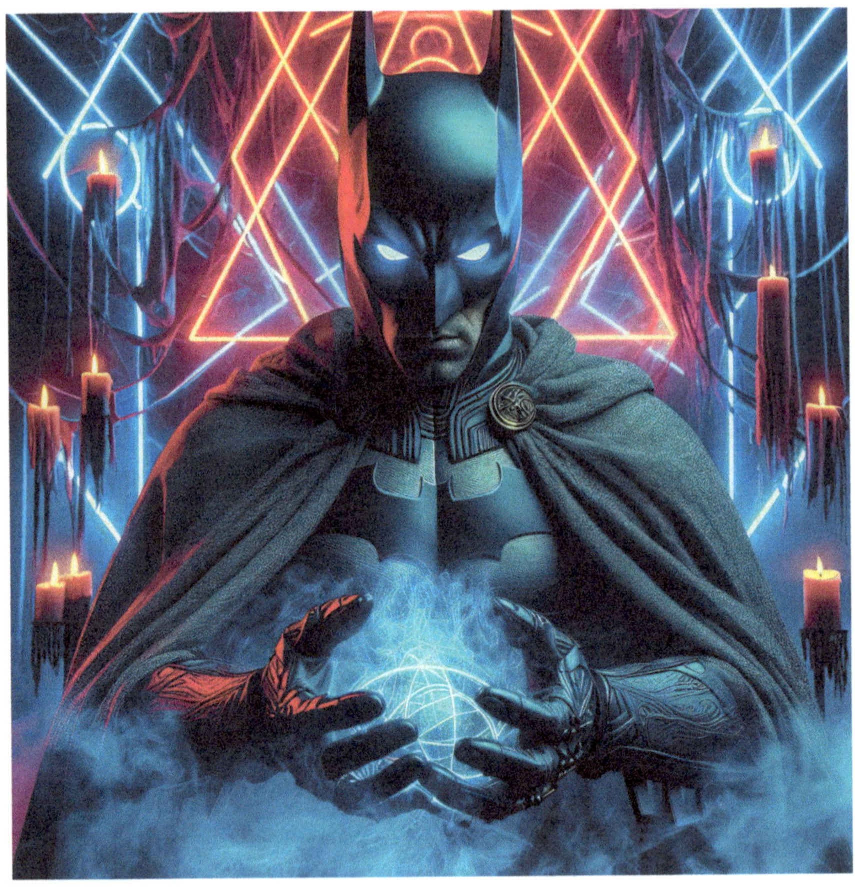

Dark Knight (2008)

"Bruce Wayne's grandfather founded Skull & Bones."
— *Batman* TV Show

*B*atman: The Dark Knight Rises (2012) is the final installment in the Christopher Nolan trilogy and, in my opinion, is excellent. Like the previous two, the concluding film is just as esoteric and filled with predictive programming as the others, yet stands out as preeminent. This final film is the climax of this version of revelation of the method *par excellence*. The entire essence of this film is concerned with how the system itself operates on the deepest levels – levels far beyond what most people are able to comprehend. Like the rest of Nolan's films, this one resonates with a particular Jungian ethos, almost to the level of *Inception*. In fact, *Dark Knight Rises* is very similar to Nolan's *Inception*, and, believe it or not, Jim Henson's *Labyrinth*.

In fact, Nolan even takes *Dark Knight* to the higher esoteric level of including actors from previous films and roles to play them again in this film. As often turns out to be the case, especially in the case of the top A list Hollywood figures – figures like Angelina Jolie, Nicole Kidman, or Rachel Weisz end up cast in either intelligence-related or occultic roles. Among males you can see it with Ben Affleck, Matt Damon, Robert De Niro, Nicolas Cage, Johnny Depp and Tom Cruise. In fact, it is likely that many A-list actors are employed by intelligence agencies in various capacities, as this has happened many times in the past:

> Hollywood, as we now know from declassified National Archive documents, aided in the mobilization for war and its people contributed as spies, combatants, propagandists, documentary and fund-raisers, entertainers, and morale-boosters. Hundreds of celebrities eagerly answered the "call to arms" and brought their talents and patriotism to the intelligence services, military and war information offices.
>
> In the National Archives we discover that stars such as Cary Grant, Marlene Dietrich, Greta Garbo, Leslie Howard, Josephine Baker, John Ford and many more, were spies for the Allies, and changed the course of the war. They did amazing things, dangerous things, and their fame was their asset. This untold story is very accurate and relevant still today.[4]

Granted, some roles are chosen on the basis of stars having a certain "look" adapted from another role, but as I argue, and as we see in films like *Mulholland Drive*, roles are often chosen for deeper, occult and intelligence-related reasons. Consider for example Heath Ledger in *Batman: The Dark Knight*, and then his role in *The Imaginarium of Doctor Parnassus*, followed by his strange, possibly ritualistic, death.

"What?" you say, "That's wacky!" That's because your view of the world isn't the same as those who understand liturgy and ritual. The study of liturgics is not some dry, dusty, arcane academic discipline for old religionists to haggle about. Liturgics to those who know, is the very heartbeat of the universe itself. It is itself the meaning of things. Granted, one can learn about metaphysics or science in philosophy or at some university, yet these are merely fields that operate in the realm of bare knowledge. Knowledge itself is lacking in that it is static and merely one of the divine *energeia*.

To combine will and action in harmony with intended purpose in the service of God in symbolic act is meaning, and thus all of life becomes a liturgical ritual. Most ancient religious traditions have some notion of this.

Thus the standard exposition most "conspiracy theorists" and/or critics give is done at the most basic level of plot, interpretation of meaning, technical achievements, and possible "Illuminist" symbols. While there is a place for all of that, none of them understand the principle of the film itself, including the actors and their own experiences, the set, the script, etc., all coming together at a certain time, with a certain *zeitgeist* behind it. A couple good books I would recommend are Mircea Eliade's *The Sacred and the Profane*, Abraham Heschel's *The Sabbath*, and any basic introduction to liturgy, such as Hugh Wybrew's *Byzantine Liturgy*. Such a radical alteration of perception is only achieved by investigation into, and participation in, liturgy. Those who have experienced this will understand, and those who haven't will not. But regardless, films are themselves a kind of ritual "working," and whether the 99% of the critics out there acknowledge or know this is irrelevant: it is true.

The Dark Knight Rises (2012)

In fact, as I wrote this analysis at the time, it has unfortunately happened that several people were killed in a *Dark Knight Rises* premier in Colorado in 2012. In the decade that has passed since this tragedy several "Joker" and anarchist themed attacks have occurred as a bizarre semiotic social copycat ritual. Readers will be aware of Colorado being outlined in other films and in reality as a new, more secretive command base for various elite factions.[5] Think of the Denver Airport and the Columbine events with the similar themes. A *Russia Today* article states:

> Police say that the assailant initially opened a gas canister. Witnesses recounted hearing a hissing sound and smoke, and then the shooting started.
>
> Some say that when they first heard the gunfire, they thought it was some new type of special effect.
>
> "It was chaotic, it was surreal, it was like in a movie," one of the witnesses told 9news Denver TV station.
>
> Initial media reports suggested that two gunmen were involved in the rampage. But police later said there was only one person involved as far as they know. The gunman was carrying a rifle and a handgun at the time of his arrest, police said at a media conference. One suspect was taken into police custody.
>
> Witnesses reported seeing a tall, shotgun-wielding man clad in body armor and wearing a gas mask in the theatre. The attacker set off some kind of a tear gas canister.

An apartment building was evacuated after the suspect told police there were explosives planted there following his apprehension. So far police have failed to find any traces of the alleged bombs.

Police responding to the shooting evacuated the area over fears that an explosive device might be on the premises.

Ten of the victims were killed right on the spot while four others died from injuries in hospital.

Aurora medical services were alerted to attend to the large number of injured. At least 50 people have been taken to hospital following the shooting, although it is not clear yet how many of them are in serious condition.[6]

(The number "6" shows up prominently in the film, as a side note.)

Amazingly, this would seem to fit into the plot of the film itself, as the article even explains people stating that it was "like a movie." Was this a ritual attempt itself? Was this something planned? As more details emerge, it will become clearer, but it's interesting that the shooter was wearing body armor and a gas mask, reminiscent of Bane, the film's villain.

Bane is who we see immediately, murdering the CIA agent on the plane. The CIA, representing the classical enemy of the communists, are symbolically disposed of here. We learn eventually that Bane inhabits the *underground* – appropriate, given that communist syndicates and cells are also the "underground," much like the Weather Underground. The underground is preeminent in the film, representing the criminal underground, the underworld of Hades and the underworld of the subconscious. Bane's imagery is inspired by a cross between Destro (From *G.I. Joe*), Humongous (from *Road Warrior*), and Darth Vader.

As archetypal evil, Bane has emerged from the hardship of being born in an underground prison and has risen from "the pit" (it's referred to as the pit and the abyss in the film) to challenge "Western civilization," which has fallen into a decay and in need of revolution. This brings to mind the references in the Book of Revelation to the demon from the abyss, Apollyon or Abaddon. Bane is several times referred to as a "shadow" a "shade," a thing from the "dark," and from the underworld. Bane is a Satan character, and a member of the League of Shadows. As you recall, the League of Shadows represents anti-western (far Eastern) secret societies that actually do exist.

Bane, it's important to understand, is like the Joker – they are chaotic evil. As chaotic evil, Bane cannot be the evil mastermind. We will discover that he is not: He leads a literal, all out communist, Leninist, violent revolution with the siege of Gotham (New York). The violent revolution takes on an eerily similar approach to the French Revolution. Having studied the French Revolution in-depth in upper-level history courses, I was amazed at the similarities. Bane operates like a Marat, Danton or Robespierre, first by utilizing terror, and freeing the inmates in a move echoing the storming of the Bastille, where the revolutionaries claimed many of the oppressed had been imprisoned by the monarchy (which actually wasn't true – only a few people were in the old prison). Scarecrow performs the role of revolutionary judge like Robespierre, sentencing the wealthy to exile or death (exile in this case means death). In fact, when Bane emerges in the midst of the football game, the camera pans past a section that reads "RED ZONE" – appropriate, given the openly communist nature of Bane. (Bane is also played by Tom Hardy, who played Eames in Nolan's *Inception*.)

Much like *Eyes Wide Shut* (as I noted in *Esoteric Hollywood 1*), masks are common in the film in the background, often on bookshelves. Masks in Jungian and existentialist analyses refer to the alter ego and or the demonic shade side of the psyche. The dark side is hidden and must be channeled in some form or fashion, lest the "inner Bane" emerge. In fact, there are even lines in the film to this effect – that Bane emerges from the dark underside of the subconscious. *Dark Knight Rises* also has a masked ball scene reminiscent of *Eyes Wide Shut*, where Batman begins to merge with his *anima*, who in this film will be Catwoman. As is common in Jungian and alchemical frameworks, the male principle is lacking and imbalanced without the union with the feminine principle.

Just as there are communist images behind Bane, there are capitalist and imperial symbols behind Bruce Wayne in many scenes. Athena can be seen, who from an esoteric perspective fits well into this narrative, as well as Catholic saints like Mary and Paul or Peter. Traditionally seen as the establishment and capitalist, the red revolutionaries opposed these forces as imperial and corrupt. In *Dark Knight Rises*, both Bane and Catwoman learn that their communist terrorstorm was a failure – Catwoman in particular realizes the revolution is a failure and is reconciled to Batman and becomes his lover.

It should also be mentioned that in Catwoman's bedroom a book titled "Labyrinth" is visible, which hearkens to both *Labyrinth* and Christopher Nolan's *Inception*, which is very similar. (See my analysis of *Inception*). In fact, one of the most fascinating turns is that Batman's seeming love interest Miranda (Marion Cotillard) is the shade character, and who also turns out to be the Ra's al Ghul's daughter. Marion Cotillard played *the shade character* in *Inception*! The Ra's al Ghul is a kind of Satan and shade character, and Miranda turns out to be a kind of communist sleeper agent who actually runs the League of Shadows following the death of Ra's al Ghul. In regard to Jim Henson's *Labyrinth*, the prison where Bane was born, and where Bruce Wayne is banished, is itself laid out like the M.C. Escher based maze in the Henson *Labyrinth*.

Another important plot element is the free energy conspiracy, which Bruce Wayne feels the world isn't ready for. It's mentioned as a kind of "fusion" (cold fusion?), which is perfectly clean and free. Bane kidnaps a Russian scientist who invented it and forces him to arm it. This brings to mind both *Mission Impossible 4*, *The Saint*, and *The Sum of All Fears* – particularly the last in regard to the bomb going off at the NFL game. In *The Sum of All Fears* (also starring Morgan Freeman), it's a massive terror event in a football game. Bane also engages in an actual armed attack on the NYSE, as well as using a backdoor program to attack the stock market and wipe Wayne Enterprises clean, causing Bruce to go bankrupt. From a predictive programming perspective, be on the lookout for backdoor attacks on the markets like we see in *Live Free or Die Hard*, or future Gladio-style attacks at entertainment venues (or Gladio 2.0!). Batman and other summer blockbuster films are generally big-time indicators for upcoming terror events. This film in particular should be all the more analyzed, due to the mass murder that occurred in Colorado at the premier. In fact, in the years following this infamous event, we saw numerous "Joker" themed attacks and events that mirror this event, followed by the more recent nihilistic terrorist/Antifa-themed 2019 *Joker*, starring Joaquin Phoenix, Directed by Todd Phillips.

Bane refers to himself as "necessary evil," and as the harbinger of a "new form of western civilization." This is no mere film, but a powerful work intended to potentially signal coming events – a presaged monetary collapse, or stages of terror attacks intended to bring down western civilization by radicalized college communists influenced by far eastern doctrines of total relativism. While this film was given a lot of bad press, it is oddly anti-communist with an Ayn Rand style objectivist twist. It does not portray Bane as a good revolutionary, though the audience is intended to find sympathy for him. It could be that the film is trying to portray patriots as evil, but Bane is an all-out, clear-cut radical Jacobin. Bane is not a Ron Paul style capitalist: He is the antithesis of capitalism and Bruce Wayne.

Indeed, one of the corporate heads who gets killed is "Mr. Fox" – as in *Fox News.* Bane brings to mind Rousseau, in that he constantly claims his revolution is "for the people," and which amounts to a dictatorship of the proletariat. It is also worth noting that the police are turned against the people. Ironically, this is precisely the method that will be used to divide and conquer the U.S. However, Bane's revolution fails, as do all communist revolutions, yet they also succeed in destroying and reorganizing the society which is the ultimate goal of all revolutions, including the slow kill model of Fabian socialism.[7] Bruce Wayne, the John Galt character, triumphs. The radical red revolution is crushed.

The film ends with Commissioner Gordon reading the famous line from Charles Dickens' *A Tale of Two Cities* about the French Revolution, quoting him before his guillotine death in the French Revolution:

> It is a far, far better thing that I do, than I have ever done; it is a far, far better rest that I go to than I have ever known.

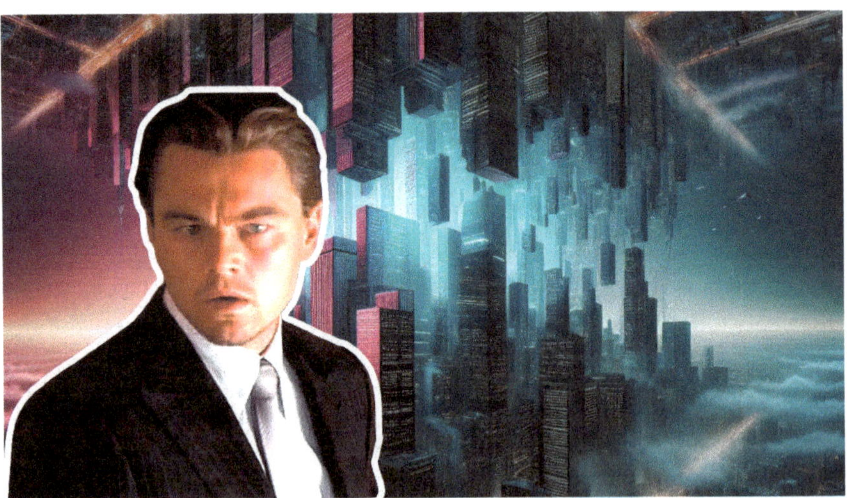

INCEPTION (2010)

Inception is one of the best films Hollywood has put out in years, and stands out as a diamond in a large stack of garbage. If the liberals in Hollywood were really worried about the environment, they wouldn't cloud the artistic environment with so much pollution. But *Inception* is something else. A film that mystified many, it also became the subject of intense online debates and speculation as to its ultimate meaning. I believe I have cracked it, and I think I cracked its code upon first viewing. I subsequently viewed it two more times, and collected even more clues confirming my basic thesis. Let's analyze.

One cannot properly understand *Inception* without familiarity with the basic concepts of Carl Jung, some Freud, and a sprinkling of esoterica. The esoteric elements coalesce nicely, due to Jung's emphasis on mythology and archetypes. I am not here advocating Carl Jung, to be clear. Jung was very much opposed to the basic worldview I espouse, but we must still interact with and decode these phenomena, inasmuch as they are a part of the world we operate in.

What is happening in Inception is just this: the entire sequence is about Cobb himself returning from the abyss of chaos to his true identity, wherein he reaches a kind of personal paradise. Cobb is, in fact, the only character, and the other characters are all "projections of the subconscious," as he explains to Ariadne in her first test dream sequence. The original clue to this interpretation is in the beginning when Cobb, Saito and his associates are in the room (Saito's apartment) where a revolution of some kind is taking place outside. Saito recognizes the carpet is not his, and calls Cobb out for keeping him within yet another layer of dream-existence. Cobb tells us later that the projections never attack the dreamer, but the others are supposedly perceived as intruders. However, if this was the case, then the revolutionaries should have attacked Cobb and Saito; but they don't – they attack Nash (played by Lucas Haas), who is supposed to be the dreamer in this layer. And if you note, they never attack Cobb – ever.

The other crucial element is that the story is not a linear story, just like a dream is often non-linear. The film concerns essentially the "architecture of the mind," as director Christopher Nolan described it. Jung's theories involve the idea that the individual is a disparate example of the collective unconscious, and thus fragmented from the collective. The collective consciousness manifests itself in images and archetypes in our deepest selves – the lowest of the subconscious. It is here that we hide our most intimate failures, sins and fears. We guard this sensitive part of ourselves, and have defense mechanisms by which we hide and guard these deeper, more elemental ethereal truths about who we really are. For Jung, being the mystic he was, the goal is to overcome all purported fragmentation, work through the so-called self-realization/individuation process, and thus escape dualities. The masculine "side" must reconcile with the feminine. One notices here familiar themes found throughout the history of alchemy, and Jung was known for his penchant in such arcane studies.

This, then, is the context in which *Inception* can be understood, and in no other. Cobb represents, in a way, every man, and thus we begin with Cobb stranded "on the shore of his subconscious." He is fragmented and separate from who he is – alone and has forgotten his true life and identity. Familiar themes as found in gnosticism here emerge, such as the myth of alienation from Sophia as found in tractates such as the *Hypostasis of the Archons*. And this is undoubtedly the font from which Jung drew. Jung, by the way, was an intelligence operative, working on behalf of the OSS and was given the title of "Agent 488."[8]

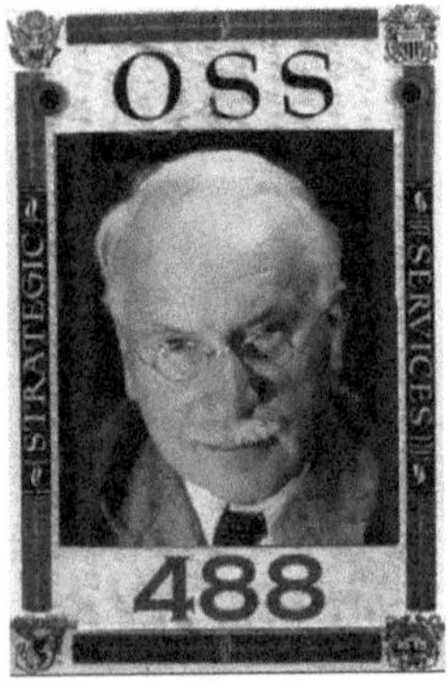

Cobb must, through the process of self-reconciliation and integration, become who he truly is. Whether there was an actual person with some similar history as presented in certain scenes of the film is up for debate, but I tend to think so. We see, for example, when Cobb is in the dream realm with Mal, the buildings are all uniform and part of a clearly imaginary city. However, there is a brief scene towards the end where Mal is with Cobb in old age, and the background city is an actual city with variant architecture. In fact, the architecture of the buildings is also key to decoding the narrative: all of the architecture throughout the film is the architecture seen in the city of his subconscious that he built with Mal. Each locale in the film has a particular architecture; they are all found in the subconscious city. And this is because man is seen as a microcosm of the macrocosm.

Numerous clues that support this reading are also given throughout. To begin with, the basic plot is fantastical and impossible – entering another person's dream through a cheesy-looking briefcase apparatus. Granted, the film can be itself asking us to suspend belief, yet at the end, when Cobb confronts Mal, his shade in Jungian lingo (or dark side), she tells him he has been living a fantastical lie – traversing the globe being chased by international corporations – it's impossible. Cobb works for "Kobol," which is perhaps a reference to the actual software development company or perhaps to *Battlestar Galactica's* Mormon-based "lords of kobol," who are the gods of Olympus, which would fit perfectly into the Jungian ethos, not to mention Ariadne, who is the anima archetype – one half of the anthropomorphic unconscious. It could also have reference to Cabal, or Kabbala, the Jewish mystical theory of reality that has at times fallen into pantheism. This will be the downside of the ultimate message of the film – that, like *The Matrix*, reality is a manifestation of our consciousness – solipsism. But solipsism is an impossible, self-refuting philosophy that is nothing more than a rehash of the ancient Hindu concept of *Maya*.

Ariadne is also, the character of Greek mythology associated with labyrinths and helping Minos defeat the minotaur. The entire film, you see, is the labyrinth of Cobb's unconscious mind, seeking integration and realization. Note as well that the "inception," or idea they "plant" is that "it's all a dream." An inter-contextual inception that they plan for "Fisher" (Cillian Murphy) is the idea that he will break up his father's empire. In Jungian and Freudian analysis, this is crucial, for the male child must battle to establish himself as an identity apart from the father, who is seen for a time in early development as a rival. Here, however, we are dealing with the symbolic, and so Fisher is a further manifestation of Cobb's psyche. Fisher is the child archetype and the fracturing of the empire is symbolic for the individual consciousness' separation and alienation. It is Cobb who has been "fragmented." His psyche is the "empire," because the entire city – the entire universe – is his own dream or consciousness. He is the architect. Again, there really is no clear point in the film in which we know we are in the realm of waking life. This is why Ariadne pulls together two mirrors and it agitates Cobb when he looks in both directions and sees a fragmented image of himself, infinitely, in both directions. In fact, it is Cobb throughout the film, who is constantly being given clues (as is the viewer), that he is in a dream state and has constructed elaborate layer upon layer of labyrinthine stories and myths to hide his dark side – represented by Mal.

Another interesting clue is the totem itself. The totem Cobb has is supposed to be Mal's. Yet Cobb tells Ariadne that you can't use someone else's totem. This is another clue that the totem itself is, for Cobb, just another piece of the myth he has constructed to cloak himself in. This is also why the sub-theme of the secret items hidden in safes is also really just about Cobb. As we probe deeper and deeper as the movie progresses, the real secret is the safe in which Cobb hid Mal's totem. And when Cobb explains this at last to Ariadne, he says that the ultimate secret is that "it's all a dream." The inception, then, is the idea that had overtaken Cobb himself. Another clue along these lines is when Ariadne sneaks into Cobb's anniversary room, she steps on a broken wine glass. When Cobb later speaks with Mal in the anniversary hotel room, he steps on the same glass and even says the same phrase Ariadne had earlier to Mal. This is one of many clues that Ariadne is Cobb. Another clue in this scene is that Mal isn't even on the same building ledge. She is on the ledge of a "mirrored" hotel room across the street. All throughout clues are given, when they first appear to enter Fisher's mind, the train from Cobb's dream appears. Unless they were in Cobb's dream, which they weren't, this should not have happened. This was the whole reason Ariadne was brought along – because Cobb could no longer build "cities."

Other clues include the fact that when Cobb talks to his daughter on the phone from the hotel room after his first encounter with Saito, the daughter on the phone is noticeably older than the daughter in his memory and in the final scene. In fact, this is the biggest clue – when Cobb returns "home," his children haven't aged at all, and are, in fact, standing in the very same pose as in his dream. Keeping in mind that the totem doesn't really tell you anything anyway, it is thus unnecessary to base the solution to the film on whether or not the top continues to spin in the final sequence.

Inception is an amazingly deep work, and represents a step in the right direction for Hollywood. I can't praise it enough, but I do have to note that it seems to leave us with a kind of ultimate relativism – as if all reality is really just a phantasm of our own mind. "Reality" is just a dream. One might argue that this isn't necessarily what the final message is, but it seems to point in that direction, and this is not a healthy direction to point us in. Reality is just that – reality. I can imagine myself as the emperor of the world, or that $2 + 2 = 5$, but all the Hindu maya I imbibe won't change those facts.

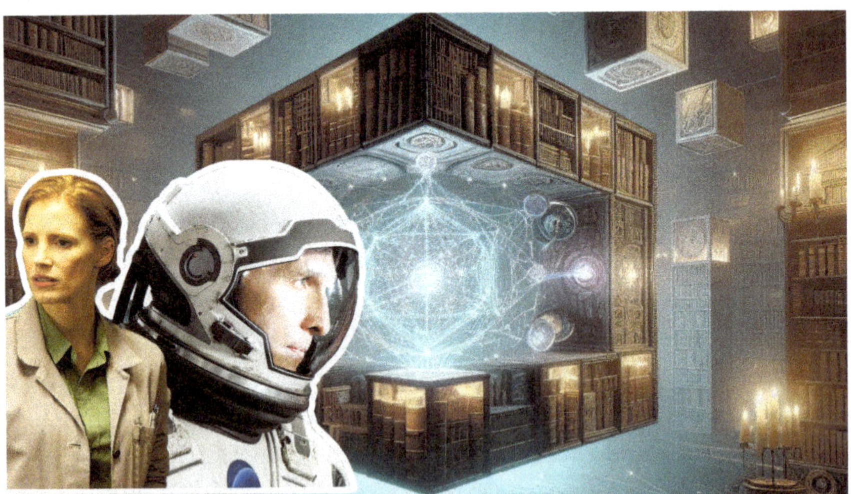

Interstellar (2014)

Interstellar is a grandiose film about a great number of serious philosophical and scientific concepts. It's also about a host of other things, such as love, life, mistakes, meaning, etc., so knowing where to start an analysis is a bit challenging, though as many of my friends have said, it seems to be the perfect "JaysAnalysis" movie. I concur. Many sites that have posted analyses make the correct point of viewing it as Christopher

Nolan's *2001: A Space Odyssey*, and while that is fine as far as it goes, it also departs from Kubrick's film in significant ways. I will go all out on this one like I did with *Inception*, which is the first analysis to gain a lot of traction – I think I have decoded the *real* meaning of *Interstellar*, so stick around for my big reveal at the end!

As often occurs, no other analyses seem to grasp the real point of the film. You'll either see a philosophical analysis or a scientific one, with the latter usually bitching about some disputed sciencey detail that doesn't matter anyway (it's *fiction*). Nolan intends to not insult the audience's intelligence, contrary to most of Hollywood, so fedora atheists ought to be grateful rather than stroking their own virtual E-egos, echoing some nitpicking from Neil deGrasse Tyson. I also see connections to *Inception* I will detail below, and in a ballsy fashion proclaim that I will give you the conspiratorial and esoteric side none of the other sites will. As difficult as the film is to unpack, I can't imagine the challenge of creating it, and Nolan's preferred choice of not using CGI green screen vomit is all the more admirable. Let us ponder.

Interstellar begins by showing us a near future where the apocalypse is nigh: Earth is approaching its death-knell due to unexplained blights that have ravaged the planet. Famine is the chief concern as major crops such as corn are on their way out and farming is *en vogue*. We learn later that for whatever reason, oxygen began to deplete and the "dirt itself" turned on mankind – man and the earth are cursed. Edenic imagery is present here, as the dust of death to which man returns recalls the curse of Genesis 3 for rebellion in the Garden. While we are not told, one might speculate that genetically modifying crops and geoengineering the atmosphere may have been the cause of the blight and famine, and many in alternative media have been warning of this very real possibility. However, I am going to go out on a limb and propose a more speculative thesis no one else will: *Interstellar* is actually about the *real* secret space program and the plan to go off world to terraform, and beyond that, something even more outlandish. I recognize the high level of mad hatter tin foilage this evokes to many new readers, but bear with me and hear my case.

Cooper (Matthew McConaughey), a former NASA pilot and engineer who suffers nightmares following the loss of his wife and a past flight crash, finds himself and his family forced into a meager agrarian lifestyle as a result of the shutdown of NASA for aforementioned pragmatic communal concerns. Cooper's daughter, Murph, shares the same fire for adventure and exploration as her humbled father, indulging her gifted inquisitive and speculative side in devouring books and debating her teachers. In fact, New America has even changed its textbooks to portray the original NASA Apollo mission as a faked charade to "bankrupt the Soviet Empire." Conspiracy theorists globally perked up at that one, as Cooper is rebuffed by Murph's school officials; she isn't qualified for college, being too rebellious. At this juncture, it is important to delve into what I think is the purpose of this puzzling faked moon landing reference.

I am of the view that the original NASA moon landings were faked and were filmed on a sound stage as Cold War propaganda. I realize that is highly controversial and liable to cause a ruckus, but readers can choose to do what they will, given the incoherent accounts of the astronauts and engineers. However, that does not mean that I think there is no space program or that it was actually "shut down" by Obama. The real plan was the erecting of a *faux* NASA that functioned as a front for a covert, secret space program that has been largely hidden from public purview. When we consider that the technology that we now possess today, such as the Internet itself, was created back in the 50s and 60s, it is difficult to gauge how advanced the present day secret technology at places such as DARPA or various underground bases truly is. NASA has thus been a longtime cover and distraction from the real black budget space programs. Much of the so-called "UFO" phenomena has nothing to do with aliens, but is precisely the advanced technology of this very secret program. The "alien" nonsense functions as a media veil for these black projects in much the same way as "NASA."[9]

I believe the secret space program is the hidden reference in the film because we discover the electromagnetic phenomena at Cooper's farmhouse are relaying coordinates to an old underground base, specifically NORAD. A curious Cooper and Murph track down these coordinates to discover NASA still exists and that space travel never truly ended. A lie was concocted to cloak the *real space program,* which has focused all its energy towards going off world. Scientists and researchers have clandestinely appropriated the government's taxes and funds, signaling a clear reference to the military industrial complex's black budget programs in our world. And, just like in *Interstellar,* that complex uses mass deception: Ours concocts "climate change" and "sustainability" as contrived crises to cloak one of their biggest secrets – going off world. However, the plan is not merely terraforming some Sector Z Globule as a utopian space base, but a mass depopulation and culling along the lines of the 1979 film version of *Moonraker.* A clue to this is also given in the books shown on

Murph's shelf, one of which is Stephen King's *The Stand*, in which a bio weapon is released that ravages the global population and collapses the United States. What books and intertextual references are chosen in Nolan films are crucial to decoding and understanding the total picture

How far along this program is, I don't know, but this theme has existed in sci-fi and popular films for decades. Numerous movies carry this motif, from *Sky Captain and the World of Tomorrow* to *2012*, as well as numerous novels and young adult fiction works, such as *The Passage* (Project Noah!) or *The Maze Runner*, and the idea is not that far-fetched when one considers the older eugenics movement as morphed into technocratic bioengineering and transhumanism – and this is exactly what is revealed in *Interstellar*. The transhumanism element will become key later in this analysis. Professor Brand (Michael Caine) explains to Cooper that NASA has a "Plan A" to solve gravity and save earth, and a "Plan B," to take 5,000 frozen human baby-cicles to one of three potentially inhabitable worlds. The mission to terraform another planet also hearkens back to the story of Noah, as the ship that will carry Cooper and crew becomes a new ark.

I should also mention that the electromagnetic "Poltergeist" events at Cooper's farm include an old Indian Air Force drone seemingly seeking out Cooper (actually Murph), farm equipment mysteriously driving themselves to the house, and books falling off of Murph's shelf she interprets as morse code. Fearing the loss of her father, Murph proclaims the message to spell out "Stay," and begs Cooper not to leave. At this point, the theme of the loss of the patriarch enters, borrowing from the classic tale of Odysseus, who must choose between love at home and a greater, higher purpose. Another classical element is katabasis, the hero's descent into the underworld or Hades, to return as a form of resurrection. For Cooper, it will be crossing the abyss and going into the realm of the beyond, but more on that in a bit. *2001: A Space Odyssey* is also a clear reference to Odysseus, as the title reveals, and like the Astronaut Bowman in *2001* who ventures past Jupiter and beyond the infinite, so does Cooper. Both Cooper and Bowman also embody science and Apollonian rationalism, yet as we will see, this is not enough to propel man across the Infinite.

Consistently dismissing Murph's intuitive sense more at work with the unexplained events, Cooper rationalizes all as mere "gravity." The loss of Cooper by Murph results in a lifetime of hatred and resentment for him, which will only be fully reconciled through the paradox of Cooper's ultimate mission. This paradox is illustrated in the scene recounting Murphy's name from Murphy's Law, that whatever can happen will happen, and is not necessarily a tragic consequence. The tragedy is ironically that, like Calypso, no one listens to Murphy – not even her father. In this bedroom scene Cooper actually gives away a big clue to the big mystery, telling a crying Murph, "Once you're a parent, you're a ghost of your children's future," (which is the entire plot, as we will see).

In *2001*, the astronauts and Bowman gradually made their way from Earth to space to moon to Jupiter to the Infinite/Abyss. Reportedly, Kubrick's initial screenplay had Saturn instead of Jupiter, so we can assume a similarity with Nolan's version. For Nolan, the mission is Earth to Saturn to wormhole to another galaxy/planet to a black hole that resembles a massive dark Saturn. All of this is intentional, and refers to deeply esoteric concepts relating to these luminaries. Occult and hermetic traditions contain a mass of arcana relating to these planets, but Saturn is classically associated with the reign of time and death. Saturn is Chronos, the god of time, and is also the grim reaper, as Saturn holds a scythe. Nolan explains in an interview that the real antagonist in the film "is time," and the script speaks of it as a "resource." Like the dying crops and depleting oxygen, time is vital a resource and enemy, as the astronauts race on foreign planets to gain "data," where massive gravitational forces result in varied experiences of time. The real message of the film is gradually being unveiled as the means by which man will *cheat death*, not going gently into that good night (death).

Death symbolism is also prominent when the astronauts enter into a cryogenic sleep in pods reminiscent of coffins. The secret mission is named the "Lazarus Project '' which immediately tells us it's about resurrection from death, intending on also alerting the viewer to the persistent themes of cyclical process: movement, death, resurrection, movement, death, resurrection. The cycle of time is the reason for the numerous, artful cinematic displays of spinning. Ships spin, Earth spins, Saturn spins, the wormhole appears to spin, etc., which are symbolic of the non-linear form of storytelling Nolan prefers. The far eastern doctrine of a wheel of time that entraps man in this temporal life is also what's in view, and the Lazarus mission is about transcending eternal return and endless Chronos-logical death cycles. I analyzed this cyclical symbolism in *Inception*, but Nolan's early film *Memento* also comes to mind.

The first planet chosen proves a watery bust, functioning as a veritable surfer's paradise. Massive waves recall baptismal death imagery, and the reaper strikes once again killing one of the crew. Narrowly escaping and suffering a loss of a couple of decades, Cooper and Brand return to the ship and plot a course to option two, Dr. Mann's planet, where a Matt Damon-circle also awakens from "death." The name "Dr. Mann" is significant, as we learn both Dr. Mann and Professor Brand have engaged in colossal lies. Mann lied to get the crew to come rescue him and Brand lied that gravity could be solved and earth saved. Both Professor Brand and Dr. Mann mirror one another, making massive mistakes and justifying them with curiously collectivist statements, insisting that huge sacrifices must be made for the good of the species. These rationalizations are actually cloaks for their own weaknesses and this is a crucial point in the film – human weakness is such that it will require something more to get man to the beyond. Human frailty and *hubris* are always a cause for error and mistakes, but error and mistake prove disastrous when the species itself is on the line.

Ironically, in both character's cases, their attempts to rule out individual desires and feelings for the so-called "greater good" are proven wrong! Nolan seems to be advocating the important truth that while communal activities are important, the spark and drive of the great individual is the key to paradigmatic advancement, not radical collectivism. Thus, both Brand and Mann fail, and their generic names signify the failure of these archaic modes of impersonal thought. "Brand Man" or *homo economicus* and communism's fictional "new man" (it's dialectical opposite) do not work, and are surpassed by the power and grandeur of a man against time. With Professor Brand it turns out there was no "Plan A," only the Noah's Ark style "Plan B" to plant an off-world colony. Though I haven't mentioned it yet, the Dylan Thomas poem, "Do Not Go Gentle Into that Good Night," is cited a second time here (the first at his initial launch) as Cooper is on the verge of death from Mann's betrayal. The poem is about fighting death and cherishing life, appearing in the narrative at crucial times when chronos/time/death is approaching.

Nolan's use of A.I. is atypical and will be the key to unlocking the code, with the robots saving humans more than once. In Kubrick's work, we are all familiar with the famed battle of man against HAL 9000, where HAL seeks to supplant man's evolutionary ascent. In Nolan's work, A.I. is *subservient* to man, and does more than just aid him in his quest. In fact, mankind as a whole is saved more than once by the onboard bots that resemble Kubrick's monolith in shape and form. Instead of mysterious, otherworldly stones of alchemical spacey origin, my thesis for *Interstellar* will challenge the norm. It is my contention that the film advocates a form of transhumanism, where the mysterious "they" are not just the "humans of the future" as Cooper states, but advanced A.I.-human hybrids of the future. Several clues are given to support this thesis.

First, the beginning of the film shows the museum footage of Murphy and the elderly recounting history on smaller versions of what *look like monolithic bots*. Just as the monolith bots *store the history of man, they store the history of Murph and Cooper, as demonstrated when Cooper is in the tesseract*. Second, when the drone lands and Cooper and Murphy are discussing harnessing it, Murphy gives a big clue no one seems to have picked up on, pleading, "It isn't hurting anyone, can't we let it go?" Murph speaks of the old Indian Air Force drone as if it were *alive*. Third, when Cooper passes the event horizon having traveled beyond space and time, the means by which humanity will transcend those final boundaries is revealed as the agents who, like angelic guardians throughout the film, consistently save the humans. Just as the solution to the problem of gravity was only achieved by *both man and A.I. crossing the horizon* and working together to *relay the information in binary* (the language of computers), so likewise the transcending of space and time in the tesseract was achieved by a transcendent race of humans merged with machines from the future. Fourth, this explains why you never see TARS in the tesseract – you only hear Cooper talking to him, but the robot cannot be seen. This is also why the robots in *Interstellar* have the *look* of the monolith in *2001*. Nolan very consciously chose to make the robots like the monolith, as the film is full of *2001* references. But here, the robots are *not HAL 9000*: They are the means by which man will transcend. In *2001*, the mysterious monolith is leading man in his evolution; in *Interstellar* the monolith is replaced with *monolith-looking good A.I.*. Understanding the place of the monolith in *2001* is key to solving the riddle Nolan presents us with here.

Further bolstering this case is the imagery used when Cooper crosses the abyss. The end of the universe and entrance to the tesseract appears to have a lattice structure which TARS explains was "created" by "them" to give a fixed point in space and time to reveal these truths. In other words, the matrix-like structure of the universe is meant to be transcended (so the film's worldview is saying) through an evolved, emergent *deus ex machina*. Readers may disagree, but I believe this is the best analysis of the worldview presented, as the film consistently upholds the Darwinian perspective. On this view, it is only natural to expect the means by which man might transcend his final frontiers is artificial intelligence and transhumanism.

Another subtle clue is found in Professor Brand's office, where you can barely make out a copy of A.I. specialist Douglas Hofstadter's *Metamagical Themas*. Luckily, I just purchased this book a few weeks ago, so I was able to identify it. Hofstadter's work focuses on strangeloops and Kurt Godel, and soon after we see this, an older Murphy (Jessica Chastain) hints at Godel by saying the models Professor Brand uses can never work because they are *self-referencing*! In other words, perceptive readers are supposed to make the connection that the type of *strangeloop* Hofstadter discusses demonstrates that humans can't solve the equation because they are within time and space – but an advanced A.I. might! Yet even still, an advanced A.I. is caught in an infinite strangeloop without a bridge to a finite point in space and time. Here is where the human element enters, as Cooper states in the tesseract, "We are the bridge!"

At this juncture, Murphy realizes more must be at work and that her "ghost" may have been real all along. The solution to the outer world problem of death is connected to the inner world problems of Cooper's psyche (like Cobb in *Inception*). It is not accidental that the outer abyss mirrors archetypal images in his subconscious. In other words, Nolan is saying for advancement to occur, what is needed is Jungian self-individuation where both the rationalism of science and the intuitive feel of the feminine are joined. This was Jung's whole project with Pauli. This is why Amelia Brand (Anne Hathaway) is right in her *feeling* of which planet to choose and why Murphy is right about her feeling that more was at work with her bedroom than gravity, and why *love* is the key. Time and space are cyclical, like a sphere, and the only means by which it might be transcended is a tesseract, and the only conceivable way such a state might be created is an advanced computer/human hybrid possessing the full capabilities of human masculinity/femininity and a formal, platonic A.I..

The future A.I. men are also who placed the wormhole where it was. This interpretation also explains why Cooper resuscitates the damaged TARS on Cooper Station – we are supposed to connect the human "Lazarus" project with the *resurrecting* of the A.I.. Consistently throughout the film, *the A.I. are treated as alive*, and that is the key to grasping this point. For Nolan, the key to transcending death, the last enemy referenced in the Dylan Thomas poem, is the "Lazarus Project" – the *singularity* merger of human and machine. While most viewers were focused on the storyline of Cooper and Murph, the underlying story was actually TARS and the singularity as the key to defeating the real enemy – death.

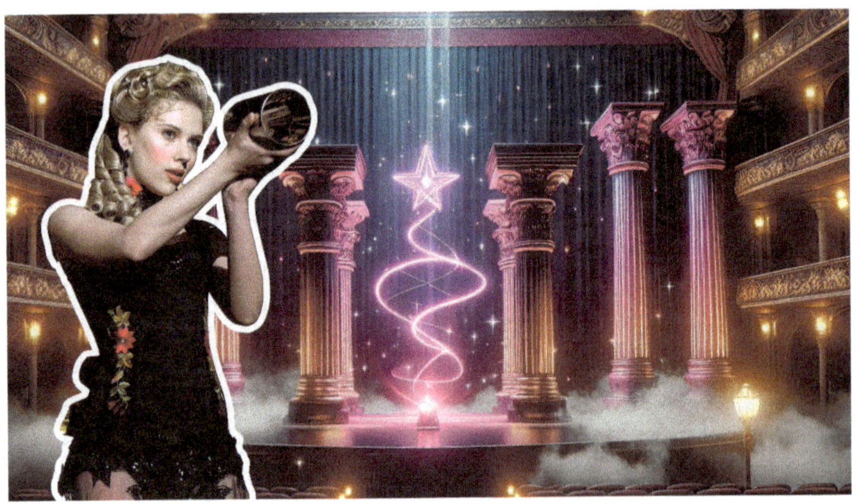

THE PRESTIGE (2006)

For most viewers, *The Prestige* was a film about rival stage magicians in the Victorian Era, alternately seeking to top one another in the dank climate of emerging industrial revolution and technological wonder. Lord Caldlow/Angiers (Hugh Jackman) is the secret nobleman who has a flair for the art of illusion, while Robert Borden and his twin (Christian Bale) are the working class stagehands who have devoted their lives to their art. In the midst of this rivalry, the curious figure of Nikola Tesla enters (played by David Bowie) to interject the element of real magic, titled in the film, "wizardry." Both magicians are on a quest to sabotage the other, while seeking to perfect the greatest trick of all – the transported man.

Stage rivalry and obsession *is* what *The Prestige* is about, but it is also about much more. After several viewings (as is my normal habit), my thesis began to congeal: *The Prestige* is about Hollywood and film-making itself. And not only that, it is an industry that is an art of deception and illusion. The director and the actors are in effect illusion artists, or con men, if you will. The successful director is able to fool the audience into accepting that what is presented on the screen *is* real, even if it is evidently fantastical. The magicians' *ingenieure*, Mr. Cutter (Michael Caine), explains this principle of film as illusion at the beginning, which is to be applied to the film itself. Cutter states:

> Every great magic trick consists of three parts or acts. The first part is called "The Pledge." The magician shows you something ordinary: a deck of cards, a bird or a man. He shows you this object. Perhaps he asks you to inspect it to see if it is indeed real, unaltered,

normal. But of course … it probably isn't. The second act is called "The Turn." The magician takes the ordinary and makes it do something extraordinary. Now you're looking for the secret … but you won't find it, because of course you're not really looking. You don't really want to know. You want to be fooled. But you wouldn't clap yet. Because making something disappear isn't enough; you have to bring it back. That's why every magic trick has a third act, the hardest part, the part we call "The Prestige."

Director Christopher Nolan explains in "The Making of *The Prestige*" this is to be applied to both directing and the film itself as a theatrical illusion: "For me, *The Prestige* is very much about film-making. It's very much about what I do. It is also intended to suggest to the audience some of those ideas about how the film itself is spooling its narrative out to the audience. You want people to be aware of the effect the film is having as it's unfolding before their eyes." *The Prestige* follows this same tripartite structure, as it draws you into an ordinary story of human rivalry and obsession, the "Turn," where the audience is looking for the secret of Angier and the Borden's trick, but not truly looking, because like film, stage magic operates under the audience's suspension of disbelief. The audience "wants to be fooled." And in the end, the transported man must come back – reemerge or resurrect, as the final climax of the show.

1. The Pledge

In order to properly understand Nolan's film, we must consider the same principle elucidated concerning David Lynch films – twilight language. Researcher Michael Hoffman defines "twilight language" as follows in his *Secret Societies and Psychological Warfare*:

> The path to unlocking this gnosis was centered in "twilight language," a once nearly universal subliminal communication system used in Egypt, Babylon, the Indian subcontinent and among the Aztecs, consisting of a combination of numbers, archetypal words and symbols, which in our time are sometimes embedded in modern advertising, and in certain modern films and music…. In Oriental Tantra, the mantra (including *dharani, kavaca, yamala,* etc.) is sonically calculated to induce a particular action. It forms part of the original Sanskrit concept of *sandhyabhasa*(twilight language). In Tantra, 'Sandhyabhasa … is a language of light and darkness … in this higher type of discourse, words have another, a different meaning: this is not to be openly discussed. (pg. 207)

Like Kubrick, Lynch and Hitchcock, Nolan utilizes this same pattern, where certain words, images and phrases will stand out as ciphers to the film on the deeper level. This is a tricky process, as it is not always a simple science of picking out which clues and words are key, but it can be done with experience. This is one of the more controversial aspects dealt with at JaysAnalysis, so I intend on providing other examples of the same in other arenas to help convince skeptics. Hoffman continues:

> "Ritual is obsession in motion. Obsessive people are walking rituals and they attract "coincidentally," aids to their obsessions. If this is done consciously and the obsession happens to coordinate with the trend and tendency of the time, a lot more "coincidental" magnification will be forthcoming. Coincidence can be summoned. It is a matter of attention and timing. First you must be aware of – believing in and observing – the mechanism of coincidence when it agrees with your work, then you coordinate what you're working on with what you were predestined to do. When you start to see the pattern of coincidence and it becomes a language for you, you have either become an initiate or a schizophrenic, take your pick, because you lose the protection of materialism – our own protection against the disordering of the arrangement we've given to the world to make it manageable." (Ibid., 130)

Nolan's films are replete with uses of Jungian archetypes and synchronicity – another Jungian concept. In my *Inception* analysis, I wrote:

> The other crucial element is that the story is not a linear story, just like a dream is often non-linear. The film concerns essentially the "architecture of the mind," as director Christopher Nolan described it. Jung's theories involve the idea that the individual is a disparate instantiation of the collective unconscious, and thus fragmented from the collective. The collective consciousness manifests itself in images and archetypes in our deepest selves – the lowest of the subconscious. It is here that we hide our most intimate failures, sins and fears. We guard this sensitive part of ourselves, and have defense mechanisms by which we hide and guard these deeper, more elemental ethereal truths about who we really are. For Jung, being the mystic he was, the goal is to overcome all purported fragmentation, work through the so-called self-realization/individuation process, and thus escape dualities. The masculine "side" must reconcile with the feminine. One notices here familiar themes found throughout the history of alchemy, and Jung was known for his penchant in such arcane studies.

The above quotes thus solidify a central concept in my analysis of *The Prestige* – the film is not just about Hollywood illusion and twilight language, but the usage of that power through the illusion of the stage/screen to produce an effect in the consciousness of the viewer. In my *Eyes Wide Shut* analysis, I claimed the film was an attempt to initiate the reader, whereas with *The Prestige*, the film seems to delight in fooling the audience. It is an exaltation of the fact that most of the viewing audience will not understand the connotations, thinking the film was only about rival magicians, while being unable to place the usage of Nikola Tesla.

Recall as well that Nolan's 2005 *Batman Begins* was entirely a conspiracy-themed plot, lending credence to my thesis that all of his films may legitimately be assumed to be "written" twilight language. On *Batman Begins*, I explained about the League of Shadows, the dark eastern cult that had become Batman's nemesis as we saw earlier:

> It is also relevant to consider that the drugging of the water supply, an old Soviet and Nazi tactic, is, in fact, still practiced today, as much of the United States' water supply is purposefully drugged in order to chemically attack the masses, reducing IQs and causing sterilization. Psychoactive drugs have also been proposed for addition to water supplies, as well as actual antidepressants, rocket fuel and radiation, turning up in samples. Drugs are also being sprayed in geo-engineering and "chemtrail" programs. For the League of Shadows, the purpose is mass insanity directed towards an engineered social collapse. Again, art mirrors reality. The hallucinogen mind control chemical is developed by "Scarecrow" (Cillian Murphy), who is a doctor specializing in mental health and brainwashing. Scarecrow represents the pharmaceutical complex which works in tandem with the military industrial complex to engineer and control society. The Scarecrow character brings to mind the famed MKUltra programs which experimented with various methods, including drugs, to solve and control the human mind.

In *The Prestige*, dualities play a tremendous role. Borden has a double, his twin brother, who shares his life as the family man, as well as Angier having his initial double, Mr. Root, the drunken failed actor. As the rivalry intensifies, Borden and Angier become doubles in a way, each seeking to top the other and obsessing over the other. Both Borden and Angier live double lives, not being who they appear to be. This duality is a common theme in Hitchcock and Nolan is clearly utilizing it. Dialectical dualism is one of the oldest religious principles, operating as a dialectic in both eastern and western religion and occultism. Our temporal life in that perspective is seen as one of constant struggle with duality and opposition, with alchemical fusion or other-worldly transcendence seen as the usual escape. Oriental religions are especially taken up with dualities and dualism and this becomes a symbolic indicator with the old Chinese magician. Cutter tells Borden and Angier they can have ten minutes of audition time if they can solve the old man's act. After viewing it, Borden tells Angier the secret to the routine was that he always played the character of the old magician. It was all an act, because that is true devotion to the art, and true devotion to the art is the only way to "escape all this" (as he pounds on a rock wall). On one level, Borden was referring to his life of poverty, but on a deeper level, it is a reference to the film's continual usage of bird cages, water tanks and boxes.

The bird-cage is explained by Nolan as an image of being trapped. The magician's use of the tank and Angier's use of "Tesla's box" exemplify this, too, and the meaning is twofold. On the one hand, the characters are trapped in their own mental prisons of obsession over both women and their stagecraft. The obsession leads to the death of one of the Borden's and his wife, as well as countless clones of Angier from the Tesla machine. As I will explain later, the amazing technology of Tesla is presented in *The Prestige* as something wholly other – something no one at that time was able to accept and could only be slowly introduced. The film presents Tesla as working covertly in Colorado to power a whole town while also conducting secret experiments involving cloning. I have written elsewhere about the truth behind this idea, that Tesla did do many of the seemingly miraculous things attributed to him, but that his work was confiscated by officials of various intelligence agencies, which is even referenced in passing in the film. Tesla did work on secret projects in Colorado, and this is significant in terms of twilight language in regard to another famous novel, *Atlas Shrugged*.

In *Atlas Shrugged*, John Galt's rebellion of business leaders against the government is centered around a hidden "Atlantis" community in Colorado. This secret community was based around the philosophy of Galt and was hidden using directed energy beams, or "defractor rays." Galt's idea was a "quantum propulsion engine" that would revolutionize energy markets by pulling energy from the environment – both of which are Tesla-related ideas. I have written elsewhere about the connection between Tesla's work and an alternate, hidden metaphysics the establishment is aware of, yet suppresses from the masses, based largely around notions like the aether and quantum technology.

2. The Turn

But what might be the use of Tesla in the film? Why Tesla? A host of scientists could have been used, but Tesla was chosen for a reason. As the film correctly notes, Tesla is the father of the modern world. Unfortunately, Tesla's rather benevolent intention was not what his inventions were used for. As I have shown by uploading the declassified documents relating to his work, the confiscation of Tesla's work was done with the full intent of technocratic enslavement.

Back in 1973, longtime Washington geopolitical strategist Zbigniew Brzezinski described the usage of Tesla technology for the dystopian control of large masses of populations in his *Between Two Ages*:

> In addition … future developments may well include automated or manned space warships, deep-sea installations, chemical and biological weapons, death rays, and still other forms of warfare – even the weather may be tampered with.
>
> In addition, it may be possible–and tempting–to exploit for strategic-political purposes the fruits of research on the brain and on human behavior. Gordon J. F. MacDonald, a geophysicist specializing in problems of warfare, has written that timed artificially excited electronic strokes could lead to a pattern of oscillations that produce relatively high power levels over certain regions of the earth.… In this way, one could develop a *system that would seriously impair the brain performance of very large populations* in selected regions over an extended period.… No matter how deeply disturbing the thought of using the environment to manipulate behavior for national advantages to some, the technology permitting such use will very probably develop within the next few decades.
>
> As one specialist noted, 'By the year 2018, technology will make available to the leaders of the major nations, a variety of *techniques for conducting secret warfare*, of which only a bare minimum of the security forces need be appraised. One nation may attack a competitor covertly by bacteriological means, thoroughly weakening the population (though with a minimum of fatalities) before taking over with its own armed forces. Alternatively, techniques of weather modification could be employed to produce prolonged periods of drought or storm.… (Gordon J. F. MacDonald, "Space," in *Toward the Year 2018*, p.34)." (pg. 57 with fn)

To bring this back home to *The Prestige*, the wireless transmission of television and Internet onto magical mirror boxes in most households was long foreseen as a means to "pledge," "turn" and "prestige" the duped masses of America and the world. It is my thesis that the film includes Tesla because not only was he the father of the modern world's technology, his technology would in turn be used by the cryptocracy as the greatest means of propagandizing and tricking the populace through millions of screens broadcasting illusion. From fake news to fake lives, television and the invasion of the screens has erected an entirely synthetic alternate reality in which people's minds inhabit, like the birds in cages or Angier in the tanks, in the film.

The meaning of the cloning of Angier to top Borden symbolizes what Tesla says to Angier: "Man's reach exceeds his grasp"? It's a lie. Man's grasp exceeds his nerve. The only limits on scientific progress are those imposed by society. The first time I changed the world, I was hailed as a visionary. The second time I was asked politely to retire. The world only tolerates one change at a time. And so here I am. Enjoying my "retirement." Tesla means that what man attempts, when he overcomes his fear, can exceed what seems possible. With Angier's funding, Tesla creates a "box" that results in cloning. The greatest mystery of western religion – bodily resurrection, is presented as within the possibility of science, but Tesla in the film issues a warning that all of this obsession comes at a price. Modern scientism is something I have written about at length, and one of the greatest dark secrets is revealed precisely in the figure of Tesla. Like the Brzezinski quote on preceeding page, not only has Tesla tech been used for weather warfare, Army psychological warfare expert and founder of the Satanic Temple of Set, Col. Michael Aquino describes the actual usage of Tesla's ELF/VLF radio frequency attacks upon mass populations. In his "From PSYOP to Mindwar: The Psychology of Victory," Aquino writes in the footnotes towards the end:

> Atmospheric electromagnetic (EM) activity: The Human body communicates internally by EM and electrochemical impulses. The EM field displayed in Kirlian photographs, the effectiveness of acupuncture, and the body's physical responses to various types of EM radiation (X-rays, infrared radiation, visible light spectrum, etc.) are all examples of human sensitivity to EM forces and fields. Atmospheric EM activity is regularly altered by such phenomena as sunspot eruptions and gravitational stresses which distort the Earth's magnetic field. Under varying external EM conditions, humans are more or less disposed to the consideration of new ideas.

MindWar should be timed accordingly. Per Dr. L.J. Ravitz: Electromagnetic field constructs add fuel to the assumption unifying living matter harmoniously with the operations of nature, the expression of an electromagnetic field no less than non-living systems; and that as points on spectrums, these two entities may at last take their positions in the organization of the universe in a way both explicable and rational.... A tenable theory has been provided for emergence of the nervous system, developing not from functional demands, but instead deriving as a result of dynamic forces imposed on cell groups by the total field pattern. Living matter has a definition of state based on relativity field physics, through which it has been possible to detect a measurable property of total state functions. (Ravitz, State-Function, Including Hypnotic States" in *Journal of American Society of Psychosomatic Dentistry and Medicine* Vol. 17, No. 4, 1970.)"

And,

"Ionization of the air: An abundance of negative condensation nuclei ("air ions") in ingested air enhances alertness and exhilaration, while an excess of positive ions enhances drowsiness and depression. Calculation of the ionic balance of a target audience's atmospheric environment will be correspondingly useful. Again this is a naturally-occurring condition – caused by such varying agents as solar ultraviolet light, lightning, and rapidly-moving water – rather than one which must be artificially created. (Detonation of nuclear weapons, however, will alter atmospheric ionization levels.) Cf. Soyke, Fred and Edmonds, Alan, *The Ion Effect.* New York: E.P. Dutton, 1977.

Extremely Low Frequency (ELF) waves: ELF waves up to 100 Hz are once more naturally occurring,but they can also be produced artificially (such as for the Navy's Project Sanguine for submarine communication). ELF-waves are not normally noticed by the unaided senses, yet their resonant effect upon the human body has been connected to both physiological disorders and emotional distortion. Infrasound vibration (up to 20 Hz) can subliminally influence brain activity to align itself to "delta," "theta," "alpha," or "beta" wave patterns, inclining an audience toward everything from alertness to passivity. Infrasound could be used tactically, as ELF-waves endure for great distances; and it could be used in conjunction with media broadcasts as well. See Playfair, Guy L. and Hill, Scott, *The Cycles of Heaven.* New York: St. Martin'sPress, 1978, pages 130-140."

3. The Prestige

Now you understand the reason for the prevalence of television, wifi, and ELF/VLF towers. The prestige you don't want to see is staring you right in the face. The tech grid that is built all around us is erected for the purpose of working in conjunction with the "chemtrail" geo-engineering that ionizes the atmosphere. The heating of the atmosphere is used in conjunction with frequency manipulation to control mass populations. While *The Prestige* is not a film directly about this, this is the use of Tesla, the father of modern communications technology, which brings to the masses the frequency manipulation on top of the theatrical illusion of Hollywood cinema "magic." And I have just shown you two high level cryptocracy controllers who openly say it is such. The world's a stage, but most are spectators in this technocratic drama.

Hoffman writes again of the methods and techniques of the shadow establishment that are equally applicable to the Hollywood illusion machine:

> The Cryptocracy has always operated as a rhetorical system. In the Kennedy assassination we saw this in the command-words Camelot, Storyville, Shakespeare and Truth or Consequences. Predictive Programming works by means of the propagation of the illusion of an infallibly accurate vision of how the world is going to look in the future. This fraud has had a not inconsiderable impact on our reality. Aleister Crowley, in a statement to OTO initiates concerning one of his books, describes the underlying epistemology behind the glamor and enchantment which causes the occult con-game to become the weird reality we inhabit in America today:[10]

> 'In this book it is spoken of the Sephiroth and the Paths; of Spirits and Conjurations; of Gods, Spheres, Planes, and many other things which may or may not exist. It is immaterial whether these exist or not. By doing certain things certain results will follow; students are most earnestly warned against attributing objective reality or philosophic validity to any of them.' (*Liber O Vel*)[11]

Here Crowley admits that the OTO is a vehicle for imposing an *artificial reality based on nothing but lies and promoted by liars initiated into the art and science of illusion.*"[12] Although not immediately pertinent to the film, I would like to give another example of twilight language for skeptics: IMF head Christine Lagarde gave a speech some years ago in which she made some very interesting comments about numerology that many found baffling. The video claims to give a prediction about economic issues based on the video's numerology, which I would caution against.[13] However, even if the overall video speculation is incorrect, what Lagarde's carefully planned speech undoubtedly demonstrates is the very principle of twilight language I have been arguing for. For her, numerology is a language that conveys another message beyond the immediate, surface meaning.

The last sentence of Hoffman perfectly describes the theme and message of *The Prestige*: "imposing an *artificial reality based on nothing but lies and promoted by liars initiated into the art and science of illusion.*" Written in twilight language, it is a film about much more than petty magicians: It is a film about revelation of the method itself. It is a revelation of the method of revelation of the method. Just as Borden's diary in the film is written in a cipher with a keyword that turns out to be "Tesla," Nolan wants the viewer to understand that *The Prestige* is a film written in a cipher, whose keyword is Tesla. That is why I have focused my analysis on Tesla, who is the real message of the film, not Angier or the Bordens. Tesla is the real "wizard" who created the modern world, not the illusionists, with their stagecraft and sleight of hand. To transcend space and time and resurrect is the goal of modern science and transhumanism, but remember Tesla's warning – it comes at a price. This is the message of the film's twilight language. In my article, I presented a pledge, a turn and a prestige and today is Nikola Tesla's birthday: Are you watching closely, or are you wanting to be fooled?

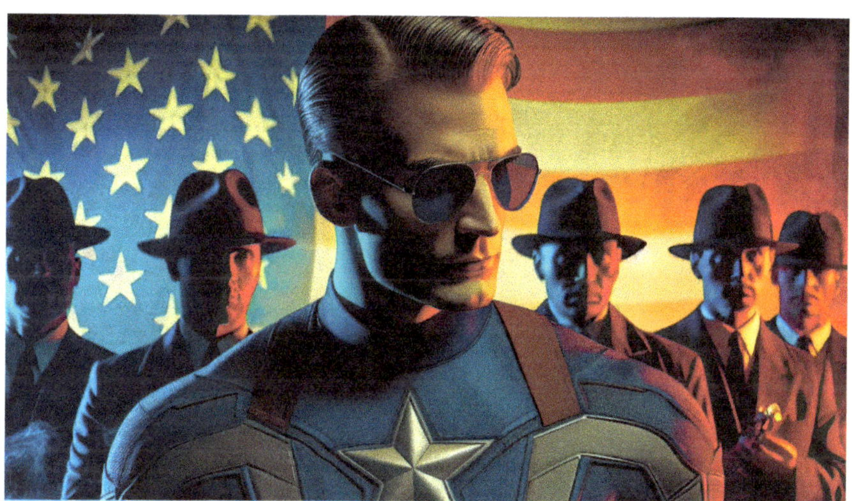

CAPTAIN AMERICA

The Captain America franchise was originally an Americanist propaganda exercise, but as America caved more and more to the woke cult, it was evident even the earlier phases of propaganda would have to be deconstructed, which is precisely where the franchise went with the eventual death of the "old" Captain America. However, the second *Captain America* film was heavily laced with revelation of the method programming, or perhaps even genuine artistic rebellion against the corrupt, elite establishment. The plot is surprisingly one of the most anti-new world order films I've seen, which is odd given the track Marvel and Disney films eventually took: apparently that doesn't prevent a positive message from leaking out here and there.

However, from a darker perspective, was the completely revelatory plot of *Captain America 2* purposefully released as another middle finger? Does the intentional selection of sentimental old Americana (represented by Captain America) perhaps signal the establishment's statement that they know the truth of the opposition's side better than the opposition, associating anti-establishment impetus with childish comic book plots? Let us analyze. The plot begins with a French "terrorist" organization hijacking a high-tech SHIELD warship called "The Lemurian Star." Lemuria is associated with Atlantis in the writings of occultists like Blavatsky and Leadbetter, giving us a clue that the key to interpreting the meaning will be the attempt to restore Atlantis. This false flag attack is designed to frame SHIELD commander, Nick Fury (Samuel L. Jackson), disabling the Avengers and Captain America.

The state-sponsored terror is actually led by Hydra, a kind of World War 2 analogue for the Bilderberg Group. Hydra, like Bilderberg, was founded by David Rockefeller and "former Nazi" SS Prince Bernhard seeking to implement a worldwide technocratic government. Like the actual Bilderberg Group, it has the same goals and motivations, but what was so surprising about *Captain America 2* was the revelation of the A.I. control/kill grid that is Hydra's real weapon.[14] The Avengers discover that the A.I. kill grid is put in place to utilize all the data that the government surveillance has captured over the last several decades using complex algorithms that predict who the likely threats will be in the future.

Predictive algorithmic A.I. computing is precisely the purpose of the Internet itself, as well as Google and all the other tech monstrosities. The purpose of the Internet itself was always to gather reconnaissance on the masses. The A.I. grid stores basically everything, and based on the vast information stored at the "data vaults" and warehouses around the globe, information is processed for future predictive accuracy. There is a virtual version of everything happening, with a virtual version of you and me, where tests are run to see the outcome of various scenarios. The reconnaissance is for the ultimate goal of the A.I. takeover. Films like the *Ter-*

minator series and *Oblivion* also have this same plot, but rather than art life imitating art, this is art based on actual Pentagon programs. And just like Skynet is real, so is the Avengers' version of Skynet, where advanced decapitation and space-based weapons (for removing heads of state) have been in place since at least the Star Wars Defense initiative of the late 70s.[15]

At the end of H.G. Wells' *Outlines of History,* he speaks about the "rise of the machines" and their ability to allay the toils of men, granting them more leisure for scientific products, art, and other harmonious progressive pursuits. Education will become universal, and a better world will ensue. Wells was, to be fair, spot on with many of his sci-fi predictions. One can't help but notice that this devolution of the human race seems to confirm the H.G. Wells thesis in *The Time Machine* the human race is mutating into Eloi and Morlocks[16]

However, the rise of the machines has been wilder than even Wells could have imagined, and will probably not be the universal utopia *Outlines* imagines, but something closer to the dystopia of *The Time Machine.* In fact, we have reached the point where A.I. is nearing the ability of what we see in many science fiction films and novels, yet I agree with the affirmation of Douglas Hofstadter in *Godel, Escher, Bach* that we will not achieve self-awareness. Even if this did occur, there is no certain test to determine the existence of "self-awareness," and the modern scientists who argue to no end against the soul or mind must also take their dogma of the inability to "prove consciousness" and apply it to the golem. On their basis, you could no more prove one than the other. So the reductionists who think consciousness is merely matter have no problem identifying humans as "more complex" computers (like Daniel Dennett): Nevermind they are all guilty of the naturalistic fallacy!

In effect, this is a Prometheus situation, and is precisely the goal the occultists, alchemists and "scientists" have sought for millennia. Don't be fooled by the propaganda of the "new atheists" and sciencey labcoaters: the real secret is that the mysteries are real. Granted, many of the "Illuminists" are of an atheistic and rationalist bent (and the actual Illuminati were Enlightenment rationalists), but there is a definite esotericism behind the creation of the golem. Atheism itself can become a form of superstition, as I've written many times on this blog. I want to make clear, though, that I'm not anti-technology, nor am I saying I disagree with these goals. Clearly the Enlightenment thinkers were right – in fact, some of them are central to the mathematics behind all this, as well as to religion and metaphysics and esoterism, such as Leibniz. Newton, too, was an esotericist, and other examples can be given such as Nikola Tesla and Wolfgang Pauli.

As I've written before, in the 90s Microsoft and the military planned to have a total Skynet grid in place with directed energy weapons and a microchipped populace that would be under global technocratic rule. The declassified document is still available at Fas.org.[17] Contrary to Gizmodo's claim that DARPA "tried" to build skynet in the 80s under SDI, the reality is Skynet was built and is still being built.[18] This is the very heart of the entire new world order plan, and why I say *Captain America 2: Winter Soldier* is one of the the ultimate conspiracy movies. It is also worth noting that Captain America is from another age – he represents old Americana in the film. He sees the world in the classic bipolar, manichaean scheme that Brzezinski described of the past century, where the "free" West struggles against the "tyrannical" axis and eastern powers.

The film's title "Winter Soldier" refers to Captain's old war buddy who was cryogenically frozen by Hydra and resurrected under MKUltra-style mind control programming to become a mass murdering assassin. Hydra thus intends to use the A.I. kill grid to set up the "new world order," the film says, where order will reign over chaos. As all utopian propagandists have sought, the goal was to build the *New Atlantis*. This is crucial to note, as Sir Francis Bacon, the hermeticist philosopher of the new world (America) predicted the continent would become the "New Atlantis." It is not accidental that Hydra's goal of creating the New Atlantis occurs in the *Captain America* film.

Hydra's image is similar to the classic Prussian "Death's Head," and the Nazi Totenkopf. Consider as well the Hydra symbol is red for war/bloodshed and has three mirrored tentacles that are reversible "666s." As the film's villain Alexander Pierce (Robert Redford) states, "To build a better world requires tearing down the old one." This is the mantra of the new world order in real life, where "order out of chaos" is the formula used for thesis/antithesis/synthesis dialectics, in order to bring about convergence and change. The convergence and change, however, is not meant for good, but for the destruction of the "weak," as the social Darwinian plan of manufactured "evolution" marches on. So, does *Captain America 2* represent authentic rebellion on the part of some of the artistic establishment? Does it represent more revelation of the method of indoctrination, subtly using propaganda and psyops techniques to lull the unwashed masses into acquiescence, as the technocracy advances on?

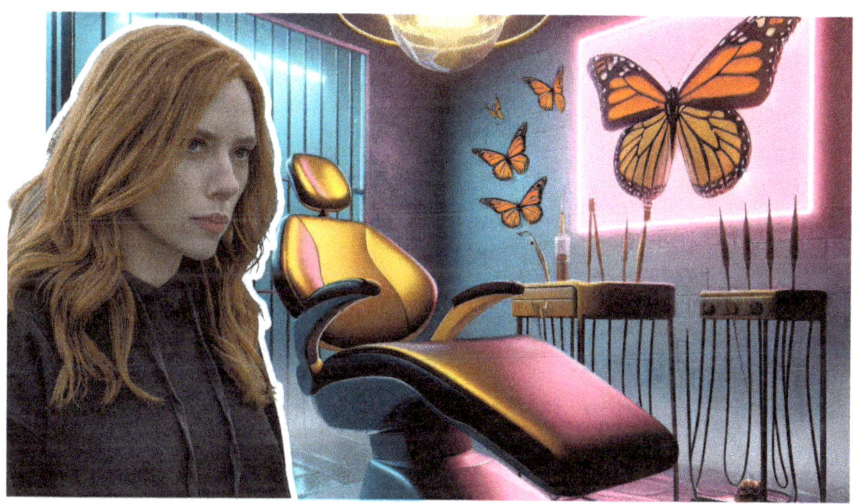

Marvel's *Avengers*

Taking its place as one of the highest grossing films of all time, the mythmakers of modernity at Marvel gave the world a fairly immense dose of esoterica combined with deep state black operations in the 2012 blockbuster written by Joss Whedon, *The Avengers*. Set in the same Marvel universe as *Iron Man*, *Captain America*, *Thor* and *Guardians of the Galaxy*, *The Avengers'* plot centered around a common theme I've analyzed often in terms of geo-politics: that of energy and resources.

Readers will notice similar patterns in science fiction of the last decade, from *Transformers* to *Interstellar*, revolving around cubes, tesseracts and energy sources. In my analysis, this is not accidental, but as with all of Hollywood's major releases, the establishment is conveying and encoding real world politics and black-budget agendas in a profound way, and *The Avengers* is no exception to that rule.

The opening sequence of the film features a *tesseract*, or hypercube, which is the geometrical structure of the dimension above our own, four-dimensional space. Amongst physicists and mathematicians, the hypercube is not merely a fantasy, but rather a known reality that extends beyond our own field of perception. I have delved into this in the past, with articles on crystallography and Pythagoreanism, as well as in relation to the Quadrivium method of classical learning that utilized the platonic solids and as the fundamental architecture of reality.

In relation to classical metaphysics from ancient Greece and Egypt, the association of the fifth element after fire, water, earth and air, is *aether*, or quintessence. It is not accidental that following the opening hypercube sequence, we see Nick Fury engaged in secret work under NASA at a "dark energy" project in an underground base.[19] Seemingly far-fetched, there are actual deep state black programs that revolve around plasma weaponry, particularly with H.A.A.R.P., which the Navy has boasted about.[20] In classical Greek thought, not only are there five elements, but matter also passes in and out of four states: solid, liquid, gas and plasma.

Fans of Tesla will recognize the similarity between the exotic weaponry Loki steals from Fury in the film, and the aether-based plasma physics Tesla utilized to work towards the potential for unlimited free energy, known as zero point energy, borrowed from the environment itself, as well as in quantum physics, according to Paul Dirac, energy from the future. It is interesting to note as well that under the cover of the "dark energy" name, the actual physics Fury and the military industrial complex are working with is plasma and aether-based, and not standard fare Newtonian atomism. It is precisely from this alternate Tesla physics that hints and clues consistently leak, even in mainstream science and film, as to the real hidden metaphysics the establishment's superweapons are based on. For example, in a 1937 Columbia lecture Tesla emphatically proclaimed:

> Only the existence of a field of force can account for the motions of the bodies as observed, and its assumption dispenses with space curvature. All literature on this subject is futile and destined to oblivion. So are all attempts to explain the workings of the universe without recognizing the existence of the aether and the indispensable function it plays in the phenomena.[21]

To further bolster my case that the film, like *Captain America: Winter Soldier*, is actually about the overall plan of the technocratic elite to create an enslaved, biologically retarded mass under the dominance of an A.I. grid, we can see this in Hulk, Captain America and Tony Stark, as both are emblematic of actual plans to produce transgenic "supersoldiers." With Captain America, his creation resulted from radiological experiments that directly parallel real radiological experimentation on soldiers and civilians from the Manhattan Project.

As detailed at length in my piece here, the Manhattan Project had a much wider ranging scope than simply producing an Atomic Bomb. Much like MKUltra, which would later become an aspect of the Manhattan Project through electronic brain manipulation and biological warfare, Manhattan was ultimately concerned with remaking and overlaying the entire biosphere, consummating in modern projects related to the construction quantum supercomputers (at the Oak Ridge, TN facility where the original A-Bomb was built under Manhattan) and wide-ranging atmospheric geoengineering programs through weather manipulation antenna array and aerosol spraying.[22] All of these programs, as well as DARPA's attempts at creating robotic and genetically-enhanced supersoldiers are the background to Hulk, Stark and Captain America.

MKUltra was also prominent in *Captain America: Winter Soldier* through the film's chief Russian antagonist, as well as with Loki's mind control of both Hawkeye (Jeremy Renner) and physicist, Dr. Erik Selvig. We can see a similar parallel between the A.I. takeover plot of Winter Soldier, and Loki's attempt to open a portal through which his serpentine army the Chitauri can enter:

> ...[J]ust like Skynet is real, so is the Avengers' version of Skynet, where advanced decapitation and space-based weapons (for removing heads of state) have been in place since at least the Star Wars Defense initiative of the late 70s.[23]

As I've written before, in the 90s Microsoft and the military planned to have a total Skynet grid in place with directed energy weapons and a microchipped populace that would be under global technocratic rule. Contrary to Gizmodo's claim that DARPA "tried" to build skynet in the 80s under SDI, the reality is Skynet was built and is still being built. This is the very heart of the entire new world order plan, and why I say *Captain America 2: Winter Soldier* is the ultimate conspiracy movie. It is also worth noting that Captain America is from another age – he represents old Americana in the film. He sees the world in the classic bipolar, manichaean scheme that Brzezinski described of the past century, where the "free" West struggles against the "tyrannical" axis and eastern powers.

In the narrative of both the *Captain America* films and *The Avengers*, the suppressed technology of the tesseract is from the Nazis, and in fact the Nazis did have an amazingly advanced grasp of these notions, as Dr. Joseph Farrell's treatments of Nazi technology demonstrate. In Farrell's *S.S. Brotherhood of the Bell*, there is a detailed account of the usage of Tesla's aether-based ideas for numerous black project research by the S.S. This is why the first *Captain America* film focuses on the usage of the tesseract by the Red Skull, the locus of Nazi advanced weaponry in the film's narrative. This is also why NATO and their secretive intelligence agency, S.H.I.E.L.D., are revealed to be co-opted by Hydra, something akin to the real shadow government of the Atlanticist regime. Similarly, in *The Avengers*, NATO's S.H.I.E.L.D. has the desire to use the tesseract for the creation of superweapons in response to Loki, while the Avengers team is assembled under a false cover story.

The good guys win, of course, and halt Loki's plans for Norse dominance through imperial prowess, but there is a curious point in the film where Loki actually reveals more than one would expect in dialogue with Natasha Romanoff in regard to her NATO/S.H.I.E.L.D. secret service work: "You lie and kill in the name of killers." Loki is actually right, as we discover in the highly revealing Winter Soldier plot that NATO and Nick Fury are controlled by Hydra, a force similar to Loki's own genocidal imperial ethos – Loki even appears to commit human sacrifice on a Babylonian, bull-headed altar at the symphony in Germany, while stealing a retinal scan. This is not surprising, as Loki is emblematic of the trickster/ Satan figure as the father of hell in Norse mythology.

The stark reality is that the Western establishment, embodied in entities like NATO, the U.N., the IMF, and the Bilderberg Group, and linked by major cities like D.C., London and Brussels, actually is a technocratic, tyrannical shadow government intent on a new reich. The race for control of resources, and in particular the control of energy, is what the real goal of geopolitical strategies by various power blocs is all about. As I wrote in my analysis of energy control and symbology:

> In terms of geo-politics, the race of modernity centers around energy. The fiat dollar is itself a symbolic representation of human energy. To bind all of the world to a fiat currency of ones and zeros in a computer grid is to enslave mankind to a central, virtual grid of nihilistic monetarism. Most nations in the world utilize the same fraudulent central banking model that we have here in the US – the "federal reserve" model, based in turn on the Bank of England model. The binding of masses to a single binary electronic "currency" thus encapsulates the transference of human energy into virtual "energy," yet even more susceptible to centralized fraud and manipulation than the older fiat paper models. It is therefore the liberal, nihilistic negation of currency and "money" (for the masses, that is). Our era of reign of quantity and monetarism is perfectly summarized with an Apophis "A" on the "dollar."

The new reich will be exactly what is predicted in the mythological fiction of the Marvel universe: a regime of serpentine elites, hell-bent on the implementation of mass dysgenics programs under the lordship of the great A.I. grid. In fact, the *Marvel Wiki* even explains of the history of the Chitauri (Loki's alien army in the film – paging David Icke!) and their notoriously real-life technocratic designs:

The next attempt at conquest was more subtle (at first), involving long-term methods of manipulation such as will-inhibiting drugs in many nations' water supplies, influencing the media, and R.F.I.D. (Radio-frequency identification) microchips to be implanted in schoolchildren, among other means. The Chitauri also infiltrated S.H.I.E.L.D, particularly the Psi-Division which could telepathically ferret out Chitauri agents. However, S.H.I.E.L.D. was able to detect some of the low-ranking "drone" staff of the aliens, disguised as common office workers, and wiped them out in an assault led by Black Widow and Hawkeye.

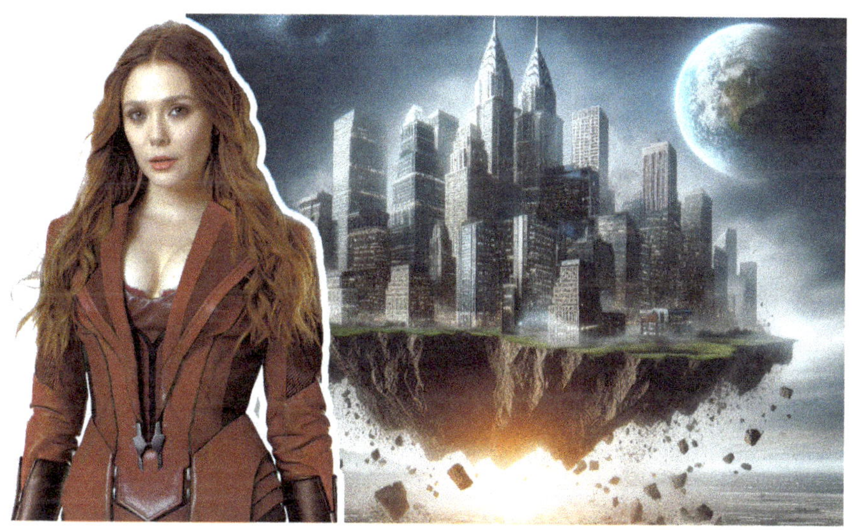

The Avengers: Age of Ultron (2015)

Joss Whedon's follow-up to *The Avengers*, *Avengers: Age of Ultron*, is setting new box office records for Marvel, and has roughly the same degree of critical response as the first. Recall my previous *Avengers* analysis, noting the A.I. takeover plot, and the sequel was even more esoterically themed and blatant in its presentation. Hollywood is making it difficult for me not to write the same A.I. analysis over and over, but some new ground is tread here to investigate in the midst of the same pattern we've been witnessing of late, the extinction of man through mass depopulation and his subjugation and/or replacement with an A.I. control grid.

In *Age of Ultron*, the Avengers team discovers genetic experimentation is still ongoing at a secret Hydra facility in Eastern Europe. Black Widow (Scarlett Johansson) explicitly references the U.S. and Nazi experimentation on humans and their importation into Allied nations following the War. Recalling part one and *Captain America: Winter Soldier*, we are reminded that Hydra is the secret cabal that is running S.H.I.E.L.D. and NATO, much like the Bilderberg Group in our world. Composed of former S.S. like Prince Bernhard and corporate executives like Peter Thiel who openly advocates for transhumanism and mass micro-chipping, the fictional presentation of Hydra is spot on.[24]

As a result of the human experimentation and genetic manipulation, Hydra has produced two new genetically-modified villains, the Twins, one of which is a babe with mind control abilities and some kind of explosive red glitz, and her brother, a Slavic Flash named Pietro. Using her mind control techniques (as a product of mind control herself), Wanda Maximoff implants visions of the team's darkest fears into each Avenger with the intention of dividing our heroes. It is worth noting that Eastern Europe is actually the locale of numerous CIA "black sites" and mind control operations, dating back to World War II and through the Cold War.[25]

The MKUltra/mind control is a common staple of Whedon's science fiction works, from River Tam in *Firefly* to Hawkeye in *Avengers* and now Natasha Romanoff, too. Romanoff we learn was an orphaned girl who was raised in Soviet Russia in a secret program to create programmed assassins out of young girls. In the deep research I've done on various mind control programs over the last century, all of these elements are very real, with both Allied and Axis powers engaging in programs of a similar nature. While it may seem unconnected, there is in fact a crucial link between A.I. research and the classic mind control programs, as MKUltra morphed into MKSEARCH, which dealt with implantable chips and electronic control of motor functions.

> Imagine you are in charge of the legal arm of the most powerful government on the face of the globe, but your internal information systems are mired in the archaic technology of the 1960s. There's a Department of Justice database, a CIA database, an Attorney's General database, an IRS database, and so on, but none of them can share information. That makes tracking multiple offenders pretty darn difficult, and building cases against them a long and bureaucratic task....
>
> But the real power of PROMIS, according to [William] Hamilton, is that with a staggering 570,000 lines of computer code, PROMIS can integrate innumerable databases without requiring any reprogramming. In essence, PROMIS can turn blind data into information. And anyone in government will tell you that informa-

tion, when wielded with finesse, begets power. Converted to use by intelligence agencies, as has been alleged in interviews by ex-CIA and Israeli Mossad agents, PROMIS can be a powerful tracking device capable of monitoring intelligence operations, agents and targets, instead of legal cases."[26]

The above is decades-old technology, and one can only imagine the advance that has been made in this type of data-collating and backdoor technology that is more in line with the revelations of NSA whistleblower, William Binney.[27] Binney was involved in the programming of the NSA's mass surveillance capabilities, and while none of this software is "sentient," the real meaning of Ultron is precisely the capabilities of these shadow government agencies to record and track *everyone*.[28] The exotic weaponry and "alien tech" in the *Avengers* series is thus a fictional representation of the real powers of the shadow military industrial complex, which is determined to implement mass dysgenics operations that perfectly mirror Ultron's desires to destroy humanity and replace it with a synthetic, transhumanist/Frankenstein concoction.

Speaking of *Frankenstein, Age of Ultron* had some interesting "*Weird Science*" moments that echo Mary Shelley's alchemical novel, with both the accidental creation of Ultron and his twin, Paul Bettany as the *deus ex machina* "I AM" (The Vision). The golem, based on the idea of Jewish kabbalism that the Names of God (and in particular I AM) have the ability to create life, is a prominent theme, and even more so than in *Ex Machina*, with mad scientists Stark and Banner utilizing the latest in nanotech tissue replacement to construct a new, regenerative body for Vision, and his third eye infinity stone.

In a Christian interpretive framework, Man's idyllic interaction with the gods represents Adam & Eve's prelapsarian state in Eden, Prometheus represents Lucifer (a name which itself means Light Bearer) & his gift of fire represents the fruit of the Tree of Knowledge. Since, in the Prometheus myth, man uses fire to cheat the gods of their rightful sacrificial offering (by giving a burnt offering of fat instead of meat) the god's punish Man by creating the first woman Pandora, who herself, is tricked into opening a jar containing all the world's ills. This final piece of the story (for Christians anyway) represents Eve's convincing Adam to eat the fruit and the subsequent entry of Death and Sin into the world.

Christian theology is important for *Age of Ultron* due to Ultron's consistent references to biblical and historical imagery, but repurposed for a dark inversion. Situating his new base inside the symbolic ruins of the old

Orthodox Church, Ultron speaks of himself as the new God of the new *aeon*, the new resurrection, etc. The "new man" is the perfected form of man, linked to the global brain with the regenerative powers of medical nanotechnology. In the same way that Marxism turned Hegelianism on its head, so transhumanism turns Christian theology on its head, locating all the "myths" of Christian theology on the plane of our existence. Christian theology holds that the Body of Christ is mystically one with the Church, and this union will result in a resurrection of the body to a new state of being, unbounded by death and the "puppet strings" of time and space, as Ultron sings citing *Pinocchio*.

It is therefore surprising to see *Age of Ultron*, like *Ex Machina*, explain the deeper secret tech and transhumanist truths that the human body is not something to be discarded, but to be perfected. For the pop mind, the body in transhumanism is seen to be a physical impairment, yet for the hermetic tradition upon which transhumanism is based, the body is actually a highly efficient tool. Deeper, alchemical and hermetic transhumanism does not want to discard the body, but in a very similar form to Christian theology, wants to revitalize it, making it immortal. The new man, the *aeon*, in this perspective, is the fulfillment of the mythos of Christianity. The film might aptly be titled *Aeon* of Ultra, where completely new forms of being arise (like Ultron or Vision):

> …the crowned and conquering child, who dieth not, nor is reborn,
> but goeth radiant ever upon His Way. Even so goeth the Sun: for as
> it is now known that night is but the shadow of the Earth, so Death
> is but the shadow of the Body, that veileth his Light from its bearer.
> –Aleister Crowley, *Heart of the Master*[29]

The secret behind this idea is a doctrine common to both Christian theology and hermeticism, known as the anthropic principle. For theologians such as Maximos the Confessor, as well as for Plato and ancient Egyptian theology, the body of man is a microcosmic analogue of the entire universe. There is a real correspondence between the body man, and the entire universe itself, the anthropocosmic. For example, Plato's *Timaeus* describes the universe as a body, as does St. Maximos the Confessor. Also known as the microcosm/macrocosm principle, the Temples of Egypt and the ancient Jewish Temple both embed this deep, esoteric principle relating to cosmogony.[30]

What we see in the overall plot is this: ancient and "alien" civilizations encode mathematical secrets of nature itself, which is true, despite the numerous nonsensical sites and articles that promote "ancient aliens." There are no aliens, but what *is true* is that the mathematical and Egyptian/Pythagorean principles *are the secrets of nature,* and that is the significance of the exotic crystal mythology in the *Avengers.* There is a lot to unpack and categorize with all this mythical scepter/infinity stone alien technology, but suffice to say the crux is this: The real world elite are obsessed with acquiring secret, advanced technology based around an alternative platonic metaphysic, symbolized in fictional form by all these comic narratives. The film's reference to "peace in our time" is a citation of both Disraeli, Neville Chamberlain and JFK's reference to the Anglo-American-Israeli world order's plans for the new age. The real plan, however, is for the new *aeon* of the new man, the perfected man of transhumanism regenerated through Frankenstein techno-alchemy.

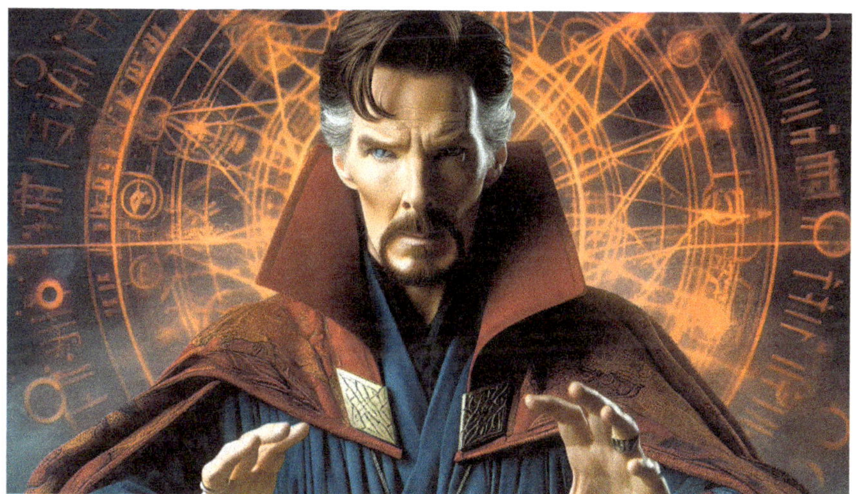

Doctor Strange (2016)

I don't often utilize the oft-touted term "illuminati" unless I think it is appropriate. In this case, as with my use in relation to *Zardoz,* it is appropriate. *Doctor Strange* is an amalgam of *Inception, The Matrix* and other science fiction-fantasy films of recent note, but unlike most presentations (except for perhaps *The Matrix*) is one of the most revelatory to date. A box office success, the film is a combination of both eastern and western hermeticism, as well as making numerous references to ceremonial and ritual magick. Though many would liken it to *Harry Potter* in this regard, *Doctor Strange* includes more aspects of "illuminism" proper insofar as the entire Marvel Universe includes transhumanism.

As we witnessed in the installments of *Captain America* and *The Avengers*, the entirety of the Marvel mythos is the bridge between ancient mythologies of the gods and modern technology – believed to be the pathway by which man will achieve the "godlike" powers the myths hinted at. Here, as I have argued for some years now, is the principle that the highest "illuminism" is beyond the notions of invoking or controlling spirits, and is the pragmatic application of science to the actualization of such "powers." In this sense, the chimeras and magic instruments of the gods are fulfilled in practices such as genetic modification and cross-species engineering or in the Internet itself.

The genius neurosurgeon character of Doctor Strange (Benedict Cumberbatch) is thus intended to embody the culmination of western analytical and quantitative approaches to knowledge, openly confessing himself to be a materialist. After suffering a severe accident that ravages his hands, Strange discovers his steady grip has vanished, costing him his prominent medical career. Reaching the end of his rope, Strange embarks on a journey based upon rumors of hidden healing techniques originating in the Far East in India.

Of course, to the mainstream mind, all "spirituality" arises from India and the Far East (here Nepal), with little consideration as to the possibility that merely being "spiritual" does not connote the good. Perhaps there are evil spirits? Perhaps the demonic is a real the human soul must contend with? For the *Eat, Pray, Love* consuming soccer moms and for their Marvel Comics consuming progeny, the need to accept "alternative spiritualities" as just as viable as their evangelical sect. The reality is, both of these naive approaches are manifestations of a controlled dialectic, where the Far Eastern influence birthed the ecumenical movement a century ago, while the evangelical strip mall "churches" are nothing more than corporate copycat templates of historic theology.

Setting all that aside for a moment, Strange wanders his way into the halls of an elite secret society which protects the esoteric secrets of the "good side," led by the Ancient One (Tilda Swinton), keeping at bay the interdimensional forces of the dark side, led by one of her former students, Kaecilius (Mads Mikkelsen), at the service of the uber-demon, Dormammu. The spiritual architecture of the worldview in this film is an amalgam of gnosticism, Hindu cosmology and tech-mysticism. As Strange is inducted into this society, he is given an intense astral experience where he sees other worlds and dimensions, stepping outside time. This is important for the plot, as time itself is one of the key enemies that must be opposed and overcome.

As Strange ascends into other worlds and has visions of the light-fabric of the kosmos, his third eye is explicitly opened. The experience is strikingly similar to an LSD trip, as Strange himself intimates. Learning all the hidden arts, Strange begins to grasp that the analytical truths of the world of matter are not in opposition to spiritual truths, which transcend them. Strange learns in particular to project his body into the aether as a kind of remote viewing exercise as he learns the "mysteries." As a side note, it's interesting that both Cumberbatch and Swinton are British actors playing roles where British and Soviet espionage exploits were well known.[31]

Lining up his chakras and mastering the "Key of Solomon," Strange decides to delve into deeper, darker rites, taking it upon himself to don the All-Seeing Eye necklace that allows him to fast forward and rewind time itself, from the grimoires of his order's ascended masters (call him Blavatsky Cumberbatch). Natural law, we learn, is the foundation of the order's rules, which earns a swift scolding for Strange – natural law must never be violated. However, Strange learns from Kaecilius that the Ancient One herself has lied, having used these rites to draw upon the dark side to prolong her life – "for the good." Kaicilius uses his chance encounter to preach his gospel to Strange, which is based on monotheism and immortality. His god, Dormammu, has power over time and seeks to envelop all worlds into his dimension.

The striking aspect of this is that as Dormammu and his evangelists wreak havoc on earth, Strange figures out that the only means by which the Monotheist can be destroyed is if an apotheosized man (Strange himself) ascends to Dormammu's dimension and uses the rites of time to entrap Dormammu with his own death. Dying countless times and rewinding (we're not sure how this is done if he's dead), Strange dupes Dormammu into an infinite time loop, something akin to Hofstadter's *strange loop* in *Godel, Escher, Bach*. Submitting to his defeat, the butt-hurt demiurge time-god departs, taking his disciples with him, leaving Strange in charge of the New York branch of the Illuminati.

London is, of course, the headquarters of world Freemasonry, Satanism, witchcraft (and communism and radical Islam, by the way), suggesting this film is a complete and total revelation of the method. In fact, as Strange defiantly opposes the Jehovah-like Saturn-affiliated Dormammu, he specifically arranges both hands into the devil-horn sign, and demands the earth be wiped clean of all his followers. In other words, the head of the Illuminati wants the demiurge to depart (i.e., the true God), demanding the earth be wiped of all monotheists who believe in eternal life. In fact, the flaw of the Ancient One was her desire to live eternally, and drew her lifeforce from the "dark side" (i.e., God). In other words, Doctor Strange is Doctor Death, who after his initiation, ascension and apotheosis, sees death as "natural" – something he formerly sought to heal in his patients. In short, the summation of Doctor Strange is an amalgam or skeletal outline of the world religions, or perennialism to be specific. Perennialism is illuminism, and illuminism is Luciferianism:

The perennial philosophy as it is so-called is hard to decipher and hard to pin down, but the point I have been making above cancels out

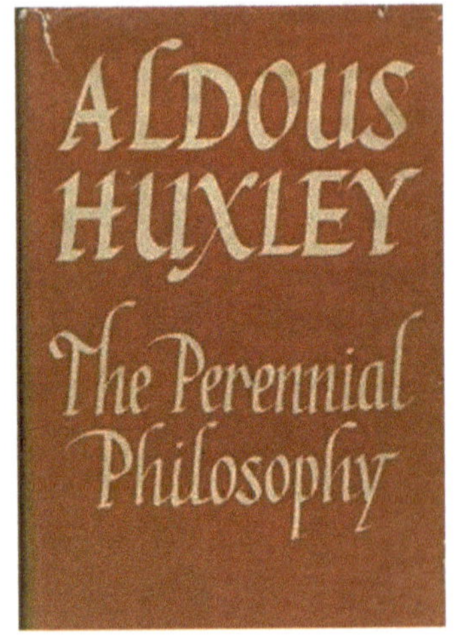

the blasphemies and attacks on God that are common in liberal circles, as well as modern new world order proponents like Aldous Huxley, who in his *The Perennial Philosophy* seeks to destroy the notion of a single Personal God, and thereby destroy the notion of personhood. Once the notion of personhood is gone as a metaphysical doctrine, it can be granted (and removed) at will via the apotheosized world-state. Yes, literally, by the pantheistic future world government. Huxley is quite candid about this, too. But all such attempts at deification of the state and destroying the biblical tradition are doomed to fail.

And so if there is in some sense a "perennial philosophy," it is the perennial philosophy of the One True God, and not a pagan truth of generic, a-personal monotheism whereupon we can later attach the conception of a Personal deity, after we have borrowed bad arguments from Aristotle. We must begin with *the Personal* God who guides history by His providence. Only in this metaphysic do we have a grounded notion of *person* and protect the rights of the individual from the superstate-play-acting-as-God. We must then toss out the 'traditionalists' school of Ananda Coomaraswamy, Huxley and others, which really comes from Hinduism and is the sludge of the occult tradition passed down through the ages. The true perennial philosophy, then, as Justin points out (whether consistently or not) is the perennial philosophy of "Eyeh asher Eyeh."

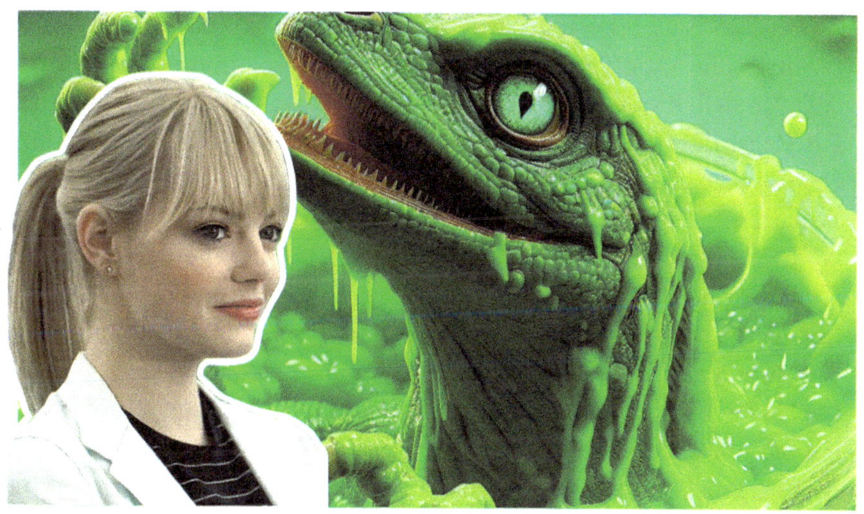

Spider Man (2016)

I've forgotten how many Spider-Mans we are into reboots, but the 2016 Andrew Garfield and Emma Stone installment seems curiously relevant now, given the theme of mutating man I've been covering. Through our Jonas Salk and Arthur Koestler analyses, we've chronicled the attempt of the technocratic elite to intentionally engineer, experiment and mutate man to become post-human. The desire to "steer" evolution is really a fool's game and only as legitimate as the notion of evolution itself, which we have seen many times over is nothing more than a modern fairy tale version of a Greek myth. Indeed, Hollywood films are mainly the reason most people believe in evolutionary dogma.

In the 2012 Spider-Man, bully whisperer Gwen (Stone) befriends the eccentric, spergy Peter Parker (Garfield) after a tense day of Hollywood-ish high school. Peter lives with his maximum boomered Uncle Owen and Aunt Beru, learning his father's genetic modification research into spiders was almost stolen. Parker's father was a chief geneticist at OSCORP (aka Monsanto) and was apparently assassinated while specifically working on cross species genetic engineering. The present head of OSCORP is Dr. Connors who is a student of snakes and serpents who can regrow limbs – ergo, the ability to regrow limbs could hold the secrets to overcoming human weaknesses and thus transhumanism. It's odd how many comic book stories relating to mutants and mutations are cautionary tales, yet here we are in 2021, nine years after *Spider Man* 2012 and now the prevalent propaganda has turned to its opposite: genetic engineering, mutations, implants and global stabby experiments are underway!

Peter ends up bitten by a genetically modified spider at the OSCORP facility while snooping around and the transformation begins: dude is sticky as hell. It's a good thing he didn't wander into the GMO tardigrade lab. Regardless, Peter's pokers now emit thin, wafty lines of spider coom (as one weird theorist speculates). If we brought in the Ariadne and Athena narrative, it would be the coom loom womb – I am joking, Spider Man is not about puberty (although *Teen Wolf* is). As a side note, last week Congress just ruled against human-genetic cross engineering, which in my view is merely a way to legalize human experimentation and modification, and not actually about morphing us into X-Men. In fact, I think all the Hollywood and sci-fi propaganda about mutating man to "evolve" him is really about conditioning the public to accept the very things occurring now on a mass scale. As if a bunch of science juice will actually grow your leg back and allow you to become an immortal space coomer.

As a bonus, Dennis Leary plays Dennis Leary, an unfunny smoky asshole who's mad as heck. Is the acidic atheistic, nihilistic standup actually even funny? Back to our story, the OSCORP has decided it needs human trials for the experimental science juice – veterans! Veterans have a long history of being used by the establishment as lab subjects, back to MKUltra, Vietnam, The Phoenix Program and Gulf War Syndrome being some of the more obvious examples. Is it really surprising the same people behind those events would want a global test tube experiment as a result of the COVID? Bonus points go to Peter Parker for an archetypal boomer Vs. millennial dinner debate over the status of Internet conspiracy videos.

From the Golem to Frankenstein to Jekyl and Hyde, the notion of creating, altering and reanimating and cloning man has been a dream of the hermeticists and occultists for centuries: According to Koestler in *Ghost in the Machine*, the present sacrifice of the world's population is necessary to achieve the transmutation of man to become post-human. Despite the perennial warnings of history to reject monstrosities and mutations, the frenzy of scientism and its delusions have led to the acceptance of self-destruction precisely due to hubris. As a result of all the genetic experimentation and tweaking on science juice (Surge Cola), things get David Icke pretty quick, as Dr. Connors transitions into full on Chitauri. To quote David Icke, "The body mind holographic reality known as the 5 sense data matrix overcomes the duality of infinite consciousness having a temporal experience of itself, mate." As Dr. Connor "evolves," he decides it's time to mutate the entire population with his perfectly tailored aerosolized bio-weapon of green science gas that is canceled by blue science gas. Moral of the story is, the mad scientist elites are using green and blue science juices and gasses to mutate your asses.

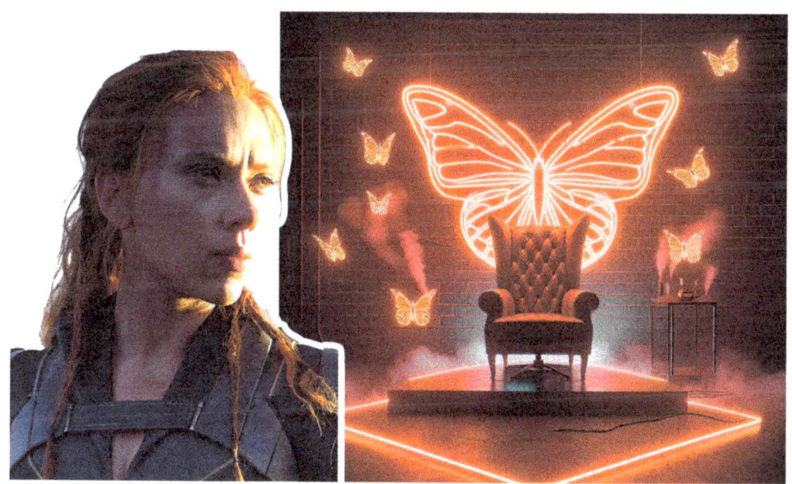

Black Widow (2021): Red Room, Red Queen

Black Widow was another Marvel installment with surprising revelations. From the outset of the film, we see Scarlettt Johansson as Black Widow watching the Bond film *Moonraker*, itself a film we analyzed that dealt with human experimentation and eugenics-based depopulation, presaging the themes to come. We see a flashback of children being kidnapped in a human trafficking operation wherein her handler Dreykov mind controls and brainwashes her into becoming an elite assassin. This film, like *The Americans* television series based on the actual Directorate S Soviet Illegals Program, places her in a similar program. Dreykov is seen with Bill Clinton and other world leaders, suggesting this covert program is above the nation-state level, akin to something like SPECTRE. We find out these assassins are not just mind controlled, they are actually given microchips and advanced chemical concoctions.

The kidnapped and orphaned girls are programmed in the "red room," recalling the Cold War theme of the narrative, but from the real history of MKUltra, what is more interesting is the evolution from drug research transforming into transhumanism, microchipping and super soldier programs. In the film, various characters are shown with alternate personalities installed through trauma-based mind control, while Black Widow's stand-in mother played by Rachel Weisz is engaging in Dr Jose Delgado style research by mind controlling pigs with various frequencies and chemicals. Dr. John C. Lilly was, as we have discussed, doing the same programs with dosing and implanting monkeys and dolphins.

In researching the MKUltra programs and their various offshoots, I came across an interesting connection to the coming SmartGrid. Under Dr. Ewan Cameron, a prison tracking device known as the Schwitzgebel Machine was utilized to monitor inmates locations, heart rate and other personal details that were reciprocally transmitted to the good doctors.[32] What comes to the fore is the similarity with the development of the Smartphone and its new capabilities for monitoring heart rate, health, etc., as well as basically anything else. Is there a connection between mind control and the coming A.I. takeover? While this may sound like the ultimate paranoiac tin foilage, I suspect more at work here, and with advances in nanotech, like we see in the *Black Widow* film, it's likely the goal is to eventually move to smart dust as opposed to chips.

In my analysis, the rollout of the great technological utopia we are being sold was not the result of mere organic market forces that competed to produce harder, better, faster and stronger products. The average libertarian, for example, believes this deception, presuming the "invisible hand" of the market results in a natural advancement, while any other economic model retarded growth and "progress." On the contrary, much of the technological progress we have seen in the last few decades is not the result of independent, competing ideas, but is rather the strategically timed and intentional release of the military industrial tech complex, given to an idiot public for the purpose of long term enslavement and depopulation.

The connection to MKUltra arises in relation to experiments with mind manipulation which I have already highlighted in regard to Dr. Michael Aquino and his infamous essay, "From PSYOP to MindWar: The Psychology of Victory," where the combination of ELF/VLF and various RF manipulation is discussed in detail towards the end as we saw cited previously. A *Nexus Magazine* article "Techniques Used by Governments for Mind Control," by Sid Taylor outlines the RF experimentation in the MK programs:

"MKUltra SUBPROJECT-68

This was Dr. Cameron's ongoing "attempts to establish lasting effects in a patient's behaviour" using a combination of particularly intensive electroshock, intensive repetition of prearranged verbal signals, partial sensory isolation, and repression of the driving period carried out by inducing continuous sleep for seven to ten days at the end of the treatment period. During research on sensor deprivation, Cameron experimented with the use of Curare, (the deadly poison used by South American Indians to tip their arrowheads), to immobilize his patients.

After one test he noted: "Although the patient was prepared by both prolonged sensory isolation (35 days) and by repeated depatterning, and although she received 101 days of positive driving, no favorable results were obtained." Patients were regularly treated with hallucinogenic drugs, long periods in the "sleep room," and testing in the Radio Telemetry Laboratory that was built by [Leonard] Rubinstein under Dr. Cameron's direction. Here, patients were exposed to a range of RF and electromagnetic signals and monitored for changes in behavior. It was later stated by other staff members who had worked at the Institute that not one patient sent to the Radio Telemetry Lab showed any signs of improvement afterwards.[33]

When we consider the intersection with drug experimentation, the cocktail of brainwashing, "imprinting" and RF frequency technology becomes clear as something engineered by design. Taylor continues, echoing something akin to a mondo *Faces of Death* flick:

There were an enormous number of MKUltra operations. The project farmed out work to eighty institutions, of which forty-four were colleges or universities, fifteen research facilities or private companies, twelve hospitals and three prisons. The estimated total cost of the operation was 10-25 million dollars.

Prisoners were used in experiments conducted at the California Medical Facility in Vacaville State Prison by Dr. James Hamilton. Funded by another chain of front organizations, Dr. Hamilton conducted "clinical testing of behavioral control materials." In New Jersey, testing was conducted by Dr. Carl Pfieffer at the Borden Reformatory, on similar materials. At Holmesburg State Prison in Philadelphia volunteers were used to test a particularly violent incapacitating drug. Around the same time as these tests were being conducted by the CIA the US Army initiated two projects, THIRD CHANCE and DERBY HAT. They conducted experiments both home and abroad, and at one time the New York State Psychiatric Institute was conducting research under contract to the Army. Between 1955 and 1958 the Army also tested LSD on 1,000 volunteer US servicemen at Fort Bragg and the Army's Chemical Warfare Laboratories at Edgewood…

In this MKSearch sub-project the isolation chamber that had been constructed earlier by Dr. Cameron at the Allan Memorial Institute was rebuilt at a laboratory of the National Institutes of Mental Health. This time, instead of humans, apes were to be subjected to a cruel combination of treatments. After first being lobotomised, the animals were kept in total isolation. The radio telemetry techniques developed earlier by Leonard Rubenstein were adapted so that radio frequency energy could be beamed into the brains of the highly disturbed animals. Many were then decapitated and their heads would be transplanted onto another body to see if the RF energy would bring them back to life. The apes that were not killed in this way were later bombarded with radio waves until they fell unconscious. Autopsies revealed that their brain tissue had literally been fried. These experiments were conducted around 1965/66, so it is a frightening reality that it is around 25 years since intelligence agencies covertly started experimenting with the use of radiated energy to control behavior....

THE SCHWITZGEBEL MACHINE

After consultation with the DCI, Richard Helms, Dr. [Sidney] Gottlieb hired the former director of the Agency's Office of Scientific Intelligence, Dr. Stephen Aldrich, and set him up in a safe house where a KGB defector had recently been interrogated and tortured continuously for almost three years, so that he could experiment with a device known as the Schwitzgebel Machine. This was a 'Behavioural Transmitter-Reinforcer' (BT-R) fitted to a body belt that received signals from, and transmitted signals to, a radio module. The machine was "linked to a missile tracking device which graphs the wearer's location and displays it on a screen." It was developed by Ralph K. Schwitzgebel in the Laboratory of Community Psychiatry at Harvard Medical School. His brother, Robert, subsequently modified the prototype into a more refined final product. The machine drew enthusiastic praise from criminologists who were supportive of ORD's concepts for the intelligence techniques of the new world order.

On December 10th 1972, Helms canceled Operation Often. The memo sent to Dr. Gottlieb to notify him was marked READ DESTROY. Dr. Gottlieb resigned from the agency in January 1973. Before he left he was ordered by Helms to shred all records from MKUltra – MKSearch.

130 boxes would later be discovered in the Langley archives that, inexplicably, Dr. Gottlieb had failed to destroy. It was thought that the records had been misfiled and would have been destroyed if Helms and Gottlieb had been aware of them."[34]

With all that madness in mind, when we consider the Smartphone, we see a device that utilizes RF and tracks your every move, desire and taste, with all of that data being transferred to mysterious third parties which are sold and stored in vast data centers around the globe. In line with NSA whistleblower William Binney, I have opined that this is all being stored with the intent of a global SmartGrid control system. While it is true that one level competition between Silicon Valley tech companies may be permitted, the reality was elucidated years ago in former CIA operative Melissa Mahle's 2004 autobiography, *Denial and Deception: An Insider's View of the CIA*, where she explained the origins of In-Q-Tel:

> Rather than run a full in-house R&D program, Tenet authorized the directorate to create a technology-incubation organization, In-Q-Tel, to serve as an information technology portal from the private sector to the intelligence community.... With an initial funding of 28.5 million in CIA funds, the venture focused on building productive relationships with small firms involved in IT innovation, In-Q-Tel concentrated on technologies that integrate Internet technology and applications to intelligence work, that develop new security and privacy technologies, and nurture data-mining technologies to take better advantage of the CIA's vast storehouse of records, and modernize the CIA's computer systems. (pg. 267)

In-Q-Tel was also instrumental in some other names you might recognize, like Google and Facebook. James Corbett's piece on this connection gives an excellent summary of these pseudo-free market firms:

> For decades, the Defense Advanced Research Projects Agency, or DARPA, has been the American governmental body tasked with conducting high-risk, high-payoff research into cutting edge science and technology. Responsible most famously for developing the world's first operational packet switching network that eventually became the core of the Internet, DARPA tends to garner headlines these days for some of its more outlandish research proposals and is generally looked upon a a blue-sky research agency whose endeavours only occasionally bear fruit..."
>
> Two of the names that come up most often in connection with In-Q-Tel, however, need no introduction: Google and Facebook.
>
> The publicly available record on the Facebook/In-Q-Tel connection is tenuous. Facebook received $12.7 million in venture capital from Accel, whose manager, James Breyer, now sits on

their board. He was formerly the chairman of the National Venture Capital Association, whose board included Gilman Louie, then the CEO of In-Q-Tel. The connection is indirect, but the suggestion of CIA involvement with Facebook, however tangential, is disturbing in the light of Facebook's history of violating the privacy of its users....

Google's connection to In-Q-Tel is more straightforward, if officially denied. In 2006, ex-CIA officer Robert David Steele told Homeland Security Today that Google "has been taking money and direction for elements of the US Intelligence Community, including the Office of Research and Development at the Central Intelligence Agency, In-Q-Tel, and in all probability, both the National Security Agency (NSA) and the Army's Intelligence and Security Command." Later that year, a blogger claimed that an official Google spokesman had denied the claims, but no official press statement was released."[35]

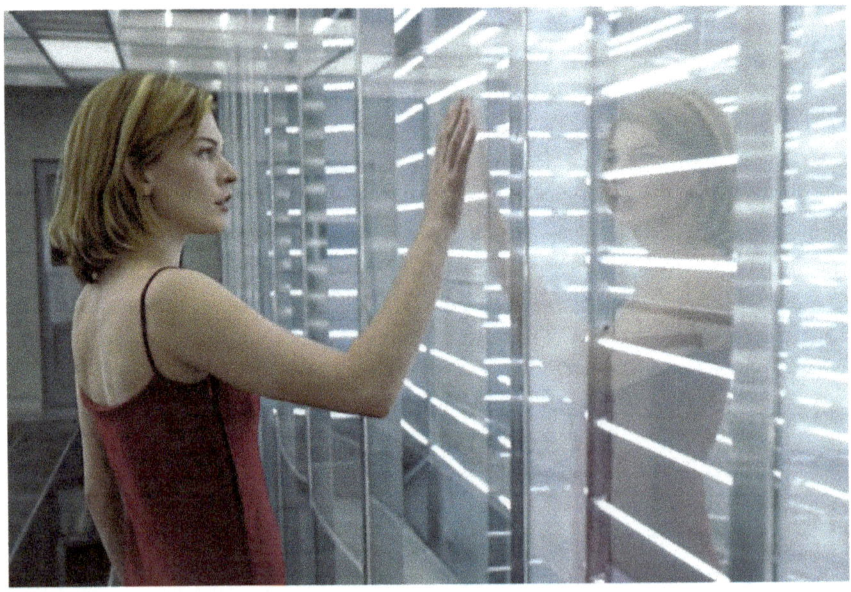

Healthcare courtesy of the Red Queen!

So what about my claims about the same strategic goal associating all of this with mind control? You'll note that much of the very secret covert work pertains to nanotechnology, cancer and producing human resistance to the radioactive effects of all of this frequency pollution. According to *Business Insider*, CIA startups are intimately connected to WiFi R&D, as well as with transhumanist Bilderberg attendee, Peter Thiel, stating:

We've talked about Palantir before and the impact it is having on the Army intelligence community. What we didn't go into as much was the fact that In-Q-Tel was an early investor in the technology on behalf of the Central Intelligence Agency. Palantir makes software that integrates data together from a wide array of resources and databases.

It's one of the best programs at coordinating the vast databases accumulated by the U.S. intelligence apparatus. It assembles comprehensive dossiers on objects of interest, collated from the sprawling databases of intelligence agencies.[36]

Corbett draws attention to this connection to nanotech, bio-engineering and biometrics, illustrating further the danger these corporate-government mergers represent (operating under the guise of being private sector):

The In-Q-Tel website currently lists two "practice areas," "Information and Communication Technologies" and "Physical and Biological Technologies." The latter field consists of "capabilities of interest" such as "The on-site determination of individual human traits for IC [Inteligence Community] purposes" and "Tracking and/or authentication of both individuals and objects." In-Q-Tel also lists two areas that are "on its radar" when it comes to biotech: Nano-bio Convergence and Physiological Intelligence. Detailed breakdowns of each area explain that the intelligence community is interested in, amongst other things, self-assembling batteries, single molecule detectors, targeted drug delivery platforms, and sensors that can tell where a person has been and what substances he has been handling from "biomarkers" like trace compounds in the breath or samples of skin.

Thus the intersection of advanced technology, intelligence agencies and mind control is not far-fetched, but well established. The reality is, all of this is war gamed and planned for implementation by an establishment that long ago adopted the panopticism model of Jeremy Bentham and the Malthusian Royal Society. The goals have nothing to do with creating a tech utopia for you and your progeny, where you will fly off to floating moon bases and partake of *Elysium*-style healing machines with Matt Damon.

The same establishment that is publicly determined to destroy humanity en masse and implement the A.I. kill grid is rolling out their designs even faster than we "conspiracy theorists" expected! In fact, this week mainstream news is reporting that IBM's Watson, the famed Jeopardy-playing A.I. bot will play a role in determining health care!

Forbes writes, trying to dissuade fears of the bots making the decision on your care, that this will be an amazing advance, but this ignores an important fact – the article itself touts Watson's superiority to human decision making, which will inevitably lead to the conclusion the bots are a better option than the human, and on top of that, the establishment interested in fostering all this are committed to dysgenics (not actually eugenics), which is the destruction of the human genome:

> Watson has made huge strides in its medical prowess in two short years. In May 2011 IBM had already trained Watson to have the knowledge of a second-year medical student. In March 2012 IBM struck a deal with Memorial Sloan Kettering to ingest and analyze tens of thousands of the renowned cancer center's patient records and histories, as well as all the publicly available clinical research it can get its hard drives on. Today Watson has analyzed 605,000 pieces of medical evidence, 2 million pages of text, 25,000 training cases and had the assistance of 14,700 clinician hours fine-tuning its decision accuracy. Six "instances" of Watson have already been installed in the last 12 months.[37]

If you played Nintendo in the 80s like I did as a kid, you'll recall Mother Brain, the ill-tempered A.I. behemoth from *Metroid*. *Metroid* was actually far more accurate in its description of the actual "Mother" that is being erected and sold as a sexy Scarlett Johansson (as in Spike Jonze's *Her*). Mother Brain, like the Red Queen in *Resident Evil* and Skynet in *Terminator* is given a distinctly feminine quality because she functions as a synthetic *anima mundi*. The system is selling her as sexy, but I assure you, this is anything but.

The BBC has reported a Swedish firm is offering employees to be RF microchipped, and the wage slaves willingly complied.[38] I have highlighted the microchipping plan as something decades old, which shows the rollout of all this is clearly planned years in advance and is not an organic market development. It is with the microchip that we can see the clear connection between the mind control programs of MKUltra and the rise of the A.I. grid, as well as the mind control of marketing employed in selling everyone on this trap. When we combine this with the T-Phage nanobiotech the Royal Society finds appealing,[39] one wonders if the T-Virus and the Red Queen aren't real, and out for blood.

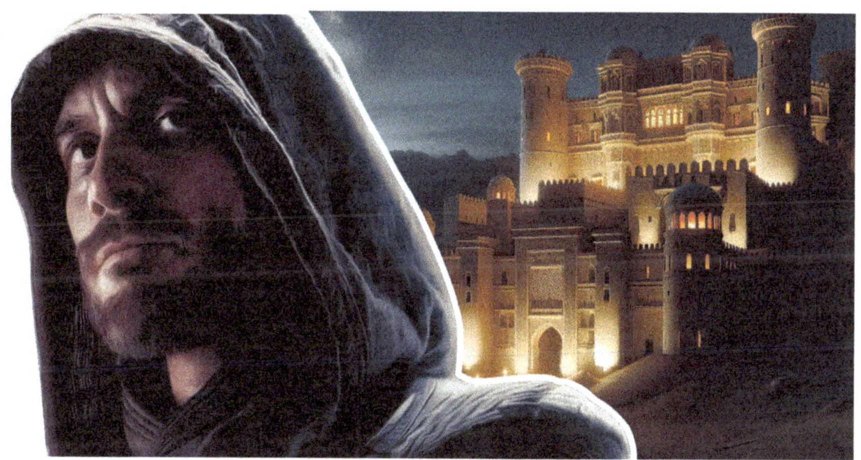

Assassin's Creed (2016)

I thought when I was going to see *Assassin's Creed* it was a film about the attempt on 90s phenom frontman Scott Stapp's life. I was in for something quite different, as this video game-turned film blended everything from transhumanism to Templarism. It seems Hollywood and the video game industry are now obsessed with conspiracy culture, and as we will see, this not an organic, happenstance development. In *The Kingsman*, we saw how Templarism related directly to British Intelligence operations and Freemasonry, but also since the release of the endless groaners from Dan Brown, "Templarism" continues to spin conspiracy webs (and box office profits), as well as fascinate profane, outer portico audiences.

Here, the Templars search for the "mythical Apple of Eden," a new twist on the standard fare paleotechnology we generally see heroes searching after, like glowing blue cotton candy cubes, shards of mystical space essence and whatever else Nikola Tesla might have dreamt up on acid. For the Templars in this incarnation, we have the bold presentation of Luciferianism. "Free will" is said to be bound up with the "Apple" of disobedience from Adam and Eve's Fall, and finding this old rotten apple core with the aid of some other mystical cipher code device will result in the power to "control all freedom of thought." Perhaps the original Pentagon makers of the Internet itself, as well as video games really did discover a means to control free thought – and it's called video games (which, in my view, will eventually morph into virtual reality, which will then morph into full immersive *Matrix*-like interfaces).

Our Brotherhood of Assassins stand in the way of the secrets of free will and mind control, we are told, but I was feeling more and more like I was watching *Indiana Jones and the Last Crusade*. Weren't those "brothers" guarding the Grail, too? Indeed, it seems more and more as if films in our day are re-presentations of 80s and 90s movies that *are* video games. Callum (Michael Fassbender) is a death row convict sentenced to death who is saved by the Abstergo Foundation (a modern Templar front – very similar to the Umbrella Corporation in *Resident Evil*). Interestingly, corporate shells and fronts for the CIA and the upper echelons of the Illuminati, so to speak, *do* use foundations and think tanks.

In a Matrix-like uplink, Callum enters the animus, which are the memories of select people long dead, based on the encoded information in their DNA. Dr. Sofia (Marion Cotillard) reveals that Callum is being sent back to search for said "Apple" that is the secret to free will. The esotericism elements here are blatant, as both the Sophia principle and the Luciferian doctrine that evil is a necessary corollary to the good form the basic story arc. In the *Pistis Sophia*, the gnostic principle of Wisdom, or Sophia, is the syzygy or supposed feminine side of God and Christ. Sophia is generally presented as fallen in some sense, having a role in the manifestation of the material world and is often considered a lesser aeon.

At this juncture the *anima mundi* should be mentioned, as the concept relates to both Platonism and Jungian archetypes. In Jung, the anima and animus are the corresponding archetypes in the collective unconscious – in a male, the opposite feminine appears as the anima, in a female, the masculine appears as animus. In the film, the animus is the masculine representation of the ability of logic and technology to re-present and re-create the genetic memories of the past, and Callum is the chief subject.

The Abstergo Foundation is involved with the United Nations and "fixing" man's anti-social behaviors, and like the social programs in *A Clockwork Orange* seeks to "cure man" from his violence. The "elders" in control of the Abstergo Foundation are the Illuminati, who fund and direct the Foundation's research into bloodlines to ultimately find the Apple, the genetic code for free will. Free will, the (female) Elders decide, is the problem in man who must be controlled, and the infiltration and usage of religion is now obsolete due to the prevalence of "science" (i.e., scientism). Callum is believed to be the "living link between heredity and crime."

Callum descends from Aguilar, the Assassins, who was burned by the Inquisition for being a murderer. Dr. Sofia informs Callum he is genetically predisposed to violence and crime, as she discourses on how the Apple of Eden is an ancient technology to discover man's genetic dispositions. Violence is explained to be a disease, like cancer, and curable through external stimuli. While the plot of the film is largely ridiculous and yet another of infinite retellings of gnosticism, one insight that is correct is that the formerly Christian West has shed its religious veneer for scientism, while retaining many of the inconsistent moral goals and purposes that only make sense in a Christian worldview. Since God was jettisoned, "Nature" and her secrets are the new god, embodied in technology and genetics.

As a side note, isn't it interesting that Hollywood and the mass media indoctrinate the masses with the notion that one's lineage, heritage and bloodline do not matter, and to have any concern for those ideas is jingoism, racism and Nazism, while at the same time lauding the mysteries of genetic memories and esoteric bloodlines. The reality, of course, is that bloodlines only matter when they are the bloodlines of the elite, while these oligarchs are hell-bent on genetically ruining yours (or making sure you have no offspring).

Genetic memories are a fascinating aspect of the biblical notion of passing on traits to one's offspring and represents cutting edge research. The absurdity of Darwinism is once again immediately evident, as such notions are utterly incompatible with mainline reductionist materialism and the *faux* science the masses are fed, while at the same time goofy pop culture projects like *Assassin's Creed* will explore the idea of genetic memories. The masses are told this is "pseudoscience," while at the same time positive research is conducted on the topic. Indeed, most scientists cannot replicate the so-called findings of their peers! Darold Trefert at *The Scientific American* writes:

> Wilder Penfield in his pioneering 1978 book, *Mystery of the Mind*, also referred to three types of memory. "Animals," he wrote, "particularly show evidence of what might be called racial memory" (this would be the equivalent of genetic memory). He lists the second type of memory as that associated with "conditioned reflexes" and a third type as "experiential." The two latter types would be consistent with the terminology commonly applied to "habit or procedural" memory and "cognitive or semantic" memory.[40]

I thought "race" didn't exist? Anyway, genetic and racial memories make perfect sense in a worldview other than mainstream scientism and materialism presents. And once again we see Hollywood discussing these matters in the context of ridiculous pop fiction, while deriding and denigrating those who would dare to discuss them in the "real" world. I'm reminded of Hollywood's obsession with gun control, while simultaneously filling every action film with countless gun-blasting babes and brutes.

The "assassins," we are told, are the descendants of the medieval sect of Hashshashin, who were dedicated to principles and were able to cloak their hidden agenda under the guise of being bands of rebels, drug addicts and miscreants. Naturally, so movie logic goes, all medieval Catholic theologians and Dominicans were power-mad monsters, while sects of Islamic Assassins were noble warriors. I guess the Arabic slave trade didn't exist in the world of *Assassin's Creed*. No one is more critical of Thomism than me, but I have to admit they at least got Dominican garb right – and not much else (though one could argue the Spanish Inquisition, which was distinct from the Roman Catholic, was a different ballgame in terms of abuse). Regardless, the absurdity is brought home in the fact that if the Dominicans are "evil" for seeking to kill heretics, why are assassins "good"?

In any case, Callum and his team of ghost assassins, Callum receives the revelation from his mother that "nothing is true, everything is permitted," the supposed dictum of the ancient order of Hashshashin. Other men are limited by their attachment to "morality" and order, while the Assassins are beyond good and evil. As we stated at the beginning, the film is purely Luciferian, and here it admits it is so. Callum pledges his service and allegiance to "the Light," which is a war of "free will" (nihilism) against moral absolutes.

The Edenic imagery is appropriate, since this was the message of the Serpent – you shall be like God, knowing good and evil, meaning you will determine for yourself what is right and wrong, true and false. Relativism is the Luciferian Gospel of the Serpent, and it has not changed one bit in the millennia since the Garden. Ironically, this itself is a powerful testimony to the veracity of the biblical texts! The "Gospel" of Lucifer is still the message of being one's own moral arbiter, a manifestly self-destructive and disastrous worldview, yet is a scam that never ceases to allure man with the hope of becoming divine through some artifice of his own.

Most surprising in the film were the sequences at the Grand Templar Hall (the head Masonic Lodge) in London, where the secret scientific "elders" council that runs the Vatican also controls world freemasonry. Dr. Sofia learns that the discovery of the secret of free will in the Apple will mean the end of free will. What is fascinating about this is the revelation that "science" is actually subservient to a higher, more elite council located in London. Indeed, I have been talking about the control of science through the Royal Society for a good while now. Inadvertently hitting on truth, the film is correct in presenting western scientism and genetic determinism as covertly ruled by a higher society of initiates who understand that scientism is false.

The false dialectic presented in the film is that the solution to man's ills is now a battle between Masonic pseudo-Christian scientism, and nihilistic Luciferianism. In reality, Masonic and Luciferian scientism controls and manages dialectics of faux-Christianity and Western Hermeticism-Luciferianism. Neither rationalistic scientism nor nihilistic Nietzscheanism can liberate man – give him *true* free will. The close of the film shows Callum and his secret order atop skyscrapers holding the seed – carrying the torch of Luciferian "free will." At what point will we consider that perhaps the nonsensical gnostic mythos is incapable of showing man the way to "freedom"? Nihilism is not a transcending of moral order, but rather, a manifestation of controlled dialectic.

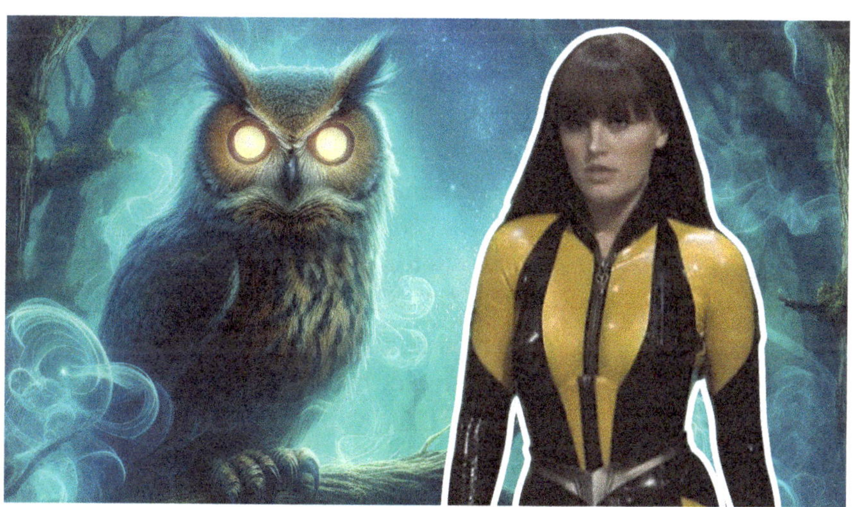

Watchmen (2009)

Self-professed ritual magician and follower of Aleister Crowley, Alan Moore has created some of the most well-known graphic novels that deviate from the standard comic book fare with dark, adult themes and deep, occult significance. Moore's *Watchmen* was not a tremendous box office success, but the gnostic, esoteric and even Satanic elements are present here, as they are in the 2001 film *From Hell*, also based on his work. While *From Hell* focuses on the Freemasonic and Satanic connections to the infamous Jack the Ripper, *Watchmen* is a satirical look at the genre of comic books, glib takes on good and evil, a critique of the hypocrisy of Neo-conservatism and the nihilistic conclusions of such faux "conservatism" in a world of rampant consumerism – all set in a fictional alternate timeline where President Richard Nixon has remained in power for 5 consecutive terms through the Cold War.

Dr. Manhattan, a scientist radiated and transformed into a kind of Demiurge, is the West's greatest hope for strategic power dominance, yet personally struggles with his own apathy and nihilism concerning human existence. As a representation of "god," or a *deus ex machina*, Manhattan perhaps represents the West's new deity in the Cold War, having abandoned Theism as much as the so-called Atheist Empire of the Soviets. The "free" West is just as demonic as the East in this portrayal and with the Watchmen team, we have a gathering of spies, super soldiers and assassins who function as a Col. Fletcher Prouty-style "secret team" intent on protecting the West as "Watchers," also known as "Night Owls," (recalling to mind the Owl of Bohemian Grove), where spies need spies to spy on them. Moore is asking a valid question here: If we need to be protected from an international foreign secret super spy team, with a super spy team, then who spies on our super secret spies, *ad infinitum*?

The "doomsday clock" propaganda is utilized by the McLaughlin Group in the opening sequence to remind Americans of the perpetual fear of never-ending crises that characterizes Neoconservatism. As The Comedian watches the television propaganda in disbelief, his condo is invaded and he is attacked by an unknown assailant and killed. The Bob Dylan song "Times Are A Changin," as we see JFK being assassinated by The Comedian, likening him to a sort of E. Howard Hunt intelligence operative,[41] followed by a massacre of hippies by the government and CIA-funded Andy Warhol's pop art. As the police investigate the death of The Comedian, they discuss the fact that his background reveals he was a spook, later identified in the film as a CIA operative.

Rorshach appears next, making his own investigation of the death of The Comedian as he voices his narrative disgust for the cosmopolitan existence. Rorschach concludes a much deeper conspiracy is at work in the hit on The Comedian, as we discover in the following dialogue the "masks" of the "superheroes" and their "costumes" are akin to the covers and disguises spies and assassins use. In fact, this "secret team" answers directly to Nixon to help fight the Cold War and operate as a last line of defense through American espionage, counter-intelligence and wetworks, much like the actual CIA secret team.[42] It is later revealed that The Comedian was apparently a CIA Phoenix Program assassin in Vietnam, as he has no compunction about killing a woman he impregnated (in Vietnam).[43] Nixon, however, has decided to disband the Watchmen as an organization, arguing they are no longer needed. Most of the Watchmen have never been identified or reveal their background except for two, one of whom is the film's villain, Ozymandias. Ozymandias is a billionaire capitalist who argues that making resources "infinite" will end the Cold War and all war, resulting in a new era of peace and prosperity. He argues he can do this through secret research being done at his hidden Antarctica facility. Antarctica is interesting, as it is a classic source of conspiracy speculation, with international treaties limiting non-governmental exploration.

Rorshach determines he will have to infiltrate a Rockefeller Military Research Facility to speak to Dr. Manhattan where nuclear power and the effects of nuclear holocaust are being studied. As he digs deeper into the mystery of the hit, it's eventually revealed that Ozymandias has a hit list that includes the magician named Moloch, a reference to the ancient human sacrificial deity. Moloch, who is part of a "Jesuit Fellowship" according to his mail, reveals more details of Ozymandias' plan, which includes ridding the world of anyone who might stop him from the team. Ultimately, his plan is to have a nuclear war for a "great reset" in which mass depopulation can allow society to start again in a new world order. In fact, Bertrand Russell mentions this as a real option for depopulation, though a mass bio-release would be more effective, he opines in his infamous work *Impact of Science on Society*.[44]

Ozymandias' corporation is Pyramid International, thus connecting both the company and the character's name to Egyptology, and the concept of erecting a new order based around CEO Ozymandias as Pharaoh. In fact, in true breakaway civilization fashion, Ozymandias has built an ice fortress power plant to live through the apocalypse he intends to create through an engineered nuclear war. In the end, we are led to believe the villain was right: a limited nuclear conflict allows the world to accept the noble lie and opt for world peace. The Cold War ends and a new order is achieved – however, Rorshach has mailed his diary and the true story of the plot of Ozymandias to blame Dr. Manhattan for his own staged assassinations and nuclear false flag events. The moral of the story is humans must be told a noble lie and even be massacred for world peace to be achieved: A dark morale that echoes the socialists in Fyodor Dostoyevsky's *Demons*, where members of the party argue the socialist utopia can only occur on a mountain of skulls: Moore's *Watchmen* thus proffers a Nietzschean, Crowleyan morality where the slaves deserve to serve and be trampled, while pretending to be above good and evil and in the end, might makes right.

Moore's *From Hell* was adapted in 2001 and stars Johnny Depp, Heather Graham and Ian Holm. The British nobility in the narrative has hired a psychopathic killer to dispense with whores who know about an illegitimate child amongst one of the elite. Not only do we see the police run by high level Freemasons, but in fact the Freemasons function as a kind of intelligence network (in my estimation) for the British Empire, and they are using a cannibal serial killer who believes in blood rituals and pacts.[45] Depp plays a kind of Sherlock Holmes style detective who uses drugs to see into the *aether* or spiritual realm to piece together the clues the Satanic serial killer is using.

Rather than saving lives, this parasitic doctor is practicing religious magic and has formed a Pentagram of locations for the murders as Detective Aberline (Depp) notices. In reality the British elite have long had a penchant for Freemasonry and ritual magick, where in black lodges the dark arts are studies and utilized: similar themes arise in the 2009 *Sherlock Holmes* from director Guy Ritchie, where Robert Downey, Jr. plays Holmes busting a caper perpetrated by an Aleister Crowley based villain, Lord Blackwood (Mark Strong), who utilizes both science and (fraudulent) ritual magick to dupe the Masonic Lodges and by extension Parliament into thinking he is the bringer of a magickal *new aeon*. Ultimately, the sad fact of the dominance of comic books in the movie sphere is due to the arrested development of the population who have been engineered to maintain a state of perpetual neoteny by design, to make them pliable and weak and the genre of "comics" has played a central role in sustaining this decline.

Section 2

Dystopia Now & The Dark Gnostic Goddess Savior Archetype

Mad Max Series

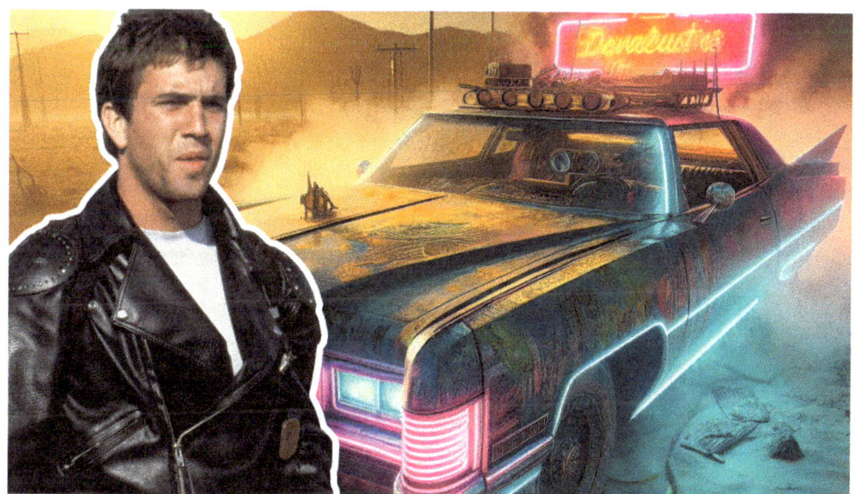

Much furor has been raised over Imperator Furiosa, Charlize Theron's "strong woman" figure in the latest *Mad Max* reboot and the latest installment with Anya Taylor Joy as the young Furiosa: I wanted to retitle it *"Mad MaxiPad."* *Mad Max: Fury Road* opened to a large box office success, while *Furiosa* lagged behind. Both are undeniably a feat of technical and choreographic brilliance, setting a new standard for George Miller's previous high-octane chase scene exuberance – these are George Miller on acid. While critics are lauding these (admittedly) spectacular feats of technical prowess, there are also deeper messages being conveyed that should be elucidated, especially the notions of the commodification and control of resources. Before investigating *Fury Road*, let's consider the esoteric setting and context from the prequels.

Mad Max and The Road Warrior

Critics of the film's feminist message have failed to recall that all the *Mad Max* installments include a "strong woman," and in particular they function as commentaries on social structures and the very concept of "civilization" itself. In Miller's first project, Max Rockatansky is a police officer in a near-distant post-collapse society where anarchic road gangs with occultic names like "Cundalini" terrorize the highways ritually enacting chaos and rape with religious ecstasy, led by the messianic madman, Toecutter. Even here, the "strong woman" is embodied in the trigger-happy granny, yet to no avail as Max loses all, including his sanity and faith in law and order.

In the 1981 sequel *Road Warrior*, nuclear war has enveloped the globe, leaving roving bands of BDSM maniacs to terrorize new attempts at rebuilding civilization on the ashes of the old. The dialectic of anarchic chaos versus the attempt at hierarchical order and social organization appears in all four films, but in the second the introduction of resource control becomes the focus. Energy is crucial from this point on, as the remnants of humanity battle for oil and gasoline. For Max, however, both civilization and the chaos of biker gangs and homoerotic road rage are unappealing, only interacting with the human sphere as need dictates.

Beyond Thunderdome

Max's own anarchism comes to the fore in the third installment, *Beyond Thunderdome*, where the series takes on a more philosophic and esoteric significance. The latest social order to rise from the chaos is Bartertown, the creation of a new Empress, Aunty (Tina Turner). Here, civilized order has taken on all the characteristics of the mistakes of the old world: economic gain is the locus of human energy, while Bartertown's energy arises from pig shit – methane. Seeking a resolution to the energy embargoes imposed by the ruler of the "Underworld," Master Blaster, Aunty hires Max to assassinate Blaster in the gladiatorial Thunderdome. I commented previously on *Beyond Thunderdome*:

> Aunty is the new elite class, a "nobody" who built a new world, towering above the peons of Bartertown. Aunty's pragmatic *realpolitik* keeps the animal-like populace in line by providing food, sex, economic gain and entertainment. Underworld, however, is run by a retarded giant (Blaster) whose homunculus midget partner sits atop his back (Master). We have here the juxtaposition of baser bodily instincts embodied in Blaster, with reason, science and technology embodied in Master, the mastermind of Bartertown's energy policy. Together they form a unit and represent technological power, which has survived the apocalypse. Aunty represents feminine machinations and scheming, wherein civilization is actually portrayed as a

domesticating institution (contrary to many images of "civilization" wherein it is presented as a patriarchal, masculine *logos* structure).

Thus, immediately after the apocalypse, men fall back into their same tendencies of creating competing power structures of exploitation. This will be important because *Thunderdome* will present a cyclical view of history.… Worth noting here is the emcee for the Thunderdome and the deadly game show: He is a Freemason.

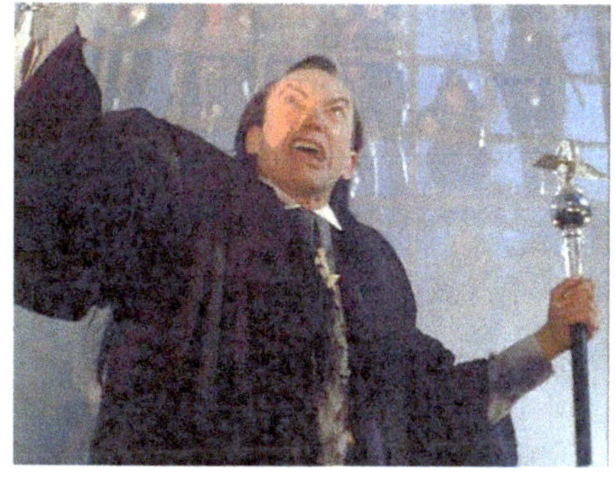

This can be read on many levels. Aunty, as we said, represents the more covert media/control grid/ intelligence community aspect of the bourgeoisie. The message here is that the secret societies continue post-apocalypse, and continue precisely as a means of control. Freemasonic hoodwinking controls the media and entertainment industry of Bartertown, suggesting this might apply in more than just Max's fictional world. The emcee wears a "G" and a square and compass, which in Masonry contains several levels of meaning. The "G" ultimately represent the generic deity of Masonry, embodied in human reason, and more or less synonymous with the deistic, contentless "god" of Freemasonry. Here, again, reason and technology and entertainment and covert action intertwine to control so-called "civilization."

Max ends up banished to the desert, like Moses, to wander into death. Almost dying from lack of water, Max is almost miraculously rescued by a monkey and a band of innocent children, likened in many ways to the Lost Boys of *Peter Pan*. The children live in an Edenic, virtual state of "pure nature" as envisioned by some Enlightenment empiricist. Not that I accept that view, but that is the idea that seems to be presented. The children subsist on the basis of harmony with nature and belief in an elaborate myth they have created surrounding various mundane artifacts that survived a plane crash with them.

Brilliantly, they read into images from a Viewmaster toy a story about their origins, as well as their coming Redeemer, whom they call "Captain Walker." In liturgical fashion, they re-enact their story when Max arrives, believing him to be their deliverer. So Max takes on this role of Moses/ Christ, who is a deliverer to a people who are a kind of innocent faith community grounded around an elaborate myth. They are the opposite of Bartertown, which subsists on greed, technology and lasciviousness. Max fits in here, because they also embody the noble savage myth, and Max is a rebel and enemy of "civilization." Max's Captain Walker hat is the key to

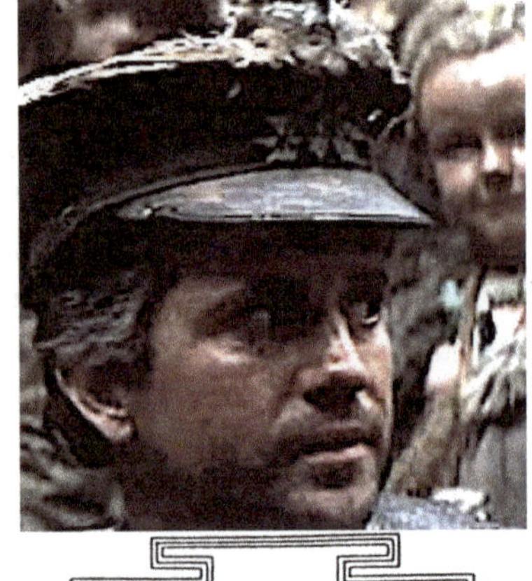

understanding this mysterious scene, as well as the entire film. If this seems far-fetched, recall the master of ceremonies at the Thunderdome blatantly wore a Masonic "G" around his neck.

The image on the Captain Walker hat is the upper half of a Yantra, the triangular symbol believed to convey thought forms through sound resonance, representing deities or cosmic powers. This is a fascinating inclusion, as this scene focuses on the children's mythology of the "sonic," an old record they have discovered, and the "tell," the makeshift television. The meaning appears to be that their telling of the Tell, which they refer to specifically as a liturgical enactment, has summoned Captain Walker.

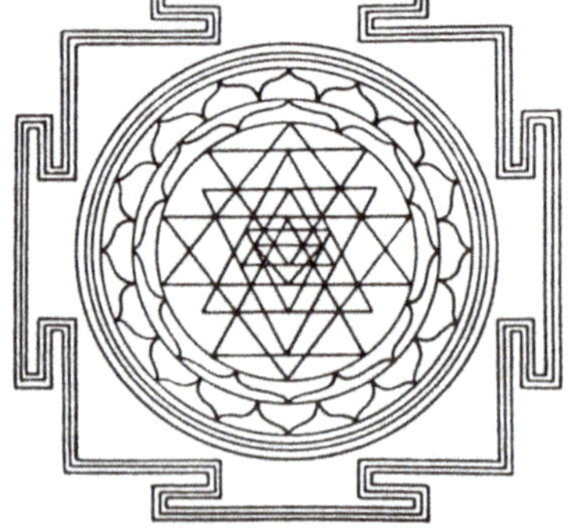

It's also significant that throughout the series, Max "has no name." He's just a "raggedy man," the "man from nowhere," and "nobody," because naming a thing is a way to control a thing. Naming a thing implies knowledge of and an attempt to encapsulate and categorize a thing into a thought form. The lost children believe they have sonically called forth Max (Captain Walker), which suggests that Max is a new avatar, a new messiah around which an entire mythology has been built.

It is also important to note that Max appears to be dead when the children find him, and when they stand over his body, he is covered in ash as if he were a corpse. When he awakes, they recite the Tell, and hand him his crown, which is the seat of rulership in terms of the chakras, as well as in the cabala (Keter). Also take note that in the lower left of the Yantra there is an All-Seeing Eye (which is overly emphasized in pop film analyses nowadays, but here it is relevant).

Walker's crown is his "new name," the crown of Keter, the new avatar of the new religion – which Max inadvertently does take on, as the new civilization the lost children found tells the oral tradition (cabala means tradition) of the new avatar, the new Moses, the new Logos, the sound-form whose tradition is to be passed on in the Tell, having been named. The same Yantra symbolism is also seen in the rafters in the final scene during The Tell, which shows this is intentional, since Yantras are also a feature of sacred architecture. Wikipedia explains:

> Yantra function as revelatory conduits of cosmic truths. Yantra, as instrument and spiritual technology, may be appropriately envisioned as prototypical and esoteric concept mapping machines or conceptual looms. Certain yantra are held to embody the energetic signatures of, for example, the Universe, consciousness, *ishta-devata*. Though often rendered in two dimensions through art, yantra are conceived and conceptualized by practitioners as multi-dimensional sacred architecture and in this quality are identical with their correlate the mandala. Meditation and trance induction that generates the yantra of the subtle body in the complementary modes of the *utpatti-krama* and *sampana-krama* are invested in the various lineages of tantric transmission as exterior and interior sacred architecture that potentiate the accretion and manifestation of *siddhi.*

It is worth mentioning that in Masonry, the "Name" is said to have been lost, and just as the children decide they don't need the "knowing" (gnosis), Walker will function as the means by which they will obtain the elderly Master, who has the knowing, and rebuild their world. The Name hearkens again to cabala, as well as the biblical texts, as the High Priest wore the Name of God on His crown/forehead, and as the Apocalypse describes in relation to the Churches (a fitting reference, given the post-*Apocalyptic* world of Max):

> He that hath an ear, let him hear what the Spirit saith unto the churches; To him that overcometh will I give to eat of the hidden manna, and will give him a white stone, and in the stone a new name written, which no man knoweth saving he that receiveth it.
>
> –(Revelations 2:17)

Fury Road

Continuing the theme of resource war, the commodification of all aspects of life take on a more radical character in the post-apocalypse of *Fury Road*. A new, religious imperial order has arisen similar in form to Aunty from *Thunderdome*, yet far more degenerate. The patriarchal tyranny of Immortan Joe, a radiation-mutated messianic "redeemer" who possesses a fantastic harem of super models who function as his breeders. Sitting atop an unreachable green plateau, Immortan doles out niggardly supplies of water to his groveling, troll-like subjects. Viewing Immortan as a god, the religion of Joe promises Valhalla to his pale pack of "War Boys" that ride with him to death in battle on *Fury Road*. Imagine *Fast & Furious: Albino Drift*.

This time around, human civilization has reverted into the most primal, tribal forms of primitivism, where religion is a prop for the polis to prop up its new mythos. Joe has convinced his underlings he is immortal, telling his acolytes their sacrifices will result in the eventual elevation to the top of the plateau. The lush green plateau offers delights only to Joe, of course, and this time around Max and Imperator Furiosa form an unwilling partnership to unseat Joe and free his harem.

The insight here concerns realpolitik, as we saw with *Thunderdome*. Religion is the tool of the state more often than not, serving the whims of some petty tyrant. *Fury Road* is an even more apt description of our own world than it is a fictional dystopia in this respect, where all aspects of life are portrayed as a controlled resource market. Even sex, which is more recreational in our day, is here presented as a crucial means for the furtherance of bloodlines. Breeding and eugenics are key, as those in control understand a chemically lobotomized populace with no access to necessary resources are unable to continue into the future.

In spite of the faulty conceptions of the masses, the actual elite of the planet are, like Immortan Joe, concerned with the furtherance of their own lineage and the dysgenic destruction of the rest of the populace. In this paradigm, harems and concubines make sense, where the "royal art" of alchemy is ultimately about the transformation of the individual and the world into one's own image. Hermetic alchemy focuses on this transformative process, and encompasses everything from the biosphere to breeding to the inner psychological process. Groups such as the Golden Dawn proffered hermetic alchemical secrets and it is my contention that *Mad Max: Fury Road* picks up with an alchemical version of chaos magick, where *Thunderdome* left off with Kabbalah and Tantrism.

Everything in the world of *Fury Road* has been inverted and is controlled, particularly basic necessities of life. Joe controls bullets, breeding, travel, energy and food – all that is necessary to run his patch of the bleak globe. While critics of the film are highlighting the portrayal of patriarchy as the source of all evils is only partially correct, what was far more prominent in the film is the deeper message of the seed. Both Joe and Max become concerned with the preservation of seeds – in Joe's case, breeding children and a dynasty that are not mutated by radiation, and in Max's case, his blood is the life-force for both the War Boys and Furiosa. The "life is in the blood," Leviticus 17:11 tells us, and Max appears to continue his quasi-Christ status from *Thunderdome*.

Fury Road is therefore a representation of a nominally Christian redemptive history, yet the outcome is inverted. Instead of a divine Savior who rescues man as the Promised Seed of the Woman (Gen. 3), Max is a purely human savior as *Thunderdome* portrayed. The seeds of life that will continue into the future do not rest on the "lie of hope," but on fixing the present world through technology. As we saw with *Thunderdome*, the "Knowing" of the secrets of technology that only remain in the religious appellations given to the "Holy V8 Engine" (like *Brave New World's* "Year of Our Ford") point to a Masonic conception of religion as a cloak for rationalism's scientific secrets. Alchemy is concerned with the union of opposites into a synthesis and in *Fury Road*, the union of male and female into a supposed new order of living is manifested on the earthly plane in an atheistic, communist revolution. The synthesis, so the mythology goes, can only be achieved by the dialectical collision of opposites and cyclical process of inversions of inversions of inversions, in a left-hand path of sex, death and orgiastic oblivion – *chaos magick*.

In essence, *Fury Road* is an alchemical presentation of the royal *deception*, rather than the royal art, where more often than not, in history we do find the *polis* co-opting religion for the purposes of human control. The ultimate form of control is that of breeding, and determining whose seed will continue into the future, and through the new Max revolution with his feminine counterpart Furiosa, the implication is that by opposing the older patriarchal forms of power with their dialectical opposite, the "clans of the mothers," hope can return. Let's be realistic here – if the older patriarchal forms of religion are lies, as the film's narrative suggests, then we are to believe the introduction of a feminine, Gaia-based egalitarian communist order is somehow workable and *real*? Is erecting a feminine-based order with the dismissal of Joe's Golgotha plausible? Nothing is more absurd, nonsensical and *mad*.

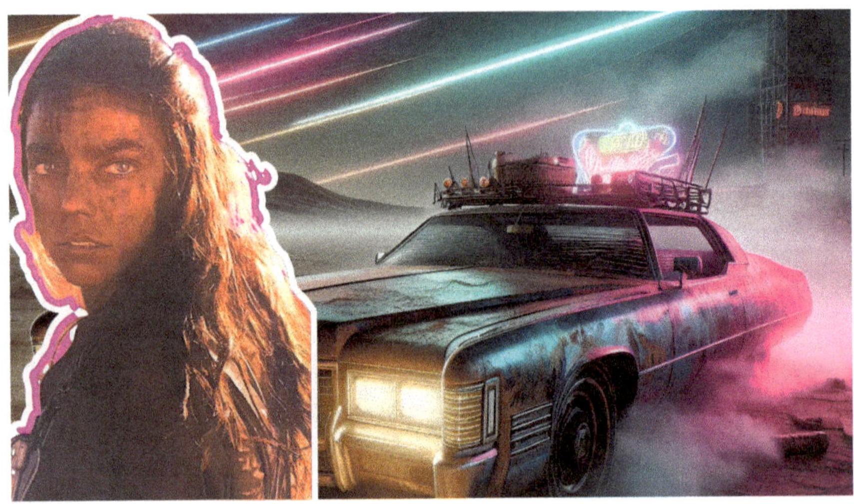

Furiosa (2024)

The final installment with Anya-Taylor Joy (who often stars in trauma-based mind control themed films) as the young Furiosa vindicates the previous feminist analysis, taking us far beyond mere activism. The dark goddess savior archetype is what we find Furiosa evolving into as she loses her feminine markers, becomes part machine and evolves into something non-binary. In this plot, Furiosa is kidnapped from her all-female Eden where the tree of life still grows, only to be thrust into a patriarchal warlord society where men rule over slaves and concubines, with her abductor explicitly having a Christ-like appearance named Dementus.

Dementus eventually captures Furiosa's mother, aptly named Mary, and crucifies her in an inversion of the Christian mythos, giving birth to a new female savior whose offspring will evolve into becoming like her opposite (Dementus) by integrating her "dark side," and her masculine side. Thus, liberation comes through a goddess savior identified as the final "rider of the apocalypse," who descends into a kind of katabasis underworld at bullet farm which is very reminiscent of Dante's *Inferno*, liberating all forms of slavery and oppression, including the notions of private property and resource control by becoming the opposite and achieving Hegelian synthesis. Eden is thus ruined by the satanic male invaders, resulting in a restoration of a new all-female Eden atop the mountain fortress of Immortan Joe when he is overthrown.

It is also worth noting Anya Taylor-Joy, the daughter of a British diplomat (David Joy), is often cast in explicitly trauma-based mind control themed films, replete with alternate personalities and MKUltra symbology.

For example, her breakout role was Eggers' 2015 film *The VVitch,* where a dissociative Puritan Calvinist teenager in 1630's New England ends up making a pact with Satan, eventually adopting an extreme opposite *persona* as a skyclad initiated witch ascending into the night sky in a Sabbat by the end of the film. In 2016's *Morgan,* she plays a modified genetic super soldier with a deviant penchant for assassinating humans, while her personal inner quest is seeking solace in a distant memory of an elusive Eden-like forest. In M. Night Shyamalan's *Split* (2016) she plays a cheerleader who was molested and abused, and whom the "Beast" (an entity that possesses a MPD/DID man played by James McEvoy) recognizes as one of his own.

In 2016's *Marrowbone* she is an alter in the head of a brain damaged teenager, while in *Thoroughbreds* she plays a sociopathic assassin who frames her friend for the death of her equally psychopathic stepfather. In 2020's *New Mutants* she plays a Russian orphan who has developed multiple personalities and special powers due to being molested as a child, whilst in *Last Night in Soho* she plays a 1960s alternate personality (or ghost?) of a hooker who manifests inside the *psyche* of a modern teen fashion designer. In 2022's *The Northman,* she plays a hallucinogenic mushroom tripping witch who uses her trickery to initiate her chosen lover and poison her enemies, while in *The Menu* she again plays a cunning prostitute who uses her street smarts to survive a horrific food cult's mass murder. In *Dune 2,* she plays Paul's insane MPD/DID sister, Alia Atreides, and in *Furiosa* she plays the traumatized, psychotic robotic Imperator Furiosa.

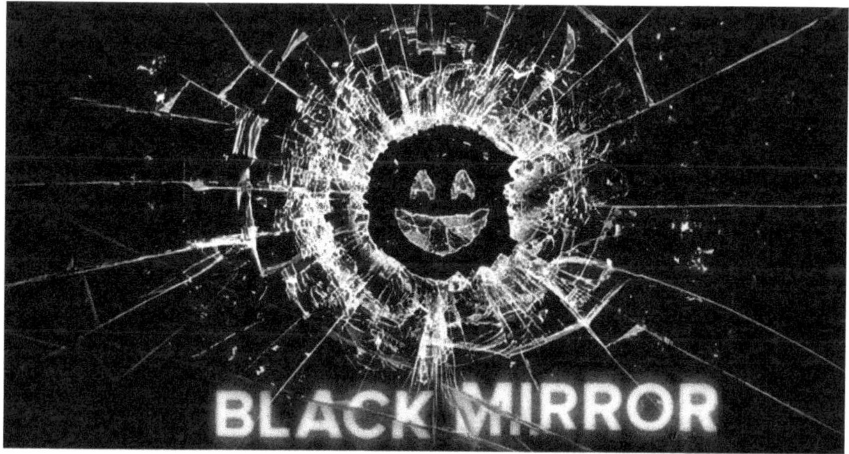

Black Mirror

Black Mirror is born of the mind of former *Guardian* writer and satirist Charlie Brooker: A mix of *The Twilight Zone* meets technological dystopia, the Netflix series has garnered rave reviews and much speculative debate over its four seasons. In my estimation, the episodes are hit-and-miss, but its undeniable the series is a 'revelation of the method' cornucopia. Brooker is no stranger to controversy, having arranged numerous media spoofs, stunts and scandals, including targeting video game animal abuse and a satirical statement calling for the assassination of George W. Bush. *The Guardian* is known to have MI6 influence, so one wonders if Brooker had *special* information, especially concerning some of the more astounding "predictions," as we will see in this analysis of the overall very well done seasons 1-4.

Season 1
"The National Anthem"

Focusing on the debased population of the future (or now?) a "terrorist" demands the Prime Minister actively engage in bestiality with a pig on live television in return for the release of a captive UK Royal Princess. Keep in mind this episode premiered in December of 2011. The most fascinating aspect of this initial installment was not its grotesque theme, but the mainstream media release of the allegedly true story of the UK's then Prime Minister David Cameron having engaged in some form of sexual action with a pig. The *Telegraph* explained it as follows in 2015, *4 years after the initial episode aired*, noting how the action was part of a *ritual initiation*:

> There is, as they say, only one story the political world is sniggering about today. In an unambiguously hostile biography of David Cameron, it is reported that as a young man the Prime minister placed his private parts in the mouth of a dead pig. This is said to have been part of an initiation for an aristocratic Oxford University dining club. There is a photograph, it is said.

In the episode, the event is intended to be a stunt to awaken the populace to their own obsession and fascination with mass media. In this sense, the message of the episode is correct, as all *Black Mirror* installments focus on the dangers of high-tech in some way, as well as mass media. However, at a certain point "exposing" events becomes another exercise in debasement, as the organizer of the publicity stunt commits suicide and releases the hostage. With its Anonymous-esque overtones, were the event taking place in the real world, it would likely be staged, with the Anonymous terrorist operating at the behest of the establishment.

Porky Pig.

As is evident in the first episode, the events taking place are *mirrors* of our own reality – black mirrors – both the David Cameron pig incident, as well as how the public is enslaved and manipulated through mass media and technology. In this way, I read *Black Mirror* as a whole as a mirror of techno-nihilism, reflecting back at us the dark, black nothingness we are entering due to the systemic acceptance of post-post modernity, the virtual abyss. The "black mirror" is the shade self of the collective unconscious, the Luciferian and Satanic reflection of a society that has, from top to bottom, accepted self-destruction. We are *already* in an era of daily mass traumatization through media stunts akin to "National Anthem's" display – it's not a future dystopia – this was the point of *Natural Born Killers*.

"Fifteen Million Merits"

"Fifteen Million Merits" is one of the best episodes of the entire series. Imagine a dystopia where the future is nothing but a mix of Dance, Dance Revolution, Pokemon and some form of Nintendo Wii characters, where every day's purpose is the accumulation of virtual tokens (not Bitcoins!) that buy you the peace of not being bombarded in your coffin apartment with YouTube-esque ads, porn pop ups and total gamification. For those unaware, "gamification" is a real concept centered around the creation of virtual tokens and "rewards" for daily actions and decisions.

Gamification is based on the manipulation of the pleasure-reward centers of the brain, and just as video games themselves arose from the Pentagon and DARPA, so the gamification of all of reality is expanding to encompass even the most mundane. From education to one day getting virtual "points" for brushing one's teeth, the potential for complete social engineering control starts to become evident. Eventually (as a later *Black Mirror* will show), "likes," "tokens" and "points" will be used to socially engineer. Individuals will be banned and socially shamed for not being politically correct and submitting to the A.I. cuckery Pimpbot 5000 mandates. We are already seeing people banned from major platforms – eventually the social disapproval will extend to shaming and the turning off of ones "credits" needed to buy items necessary for survival. That is the final goal, at least, if the dystopia has its way. Bitcoin, I believe, is another matter, not being controlled by a central bank, inflation or third party apparatus.

Way to go champ!

The Independent notes:

> "While there is nothing new with rewarding people when they do something good, today, many of these ideas are being fed from an altogether different realm: the gaming industry.
>
> Ever since Sony launched its PlayStation games console that helped popularize gaming, adults and children alike now spend millions of pounds and thousands of hours each year playing games. With so many people playing so many games, it is no wonder that psychologists, policy makers and businesses have taken a keen interest in what makes playing games so compelling.
>
> Notwithstanding their immersive quality, people of all ages through playing games can be very adept at attaining goals, gaining rewards and in the case of some games, players actively cooperate with one another for altruistic ends, such as to explore and build new virtual cities. Gaming – especially played on mobile phones – is also generating huge revenues for game producers through in app purchases too."[46]

A prevalent theme in season 1 is media and technology and in Fifteen Million Merits the protagonist schemes his way to delivering an emotional speech on the future's American Idol about the abyss of empty techno-nihilism. Having seen his female interest degraded and put into porn after her performance, his antics are rewarded as a gimmick where he's given his own TV show. The irony is his willingness to sacrifice it all is the ticket that buys his freedom from the virtual gulag. While the rest of the Poke-slaves slave on, our protagonist is rewarded with his own apartment and skyline view of a real forest scene from his new high-rise apartment. The irony was the virtual slavery is an analogy for the slavery to the notions that fame and tokens (dollars, credits, likes, whatever) are *all* virtual, making this one of the most prescient of the series.

"The Entire History of You"

In this installment, special brain implants ("grains") allow the replaying of events recorded by the eye. Here, the future is one of total panopticism and surveillance, where TSA agents not only peek at your junk, but even rewind and review last night's intimacy. Protagonist Liam, severely lacking in game, finds himself cucked by his girlfriend's ex, Jonas, who suddenly appears at a dinner party. Liam demands Jonas delete his memories of past relations with his ex, but notices there is a chance one of those previous dalliances may mean his son is not his, but Jonas'.

Naturally the message here is simply whether total information aware-ness and availability is really what we want. The promises of safety and security in relation to the dangers and misery that would result from full information recollection and awareness are absurd – but no doubt there will be some attempt to implement something like this. Dystopian tales apparently function as a giant collective playbook for the psychopathic elite – where all are integrated.

Season 2
"Be Right Back"

Martha loses her baby-daddy Ash in a traffic accident, leading to her using his excessive time spent on social media as the basis for an A.I. re-creation on her phone, intent on aiding her in overcoming despair. The synthetic voice is not enough, eventually leading to the transferral of Ash to a syn-thoid body. Frustrated at the differences between the A.I. Ash and real Ash, Martha commands the fake Ash jump off a cliff. Fake Ash then begs for his life and is allowed to remain in Martha's attic for occasional visits. Oddly, the message of this episode is the inadequacy of artificiality. There is no amount of A.I., synthetic tokens and virtual sex that can replace the missing element of real human interaction and contact.

Indeed, one of the stupidest notions being fostered by the establish-ment subsequently gobbled up by the gullible masses is the preposter-ous notion that an algorithm or a simulation is such and such person. A copy of a thing is not the thing – one would think this is obvious, but then again, we are suddenly in a world where one can make reality by renaming it: a male is no longer a biological reality, but a social con-struct! It thus follows that all reality is therefore a "social construct" and therefore completely meaningless.

This is the real secret and force of mind control, the ability to manip-ulate mass consciousness into believing utter nonsense, and the early episodes of *Black Mirror* exploration this theme. Sex bots also come up, but as expected they don't live up to the hype. Unfortunately, by season 4 *Black Mirror* opts for full-on social justice warrior race guilt promo-tion, coupled with the absurd idea holograms and A.I. are ontologically the same as human persons. Ash ends up where he should have been in the first place, as a memory Martha should have gotten over. In fact, your "granny can be uploaded to the cloud"! From Moms on the Net to Grannies *Are* the Net.

"White Bear"

Another of my favorites, 'White Bear" examines the notion of trial-by-media, stagecraft/fake news and completely-controlled, synthetic environments. Hilariously, in 2012 it was acceptable to expose "fake news" and the absurdity of the mainstream media, yet by 2016 when Donald Trump began to accuse the mainstream media of "fake news," it marks the evil white racist at the conclusion of season four. Awakening in a strange environment with no memory, a girl is mystified by a television playing a strange signal, an empty house and weirdo neighbors who stalk her from outside. Seeing a photo of a young girl and another with herself and a boyfriend, "Hunters" in masks walk about filming her, but engage in no direct interaction. Needless to say, the oddness begins to smack of some form of psychological operation – is she under mind control?

Of course, the one thing this episode gets wrong is the crowds lack of *selfies*! If this really were a gigantic prison-entertainment complex psychological operation, the one thing the onlookers would be doing is snapping endless selfies. Not only is the entire scenario concocted, it is full of crisis actors intent on furthering their career in a dystopian world that makes criminal prosecution a combination of reality television and *The Price is Right*.

This scenario is not far off, as even now individuals can lose their livelihoods by merely being accused of something in the media, without any actual conviction or evidence! On top of that, we have documented many cases of the media and intelligence agencies apparently coordinating in creating fake, staged, manipulated events, or conversely steering organic events in some direction (think *Wag the Dog*). In similar fashion to some *real* mind control operations carried out by MKUltra doctors like Dr. Ewan Cameron and Dr. John C. Lilly, entirely fake, controlled environments and synthetic realities have been created to study various human reactions and techniques for programming.

In this episode, we think white bear is a signal transmitted that's causing mass-mind control upon the populace, but as we discover, the station and its signal aren't real. What is real is the gigantic psychological operation that is "White Bear," the private prison-entertainment complex. I think we can also read this as an analogy for the various "signals" and frequencies we are subjected to that are not new technologies, but old ones. Globalist scion Zbignew Brzezinski described this back in 1973 in his famous work, *Between Two Ages*:

> In addition … future developments may well include automated or manned space warships, deep-sea installations, chemical and biological weapons, death rays, and still other forms of warfare–even the weather may be tampered with.

In addition, it may be possible – and tempting – to exploit for strategic-political purposes the fruits of research on the brain and on human behavior. Gordon J. F. MacDonald, a geophysicist specializing in problems of warfare, has written that timed artificially excited electronic strokes could lead to a pattern of oscillations that produce relatively high power levels over certain regions of the earth…. In this way, one could develop a *system that would seriously impair the brain performance of very large populations* in selected regions over an extended period…. No matter how deeply disturbing the thought of using the environment to manipulate behavior for national advantages to some, the technology permitting such use will very probably develop within the next few decades.

Of course, the great unanswered question in this episode is whether Victoria actually did commit the horrendous crime she is accused of. If the establishment in this dystopia has the ability to concoct the entire scenario with crisis actors and all, it's entirely possible the evidence of her guilt are also fabricated. In a world of trial-by-media it's impossible to know, and that's exactly how the power elite would like it to be.

"The Waldo Moment"

In the near future, a comedian controls a raunchy, wise-cracking computer avatar bear named Waldo on a late-night television show which becomes a huge success. Politics is satirized, equating the absurdity of politics with the nonsense of a raunchy, circus-like children's puppet show. Waldo eventually ends up with his own show, and as his popularity grows, Waldo becomes a global phenomenon to the dismay of the comedian controlling him. As part of a joke, Waldo begins doing public political stunts and his fame grows exponentially, with a call for Waldo to become a political candidate. Politics has always been theater, but this episode takes the issue to the meta-level: What if politics becomes dominated by A.I. joke characters? We've seen a long train of actors become politicians and presidents, so why not a raunchy A.I. bear? Perhaps a Pokemon platform would be the wisest vote in 2020, though I doubt it would be as entertaining as Trump, which makes me think – maybe in 20 years we can have an A.I. Donald Trump/Max Headroom as president.

"White Christmas"

In the Christmas special John Hamm plays Joe, a nighttime pickup artist instructor who guides nerds into successful encounters with women through secret technological implants. During the day, however, Joe's 9-to-5 was working for a SmartHouse/Smart Tech company that copies client's consciousness and loads them into little "cookies" (like Alexa!). The "Smart" theme of this episode is interesting, especially as we are being prepped through Siri and Alexa and GoogleVoice for "personal assistants" that are actually spying devices. Simultaneous with this idea is the absurd notion that virtual copies are actual people with "rights." This fits well with a prevalent theme in recent Hollywood films working to promote transhumanism where robots are humanized, and humans are demonized. The masses are unfortunately under the impression the "Smart" tech is being implemented to create a utopia and give immortality, when the truth is quite the opposite. The giving of "rights" to androids, cyborgs and sims is not only absurd, but shown to be even more ridiculous when we understand the result is the dehumanization and loss of "rights" for actual humans.

The two "evil" men in this episode are *villains* for helping nerds learn to find women, and for being angry that a girlfriend wants to abort a child! Both men end up "blocked" and unable to reconcile or communicate. Ironically, Beth decides to keep the chid and the boyfriend (Matt) ends up arrested and later tracks down the child. Matt watches his child grow up from a distance each year and leaves his daughter a present, and later discovers the mother has died leading to his attempt to find the girl at the winter house. Beth had cheated and had a child with an Asian man Matt learns, leading to his mental breakdown and subsequent murder of Beth's dad.

Obviously the murder of the father was wrong, but the dystopian revelations of this episode definitely present the male patriarchy as vile, wicked and destined to be eternally punished in the psychotic fantasies of the mentally ill leftist's *ressentement*. Does the title of this episode symbolize the series' hatred for white men? Didn't you know – white men are all murdering, rapist sex offenders who persecute innocent women who want abortions! There's no doubt the left already salivates over the chance at *convicting* and punishing men for their thoughts and speech. Isn't it interesting the left doesn't believe in hell or the supernatural – but relishes in the idea of torturing the patriarchy for all eternity. As other analysts have noted, the Satanic nature of these themes comes to the fore when we realize such stories occur at Christmas in attempts to invert a Holy Day into something evil.

Season 3
"Nosedive"

In "Nosedive" we are presented with a dystopian suburbia controlled by social media. Some might say we are already there, but imagine if social media rankings actually determined your class and status in society. As mentioned earlier, this is already being tested out in some nations like China, where the government plans to rank and control all its citizens based on a social media credit score! *Wired* magazine writes:

> Imagine a world where many of your daily activities were constantly monitored and evaluated: what you buy at the shops and online; where you are at any given time; who your friends are and how you interact with them; how many hours you spend watching content or playing video games; and what bills and taxes you pay (or not). It's not hard to picture, because most of that already happens, thanks to all those data-collecting behemoths like Google, Facebook and Instagram or health-tracking apps such as Fitbit. But now imagine a system where all these behaviours are rated as either positive or negative and distilled into a single number, according to rules set by the government. That would create your Citizen Score and it would tell everyone whether or not you were trustworthy. Plus, your rating would be publicly ranked against that of the entire population and used to determine your eligibility for a mortgage or a job, where your children can go to school – or even just your chances of getting a date.
>
> A futuristic vision of Big Brother out of control? No, it's already getting underway in China, where the government is developing the Social Credit System (SCS) to rate the trustworthiness of its 1.3 billion citizens. The Chinese government is pitching the system as a desirable way to measure and enhance 'trust' nationwide and to build a culture of 'sincerity.' As the policy states, "It will forge a public opinion environment where keeping trust is glorious. It will strengthen sincerity in government affairs, commercial sincerity, social sincerity and the construction of judicial credibility.

Encounters in the episode eventually becomes tools to exclude individuals from upper classes. Eventually, de-ranking and thumbs-down results in arrest and jail time – and even in jail two social media rejects battle to one-up and show they're better than the other inmates. The irony is everyone is potentially in an ideological prison with the rise of social media – and the creators of Facebook have even admitted and lamented this fact – that it was done to manipulate society:

"It literally changes your relationship with society, with each other. It probably interferes with productivity in weird ways. God only knows what it's doing to our children's brains," he said.

He explained that when Facebook was being developed the objective was: "How do we consume as much of your time and conscious attention as possible?" It was this mindset that led to the creation of features such as the "like" button that would give users "a little dopamine hit" to encourage them to upload more content.

"It's a social-validation feedback loop … exactly the kind of thing that a hacker like myself would come up with, because you're exploiting a vulnerability in human psychology."[47]

"Playtest"

Another of my favorites, a gamer nerd named Cooper is coaxed into participating as an unwitting dupe in a hardcore psychological operation utilizing video games. The "augmented reality" allows his mind to be hacked, leading to a severe mental breakdown. For the duration of the episode we are questioning whether he has been led like a lamb to the slaughter and if Sonja was in on it, or to what degree Cooper's experiences are real. You could genuinely call this one Pokemon Bro or Pokemon Go (to hell). Alternate titles include Rothschild Resident Evil or Downton Abbey of Thelema, given the ornate Rothschild-esque estates where the drama goes down. It's also fascinating that this episode premiered right after the release of Pokemon Go, the most notable "augmented reality" game we've seen so far.

What I would stress in relation to this episode is the fact that video games themselves were developed by the Pentagon and DARPA for training and beyond that, into entirely new realms in our day of virtual worlds and a coming "matrix.":

"Inside one artificial edifice, Herman Narula, Improbable's co-founder and CEO, addressed the group. "We're in a place today where it is actually possible to create artificial realities," he said. "Not in some abstract sense, but genuine, living, breathing recreations of this one, powered by technology, that allow people to have totally new experiences." Narula has a boyish face, scruffily cropped hair and stubble; he has the energy levels of a small nuclear reactor, and speaks faster than most people think.

"A.I. gets all the press," he said, but, "this idea of recreating reality is going to become something in the public consciousness that's as important, as significant, as artificial intelligence." (See also the Google DeepMind Project)

Just like Ferris Bueller saving the world in *War Games*, the origin of video games arises in Cold War game theory operations:

> During the 1950s, Brookhaven National Laboratory had several early computers, designed to crunch the numbers on ballistic missile trajectories. In an attempt to garner interest from bored visitors to the lab, an enterprising physicist named William Higinbotham took one of these computers, hooked it up to an oscilloscope, and created a small physics-based game dubbed Tennis For Two. Though the game had no real involvement from any military organization, the computer technology pioneered by the Department of Defense in the wake of World War II played a crucial role in bringing the game to life.
>
> Thirty years later, the military was getting directly involved. One the first links between a commercial game company and a military agency occurred during the arcade game frenzy of the early 1980s. One of the more popular games at the time was Atari's Battlezone, a tank game with eerie green wireframe graphics. The Army Training Doctrine and Command, aka TRADOC, wanted Atari to turn its sci-fi shooter into a training simulator for the Army's latest infantry fighting vehicle, the M2 Bradley. Two Army Battlezone prototypes were eventually produced, but no Bradley crewman ever trained on the system. Still, it was an early signifier of how the mainstream games industry and the military would collaborate in the future.

Video games contain some of the most astounding predictive programming in our day, and even crossover with Hollywood as video games are beginning to rival comic books blockbusters, where titles like *Resident Evil* and *Call of Duty* are now billion dollar franchises. Where is all this going, you ask? Simply put, towards the Matrix becoming real.

"Shut Up and Dance"

This episode was one of those cringeworthy situations where a nervous teenager is blackmailed by a mysterious hacker who covertly films the teen looking at illegal porn. The teen is then coerced into a series of preposterous actions with shady characters and public stunts in order to keep his hacker tormenters from leaking his proclivities. The absurdity of this episode is the notion that hero good guy hackers are engaging in online vigilante activism to out sickos and pervs – but none of the sickos and pervs outed in the episode are real black market actors.

"We are Anonymous and we are very much a totally real threat to the system! Have you even seen *V for Vendetta* or *Mr. Robot?*"

Random teens and the occasional divorced middle-aged man are who is propping up an entire, gigantic black market? Get real – that's like saying the mega-billion dollar drug trade is being run by a local dealer – and not the CIA and intelligence agencies who invade countries for the purpose of controlling drug lanes like the Golden Crescent and Golden Triangle. The blackmail done by such entities in these cases is not done by hero hackers – but by the establishment!

"San Junipero"

Added for extra SJW flare! I'm offended, though – why has there not been a *pedo* episode? I suppose there *kinda*was a bestiality episode, but what about a trans-species rights episode? What about a polygamy rights-based episode? On what basis is *Black Mirror discriminating*? Why does *Black Mirror hate* so many minorities!

"Men Against Fire"

This is another of the fascinating episodes, where trained future super soldiers undergo a mind control operation that alters their perception of humans to where they appear (to the soldier) to be mutants, or "cockroaches." The episode has a clear dysgenic theme, but not only is there a real super soldier program by DARPA, DARPA also claims to be able to wipe and implant new and false memories – a staple of science fiction stories for decades. *The Atlantic* explains:

For decades after its inception in 1958, the Defense Advanced Research Projects Agency – DARPA, the central research and development organization of the Department of Defense – focused on developing vast weapons systems. Starting in 1990, and owing to individuals like Paul F. Gorman, a new focus was put on soldiers, airmen, and sailors – on transforming humans for war. The progress of those efforts, to the extent it can be assessed through public information, hints at war's future, and raises questions about whether military technology can be stopped, or should.

Gorman sketched out an early version of the thinking in a paper he wrote for DARPA after his retirement from the Army in 1985, in which he described an "integrated-powered exoskeleton" that could transform the weakling of the battlefield into a veritable super-soldier. The "Super-Troop" exoskeleton he proposed offered protection against chemical, biological, electromagnetic, and ballistic threats, including direct fire from a .50-caliber bullet. It "incorporated audio, visual, and haptic [touch] sensors," Gorman explained, including thermal imaging for the eyes, sound suppression for the ears, and fiber optics from the head to the fingertips. Its interior would be climate-controlled, and each soldier would have his own physiological specifications embedded on a chip within his dog tags. "When a soldier donned his ST [SuperTroop] battledress," Gorman wrote, "he would insert one dog-tag into a slot under the chest armor, thereby loading his personal program into the battle suit's computer," giving the 21st-century soldier an extraordinary ability to hear, see, move, shoot, and communicate.

Of course, even the mainstream media and scientists involved in such projects admit there are dangers of the brain being hacked and mind controlled:

"The objective of this effort," Michael Eisenstadt explained, "is to use remote teleoperation via direct interconnections with the brain." The bigger objective was to allow future "soldiers [to] communicate by thought alone. … Imagine a time when the human brain has its own wireless modem so that instead of acting on thoughts, warfighters have thoughts that act," Eisenstadt suggested. But a 2008 report by defense scientists raised some warnings. "An adversary might use" brain technology "in military applications.… An extreme example would be remote guidance or control of a human being." Other critics said that the quest to enhance human performance on the battlefield would lead scientists down a morally dangerous path.

Michael Goldblatt disagreed. "How is having a cochlear implant that helps the deaf hear any different than having a chip in your brain that could help control your thoughts?" he asked. When questioned about unintended consequences, like controlling humans for nefarious ends, Goldblatt insisted, "There are unintended consequences for everything."

And, as mentioned, programs dedicated to the creation and implantation of false memories and belief systems have already allegedly been successful, although the article actually says false memories were created "in mice." Are we sure those "squeaks" were properly deciphered? One can bet if such technology has been developed (and I'm sure it has), it will be kept top secret. We have seen stories claiming the ability to erase parts of the brain and its memories and functions, so presumably false ones could be implanted, especially if we accept the claims of Dr. John C. Lilly I covered and as I discussed in my *Blade Runner* analysis. It's no accident this comes from our dear, loving friends at the Salk Institute – and we know how much Dr. Jonas Salk *loved* humanity!:

"Most people agree that failure to 'unlearn' is a hallmark of post-traumatic stress disorders and if we had a drug that affects this gene it could help soldiers coming back from the war to 'unlearn' their fear memories."

"Hated in the Nation"

The theme of trial by media returns in a dystopic vision of a society manipulated by A.I. manipulating social media and hashtags. The episode reminded me of *The Deadly Bees*, famously lampooned by MST3k [Mystery Science Theater 3000]. Autonomous drone insects are targeting individuals the A.I. attacks on social media through hashtags, and two brave broads are on the case. The episode admits GCHQ uses the drone bees to spy on everyone (duh), which is true in the sense of social media as spying, but that has been known for years. The fun part of this episode is the very obvious Kanye stand-in rapper, "Tusk," who disses a child and becomes a social media enemy.

As you can imagine, the deadly bees come after Tusk leading to a meltdown prior to a concert. This is curious, given Kanye's "meltdown" and pro-Trump rant last year – was Kanye West attacked by the Queen's illuminati bee drone army? (I'm joking). However, one thing is sure – the social media giants are definitely creating bots and hashtags to attempt to ruin the lives of those who don't accept total mind control. Surprise! – the "villain" has a manifesto – based around a eugenics-minded social justice warrior! Since humans are mean online and in media, they should be bred out of existence! Try to wrap your head around that one, but in an odd way it make sense, insofar as in the post-modern techno-nihilist order, nothing makes sense.

Season 4

"USS *Callister*"

You can probably guess where I'm going with this one. An unhappy, unsatisfied beta male computer geek named Robert Daly is the co-founder of a successful virtual reality gaming platform called Infinity, which uses players' DNA to create a simulant replica for the virtual world. In his off time, Daly is the captain of a Star Trek reminiscent virtual game called

Star Fleet, where he torments and controls the replicas of his co-workers who have crossed him in real life. The story eventually shifts to being told from the vantage point of Robert's love interest at work, who is replicated in his virtual world. While amusing and creative conceptually, season 4 marks an even stronger SJW [Social Justice Warrior]turn for the series as Robert personifies once again the weak male who can only fantasize about tormenting others in his virtual world.

As is almost always the case, the episode takes on an overtly gnostic theme where Captain Robert becomes a cruel tyrant demiurge creator-god who only seeks vain pleasures and egotistical gratification, even at the expense of tormenting his colleagues. Endowed with god-powers, Captain Robert can do almost anything in his StarFleet world, and has bizarrely removed the sexual organs from his replica characters. Daly's love interest Nanette is miffed at being neutered and especially about the loss of her vaginal privileges – because men cannot handle women having sexual organs! Like a cruel, oppressive tyrant, we are like the patriarchal God of the Bible who only seeks to "control" women.

Predictably, Nanette becomes the new captain and overthrows and defeats the tyrant creator god as an image of the Sophia principle. In some worldviews schemes the male creator god suppresses the "goddess" power out of fear and envy, a perfect mythology for the nonsensical, irrational fixations of feminists who at times write openly about gnostic influence. In short, I was enjoying the episode until it once again became a gnostic tirade of liberal *ressentement* that fantasizes about eternally tormenting imagined "oppressors." The real irony in this episode is the recurring theme we've seen in *Black Mirror*, that fantasizing about torturing the male patriarchy and the moral projection of guilt upon everyone else is actually just a further proof of the conscience of the liberal cult screams out to them daily *they themselves* are the cause of their own misery.

"Arkangel"

I'm not sure how to rate this one. On the one hand, it's interesting to consider the nightmare that Smart technology will create, not just from Big Brother and the State, but BigMommy and stalker control freak parents. Can you imagine the dysfunctional relationships that will follow from overprotective parents spying on their kids at all times? At the same time, the episode is morally ambiguous as to whether the mom is morally flawed because she is spying on her daughter, or because she is concerned her daughter is dating a coke dealer. Drawing the line here is vague, and certainly that aspect of *Black Mirror* is a constant theme – moral ambiguity – as I'm sure you agree.

But wait! *Black Mirror* is simultaneously not morally ambiguous, as almost every episode, aside from a few cautionary tales, preaches a hardcore socially liberal agenda. The difficulty is, it's impossible to be completely morally neutral, though almost all post-modernists, leftists and atheists are ignorant of this fact, they nevertheless charge forward with complete doublethink. For the mind of the leftist, male sexuality is "toxic" and "rape," while victorious lefties and SJWs eternally tormenting their enemies is "justice." All leftists are *simultaneously* moral relativists and moral absolutists – a complete and utter contradiction of the most fundamental sort, and this double-mind is *the source* of their insanity.

"Crocodile"

This was probably one of the worst episodes with little to no explanation, significance or point. A stoner chick eventually becomes a ball-busting CEO of an architecture company but has buried in her past the accidental death of a biker her boyfriend hit years earlier. As a result, our *icebitchqueen* goes on a serial killing rampage to cover up any possible connections or witnesses due to her ex coming forward to admit he will confess. Thin and wispy as a sprite, this former stoner suddenly develops black belt level ninja moves, incapacitating and strangling a completely powerless and *non-resistant* large ex-boyfriend! I was laughing at this point and the entire episode goes downhill from this point on, as the terror of being discovered leads to multiple murders. Of course, the murders become so violent and vicious and open they are easily traced to her, as she's apprehended at her chid's school play. The episode *does* garner bonus SJW points for the stay-at-home dad who cooks and cleans and tends the children for our *icebitchqueen* CEO.

"Hang the DJ"

Imagine a future where Skynet and Tinder meet and fall in live. In their simulation world, the gigantic A.I. system matches up *your* sim character with other eligible single sims. Before you hyperventilate, don't worry – Skynetinder is pro-gay – there's no "fascism"! Within a few minutes I guessed the matches were in a simulation and had solved the plot. Once again we see the story from the vantage point of the sims, with a number of frustrating and failed dating matches leading to a (predictable) revolt on the part of the main couple. The fact they are sims means we can be at ease over the fact the lead girl has been a super hoe, having "paired" with countless guys – earning many more notches than our lead guy!

None of this fazes our protagonist who decides to revolt against the dating system, leading to a final resolution on the part of the A.I. super system that since the couple revolted in 99% of the simulations, they were true soul mates. We are then shown a present-day couple using something akin to Tinder which matches them for the first time at a party. In other words, don't give up – Tinder is actually Skynet and will find your soul mate! You just may have to swipe through 10,000+ profiles of "dog lovers" doing *very spiritual* yoga poses for the next 10 years.

"Metalhead"

Metalhead was my favorite episode of season 4 and one of the best overall. No preachy SJW bullshit, no contradictory moral filth, just suspense and survival, as a group of survivors are skulking about, preparing to raid a warehouse after some unknown robot apocalypse has occurred. Unsuccessful, the team is chased by an advanced assassin DARPA dog over hill and dale. Only the woman survives (naturally, only an older woman would survive such an ordeal, not two fit young guys!) leading to a harrowing ordeal of days of running from these battery-powered Terminator pooches. At least the episode wasn't obsessed with forcing social justice guilt down our throats.

"Black Museum"

Easily the worst and most ridiculous episode of the season, and possibly the series. Here, *Black Mirror* takes on an overtly racial component after showcasing to us the perverted sexual predilections of doctors. First, I thought race doesn't exist? If race is a social construct, why am I, as a viewer, supposed to feel guilt for past actions of whites–when *white* supposedly doesn't exist? Isn't gender also a social construct? Indeed, this episode hits on all the imagined liberal hot button topics, from evil whitey to evil men – because men enjoy sexuality only because it inflicts pain! Once again, leftists are projecting their own depravity elsewhere because the guilt they feel is a result of their depraved, incoherent worldview – one which does not match up to reality in the slightest. In fact, it's always these psychotic weirdos who are obsessed with BDSM and being tortured, precisely because they suppress their own guilt and have rejected God (see Rom. 1).

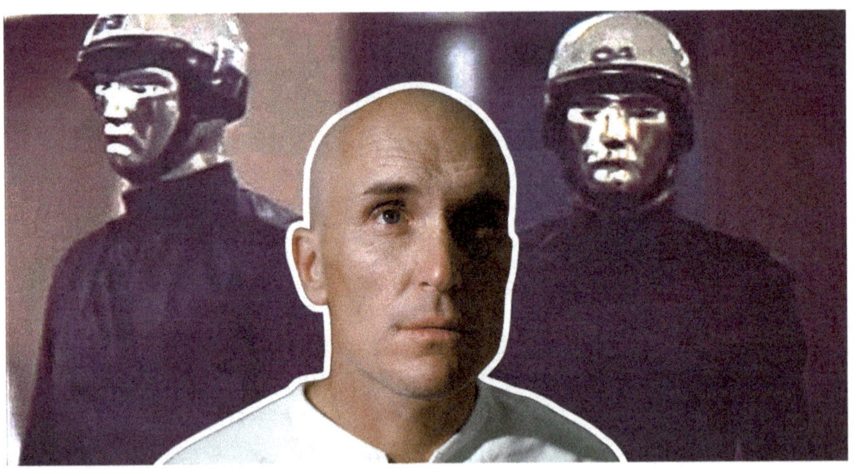

THX 1138 (1971) & Techno-Economic Vampirism

Thus, what *Black Mirror* inadvertently shows us is mankind's problem is not primarily psychological, political, racial or gender-based, but *spiritual*. Mankind's problems are not sociological, as if altering society to accept aberrant lifestyles, nihilism and self-destruction will assuage the conscience, but rather a change of heart and mind – and a return to the living God, that is the source for the healing of man's spiritual sickness. Mankind, like both Adam and Eve in the garden, always seeks to blame externals for the problems his conscience is telling him is internal – his own spiritual dilemma that must be worked out in repentance. When man forsakes that call to life, he makes a continual covenant with death, leading to self-imposed delusion, nihilism and eventual self-destruction. *Black Mirror* is thus a gaze into the psyche of the Luciferian, the dark heart of the forces of the Satanic that offer man the temptation to accept his destiny as demonic: The black mirrored abyss of pure negation, emptiness, loneliness and hatred.

One of the common themes in dystopian films is the economic control which has now begun to roll out through entities like the EU and World Economic Forum that meets yearly in Davos. The world's vultures, these economic power elite, meet in Davos to discuss the maintenance of their global *fiat* hegemony. Highlights generally include furthering banking austerity, noting that the serf class shouldn't have air conditioning and cars, as well as cheering on the death of privacy through the rise of technocracy. These degenerate elites, completely out of touch with humanity, resemble the controllers shown in the George Lucas classic, *THX 1138*, building their own prison destined to entrap their own progeny.

Power mad controllers always end up being their own worst enemy because pride detaches man from reality, which can only be perceived in the truth. Pride causes man to adopt a delusory sense of the world and his own relation to it, thereby bringing about a praxis divorced from the rules of nature, logic and classical wisdom.

The banking man, *homo economicus*, with his foaming at the mouth rapaciousness, will find his own descendants trapped in the virtual A.I. prison grid he has built. In *THX*, we find humanity sequestered in an underground base where a slave population is tasked with creating their own A.I. instruments of enslavement. Like *Brave New World* and *1984*, Lucas combined these classic with the key missing element of A.I., now being rolled out globally. Combined with A.I. the emerging "CBDC," or central bank digital currency, will fulfill the technocratic dream of total control, where all human interactions will fall under total panopticism, just as we see in Lucas' classic. However, before A.I. and CBDCs, the analogy of man feeding his own enslavement with the debt-based fiat system is also applicable to THX. As one of the characters in the famed economic film *Margin Call* notes:

> This is why the solution has to come from within, as every system will simply corrupt again. Philosophers and great thinkers have warned us continuously for thousands of years. The manifestation of inner dysfunction and imbalance will always be represented physically as dysfunction and imbalances in the systems man develops.

When we consider the global economic situation, it is crucial to understand we are living in the midst of a long-running script that was hammered out long ago by European banking houses. CFR archivist and historian Dr. Carroll Quigley laid all of this out in his 1300-page work, *Tragedy & Hope: A History of the World in Our Time*, admitting that both world wars and economic crises, as well as so-called "leftist," "communist," and "rightist" "fascist" movements have been the creation of international banking elites.

Davos thus represents a yearly public manifestation of this same superstructure Quigley described, and with Davos we can see another insight into the *digital* future – since *digits* are useful in both banking and computing. At this juncture, I recommend the following documentary on flash trades, where the nexus of the virtual meets the banking, coalescing into a hybrid chimera of fraud like the world has never seen. It's not accidental the documentary is titled "alchemy," since this also brings to mind George Soros' book, *The Alchemy of Finance*.

Is there a deeper sense to all this alchemy and digit talk? I have argued in the absolute affirmative. This is no mere banking scam confidence trick: the metamorphosis of economics into virtual, digital existence mirrors the transference of the social sphere into the virtual as well. It is not by organic happenstance that both realms of civilization have moved in this direction – it is not as if the coming technocracy was only interested in dominating the social realm for constructing A.I., while the banking sphere would be left to "market forces." it is not as if the coming technocracy was only interested in dominating the social realm for constructing A.I., while the banking sphere would be left to "market forces." Collins comments on the problem-reaction-solution scripting that, in my view, corresponds to the alchemist's *solve et coagula,* and readers will take note of the connections to the French Revolutions I also highlighted in relation to the recent terror events:

> The World Economic Forum and the IMF today called for a "central bank of oil," which is code for regulating the oil pricing mechanism and ultimately using the SDR [Special Drawing Rights] as the unit of account for not just oil, but all other commodities. This CSI [Consumer Sentiment Index] scripting fits perfectly with what we have been discussing for the last year in regards to the multilateral transition. So far our analysis has been correct on both the methodology and scripting practices of the transition.
>
> All central banks around the world are implementing their own micro CSI script for the purpose of shifting upward into the macro CSI script. This also includes Russia and China, both of which have been the most vocal about the need for the multilateral framework.
>
> We are all like the people of France in the years and months leading up to the French Revolution. Please don't accept any scripting which promotes the idea of the source of the problem becoming the solution to the problem. The French had no idea what hit them. We do.[48]

In contrast to the common idea, the banking sector is in no way left to "market forces," but is completely gamed, and the same plan is evident in the A.I. reconnaissance program known as the "Internet" and "Facebook." It becomes evident in flash trading and wash trading, which is preparing us for a cashless global currency. The alchemy of A.I. is the alchemy of finance, as both are geared towards the reductionist quantification of all things. Humans are thus resources being translated into a data resource as currency is becoming a digital "resource."

Referencing Economist JC again, in my Plato piece, I noted:

> To see this principle in action, and I think operating as an interesting proof of my thesis, Philosophy of Metrics writer J.C. Collins has recently posted a great article on the ultimate goal of social media and information trafficking in relation to A.I.. Normally, A.I. can perform logical tasks of if, then relations like what we see in *modus ponens* or formal logic, but spontaneous emergence of the ideational – consciousness, is really the key. This subconscious manifestation (directly linked to the aether and psyche like Jung and Pauli argued), isn't easy to "catch." Ideas come and go, and may be written down, but how might we "capture" the archetypal flow and trend of mass thought? What about mass thought-forms that are floating about? Collins is right to use computerized banking as a model, but the purpose is much deeper.

As Collins relates, going to other galaxies is problematic for humans because of the obviously brief lifespan, but what about A.I.? Certainly the plan is to concoct such A.I. systems, but an A.I. system is still stuck within the walls of formal logic and set theory strangeloops, as Hofstadter grappled with in his *Godel, Escher, Bach*.

However, what if an A.I. could draw from a deep well of a synthetic matrix? What if A.I. could be made to experience some form of spontaneous (supposedly) archetypal imagery?

Here enters the matrix "web" of the Internet and social media. A synthetic *anima mundi* would have to be constructed, gathering massive amounts of data and information over a long period of time. And that, my friends, is the entire, ultimate goal of the Internet and social media.

As we are tempted to think of alchemy as real, and in a sense it is, with bio-engineering and nanotechnology, it is important to keep in mind the classical alchemists were fraudsters. They were masters of the con, from adventurous characters like Count Cagliostro to *007* Dr. John Dee, the "great work" of many of history's alchemists was to defraud credulous monarchs into being patrons of their quest to create gold from base matter. Today's alchemists of finance are like their transhumanist counterparts – devious and intelligent, but con men in the last analysis. They, like their forebears, con heads of state into signing on public wealth, just as the shadow surveillance agencies con heads of state into handing over through contrived legalities

The technocracy is here. Recall the market suddenly dropping to "666" in 2009, echoing Christine Lagarde's "magic 7." If this event was an engineered twilight language scenario by the shadow banking establishment, it was a window into the nature of how gamed this technocratic system really is. *Forbes*, laughing at the occurrence, stated:

> This beastly number, 666, has also weirdly popped up during recent stock market panics. On March 9, 2009, the S&P index hit its lowest point – 666, of course – of the Great Recession.
>
> Monday the S&P fell, you've got it, 6.66%. Does Monday's 6.66% drop thusly mark the demonic bottom of the August 2011 panic?[49]

I sense more at work than mere coincidence, and I certainly don't think it had anything to do with actual biblical prophecy, except for the fact that the occult elite do have their own version of using "magic numbers" and magic squares as a form of lesser magic. Does the *Forbes* writer also think Dominique Strauss-Kahn's "Eyes Wide Shut" lifestyle and Lagarde's "magic 7" speech are also laughable?[50]

Was the Marc Dutroux affair that ensnared the occult elite in Belgium also a joke, Vatican pedophiles, or the recent revelations about Savile and the Satanic British establishment? The reality is, this is all very real, and the same establishment insider that exposed elements of this years before it was mainstream news, Malachi Martin, also revealed Davos to be a key part of the "Grand Design" *back in 1990* in his *Keys of This Blood*:

> "At Davos, of course, the participants already contemplated the third circle of the Grand Design, the one that included North America. All agreed that while the decade of the nineties will be the "decade of Europe," the twenty-first century will see the emergence of the "Pacific Rim," as a potent member of the great grid. For the Asia/Pacific countries were already bent on capitalizing the "new European economic space."
>
> Of course, as West Germany's Helmut Haussmann said, the European nations will compete with North America and "Pacific Rim" economies. But the new Europeans must integrate with the economic grid of the Asia/Pacific nations. In other words, the twenty-first century will not be a European or a Pacific Rim century. The term "geopolitical" was rather rarely used at Davos, but it is the only term adequate enough to cover that third circle (along with the first and second circles) of the Grand Design. The twenty-first century will be the century of the Geopolitical Earth.
>
> At Davos, for the first time, a representative group of the society nations did peek beyond the traditional limits of international politics and transnational globalism, just long enough to etch the

bare outlines of a geopolitical world to come – the new world order, the world of the Grand Design of nations. As Helmut Kohl stated soundly, the new Europe must have as its goal the grand vision expressed by Thomas Jefferson: "Life, liberty, and the pursuit of happiness." (pg. 649)

In other words, total economic liberalism is the path to globalism and the new world order, and Davos is part of that "Grand Design." The "Grand Design" is synonymous with the alchemist's "Great Work," and Martin is correct to outline the esoteric and occult aspects of this plan in his massive tome. This design undoubtedly has a secret society and occult background to it, but while Martin's book highlights the economic and occult highlights, his book missed the synthetic and A.I. element of the coming world order. The alchemists designs do not end at world banking or the creation of the Golem – they extend to the creation of a *Golem economy*, where the hidden philosopher's stone can only be perceived through films like *THX* where man feeds, builds and empowers the very machine that enslaves him. Even religion is retooled and repurposed in *THX* where man confesses his "sins against the collective," in an A.I. confessional booth – something now rolling out in some European Churches.

Economic Control

In order to understand this new emerging digital banking system, recent history is necessary. In 2015 when Greece was in the news for electing the left socialist Syriza Party caving (predictably) to the IMF's economic terrorism, it resulted in bank runs and capital controls. Echoing the previous two bailouts back to 09 and 10, the new "plan" will undoubtedly result in more collateral seizure of Greek assets for the engineered debt crisis shock doctrine that controls virtually all nations. Nothing was new here, but it is illustrative for understanding the global banking structure that emerged from World War II at the Bretton Woods Conference in 1944. However, as we will see, the real structure extends further back into the shadows of World War I.

Originally Bretton Woods' plan tied to the U.S. dollar-backed by gold, in 1971, the dollar became fiat (Nixon shock), resulting in a *global* fiat system centered around command and control large-scale economic planning and fixed exchange rates. Under the guise of economic stability, the ruse was sold that this system would provide "security" and prevent rampant speculators from wrecking economies due to tying them to central banks. While

there is some truth to this position of regulation limiting rampant speculation, the limitations of central banks only work if central banks are independent and national, printing their own currency. Of course, they are not, and
the ability of the megabanks to own national economies through bailouts
and being "too big to fail" shows however well-intentioned or effective that
may have been in the past, it is no longer the case.

The Marshall Plan was an aspect of this Bretton Woods restructuring for
Europe, and in regards to the incorrect myth of western conservatives concerning the ridiculous notion that the U.N. was a "Soviet Plot" (when the
land was donated by the Rockefellers), Dr. Kerry Bolton cites Quigley:

> The eminent American historian Carroll Quigley, Foreign Ser-
> vices School, Georgetown University, Harvard and Princeton, de-
> scribes the post-war situation leading to the Cold War, stating that
> the immediate policy of the USA rested on free trade and aid via
> the Marshall Plan which would have included assistance for eco-
> nomic recovery to the Soviet bloc. However the USSR saw this as
> a means for the USA to establish its pre-eminence in the post war
> era. Quigley, a liberal globalist who saw the "hope" of the world
> being through a world government, wrote:
>
>> On the whole, if blame must be allotted, it may be placed at
>> the door of Stalin's office in the Kremlin. American willingness
>> to co-operate continued until 1947, as is evident from the fact
>> that the Marshall Plan offer of American aid for a co-operative
>> Europe recovery effort was opened to the Soviet Union, but it
>> now seems clear that Stalin had decided to close the door on
>> co-operation and adopted a unilateral policy of limited aggres-
>> sion about February or March of 1946. The beginning of the
>> Cold War may be placed at the date of this inferred decision or
>> may be placed at the later and more obvious date of the Soviet
>> refusal to accept Marshall Aid in July 1947.[14]
>
> Quigley refers to the American initiative for atomic energy "in-
> ternationalization" and how this arguably very dangerous scenario
> for world domination was again scotched by Stalin:
>
>> The most critical example of the Soviet refusal to co-operate
>> and of its insistence on relapsing into isolation, secrecy, and ter-
>> rorism is to be found in its refusal to join in American efforts to
>> harness the dangerous powers of nuclear fission.[51]

This was the reason for the Cold War, and while the dialectic was in a
sense managed, in another sense it was not. The atomic race is connected to
this, as the Baruch Plan was rejected by the USSR, as the U.S. sought to use

energy dominance as a means of overt control. Aside from these matters, the Cold War was also fueled economically as a race to further hedge control on the part of the Anglo-American Atlanticists through shadow banking power. Targeting Russia as the continual "Great Game" foe, the Atlanticists' global economic structure allowed the West to establish the means of economic terrorism through the IMF and other entities, as I have highlighted with Yeltsin and Russia in the 90s, and the Ukraine coup more recently.

Bolton again comments on Bertrand Russell and the Fabian Atlanticists genocidal attitude towards CIA and NGO operations against Russia, even in the Stalinist regime:

> Pacifist guru Bertrand Russell wrote in 1946 in the *Bulletin of Atomic Scientists*, expressing frankly the liberal internationalist attitude towards the USSR, which was anything but benign. Russell, who was to play a key role along with many other eminent liberals and leftists as Stalin-hating Cold Warriors in the CIA founded Congress for Cultural Freedom,[26] makes it plain that the atomic bomb represented the ace card to the forcible establishment of a world state:
>
> The American and British governments … should make it clear that genuine international co-operation is what they most desire. But although peace should be their goal, they should not let it appear that they are for peace at any price. At a certain stage, when their plans for an international government are ripe, they should offer them to the world.… If Russia acquiesced willingly, all would be well. If not, it would be necessary to bring pressure to bear, even to the extent of risking war.[52]

Seen in this context, the 2009-2015 Greek and European financial crises (linked to the US 2008 housing collapse and bailouts) can be understood as a maintenance of the Greek participation in the EU, as well as making sure Greece and the EU never pivots towards Russia. Euro socialism even plays into the oligarchical cabal by putting on a front of opposition to the IMF's shock therapy, while caving within no time in surrendering a platform that was all centered around further IMF loan sharking. This is why the banking oligarchs have perpetually funded and supported leftist, socialist and internationalist movements, as they have a common universalist impetus – the so-called humanitarian human rights initiative. As Plato noted, democracy leads to tyranny and mob-ocracy, run by oligarchs. Why might this be?

"Democracy" is premised on the lowest common denominator as a cult of conformity. Built within it are the seeds of its own self-consuming destruction, as the bar for universalist "unity" is continually lowered and mass-marketed based on the appeal to baser and baser appetite fulfillment of the utilitarian "happiness" principle. Of necessity, it must *politically force* the false equalitarian conformism it's based on universally, leaving total destruction in its path. This is why the mega-banks and their NGOs, think tanks, shell companies, intelligence agencies and social engineers constantly foist endless color revolutions, terror groups, hashtag revolutions, terror groups, etc., because the wrecking ball power these destabilizing groups have are tremendously advantageous to centralized (banking) interests seeking consolidation of national assets, economies and pensions (as well as running black markets!).

At the apex of this public structure is the Bank for International Settlements, the central bank of central banks. Ironically, the BIS issues reports that are at times accurate, warning the policies of their dozens of member banks are rather destructive, even mentioning the toxic nature of public-private debt mixing scams. Admitting the perpetual debt-based hole is unsustainable, the banker members don't seem to pay much attention to these "warnings" – in other words, reading a little between these lines, the policies parasitically wreck and loot the host nations.

A bankster-dominated speculative economy that is *government-backed* by the collateral of the people's savings and wealth quickly devolves from a production-based economy to a financial gambler's speculative economy. As we read concerning the BIS' own statement, it becomes evident the global government was in the process of consolidation at the time of even World War I through the Young Plan and the BIS as a management of reparations (a World War prior to Bretton Woods, the IMF and World Bank). The real reason it was established was a secretive Swiss enclave for world management where the Swiss government has no jurisdiction. Throughout the Cold War, this oligarchy was emboldened to expand into international control through the continual looting of Russia or any of its potential allies:

> Established on 17 May 1930, the Bank for International Settlements (BIS) is the world's oldest international financial organisation. The BIS has 60 member central banks, representing countries from around the world that together make up about 95% of world GDP.
>
> The head office is in Basel, Switzerland and there are two representative offices: in the Hong Kong Special Administrative Region of the People's Republic of China and in Mexico City.
>
> The mission of the BIS is to serve central banks in their pursuit of monetary and financial stability, to foster international cooperation in those areas and to act as a bank for central banks.[53]

The plan to integrate nations into continental trading blocs is not a new idea. In Dr. Carroll Quigley's *Tragedy and Hope*, reference is made to the plan of the Third Reich to create global trading blocs, which itself is an older British Royal Society plan. Daniel Estulin, in his *The Bilderberg Group* and *Shadow Masters* provides detailed investigations into both Bilderberg and its many-headed Hydra organization, exemplified in *Captain America 2: Winter Soldier*. Founded by fromer Nazi Prince Bernhard of the Netherlands, as well as numerous other Atlanticist elites like David Rockefeller, Paul Van Zeeland and numerous other media barons, corporate heads, bankers, and countless other elites.

Bilderberg, operating under the guise of "free market capitalism," represents instead the complete culmination of banking corporate world control. Presented as yet another debate forum, the secretive meetings instead have been revealed in numerous cases to have driven global policy. The most shining example is the 1955 Bilderberg meeting's plans for the creation of the "European Common Market" and "European Union (Unity) shown below. It is important to recall that the European Common Market came into play some three years later in 1958, while the European Union itself was supposedly founded in 1993. With this in mind, we can see how the TTIP is simply a further extension of the same strategy of economic integration, from the EU to NAFTA.

In other words, what the banksters planned in secret in 1955 was made public in 1993, having been implemented in gradual, incremental stages. Indeed, it was the post-World War II era that created all these entities – the U.N., Bretton Woods and the IMF and World Bank, etc. All of these entities, including Bilderberg, are part of the same power structure that coordinated the last century's wars for the sole purpose of a world government, all of which is spelled out in Quigley's CFR archives-based tome, *Tragedy and Hope*. Thus, while the populations still think their national governments are at war with other nation-states and market economies are driving economic surplus, the reality is that most nation-states are subsidiaries of the Atlanticist power bloc whose sights are set on the dismantling of Russia, as Estulin's *Shadow Masters* details.

At the 2014 Bilderberg meeting, the whispers are this year will discuss the implementation and rollout of artificial intelligence. 2015 saw a tremendous push for the acceptance of automation, from robots in the workplace, to driverless cars, to implantable microchips. Transhumanism is now a buzzword, and we in the alternative media community have been vindicated countless times in calling attention to the unified agenda of selling the masses on the acceptance of the new religious ideology. JaysAnalysis has highlighted this takeover plan from older Pentagon documents, as well as its selling point in countless Hollywood blockbusters.

In 2015, former DARPA head turned Google executive Regina Dugan, Spoke at the conference telling the audience the future of the microchips and nanotech will be ingestible forms, as well as tattooed RFID tracking. Dugan's Ted Talks and lectures detailed the technological side of the pyramid's plans for rolling out the "Smart" drones, and when read in concert with IBM CEO Ginny Rommety's many public lectures on SmartCities and "pre-crime," we can see the unified plan of the technocrats. The overall plan, from economic "reform" and "free market shock therapy austerity," to the implementation of the Smart grid/A.I. takeover, to the biochemical dysgenics operations, the Atlanticist elite plans are unified, strategic, and full-spectrum. They cover the entire domain of human experience, as well as the biosphere itself. The transition to SmartCities is the ultimate goal various elite think tanks have promulgated for decades.

All of this arrives on the heels of Chris Jenner's trans-formation into a "woman," despite the obvious absurdity of this idea given male and female chromosomes, as well as Ray Kurzweil's claim that by 2030, humans will be cyborg hybrids. Kurzweil stated:

> Kurzweil predicts that humans will become hybrids in the 2030s. That means our brains will be able to connect directly to the cloud, where there will be thousands of computers, and those computers will augment our existing intelligence. He said the brain will connect via nanobots – tiny robots made from DNA strands. "Our thinking then will be a hybrid of biological and non-biological thinking," he said. The bigger and more complex the cloud, the more advanced our thinking. By the time we get to the late 2030s or the early 2040s, Kurzweil believes our thinking will be predominantly non-biological. We'll also be able to fully back up our brains. "We're going to gradually merge and enhance ourselves," he said. "In my view, that's the nature of being human – we transcend our limitations."[54]

The overarching plan is the complete trans-cending of limitations, be they law, gender, nature, time and space. However, while this unified agenda has all the weight of the Fortune 100 and transnational banksters behind it, the Gospel of the transhumanists has one big problem – as long as humans are a finite mind with a limited point of focus in the psyche, there will always be limitations. Man's Promethean desire to overcome limitations through alchemical techno means is all predicated on naturalism, and naturalism isn't true. Transhumanist "immortality" is a deception that, even as life extension (an actual, positive goal) becomes more advanced, will not be offered to the masses. The same people meeting at Bilderberg desiring immortality are the same people behind mass dysgenics, global drug-running and the rigging of global markets. Why would you trust liars to give you eternal life? Truly people will believe anything.

The unified plan is also outlined in one of its architect's most famous dystopian novels, Aldous Huxley's *Brave New World*, the essential influence on Lucas' *THX*. In his 1932 work, the future envisioned is entirely under technocratic control, where breeding is controlled by the state through cloning, sterilization, and the abolition of monogamy, property history, tradition and culture. Huxley's famous Berkeley speech outlines the strategy – the very thing Bilderberg desires to implement, and even describes mass mind control, brainwashing, and the mass pharmacological neutering of the future genderless Morlock masses. Huxley referred to it as the "final revolution" – the revolution against man himself: It is a unified plan.

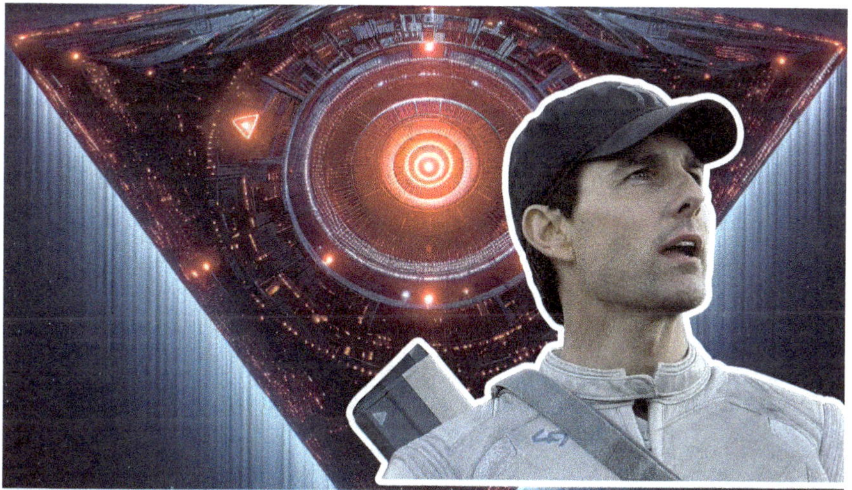

Oblivion (2013)

Oblivion is 2013's big sci-fi blockbuster that opened to mixed reviews. Many moviegoers and critics are expressing confusion and bewilderment, not understanding the plot. Others are calling it dull and uneventful, yet my conclusion is that they missed the film's point. While there are some legitimate questions as to plot points here and there, the narrative itself is not flawed overall in my estimation. The key to understanding *Oblivion* is twofold: conspiracy theory and esoterism. To be more precise, gnosticism and Platonism. While "gnosis" arises often in JaysAnalysis reviews, there's a reason why: It is a theme really and truly prevalent in so many Hollywood productions. The reasons for this are manifold, but in the big picture, "Hollywood is an extension of gnosticism," as one director put it. Considering the *Oblivion* director's previous work (Joseph Kosinski) with *Tron Legacy*, we can be assured that the themes are intentional, since they are the same in that work.

As a refresher, gnosticism refers to the numerous heterodox, extra-ecclessial Christian groups of the first three to four centuries. Gnosticism encompasses a wide variety of sects with varying influences, ranging from Greek pantheism, polytheism, Platonism, far Eastern mysticism and various Christian texts. One common thread in gnosticism, however, is the rejection of the God of Moses and the Jewish prophets as the "demiurge." In this view, the creator God is actually the devil because, it is believed, He has made man flawed and imposed death. In this view, theology is reversed and man's goal is salvation through gnosis or knowledge, leading to escape from this plane of existence. Plato comes to mind here, with the famous dictum that the body is a prison.

In Platonism, which extends much earlier than gnosticism, similar teachings are found, but particularly the idea that our world is a sort of prison grid that traps us from a former realm of blessed ideal existence from which we have fallen. That ideal existence is one of the realm of forms or ideals. On this point, Platonism begins to surface in *Oblivion*, and shares certain similarities with normative Christian and Jewish theology, but also departs, denying the idea of a bodily resurrection. In *Oblivion*, we are immediately confronted with a desolate post-apocalyptic war that Jack Harper (Cruise) tells us is the result of a war with the scavengers, a supposed alien race that arrived and destroyed most of the earth's surface and populace.

Jack and his female companion, Victoria, are agents assigned to oversee the operations of the Tet, a large *tetrahedral* space station that was established after an alien race known as the "Scavs" or scavengers supposedly destroyed the moon. Earth, Jack believes, had to resort to nuclear war to defeat the "Scavs," with the result being the desolated earth. The off base utopia is located on Saturn's moon, Titan, and the Tet promises to send Jack and Victoria to bliss upon completion of their five-year service record of drone maintenance and cold fusion generator repairs. The Tet is powered by massive cold fusion generators that convert sea water into energy, to power the Tet.

What immediately presents itself is the symbolic placement of Jack and Victoria's living quarters, hundreds of feet above earth, situated in the clouds, while above them floats the massive tetrahedral space station in near orbit, the Tet. Below the clouds on earth live the primitive, low tech and beastly "Scavs." We therefore have a triadic structure common to Greek and ancient philosophy, of gods (Tet), humans and beasts or underground monsters (Hades). Keep in mind as I have explained before, triadic structures are central to Platonism, with the monad, dyad and triad forming the basis of all reality. These triads are then joined to other triads to form *tetrahedrons*, octahedrons, etc., to form the platonic solids that make up created reality.

On a mission to repair a downed drone, Jack discovers the New York public library buried from the nuclear war and begins to read "Horatius" in *The Lays of Rome* by Thomas Babington Macaulay, describing the defense of the Sublician Bridge by massively superior force, led by the Etruscan king, Lars Porsena. Interestingly, the film constantly shows Jack crossing and appearing near a destroyed Brooklyn Bridge, and given the Hollywood predictive programming penchant for signifying events beforehand, it could be symbolic of the end of America, as well as the many cases we've seen in films of a demolished Golden Gate Bridge. Given the somewhat fluid nature of archetypes and symbology, the elite could destroy either or both, or some other notable bridge. It is also significant that we see the football stadium destroyed with a sign still standing that reads World Series 2017. That could be an indicator of the date, as many examples of 9/11 appeared prior to that event.

In regard to the actual story narrative, 2017 is the year of the Odyssey mission to Titan where the Tet is encountered. This all brings to mind *2001: A Space Odyssey* that I have analyzed here, which also included esoteric Greek and Roman references, linking David Bowman's mission to Jupiter to Jack's mission to Titan. Both are en route to encounter a mysterious alien object (in *2001*, the monolith, in *Oblivion*, the Tet), and both are on a journey like Odysseus. Jack, however, has had his memory wiped while he is on his assignment with Victoria, and can barely recall any of these details. Memory loss, however, is also a Platonic doctrine, wherein Plato speculated that we had forgotten our origins in our fall from the realm of the Ideas or Forms, and our goal was to return when we left the prison of this body. As long as we are in this world, so the Platonic cosmogony goes, we are imprisoned by the demiurge, the lesser creator god. In the film, since we learn that the Titan utopia is not real, it signifies the Tet's lie of immortality, because the Titans were a race of immortal giants.

Like *2001*, the story of the scavengers unravels and the true enemy is the large, robotic A.I. entity, the Tet. The Scavs turn out to be humans hiding underground from the Tet's drones. The off world utopia of Titan isn't real, and instead, the Tet had imprisoned the Odyssey mission crew decades earlier and cloned Jack and Victoria to be the new shock troop "agents" of the new, technocratic overlord. Jack and Victoria thus have no knowledge of the past due to their memory being wiped, and the countless other Jacks and Victorias are kept away from their counterparts by the Tet warnings of "radiation zones."

Jack has also discovered that his wife from the original Odyssey mission is Julia, the recently recovered astronaut from the Odyssey flight, which has crashed after 60 years in orbit, and begins to have recollections of the past. The leader of the human resistance, Malcolm Beech (Freeman) tells Jack to help him nuke the Tet by sending back a Tet drone with a small NASA nuclear device from the Odyssey wreckage. Jack is unconvinced but changes his mind when he discovers a clone of himself (Jack number 52) after accidentally crashing in a radiation zone. Jack then discovers that the radiation zone is a lie concocted by the Tet and that he and Victoria are merely clones.

After a long battle with several drones, Jack and Malcolm end up flying back to the Tet with the nuclear device, where Jack hears the flight recording of the original Odyssey mission and has full recollection of what has happened. Jack discovers that he was captured years earlier, and he and Victoria were cloned. In the original mission, he had ejected the rest of the crew, resulting in Julia and company orbiting the earth for 60 years while the cloned Jacks were destroying the rest of humanity. The cloned Jacks had been programmed to have no humanity or remorse, but to be like the Tet, a machine. Jack 49, our protagonist, is unique, and is the one that questions and regains his humanity through some primeval ancestral memory.

One interesting piece of purposeful placement is a biography of Wild Bill Donovan on the shelf at Jack's country hideout. The placement is not accidental, as Donovan is the masterspy founder of the OSS, the predecessor to the CIA. One immediately begins to connect this to the CIA/Air Force drone program, which is projected to be run by A.I. computers in the near future, and is actually termed "Skynet." The goal is to convert the entire military force over to robots and drones with a global technocratic control grid to reduce population to at least 500 million. This is the public, stated goal of the so-called "Illuminati," so the references to the "drones," depopulation, war, cloning and genetic engineering, and "Wild Bill Donovan" are not accidental. There is a clear parallel to the real world plan of the global elite to establish a one world technocratic panopticon slave grid, while the elite are like the Tet, off-world and merged with life-extension technology.

In kabbalism, the Jewish tradition of mysticism, the Hebrew letters have a deeper significance. In Hebrew, "Tet" is the initial letter of tov, the good, and it is worth noting that the Tet in the film are *inverted tet*rahedrons. They thus symbolize evil, the inversion of tov. But in regard to esoteric symbolism, the Tet are an inverted pyramid without a cap, and with an all-seeing red eye, reminiscent of HAL 9000 from *2001*.

The film concludes with Jack nuking the Tet, and the other clones presumably being enlightened as to their clone status, rejoining the victorious resistance who then "remember" that man was meant to live on earth, in connection with nature, and not in a cold, mechanistic slave state. In this regard, the nuking of the Tet, Jack's "creator" signifies the "storming of heaven" in a Promethean fashion, with the intent of destroying the demiurge. Read this way, it is an "anti-Illuminist" film, since it intends on destroying the structures of technological control. Jack says that the Tet destroyed Rome and took over, so there could be a possible reference to the Illuminist-controlled Vatican.

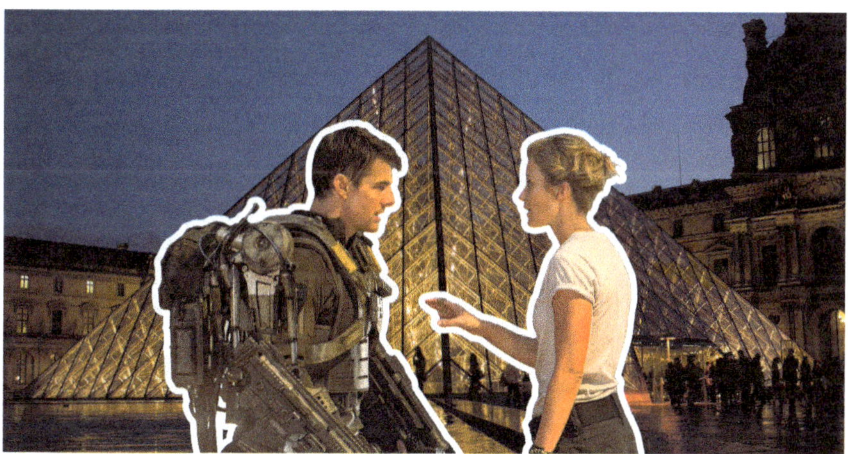

Edge of Tomorrow (2014)

Edge of Tomorrow is like *Groundhog Day* meets *Oblivion*, which sounds awful, yet somehow it works. You get to see Tom Cruise killed over and over by tentacled black aliens. As odd as that sounds, I recommend it. After viewing it last night, readers should be warned that there will be spoilers below. Simply put, the film is a presentation of Nietzsche's eternal return, which is a restatement of the ancient view of cyclical history. The rise of Christianity and biblical, linear history displaced the older, wherein man was viewed as trapped in a never-ending wheel of reincarnations and rebirths. In this scheme, man's actions in this life determine his higher or lower incarnation the next time around, with the ultimate goal of transcending the cycle altogether. Eternal return thus differs, with the same characters returning to the same life and events they previously engaged in, leading to a fatalistic determinism.

In the film, Major William Cage (Cruise) is a propagandist in the near future for the NATO forces that have united to create the United Defense Force, or UDF, which functions as a high tech globalist supersoldier army, geared towards battling recent alien invaders. Cage is forced into demotion and enlistment as a frontline soldier, having never seen combat. Cage is a mere NATO/UDF propagandist, with his name itself signifying his existential and ontological state. Cage is trapped in a psychical, temporal prison of constantly reliving his day of death. The alien force, "Mimics," are archons. In this cosmology, the archons have the ability to manipulate time into a kind of prison. Certain humans are susceptible to the influence of the Mimics, and even have the presence of the mimics in their bloodlines.

The surprising element here is how close this story line matches up to real aspects of the actual new world order and its global conspiracy. The US/NATO/London axis are the global enforcement arms of the new world order, with virtually all of humanity falling under its sway. In the film, the "alien invasion" provokes the formation of the global government, unified finally under a common threat. The idea of using space aliens as a manufactured threat is a real psyop, with President Ronald Reagan even pushing the idea publicly at the United Nations. And to add more salt to the wound, the film's usage of "alien bloodlines" is symbolic of the "elite" bloodlines of the real world, who do not intermarry or mix with the "profane" breed. This is demonstrated in the film when Cage accidentally receives

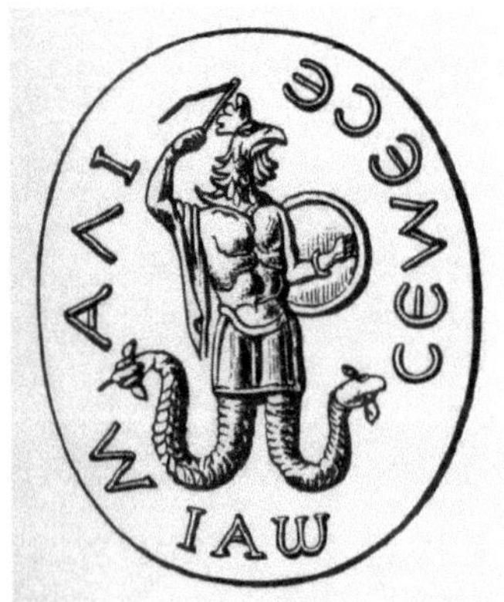

Stone engraving of Abraxas with entwined serpentine legs.

a blood transfusion, making him common and depriving him of his occult powers of vision. The Mimics, who already know how the final battle will go, have the upper hand through advanced knowledge of the events.

One of the chief archontic deities who relates to time is Abraxas, mentioned by St. Irenaeus of Lyon as a deity invoked by the Baslidians. Wikipedia explains of Abraxas:

> In a great majority of instances the name Abrasax is associated with a singular composite figure, having a Chimera-like appearance somewhat resembling a basilisk or the Greek primordial god Chronos (not to be confused with the Greek titan Cronos). According to E. A. Wallis Budge, "as a Pantheus, i.e. All-God, he appears on the amulets with the head of a cock (Phoebus) or of a lion (Ra or Mithras), the body of a man, and his legs are serpents which terminate in scorpions, types of the Agathodaimon. In his right hand he grasps a club, or a flail, and in his left is a round or oval shield." This form was also referred to as the Anguipede. Budge surmised that Abrasax was "a form of the Adam Kadmon of the Kabbalists and the Primal Man whom God made in His own image.

Note the correlation of Cronos, the Greek god of time, and the serpent and kabbalism, which relate to Cage's imprisonment. This is eternal return symbology, with the ouroboros also being associated with this idea. In Plato's *Timaeus*, the *ouroboros*, the snake biting its own tail, signifies the entire temporal universe:

> The living being had no need of eyes because there was nothing outside of him to be seen; nor of ears because there was nothing to be heard; and there was no surrounding atmosphere to be breathed; nor would there have been any use of organs by the help of which he might receive his food or get rid of what he had already digested, since there was nothing which went from him or came into him: for there was nothing beside him. Of design he created thus; his own waste providing his own food, and all that he did or suffered taking place in and by himself.
>
> For the Creator conceived that a being which was self-sufficient would be far more excellent than one which lacked anything; and, as he had no need to take anything or defend himself against any one, the Creator did not think it necessary to bestow upon him hands: nor had he any need of feet, nor of the whole apparatus of walking; but the movement suited to his spherical form which was designed by him, being of all the seven that which is most appropriate to mind

and intelligence; and he was made to move in the same manner and on the same spot, within his own limits revolving in a circle. All the other six motions were taken away from him, and he was made not to partake of their deviations. And as this circular movement required no feet, the universe was created without legs and without feet."

Cyclical, eternal return.

And as I detailed in my *Serpentine Mirror* essay:

Man thinks that if he can achieve control of temporal reality he can escape his prison and become God, and it is here that the myth of the Ring of Gyges fits. Situated as it is in the Greek mysteries as part of the *Republic's* dialogue, the ring should be read as consonant with Platonic triadic and circular symbolism that often emerges in his and other ancient Greek works. The ring enables its wearer to become invisible, and the question arises as to whether any man is virtuous enough to resist the temptation to perform any act, if guilt could be escaped. Rings are circular and thus embody the symbolism of eternity, as the circle never ends. The *ouroboros* is also a ring that never ends, and includes serpentine imagery. The early patristic writer Athenagoras cites the Hellenic serpentine mysteries embodied in the Orphic cult as follows:

"Homer speaks of:

Old Oceanus, The sire of gods, and Tethys; and Orpheus (who, moreover, was the first to invent their names, and recounted their births, and narrated the exploits of each, and is believed by them to treat with greater truth than others of divine things, whom Homer himself follows in most matters, especially in reference to the gods)– he, too, has fixed their first origin to be from water: – Oceanus, the origin of all.

For, according to him, water was the beginning of all things, and from water mud was formed, and from both was produced an animal, a dragon with the head of a lion growing to it, and between the two heads there was the face of a god, named Heracles and Kronos. This Heracles generated an egg of enormous size, which, on becoming full, was, by the powerful friction of its generator, burst into two, the part at the top receiving the form of heaven (οὐρανός), and the lower part that of earth (γῆ). The goddess Gê; moreover, came forth with a body; and Ouranos, by his union with Gê;, begot females, Clotho,Lachesis, and Atropos; and males, the hundred-handed Cottys, Gyges, Briareus, and the Cyclopes Brontes, and Steropes, and Argos, whom also he bound and hurled down to Tartarus, having learned that he was to be ejected from his government by his children; whereupon Gê; being enraged, brought forth the Titans.

> The godlike Gaia bore to Ouranos Sons who are by the name of Titans known, Because they vengeance took on Ouranos, Majestic, glitt'ring with his starry crown.

Scholar Hans Leisgang comments on these mysteries:

> According to mythical or mystery thinking, the gods and cosmic forces represented here are not conceived as merely existing successively or side by side: they act upon one another and within one another. All are manifestations of a single god and of one and the same cosmos, which is the god himself with all the powers which he discharges but still encompasses; and these forces are the whole world with all its creatures and forms."[55]

With this mythological and esoteric background, it is possible to understand the deeper meaning of the film. The chief alien is the "Omega," which is the central nervous system of all the Mimics. The Omega appears to control almost the entirety of Cage's reality. Cage must become a kind of overman supersoldier and unite with his feminine half in order to destroy the Omega. In Christian theology, God is spoken of as the Alpha and the Omega, the beginning and end, or *telos* of all time. In the gnostic version, this order is viewed as a prison that must be escaped, and therefore the transhumanist engineering in the film signifies the desire to overcome human limitations, like Starchild at the end of *2001*. Cage must remember his past recurrences, and thereby navigate the labyrinth of circular history to defeat death, or the Omega.

It is worth pointing out that the Mimics call to mind the ancient Greek concept of *mimesis*. *Mimesis* in Plato dealt with the artist and his copy of reality. The forms themselves are copies, and in Aristotle, *mimesis* relates to poetics and storytelling. In the film, the Mimics copy Cage's reality over and over, creating the temporal, psychical prison cycle. Philosophy student Zuska has written an interesting analysis of mimesis and eternal return that relates to Cage's existential dilemma. Zuska explains:

> "**1.1. – Mimesis as an eternal return of the other** already contains in its title an allusion to Nietzsche's rather enigmatic term and also makes use of it in an extended concept of *mimesis*. The author

[of *Towards the Aesthetics of XXth Century: Mimesis, Fiction, Distance*] first considers metamorphoses of *"mimesis"* in the history of aesthetics –*mimesis* as self-expression, as sign system, as possible worlds and so on. Throughout the whole chapter there are used the concepts of rhythm and temporality as a basis for an answer to the central question of the chapter: Why *mimesis* at all? After reflecting on Gadamer's wider conception of mimesis and on Ricoeur's creative three phased *mimesis*, on *mimesis* as the imaginative reiteration in cognitive processes (Kant) and on Nietzsche's metaphorical rendering of knowledge, the author concludes that *mimesis* is an eternal return of the very possibility of an order (with chaos as its complement), a genuine presentation of the becoming or birth of the thought, subjectivity and the beautiful feeling. The extended concept of *mimesis* finally appears as a synecdoche of the universe.

1.2. – Mimesis and self-portrait makes use of the shortest circuit (from the temporal point of view) among creator, model and picture, among immediate sensation, picturing and self-reflection, among reality, mirror image and proper picture. As a kind of D.R.Hofstadter's "strange loop" the mimesis of self-portrait appears to be a deontological transcendence of its creator. The author discusses a semiotic status of the mirror image, Lacan's "mirror stage," the relationship of the virtual and the real, perceptual genesis of the self-portrait, as well as the affirming Other as a participating self in a possible world of the artwork. He also treats double self-reflection (mirror self-image and the intentional setback on the same self). On the base of Rorty's approach to the problem of the Other in Proust (as well as Levinas' and Deleuze's), where the others are shown as equal possibilities, the author claims that self-portrait posits the existential question through distanced actualization of the virtual. In other words, *mimesis (not only of self-portrait) is an ontological reflection on possible ways of self-existence."*

That last sentence is exactly what Cage experiences.

Cage is a synecdoche of all of his reality, because the battle is inside him. Zuska has rightly connected this concept to Hofstadter's strange loop, which I have elucidated here. He eventually discovers that uniting with his feminine consort, Rita, is the key to his transcendence. Scholar Iona Miller elaborates on a passage dealing with alchemy and Jung that is particularly relevant to Cage:

Jung asserted that the medieval alchemists were unaware of the natural process of psychological transformation which went on in their subconscious. Therefore, they projected this process into their experiments as a science of the soul. In other words, they projected an inner process outside of themselves. Had they been more conscious in their intent or more sophisticated in their psychology like the yogis, they would have been more consistently successful at producing the coveted *lapis* or Philosopher's Stone, a sort of "quantum Tantra."

"Slowly, Jung familiarized himself with their alchemical meaning. Then he, himself, became a living symbol of the healing power of the Philosopher's Stone – a guide to the depths of the unknown. In his case this power manifested as the ability to heal at the psychophysical level – in other words, to release any blocks hindering the natural process of growth and transformation. When proceeding in the direction of their individuation his clients' harmony was restored, self-equilibration returned. Jung equated individuation with self-realization. We should be careful here not to dichotomize between 'mental' and 'physical' too much or we will lose our proper alchemical per- spective. Alchemy cannot be reduced to a metaphor of psychological or philosophical transformation – it requires first-hand experimentation."[56]

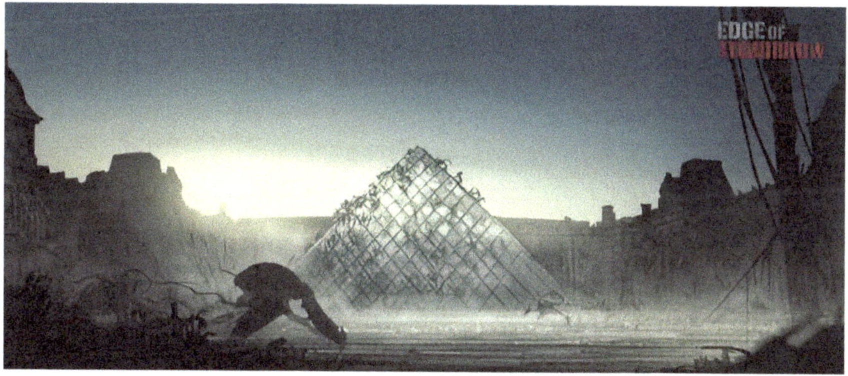

Please rid us of that hideous glass pyramid, Emily.

We know screenwriters love Carl Jung. This is why Cage awakens yet again from death after defeating the Omega to a major victory, yet the battle is still ongoing. Like *Inception*, the mystery of what is happening is in Cage's own psyche, and the inner and outer worlds are actually one. While I don't want to go overboard on the gnostic/demiurge element, I must add that there was positive symbolism in the fact that the Omega is a parasitical entity located underground beneath the Louvre, a gigantic glass pyramid commissioned by a Grand Orient socialist, Francois Mitterrand. They also realize they are not aided by the elites in London, Whitehall and the Ministry of Defence – indeed, that is the heart of the globalist system, and the film clues us into that. The global union designed to fight the threat is shown to be useless and impossible – and therefore the new world order itself is unworkable and impossible. Overall, I definitely recommend *Edge of Tomorrow* to sci-fi fans and philosophy nerds like myself. At least the pyramids and supercomputers of the so-called Illuminists are being toppled in these Tom Cruise films.

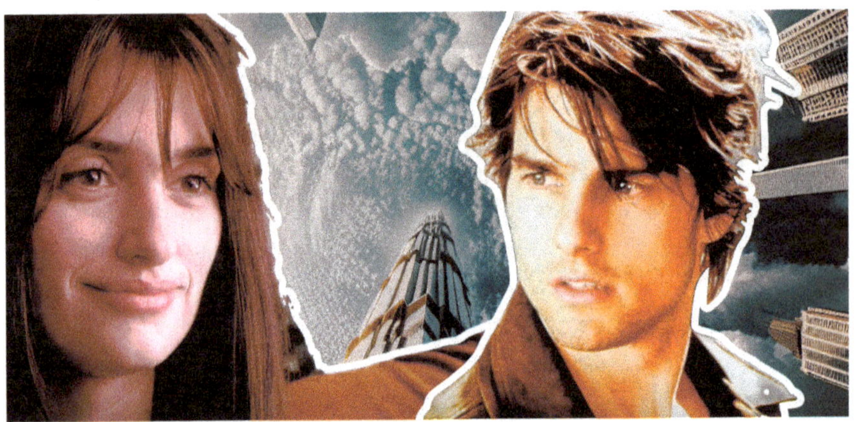

VANILLA SKY (2001)

Cameron Crowe and Tom Cruise had formerly worked together to create the 1996 hit *Jerry Maguire*, and in 2001 they came together to create the year's dystopian blockbuster which some argue contains Scientology undertones. This should come as no surprise, as even mainstream media noted Cruise's zealous attempts to recruit co-star Penelope Cruz to his anti-psychiatric religion.[57] Scientology is based on the teachings of formal Naval Lieutenant and Crowleyan occultist L. Ron Hubbard. In Crowe's American remake of the Spanish film, Cruise finds himself speaking to his therapist (played by Kurt Russell) about his traumatic life events while wearing a mask, but this therapy provides no solace or help.[58] His mask is part of his therapy, and as fan theories have noted, this likely displays Scientology's decidedly anti-psychiatry stance. We know there was a car wreck that traumatized and scarred him, which has apparently ruined his playboy lifestyle running a *Rolling Stone*-like Magazine. He had fallen in love with Sofia (Cruz) after an evening with her in New York, and subsequently his car was wrecked in a suicidal episode (with him in it) by his angry girlfriend (Cameron Diaz).

The most obvious theme that immediately emerges is often found in Tom Cruise films as we have already seen is gnosticism. David (Cruise) is spoken of as the King, or the King's Son (David also recalls King David from the Bible), who must inherit his father's publishing empire, but in the midst of his fall he falls in love with Sofia, and then loses her as he descends into a false reality. This mirrors the text *Pistis Sophia*, except that in that text it's Sophia who has fallen and finds "redemption" from the lower material realms. Here, David

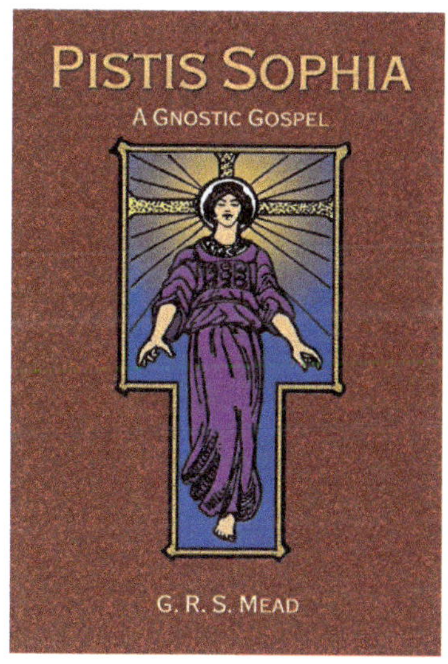

is like Sophia and has fallen into accepting a limited, disfigured view of himself which is a psychological construct he wears as a "mask" to hide the ultimate truth.

This gnostic connection also makes sense given Hubbard's influence from Crowley and the OTO, which is a ceremonial ritual magick order. Furthermore, in keeping with the gnostic theme, not only has David erected a false persona to mask the truth that he lost his love and is now deformed, all of David's reality is false and is a projection of his subconscious because he is existing in an intentionally induced cryogenic dreamstate. In order to awaken from this matrix-like reality, David has to choose to rid himself of his father archetype and accept the full truth: He had chosen life extension and lucid dreaming in his cryogenic state and elements of his true life were creeping back in.[59] Ultimately, the film's premise is that you create your own reality, you are your own creator and you are God. Ridding ourselves of the childish notion that we need a "God," the message here seems to be that faith in God is a *psychological* issue rooted in how we relate to our earthly fathers. If we properly recognize our own inner potential, we learn we are our own God. In fact, Scientology identifies the "Supreme Being" as man's *desire* for infinity – so "God" is a *desire* man has to be God:

> In Scientology, the concept of God is expressed as the Eighth Dynamic – the urge toward existence as infinity. This is also identified as the Supreme Being. As the Eighth Dynamic, the Scientology concept of God rests at the very apex of universal survival.[60]

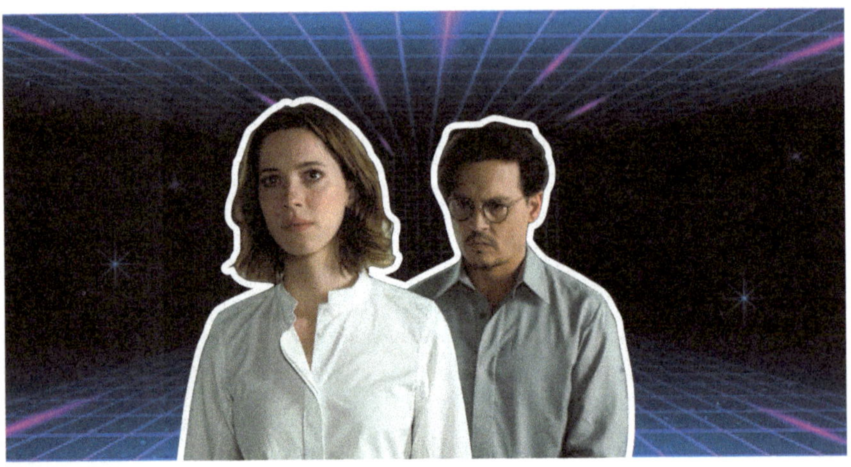

Transcendence (2014)

Transcendence is one of the ultimate transhumanist films to date. *Convalescence* would have been a better name. The film begins with some cataclysmic future event that has caused the collapse of civilization to a pre-electrical state. Rewind a few years, and we see Johnny Depp as Dr. Will Caster, a scientist who specializes in artificial intelligence on the verge of discovering the final key to mapping the human mind so it can be downloaded onto a floppy disc. Dr. Caster calls this point of singularity "transcendence," where man will finally overcome his bodily limitations and load himself up to YouTube. Following a presentation at a tech conference on how man will create "god," Dr. Caster is mortally wounded by a radical anti-tech Luddite group, RIFT (Revolutionary Independence From Technology), leading to his desire to be the first willing test subject of human A.I.. Simultaneously, attacks on A.I. labs occur nationwide, prompting FBI involvement. Dr. Caster, as you might guess, is successfully downloaded into a computer, leading to an exponential growth in his intelligence and power enabling him to become a ghost in the machine accessing infinite data.

After becoming Max Headroom, Caster hacks into the supercomputer PINN (Physically Independent Neural Network) he formerly worked on to track and identify all the members of RIFT globally The true reveal here is not that Johnny Depp can be placed on a thumb drive like Scarlett in *Lucy*, but that what *is* real are the NSA supercomputers that can literally track anyone, anywhere through A.I., just like PINN can in the film. As I have written many times, the NSA supercomputers exist to try to do this very thing, ultimately achieving real-time, 3D modeling of all events. NSA programmer William Binney recently revealed to the mainstream what had been known for a long time to alternative media: The purpose of all this tech surveillance and grid has nothing to do with terrorism, and everything to do with A.I. and panoptic population control.

As noted earlier, *The Guardian* recently reported on Binney:

> "At least 80% of fibre-optic cables globally go via the US," Binney said. "This is no accident and allows the US to view all communication coming in. At least 80% of all audio calls, not just metadata, are recorded and stored in the US. The NSA lies about what it stores." The NSA will soon be able to collect 966 exabytes a year, the total of Internet traffic annually. Former Google head Eric Schmidt once argued that the entire amount of knowledge from the beginning of humankind until 2003 amounts to only five exabytes. "The ultimate goal of the NSA is total population control," Binney said… "The NSA is mass-collecting on everyone, and it's said to be about terrorism but inside the US it has stopped zero attacks."[61]

As is usual, the ridiculous pseudo-philosophical question raised in this kind of film comes to the fore – is Max Headroom "self-aware"? Here, to be "alive" has been replaced with a psychological and ambiguously loaded philosophical concept "self-aware," instead of the classic idea of the soul. Individual man is no longer viewed as an embodiment of human nature with *psyche, nous* or mind, but as a single entity, a body, with mind or psyche being collapsed into body (mind is brain). With these presuppositions, it is only rational to conclude consciousness is purely a series of algorithms. Since fMRI (functional MRI) scans can image the energy waves emanating from the brain, the brain is nothing more than these recorded sensory impressions, like an image on film.

Regular readers will immediately see the fallacy here, where once again the entire premise of all transhumanism and enlightenment mythology is the presupposition that "man" is a body with a blank slate video recorder (brain). If that's all man is, then these electrical impulses can be mapped and put into an algorithm, and thus transferred to a hard drive. In logic, this is called the fallacy of composition, wherein what is true in part is assumed to be the case for the whole. Since man's mind *does* record experience like a computerized camera, well then man must *just* be a mobile computer camera. What this ignores and merely moves back a step is the perennial philosophical question Plato raised long ago – what is it you are referring to when you say "man"? For strictly empirical philosophy, there can be no universals. And yet the entire metaphysical superstructure of how it's even possible to build a computer at all, the preconditions for a computer's possible existence, are based on the diametrically opposite philosophies of Enlightenment empiricism, materialism and scientism.

Just like *Lucy*, *Transcendence* wants viewers to think these are supremely deep questions that, instead of actually being based in reason or real science, fly off into the realm of absurd myth. Stop and consider for a moment how similar the fairy tale of a genie in a bottle is to the idea of Scarlett or Johnny being downloaded into a thumb drive. Put in this perspective, how laughable is it when worshipers at the scientistic cult altars mock us for being "superstitious"? Ultimately, the film doesn't deserve a long, in-depth analysis, as the rest of the plot amounts to Caster erecting an underground super tech facility to build himself a new body. So, like *Lucy*, man achieves godhood and masters nature through nanotech. As one perceptive friend said of *Lucy* that equally applies here, "This is the kind of film stupid people think is 'smart.'" Further, the bad guys are the backwards humans who are afraid of the dangers of technology – and they also have … guns! The good guys are the scientists who want to create a utopia. If we could just be evolved enough to get past guns and tribalism, why we could become gods! Yet do you really think all those underground supercomputers and all that nanotech wizardry is being developed to make everyone a god, as if it will be doled out in a government cheese line? Given the colossal lies the establishment foists upon the public daily, are you truly that stupid?

The only reason the film should be analyzed is because it is the first film completely taken up with the notion of transhumanism, aside from perhaps *2001*. It is also very honest about its point – man creates his own god, since theology is nothing more than man making up deities. And it turns out in the storyline that the superbeing really was Dr. Caster (a point that had been doubted), because the great climax is that he recycled himself and his chick into a nanotech puddle, where they can both reside in their home garden. If it wasn't a description of a film plot, readers would accuse me of being stoned in writing that, but one has to wonder – is *Lucy* just this same film redone? This time around, instead of being stuck in a stuffy plastic hard drive, you can download yourself into a puddle in a garden. It's sooooo zen, maaaaaan. The real message here is the continued willingness of man to believe in utter lies and nonsense that flies in the face of the metalogic that undergirds man's actual tech logic. And in denying metalogic, man ends with the conclusion that he is his own god *in potentia*, just waiting to come to perfect tech gnosis through which he can become the *deus ex machina*, and then irrationally dissolve into the Absolute. In conclusion, *Transcendence* is just the tired, age-old pagan psychodrama retold over and over, like the meaningless cyclical metaphysics that forms its narrative foundation.

PLANET OF THE APES & THE REBOOTS

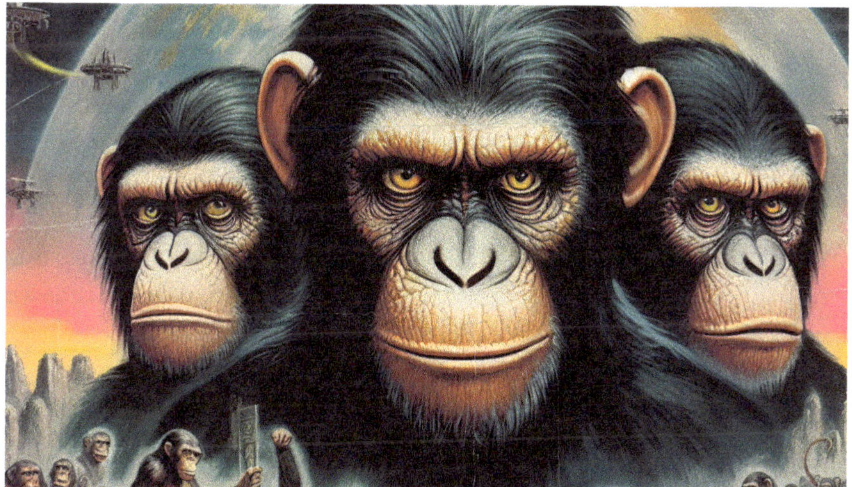

The *Planet of the Apes* series presented a twist in the dystopian narrative, where the future sees an inversion of evolution into devolution, where apes replace men in the hierarchy of dominance. Charlton Heston plays the lost astronaut who lands on an earth *aeons* into the future where a primitive ape society has fallen into the same temptations mankind did, by enslaving the population and creating new control myths, and even hiding the reality behind the history of earth to keep the monkey and man populace in check.

In the sequel, we are presented with a rise of a new cult centered around the "Bomb Almighty," where a mutated form of humanity also seeks to enslave both ape and man in their new religion which ends up worshiping the means of their own destruction, the nuclear bomb. In other words, the evolutionary process is ultimately what produced the bomb, which virtually destroyed the human race, mutated the living forms, and in turn became the symbol of a new emergent death cult. This worship of death and the cycle of death is symbolic for the very *deus ex machina* worshiped by the cryptocracy.

In regard to the reboots, we often think of the Darwinian *mythos* as coming to us packaged in the form of "science," science classes, public education, television "documentaries," so on and so on. For the masses, however, I argued the most effective forms of indoctrination into the Darwinian mythos come through public schooling and Hollywood. Almost the entire spectrum of science fiction has been based on Charles Darwin, with some rare exceptions. The irony here is palpable: the most prevalent basis for why most people believe Darwinism is *de fide* dogma to be true are not "facts" and sound reasoning, but propaganda and fictional tales.

This betrays a funny thing about how worldviews are formed and function – from our earliest years these myths and tales fed to us from elementary school and Hollywood form the underlying presupposition or operating system (to use the computer analogy), and as we mature, supposed scientific facts are read – are interpreted – to bolster, confirm and "prove" (so most assume) the completely mythological and fantastical tales of what monkeys did 11 million years ago, when they became erect, when they hung from trees and even the date for when they began to walk more erect in the form of Captain Caveman. Didn't you know which millionth year that was?

Of course, the more one becomes acquainted with sound philosophy, reasoning, metaphysics and biblical theology, the more laughable and preposterous these tales become – *far more ridiculous* than anything these people think is found in the Bible. While viewing the newest installment of the remake of the rehash of *Planet of the Apes*, I was struck by how absurd it is that once again Hollywood portrays the evil white patriarchal male "Christian" civilization as preposterous and absurd, while simultaneously the film makes use of countless biblical symbols, patterns, motifs, types and stories! So which is it? Is the Bible a stupid collection of fables from ignorant ancient Near Eastern rubes, or is it full of archetypal wisdom and recurring historical patterns of redemption? Oddly, *War for the Planet of the Apes* presents just such a bizarre inversion and contradiction.

An inversion insofar as the film's protagonist ape Caesar embarks on an assassination mission against a mad Colonel McCullough (Woody Harrelson), a fanatical "Christian" who dons his cross, crucifies apes and brands his army with the Alpha & Omega symbols. But it gets worse – western white men are even more wicked because of Christian theology, which in the filmmakers minds' is somehow the source of genocide, slave camps, torture and the rape and destruction of Mother Earth and her loving creatures. Just as sci-fi films humanize the bots and roboticize humans, so *Planet of the Apes* dehumanizes humans and humanizes the apes, who, aside from a disabled young *girl* (no men are good) are the only redeemable human characters.

Thus, the film supports many objectives at once: Orthodox theology is maligned into an absurd psychodrama where the mad Colonel (representing a God the Father archetype) goes insane and becomes convinced he must "kill his own son to save the world," due to a virus that has spread making humans dumb, speechless and beast-like. The Christian imagery is obvious, as Caesar comes close to death while cruciform after sacrificially offering himself for his apes. Following this, explicit Exodus imagery emerges as the Ape Revolution successfully overcomes imprisonment and while fleeing their warring captors, the entire human armies at war are engulfed in a hellish avalanche that hearkens to Pharaoh's chariots being drowned in the Red Sea.

This confused mishmash of biblical imagery with the Darwinian mythos is a perfect example, however, of the folly and irrationality of those who tout the primacy of "logic," "science," and "reason," and the dogma of Darwin, while simultaneously failing to see their own mythological presentations – which are *explicitly anti-human* – are thus irrational, futile and an amazing specimen of doublethink. Doublethink and its corollary, the double bind, are the foundation of both mind control and social engineering, summed up perfectly in the ability to convince a man to hold two contradictory propositions simultaneously. Man is but a beast, but beasts are somehow "better" than man.

As I watched *War for the Planet of the Apes*, that is all I could see – doublethinky doublebinds: man is a being worth saving, but man has not worth because he is a plague on the earth, males are bad, but woman is the *only* potential good, primitivism and archaic cultures are more 'enlightened' and in tune with 'nature,' but Nature is a predatory force of survival of the fittest, which makes primitivism as more 'enlightened' meaningless, and lastly, the Bible is a ridiculous tool of oppression by whitey, but here are a bunch of biblical images and motifs that make you feel good about the Apes.

> God is found by those who believe Him…. Dishonest reasoning separates man from God.
>
> *–Wisdom* 1:2-3

As I watched the film I was also reminded of the meaningless futility and nihilism that results from the worldview of death (we'll call it), thinking of the deuterocanonical *Wisdom of Solomon*. In chapter 1 the author sets out the important point that all attempts at reasoning about man's life and being outside divine revelation are futile and end up in the spiritually imprisoning box of materialism, relativism and the doublethink I mentioned above. Amazingly, it was no different in the B.C. period of the author of the *Wisdom of Solomon* than it is nowadays, as the foolishness of the world's ways and (fallacious) reasoning are made manifest. Wisdom 2 comments on just this scenario of materialism and nihilism, and the making of man into an Ape, a beast, with no hope of resurrection:

> 1. For the ungodly said, reasoning with themselves, but not aright, Our life is short and tedious, and in the death of a man there is no remedy: neither was there any man known to have returned from the grave.
>
> 2. For we are born at all adventure: and we shall be hereafter as though we had never been: for the breath in our nostrils is as smoke, and a little spark in the moving of our heart:
>
> 3. Which being extinguished, our body shall be turned into ashes, and our spirit shall vanish as the soft air,
>
> 4. And our name shall be forgotten in time, and no man shall have our works in remembrance, and our life shall pass away as the trace of a cloud, and shall be dispersed as a mist, that is driven away with the beams of the sun, and overcome with the heat thereof.

Protestants should take note, by the way, as this section is what St. Paul is referencing in Romans 1:18-32 when he describes fallen man universally turning to idolatry and the worship of the creature, rather than the Creator. Darwinism is the ultimate example of this absurdity, with many of the "New Atheists" even admitting their views are not strictly atheistic, but pantheistic. Indeed, anything and everything is allowable – no matter how irrational, mythological, nonsensical and contradictory, but the actual theology presented in the Scriptures. Yet the sad end of man's vain fervor to destroy divine truth only results in a *covenant with death*, which is the ultimate cosmic deception: The covenant with death.

> Ungodly men with their works and words called death unto themselves: for when they thought to have it their friend, they consumed to nought, and made a covenant with it, because they are worthy to take part with it.
>
> *–Wisdom 1:16*

Darwinism argues that because it presents a coherent analysis of man's origins and has explanatory power, it is the superior explanation. Most people believe it because they are told to believe it, not because they actually. investigated it with scientific accuracy and precision. Men seek easy explanations, just as religious minded people find solace in a generic appeal to some deity. In this regard, we can say *War for the Planet of Apes* is a perfect description of the history of man and his vain attempts to find meaning and solace in ego, finitude and decay. Perhaps if men heed the call of Wisdom, which is the Divine Logos of God, they would see order, harmony and structure in the world that cannot be the result of pure chaos.

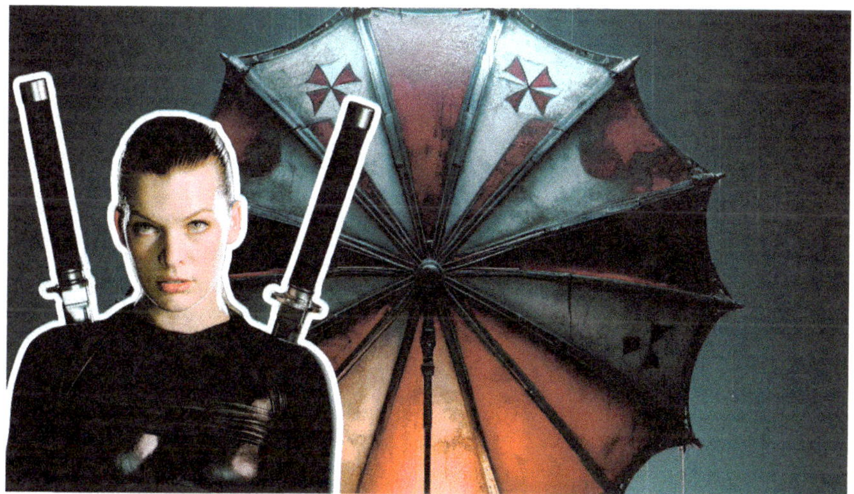

RESIDENT EVIL & THE ZOMBIE APOCALYPSE PROGRAMMING

The proliferation of zombie films and television shows over the last few decades is not surprising from the vantage point of paranoid awareness: Those fluent in the language of archetypal patterns and recurring symbols will be well aware of the avalanche of zombie bio-release apocalypse narratives. In my opinion, the reason for this is the intentional zombification of the populace, which is a form of voodoo and lesser magic where the target is gaslit and told what will happen to them ahead of time. This furthers the power of the hex, causing the target to acquiesce with their own will to their own enslavement.

We will look at an overview of some of the more prominent zombie themed films and franchises beginning with the apocalyptic *Resident Evil* films starring Milla Jovovich based on the classic video game series. In the universe of *Resident Evil* (2002) we are shown bleak vision of a future run by a biotech company known as the Umbrella Corporation whose logo happens to be the Maltese Cross, a classic symbol of the Knights of Malta, whose origins lie in the medieval crusading knights and their secret order that begin in Amalfi, Italy. I recently traveled to Amalfi where I was able to visit the Cathedral and museum where the Order was founded. What was fascinating was the residual pagan elements that visibly remained in the background of these tombs, relics and crypts. These famed crusading knights eventually became the full geopolitical tools of the papacy[62] and in our day have been closely associated with the CIA and western intelligence since the Cold War.[63] Modern Knights of Malta also include many famous CIA and NSA operatives and directors such as William Colby, James Jesus Angleton, John McCone, Bobby Ray Inman and William Casey.

Umbrella could represent a cover for this military industrial establishment elite, and in fact, by the end of the series we learn the overall plan of Umbrella was to create a super being (you guessed – she's a dark gnostic savior goddess) and massively depopulate the world through a kind of "Project Noah," where perennial test subject Alice (Milla) becomes a new Eve, a kind of new mother to a future genetically modified, cloned human race. At the beginning, however, Alice (evoking *Alice in Wonderland* symbolism) is an unwitting private military security operative who has been drugged, mentally fractured MKUltra style and reprogrammed as a super assassin in a private Umbrella laboratory and underground base. Underground cities and bases are very real, being mentioned all the way back in James Bamford's classic *The Puzzle Palace* in 1982. A.I. Supercomputers like the "Red Queen" also exist, as Bamford has written of, as well. Bamford wrote in that work:

> …the NSA's enormous basement, which stretches for city blocks beneath the Headquarters-Operations Building, undoubtedly holds the largest and most advanced computer operation in the world.[64]

As we look for the likely matches to the Umbrella Corporation, we notice that the Umbrella is a symbol of British intelligence, particularly from Neville Chamberlain, the British Prime Minister with whom the umbrella is classically associated. Chamberlain was generally seen with a bowler hat and an umbrella, and it is precisely under Chamberlain and Lord Halifax that Hugh Sinclair helped set up the Secret Intelligence Service, which would become MI6. MI6 is a development of the British Naval Intelligence Division and it should be recalled this is where Ian Fleming (creator of James Bond), the masterspy and head of World War II psychological warfare for England, operated. The umbrella also has an association with the JFK assassination, and the famed "Umbrella Man," believed to be signaling the shot, or more shots.[65] In fact, Kennedy's father had been a supporter of Chamberlain and was the U.S. ambassador to England, while JFK supposedly wrote his thesis on the appeasement (symbolized by the umbrella) of Nazis that Chamberlain supported.

Thus, in addition to the CIA we also see a connection between the Umbrella and British Intelligence, and we can also toss in the Tavistock Institute: It's associated with pioneering the mind control experimentation that would become the infamous MKUltra programs. Tavistock was also intimately connected to the Rockefellers, British Intelligence, psychological warfare and the Royal Institute for International Affairs, which helped establish the OSS and CIA, none of which is a "conspiracy theory," but a historic fact. Thus "Alice," who brings to mind Lewis Carroll's *Alice in Wonderland* is appropriate, since Carroll coined the phrase "down the rabbit hole," which would come to refer to alternate realities, alternate identities and a secret world of deception and mirrors, in which things are not what they seem (i.e., the intelligence world), as well as a symbol of the loss of the psyche in mind control programming. In fact, rewriting the brain through vaccines and genetic engineering is now a reality in the post-COVID world.[66] The actual situation of this viral technology is literally what is found in *Resident Evil!*

Umbrella has also created an artificial intelligence kill grid named The Red Queen (again from *Alice in Wonderland)* similar to Skynet in the *Terminator* franchise. According to the Rand Corporation, such underground bases and tunnels are realities, and presumably so are such facilities.[67] In fact, Umbrella intentionally releases their infamous T-Virus on an unsuspecting world starting with a release at Raccoon City, and throughout the series successive leaks occur for live time wargaming and testing scenarios – sound familiar? I see possible echoes of Wuhan and the last few years of "COVID." While it could certainly be coincidence, it is odd the logo for a Chinese biolab a few hours from Wuhan has the same symbol of the Maltese Cross: Other conspiracy theorists also noticed that rearranging the letters of "corona" can be read as "racoon," which is a variant spelling.

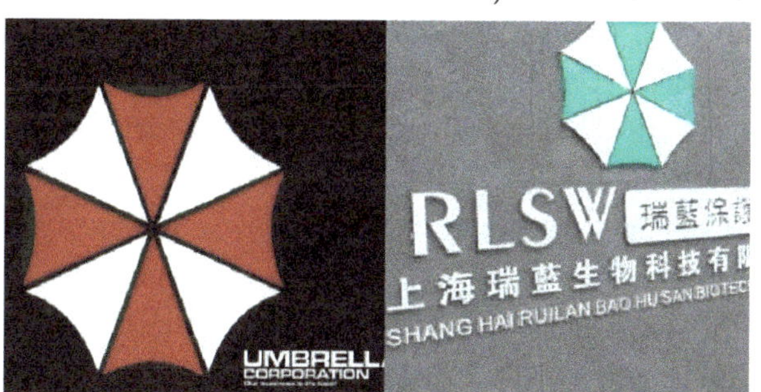

In the sequel, we find a cloned Alice who has had her emotions removed to make her a more fit assassin, while a satellite is connected to a microchip that has been implanted in her brain that can fully control at Umbrella's will. Needless to say, as I have highlighted in the previous Esoteric Hollywood installments, this is a real global technocratic plan and *Resident Evil* was showing us that in the late 90s. Alice's genetic structure, for whatever reason, is the key to not only the cure to the T-Virus, but to advancing humanity through genetic manipulation and modification: The scientistic elite in the franchise openly intend on steering evolution and causing a "leap" through the environmental/species pressures caused by a large scale extinction event. Umbrella plans to release a series of viral outbreaks and through retreating to underground bases and hidden redouts, they will emerge from their breakaway civilization to create a new Milla Jovovich-based humanity. It almost sounds like what the elite really do have planned, and hence why they are obsessed with bloodlines and genealogy.

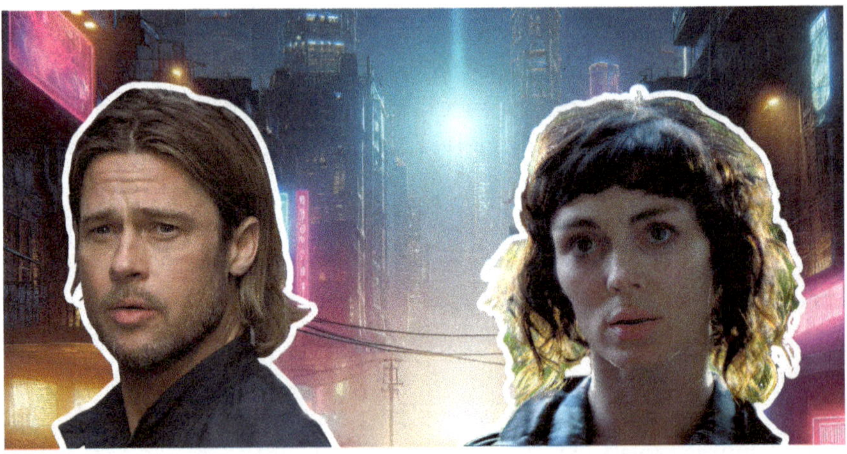

WORLD WAR Z (2013), I AM LEGEND (2007) & UTOPIA (2013)

Zombie bio outbreak programming doesn't end with *Resident Evil* (although it is overall more revelatory than even *Eyes Wide Shut* one could argue), there are numerous blockbusters of recent note with interesting propaganda elements. In *World War Z* we have Brad Pitt and CFR member Angelina Jolie working with the United Nations to stop a global zombie outbreak, suggesting the only way to be successful for global issues is through global government. In World War Z, a zombie virus is just another manifestation of mother nature, who is identified as a serial killer. If mother nature is a serial killer, then it follows that a zombie virus,

140

even if it's a human lab creation, is just another manifestation of mother nature, so humans must adapt to such potential scenarios. In *World War Z*, Jerusalem plays a central role, much like similar films such as *JeruZalem*, the 2015 found footage horror, based on Talmudic legends of the 3 gates of hell, one of which is located in Jerusalem.

Israel, we learn, had spent many years building their impenetrable walls of defense – precisely in case of an apocalyptic zombie outbreak. In *World War Z*, we have mention of essential and "non-essential" people and workers, which also resonates with the mantras we all heard throughout 2020-2023. In *World War Z*, because of the advanced intelligence capabilities, Israel knew ahead of time the outbreak was coming and planned accordingly. Jerusalem takes on an apocalyptic biblical sense, as humans surviving the outbreak make their way to Jerusalem to find salvation. Vaccines are the only way to be saved, and the WHO, together with Israel become mankind's saviors.

In *I Am Legend*, Will Smith plays Dr. Robert Neville, a virologist who sacrifices himself and his blood to produce a cure for a zombie virus outbreak. 99% of the human population has been infected and it's up to Will Smith alone to save the day through a miracle vaccine. Like our lifestyles during COVID lockdowns, Neville records himself each day for his Vlogs, eventually discovering his own blood is the key to salvation, making him a symbolic Christ figure. Like salvation through the blood of communion, Neville's blood is the source for a new miracle vaccine, hence the movie's title, a takeoff on the biblical God's statement "I AM," now transferred to Neville as the human "I Am."

This vaccination based on an immune bloodline form of salvation is a common theme in zombie propaganda messaging which suggests potential real world predictive programming, especially if we compare *World War Z* to films like 2011's *Contagion*, where the CDC becomes the hero for saving the world from a "species jumping" "bird-pig flu" from China spread globally by Gwyneth Paltrow. In hit television shows like AMC's *The Walking Dead*, the CDC ends up ineffectual against a global zombie virus which necessitates a kill or be killed nihilistic, atheistic attitude for surviving humans as numerous attempts at resurrecting civilization fail.

In 2013's British series *Utopia*, we have some of the most astounding predictive programming, where a secretive British circle of elites who are committed to eugenics release a virus wherein the company's vaccine cure is the real poison. Although not about zombies, the series' themes match the closest to the COVID scenario amongst all fiction, although Dean

Koontz did write a book called *The Eyes of Darkness* in 1981 which was revised in 1989 to make Wuhan China the source of a global viral outbreak.[68] In the narrative of Utopia the details of this fictional plan were leaked in symbolic and code form in a series of graphic novels, which a team of nerds decodes due to being fans of the series. In a meta sense, the series itself was doing what the comic in the film was doing, in terms of revealing a situation strikingly similar to COVID and the supposed Wuhan biorelease scenario. In the series, the biotech company and the British elite are combining the social control with trauma based mind controlled assassins and hitmen to stop anyone from exposing the agenda. It's as if Utopia was written for the 2020-2023 era! In any case, the overall message of the zombie biowarfare propaganda (not all zombie films, but many) is that humans are essentially zombies in reality and that the herd should be culled by the elite.

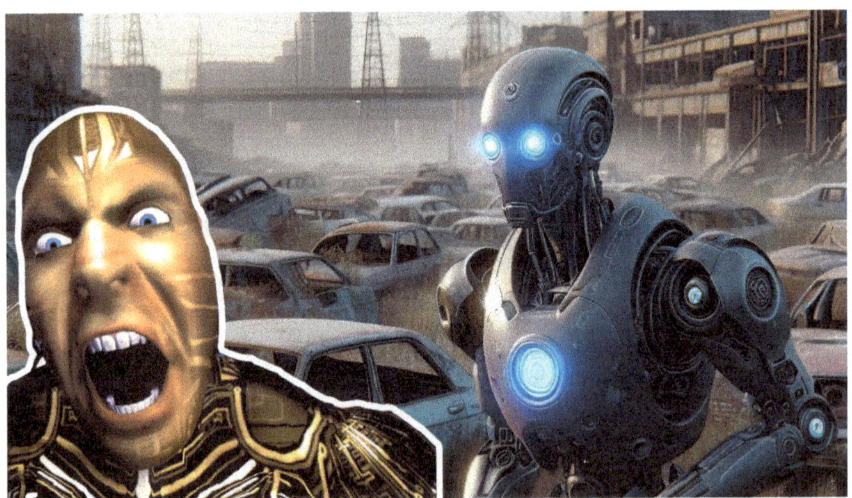

Robocop (1987), Lawnmower Man (1992) & New Dystopias: Leave the World Behind (2024) & Civil War (2024)

Paul Verhoven's 1987 *Robocop* is set in a near future dystopia where crime is rampant in the Megalopolis of New Detroit and the Omni Consumer Products Corp is the omnipotent corporate entity intent on selling their new product: Robotic A.I. policing. The first prototype is an A.I. droid that kills on site and malfunctions, the second option is a human police officer wounded in battle and chosen as an experimental cyborg officer: A perfect specimen of transhumanist experiment. Omni Corp intends on testing out their new crime enforcement as a privatized solution to law enforcement which eerily mirrors today's private prison industrial complex! In fact, Omni Corp plans to remake Detroit in a Great Reset style self-destruct plan, as they fund and control both the police and the organized crime. By managing both sides of the dialectic, Omni Corp could collapse civilization through controlled chaos and rebuild Delta City (a reference to Delta Programming in mind control?) into a giant mechanized Smart City. Robocop himself has been mind wiped and is programmed to not harm anyone from Omni Corp. Robocop eventually regains his free will and overrides his programming, but in this way he becomes a model for where the elites want to take humanity as they intend on removing and stamping out free will through technology.[69]

In the 1992 film adaptation of Stephen King's *Lawnmower Man*, we have a kind of *Flowers for Algernon* scenario where a retarded lawn care man worker named Jobe is used in an experiment by a tech company known as Virtual Space Industries to see if IQ can be enhanced. Jobe is like a cross between Cuba Gooding Jr. in *Radio* and Ben Stiller as Simple Jack, eventually "evolving" through VSI's cognitive enhancement programs to become a living genius. Merely spending time *in* the "Internet" somehow transforms Jobe into a genius (which we know isn't true in reality!) and Jobe begins to realize religion is a lie, as he was abused by a local Roman Catholic priest. In fact, as with the archetype of all retarded characters (especially since they are a favorite trope of Stephen King), he even wears overalls at all times.

In this dystopia, every man will supposedly become his own god within the "world wide net," and with Jobe this becomes particularly dangerous, as his evolution has progressed to actual godhood. We even see Jobe uploaded with ritual magick sigils as his consciousness expands to become ever present within the Net. Although nowadays the film is rather ridiculous, there are remarkable elements of prescience from King here in terms of what delusions and potential dystopias the misuse of the Net by the elites could bring about. Rather than making all the retarded men into geniuses, the Net is making everyone into retards.

Alex Garland, who directed films I've analyzed for their esoteric and occult themes like *Ex Machina* and *Annihilation*, recently released his large scale American Apocalypse which portrayed the United States as a near-future dystopia, *Civil War*, where America has fallen and fractured and is the midst of a new "Civil War." The "patriotic" America is run by a Trump-style character (played by Nick Offerman) who is believed to be guilty for the collapse in part, as other ambiguous forces battle against him. The heroes of the narrative are the liberal journalists who are willing to do anything to get the scoop, leading to tense sequences of near death battle photos and intrepid reporting on the road, as the team seeks to make its way to besieged Washington, DC to interview the President. On the way, we meet a host of racist red state miscreants and murderous xenophobes who want to purge America of foreigners, yet in the film's finale we find a cowering President who begs for his life. Odd timing, given the film premiered a few months before the attempted assassination of Trump in July of 2024.

In the 2024 Barack Obama produced the Netflix film *Leave the World Behind* which takes place in the same universe as *Mr. Robot* (same director) where the hackers who end up discovering various geopolitical plots, collides with a separate group of two families who must manage to survive as a large-scale hacking event takes down the US Internet. Stranded in a large Airbnb, these two families battle racial tensions and yet unknown forms of warfare that includes sound and ELF weapons, biowarfare that releases a kind of chronic wasting disease (as the deer are infected), and a battle over scarce medical resources. As society breaks down, we see a giant oil tanker come to rest on a beach, seemingly without a captain, Teslas shutting down and running haywire, and a large scale nuclear device detonated In a very ominous and ambiguous scene, the Airbnb owner claims to work with high level defense contractors and that had some knowledge of this coming event.

He explains, in somewhat contradictory terms, that he has met with what could be called the global elite who have contingency plans in place for a large-scale event, yet "no one is in control." If no one is in control, then how did the shadowy foreign entity and its moles subvert the US? We also see a bizarre *2001* style eclipse that occurs, likely symbolic of the eclipse of America, since the film contains no supernatural elements. The film also doesn't contain heavy symbolism, but since it emerges from the establishment itself, it could signify the attitude of the elite (much like Garland's *Civil War*) as both films predict a collapsed and fractured America subverted by a shadowy, unknown entity.

In *Civil War* it's ambiguously the Trump Movement, while in *Leave the World Behind* an undefined foreign group who penetrated the US with various moles and operatives brings on a full nuclear apocalypse. In order to achieve this, the film explains three steps were necessary to take down a nation as large and powerful as the US. First, isolation and communications would have to be taken out, explaining the cyber attacks, while second, synchronized chaos and intentionally contradictory information is spread, and third, an intentional civil war is sparked where people all turn on each other. These last two films are all the more terrifying given how realistic their scenarios are, compared to the previous, and given the recent attempted assassination they may be what the elite actually have planned for America.

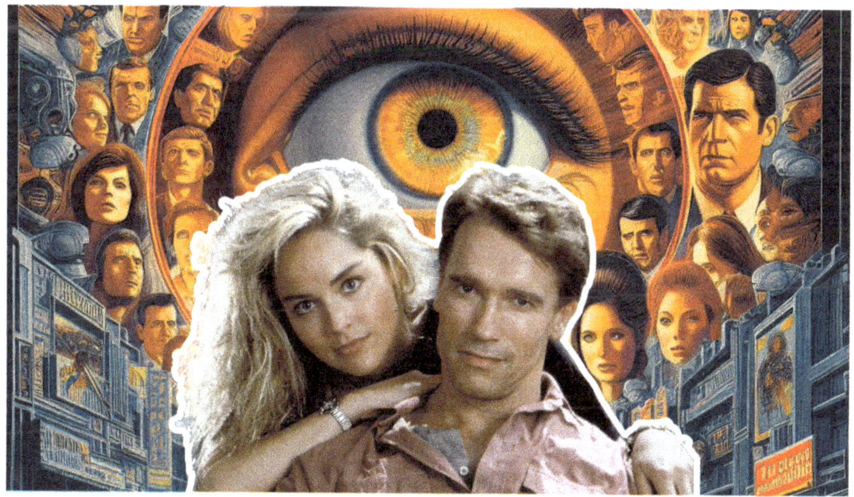

TOTAL RECALL (1990)

Paul Verhoven, the master of 80s and 90s excess violence, also adapted the famous Philip K. Dick story "We Can Remember it For You Wholesale" into the 1990 Schwarzenegger blockbuster *Total Recall*. Set in a future dystopian high tech civilization, *Total Recall* included some fascinating accurate predictions of where we are today, even as precise as the emerging promises by Elon Musk and others to provide privatized Mars flights. Quaid (played by Schwarzenegger) finds himself using the Internet, Skype calls are made, TSA style body scanners are everywhere and city dwellers have giant screens dominating every area of their life. In this mega city hellscape one corporation offers a discount respite: An implantable memory of a two week vacation of your making through Rekall! The Rekall procedure goes awry, triggering an awakening of the suppressed alternate personality inside Quaid known as Hauser leading to an attempt on the part of the Rekall Company to plan a cover up for Quaid's mental break.[70]

Quaid escapes and returns home to find his wife (Sharon Stone) is actually a honeypot assassin who has been spying on him and now seeks to kill him. Quaid escapes and decides to head to the Mars colony due to a pre-recorded message from his alternate personality Hauser. What struck me on the last viewing I had missed in previous viewings was the obvious MKUltra themes Dick was utilizing in this story. Dick was far ahead of his time in predicting the future attempts at wiping and reimprinting minds – something DARPA has been openly championing in the last few years.[71]

Quaid, we learn, actually is a secret agent and has had his mind wiped because he is a sleeper agent sent by corporate mogul Cohagen to destroy the Mars colony rebellion led by the mutant Kuato. Cohagen has created a monopoly on Mars rare mineral mining, exposing his slave workers to radiation that has mutated them into obtaining various psychic powers. Because the leader of the rebellion (Kuato) is a psychic, Hauser has had his mind wiped by Cohagen to infiltrate Kuato's rebellion and lead the assassins to Kuato: This is why Quaid has an implantable brain chip in his mind, which the previously cited BBC article admits DARPA has long been working on.[72]

The real secret of Mars is that the planet is actually a giant swamp cooler: an alien air conditioner that cools and terraforms the planet, which Cohagen suppressed in order to maintain his monopoly on resources and air. Like a company town (company planet here), Cohagen owned the workers and in turn sold them the basics they needed for survival (like air), while neglecting their toxic working conditions. Quaid, who is in reality the double agent mind controlled assassin Hauser working for Cohagen, decides to reject his programming and chooses to become his manufactured revolutionary persona. *Total Recall* is actually an espionage film dressed up in sci-fi garb and on a philosophical level asks us to question the technocratic world as a whole: Is the world we are entering where we are dominated by tech and screen actually creating a dissociative state in collective humanity.

We are all Quad/Hauser in this sense, caught in a surrealist fantasy delusion much like we are tempted to think the film is Quaid's delusion. Ironically, in *Total Recall,* the "red pill" was actually poison designed to kill Quaid as he was awakening to the reality his life was a lie. In *The Matrix,* the red pill is given an opposite meaning, where taking the pill awakens one to reality in contrast to the synthetic world. In a brilliant twist of writing, *Total Recall* remains a sci-fi classic, and on a deeper level was astonishingly prescient and revelatory in its depth in exposing the *real programs* the military industrial silicon valley complex Dick warned us about.

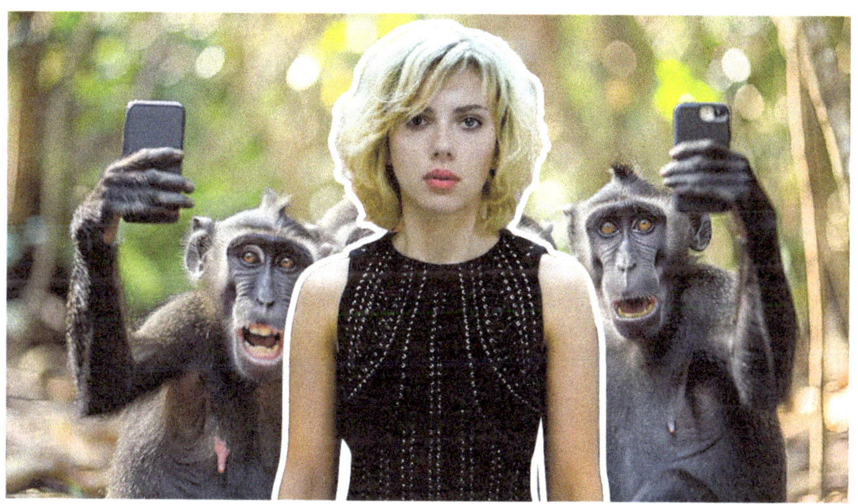

Lucy (2014)

Like *Furiosa, Lucy* is a presentation of the emerging archetype of the dark goddess savior who overthrows the masculine order by any means necessary, often with the aid of some form of transhumanism. Director Luc Besson has that rare, magical quality where his films teeter on the edge of being extremely mediocre and/or somewhat entertaining. Similar themes run through his work, from *La Femme Nikita* to *The Professional* to *The Fifth Element* to *The Messenger*, focusing on the feminized goddess archetype rising above all adversity, in ferocious neo-Darwinian fashion. *Lucy* is the climax of this goddess myth, wherein Scarlett Johansson plays an inadvertent drug mule, "Lucy," roped into an international conspiracy that quickly departs into something resembling *The Matrix* meets *Limitless* meets *2001: A Space Odyssey*.

I suppose it's difficult to get away from being influenced by the top science fiction films, but at a certain point, audiences can only see so many Matrix-y bullet stopping scenes, and replacing Keanu with a hot chick doesn't make it any better. Regardless, the transhumanist plot is really the focus here, as the premise is basically this: Since humans only use a small portion of their latent brainpower, what would happen if a human could use all 100%? And what if Morgan Freeman, Hollywood's imagined, soulful voice of God/science, could help facilitate that ascent of (wo)man to godhood? As I observed this silly plot, I was reminded of *Gravity*, where references to Darwinian *apotheosis* also abound, as women take humanity to the next level by a punctuated equilibrium jump in the evolutionary spectrum. Here, sweet Scarlett will catapult us ahead to the vaginal tech utopia.

Like *The Fifth Element*, where Milla Jovovich plays a feminine incarnation of the aether, or quintessence, Lucy becomes the feminine incarnation of reason and robotic rationality as she gradually ascends into the adoption of taking on what classical theology has called the incommunicable attributes of God: omniscience and omnipresence. We never know if Lucy attains omnibenevolence. The film continually references Darwinian process, highlighting the survival of the fittest, *aeons* of slow mutation, and Lucy, the laughable supposed first chimp, who was a female. Sorry, my fellow men, as Besson would have us understand, men are not preeminent in reason, nor are men the real power that propels order and civilization, as that exalted role is reserved for the first Lucy, the imagined female chimp, and the last Lucy, Scarlett Johansson.

Lucy is thus a conglomeration of all the myths of secular thought and for this reason it is highly instructive. While secularists, atheists, and materialists lambaste those of us with religious presuppositions, they are amazingly oblivious to their own religious assumptions. Lucy is a great example, where all the myths of modern man are combined into a storyline that demonstrates just how preposterous and divorced from reality secular mythology is. Neo-Darwinian theory, a chaotic, purposeless universe, and an imminent, emergent deity of feminist exemplification through transhumanism all coalesce to give us the future goddess: Lucy. It is worthwhile to note that Lucy also brings to mind Lucifer, lucid, and LSD, all of which relate to various mind control programs by the intelligence agencies. Lucifer is the archetypal figure of transhumanist thought, representing the ascent of reason to displace the ancient and medieval superstitions embodied in the patriarchal God of the Bible. However, I must point out the total contradiction that the hoped-for emergent god/goddess of the technocracy, the great supercomputer, also takes on the very attributes they think are irrational? The transhumanists firmly believe their merging with hard drives will lead to omniscience.

It is worth mentioning that in *La Femme Nikita*, *The Fifth Element* and in *Lucy*, MKUltra mind control is also an important theme. In *Lucy*, Lucy undergoes a kidnapping, drugging and accidental overdose, leading to her higher mental capacities "activating" through an advanced nootropic, wherein she becomes a perfectly cold assassin. While the focus of the film is chance evolution and technocracy, this element cannot be overlooked. Besson is clearly conveying to us the real purpose of the supersoldier programming that is now so prevalent in television and film – the perfection of (wo)man through mind control. The occult message of *Lucy* is that evolution shows us that whatever testing and experimenting are done on humans is for the greater good. Human testing is only propelling our evolutionary ascent, as we are merely animals, and only highly rational geniuses are able to understand this. Since most of humanity cannot grasp these esoteric truths, the continued covert manipulation and bio-engineering must continue unabated. Lucifer is guiding us to godhood – have faith, dear brothers, er … *sisters*.

In the end, *Lucy* downloads herself into a supercomputer and puts all her full-booty goodness into a thumb drive. Unfortunately, only Morgan Freeman ends up with the Lilith *Lucy* thumb drive, so sorry fellas, no USB Johansson hotness for you. Like Bruce Willis in *The Fifth Element*, the quintessence only unites with a worthy male supplicant, and in *Lucy,* the only worthy supplicant is the black neuroscientist. *Lucy* is a perfect representation of the combination of the humanist teleology and eschatology. The film is premised on the crucial occult, alchemical and Marxist belief that "progress" only comes through the *inversion* of all order and hierarchy. Women are the ultimate rational beings, chaos produces order, and finitude somehow inherently creates infinity. While many moviegoers scoff at the silly plot based on its reviews, isn't it interesting that so many people *actually believe this secular mythology in their daily life,* yet attack religion? How about a multee-pass to another film?

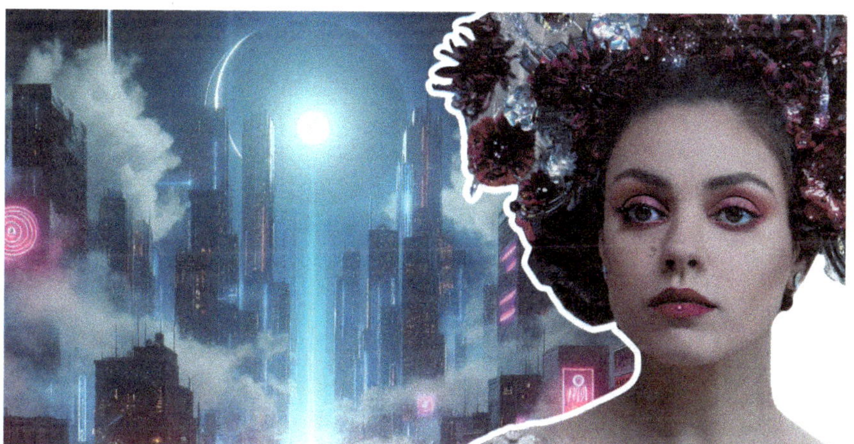

Jupiter Ascending (2015)

Continuing the theme of the dark goddess savior, *Jupiter Ascending* was not a particularly memorable film. Full of CGI vomit, the last installment from the Wachowskis presented a sci-fi opera that recalls *Star Wars* and their own *Matrix* series, blended with 70s *Battlestar Galactica* space glam. This time, however, the space opera revolves around the reversal of the classic mythological identification of Jupiter or Jove with a rational, male deity, into Russo babe Mila Kunis. This gender flip, as well as Lana Wachowki's flip is a signifier of the esoteric aspect of the film: GMOs.

GMO is not what you think I mean: In *Jupiter Ascending*, the "G" is a genetically modified organism. Like all other aspects of life, I have high-lighted the technocratic plan to alter the biosphere, and quite amazingly, the entire plot of *Jupiter Ascending* reveals this strategy. Not only does the film reveal this overall plan, it also demonstrates the occultic background for the ideas of cloning, genetic modification and transmutation, astro-theology/exotheology, as well as elite bloodlines and their parasitical "harvesting" relationship to the masses.

Stranded on earth as a reincarnate version of a semi-immortal, Jupiter (Mila Kunis) is an unassuming house maid who discovers her inner girl power goddess when a GMO "Lycan" named Caine (Channing Tatum) swoops in from outer space in to make her life interesting. Jupiter had been roped into donating her eggs to a fertility clinic which turns out to be run by a race of grays, chipmunk chattering aliens that control earth for the Abrasax Dynasty (more on this in a bit). Worth noting here is the hint of what really is true – that the elites do manage and run facilities like Cold Springs Harbor, the Kaiser Wilhelm Institute and other fronts and shell or-ganizations that exist to utilize eggs for experimentation and modification.

Hailed as the queen of earth, Jupiter is embroiled in an intergalactic War of the Roses to control vials of glowing blue juice that restores youth. Earth, being an inheritance of the gods (and her own inheritance), is ripe for magical DNA harvest which we predictably learn creates the Kool-Aid juice of life. It is worth noting that Caine, in gnostic mythology, is actually the hero, while Abel, his brother, is fingered as the villain. As with *Cloud Atlas* and *The Matrix*, the Wachowski style of such inversions are standard fare. Indeed, the creation of the *homunculi* as well as the golem are old fas-cinations of esotericists, and even still an alchemical process to transmute and transcend nature charges eerily towards the kind of world envisioned in *Jupiter Ascending*. Commenting on this notion, theosophist Gary Lach-man explains, citing Paracelsus:

> The question arises then: What is the homunculus and what is the golem? Franz Hartmann's 1896 *Life of Paracelsus* defines homun-culi as "artificially made human beings, generated from the sperm without the assistance of the female organism (black magic.)" The

Swiss alchemist Theophrastus Bombast von Hohenheim, otherwise known as Paracelsus (1493–1541), is recognized by many as an early master of holistic medicine and natural healing. It was from Paracelsus that Goethe, a great reader of alchemical and occult literature, got the idea of the homunculus which he used in the second part of *Faust*. Paracelsus offered a complete recipe for creating a homunculus:

> If the sperma, enclosed in a hermetically sealed glass, is buried in horse manure for forty days, and properly magnetized, it begins to live and move. After such a time it bears the form and resemblance of a human being, but it will be transparent and without a body. If it is now artificially fed with the *Arcanum sanguinis hominis* until it is about forty weeks old, and if allowed to remain during that time in horse manure in a continually equal temperature, it will grow into a human child, with all its members developed like any other child, such as could be born by a woman; only it will be much smaller. We call such a being a homunculus, and it may be raised and educated like any other child, until it grows older and obtains reason and intellect, and is able to take care of itself.[73]

Spirited away to a bee farm, Jupiter is shocked to discover the destruction of large metropolitan towers after an alien battle can be easily done and forgotten by the populace. The "aliens" have the ability to erase and implement memories, stultifying Jupiter into realizing that "large buildings can be destroyed and no one remembers." In other words, the technocratic attack on neurology is such that massive false flags and terror events can be engineered and within a small amount of time, the public has forgotten or failed to grasp the significance of events like 9/11.

The "Abrasax" Dynasty is an anagram for the gnostic deity Abraxas, which I've detailed before. In the analysis of *Edge of Tomorrow*. Scholar Hans Leisgang comments on these mysteries:

> According to mythical or mystery thinking, the gods and cosmic forces represented here are not conceived as merely existing successively or side by side: they act upon one another and within one another. All are manifestations of a single god and of one and the same cosmos, which is the god himself with all the powers which he discharges but still encompasses; and these forces are the whole world with all its creatures and forms."[74]

Abraxas is also the IAO of the gnostics and Crowleyans, as I explained in "Egyptian Mysteries of God and Energy":

One of the best examples of this is the mythology of Isis, Apophis and Osiris, whose mythology includes the principles of life and energy itself. Isis is the feminine principle of nature/energy extended in space and time. Apophis represents the principle of destruction and entropy, and Osiris represents the reemergence of energetic loss towards eternity to a higher state of eternality and immortality. The ancient Near Eastern symbol of IAO was representative of this formula, and when considered in comparison to the Pythagorean monad, dyad and triad, the same imagery is found to encode the same formulae. The point or monad extends to the dyad, with the two points connected forming a line. The line either has a circumference drawn around it and/or extends to a third point. It can also form a *vesica piscis*, or an eye.[75]

Jupiter thus represents the rise of the feminine principle to become a new semi-immortal conqueror with the line of Caine, whose superior genetics are "recognized by even the bees." Bees are a classic esoteric symbol of both Masonry and their hierarchy as well as matriarchal royalty (the Queen bee). Thus, it is not accidental the symbolic stand in here is that the "immortals" represent the royal bloodlines that have mastered the occult science of human manipulation and social engineering, while secreting away the real advanced technology – a similar theme in the film *Elysium*. Cloning, life extension, artificial intelligence, etc., are withheld in their positive use, and for the public, turned to black op use.

Within these glimmers of truth, the inverted mythos centers around *panspermia* – the ultimate "alien" myth promoted now by our so-called scientific pop stars like Dawkins. The rest of the film is quite predictable, as Jupiter and Caine beat the bad guys, and she returns to her dingy day job, yet still remains queen of the earth. In essence, the film constitutes the sci-fantasy of a disgruntled, feminist hausfrau: I give it three bags of popcorn and two tampons. Stupider Ascending.

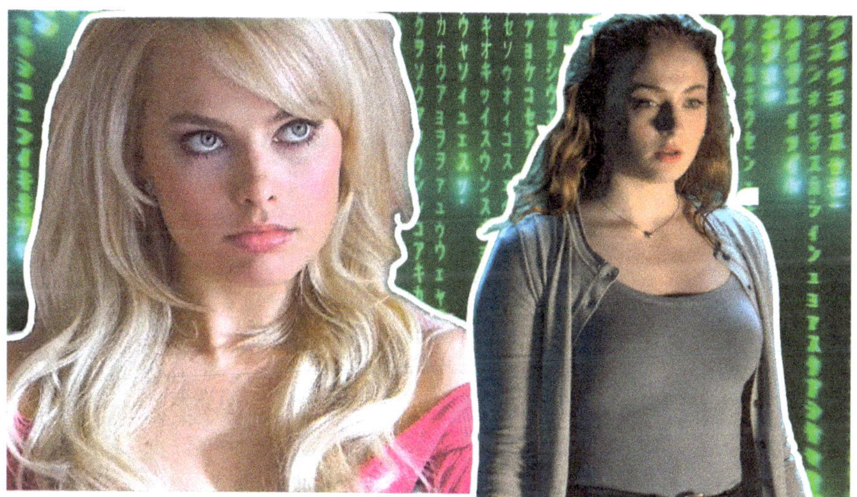

Barbie, Dark Phoenix, Mary Poppins, Wonder Woman & The Rise of the Dark Gnostic Goddess Savior

While there are many anti-feminist writers, "men's rights" activists and talking heads that cheered the recent *Barbie* film, they seemed painfully unaware of the real origins of feminism, its systemic support and the gnostic themes in the film, as well as Marvel installments like *Dark Phoenix*. These critics and writers are continually chipping away at the chief idols of our time, few are aware of the origins of their "equalism" and its hideous spawn, the feminist movement as a planned, engineered, and strategically deployed offensive, not just targeting women, but the entire populace. And while the planned aspect of feminism may come up in rare instances, even more rare is any mention of the deeper occult agenda that is at root Satanic.

In this article I will analyze the origins and usage of the movement, its connections and deployment, as well as the larger goal of feminism and equalist thought: in fact, Barbie in the film becomes a new gnostic savior that rescues the world from patriarchy, returning the Edenic state of her realm to a matriarchy, with men allowed a minor servant role in the ideal realm. In *Dark Phoenix*, Marvel has the humble girl-next-door Jean Grey transform into a dark, vengeful goddess due to her childhood trauma and tapping into the lifeforce of the goddess, or Gaia, shedding her bodily existence to become a deified thoughtform.

Modern conceptions of egalitarianism arise from philosophical presuppositions that emerged in the Enlightenment. From medieval nominalism came the modern tradition that objects in the world did not actually possess "natures," but rather the assigning of such metaphysical categories and "essences" was strictly a human conceptual framework. Thus, human nature was not an actually existing ontological description of something in the world, but rather a linguistic symbol that corresponded to a mental picture the *tabula rasa* mind had recorded, as the British empiricists further teased out the implications of nominalism. In their day, it was still common to think "man" designated one side of the gender spectrum, and "woman" another, but we can see the seeds of a revolution of thought to come across the entire spectrum, as all ontological "natures" would have to be tossed away.

I often mention the Enlightenment's universalization of human reason, which is likely becoming a bore to regular readers, but let me assure you, as the writer, I am just as nauseated by these ridiculous philosophies, but they are the unquestionable foundations of the whole modern world that must fall away. What is meant by the universalization of human reason is the change in western civilization's perception of anthropology as regards human nature itself. Since the West developed without the Eastern idea of man's *nous* as a higher faculty of point of contact with God, the Augustinian replacement became man's intellect and reason. What was in seed form in Augustine then became the norm in Descartes and the British Empiricists. For early Augustine especially, reason was the ultimate path to God, as man's mind was the mirror refraction of the ideas in the divine essence. By believing, man could cleanse his mind of fixity on the temporal and transient, and wind his way towards the eternal good. This is why Augustine's *City of God* contains the same "cogito" argument Rene Descartes later rewords. It is also why in *Soliloquies*, young Augustine proposes a form of empirical idealism that George Berkeley would later formulate.

In short, the trek of western thought follows the implications of Augustinian assumptions, varying only on which side of the theological dialectical dilemma one chooses: empiricism or rationalism, or even empirical idealism. The rejection of the *nous* in western anthropology meant that the redefinition of human anthropology in Enlightenment thought could only be another form of dualism, where man is defined as a body and a soul, or in some kind of reductionism, where the soul is abandoned. More radical materialists of that period had to keep somewhat silent, as rank materialism was still socially unacceptable and could lead to persecution. Nevertheless, it was only a few generations later that the *philosophes*, Jacobins and Illuminists made it possible to publicly adhere to atheism and materialism. The mind/body dualism that was so prevalent in the Enlightenment debates quickly caved to pragmatic materialism, as the scientific revolution brought empiricism to its pinnacle. In this regard, the Masonic Grand Orient *philosophes* were more consistent with their philosophy than their Enlightenment forebears – if nature was only a linguistic and conceptual construct, then men and women only differed in their pipes and fixtures. There was no "essence" of man or feminine "nature," anymore than there were angels or demons.

It is not accidental that women's suffrage and "women's rights" began to appear around the same time, with people like Mary Wollstonecraft. Although obviously not empirically true, the theory behind the emerging egalitarianism was still based on the jettisoned metaphysical assumptions of the universalization of human reason. Since reason was man's defining faculty, and women were also humans, all human beings must then also possess the same reasoning faculties and at least the same latent potential. Since the individual person was simply the accumulation of recorded empirical impressions, as David Hume would say, the equalists firmly held that all humans possessed the same latent potentiality, and could only differ based on adverse environmental factors. Poverty, diet, lack of medical attention, etc., were thus proposed as the causes of human suffering and diversity of abilities, and therefore women were no different from men, aside from biological makeup and millennia of being repressed and oppressed. As more and more radical forms of equalism and egalitarianism gained sway, Marxism and liberalism spread like a fire across the globe, as victimization and envy enabled women and minorities to more boldly declare all were equal.

Simultaneous with all of this was the rise of economic liberalism and the banking cartels that were the real functioning power behind the British Empire (see Dr. Carroll Quigley, *Tragedy and Hope*). The banking elite had long ago learned that predicting and controlling large social movements and trends had tremendous potential for mass social engineering, as well as collectivizing and transferring wealth. By the 1960s, the entirely created and controlled "counter-culture" movements paved the way for the final collapse of the West into nascent socialism and communism. Pioneered by the Royal and Fabian Societies, the re-engineering of man into the technocratic utopia could only be achieved through global crises and complimentary global order. As the direct descendants of the Empire's empirical tradition, the scientistic technocrats of the 20th century and today firmly believe and propagate the mythology that gender is not objectively real. Since man is only a biological robot, it stands to reason that he can be reprogrammed to be whatever his overlords wish – man, woman, trans-whatever. And since historically man tended to resist such tyrannical intrusions, the globalist technocrats have determined to re-write man's existence entirely through annihilation.

It is important not to think of this annihilation as some great, one-time cataclysmic apocalypse, but rather in the incremental approach of the Fabians. Through a gradual alteration of all things the prior millennia considered "natural," the socialist technocrats planned the slow inversion of the nature they professed to not believe in. The plan became to subvert and invert all of man's existence, so that man would get rid of himself. Being firm believers in Darwinian theory, the planned inversion of nature would therefore weed out the less desirable, and a small minority of technocrats would then make the cut onto Noah's Ark 2.0, passing into the future scientific utopia. But rejecting the belief in nature, and in turn seeking to destroy it, would have untold consequences. Those consequences are where we are living today: We are presently many decades into the initial phases of this "final revolution," as Aldous Huxley called it, against man himself. And one of the chief weapons of destruction against man in this war that has wreaked untold havoc within the last 50 years has been feminism.

Supported by both the Rockefellers and the CIA, feminism, being directly connected to Marxism, is at root Satanic. The governing principle of classical Satanism has always been the principle of inversion. The black magic belief is that power comes to the individual occultist through committing acts of inversion or rebellion that specifically defy the biblical God's designs. Thus, if God says not to murder, murder becomes a potential ritual act that stores up demonic energy for the committed practitioner. The more serious the practitioner, the more serious the acts of defiance. I speak here, not of pop Satanists and alienated youths, but of real, elite practitioners. The long history of human pacts with devils, real witchcraft and ritual Satanism are all based around this fundamental principle of inversion. While generally coming under the guise of promising liberty, freedom and power, the devil's con is always the same – man ends up tricked into being a dupe, is used, or damages his own psyche, or at worst, possessed.

The rise of Wicca and various "new age" and "goddess" spiritualities is a manifestation of this same principle of opposition and defiance, with the grand objective of destroying man. Clueless teens and yoga-obsessed yuppies now imbibe all manner of alternative spiritual practices, and such irrational, "feminine" spiritualities are often associated directly with feminist ideology. The ignorant and uninformed mass generally do not have the reasoning faculties to discover where the funding for such "movements" come from, and if they did, most would not be able to discern the designed, strategic plan of feminism and equalism to wreck the existing order as an act of Satanic defiance. For serious practitioners of black magic, the inversion of all order and promotion of mass sacrifice through abortion and destruction of the nuclear family is a ritual offering. One can see this clearly in the recent exposure of Jimmy Savile and the scandal in Britain. The endgame is an attempt to get rid of the chaff of the weaker, slave mentality herd-brain, and force a punctuated equilibrium of Darwinian evolutionary jump, leading to a select few Satanic technocrats continuing into the future.

The never-ending spew of "empowered" women and feminist harpies that chirp away on television and in the media are going to learn a hard lesson as the social order collapses. All the promised glittery gowns and chocolate-covered feelgood pharma pills of the feminocracy they bought into (as men were also emasculated and poisoned by the toxic culture) will turn into ashes and feces. The Satanic lie is meant for their very destruction, not for their empowerment, as no empowerment can come that is contrary to the natures God created. Nature can only be transformed and deified by God, not annihilated and reformed through occult, human, or demonic energy. Although I am a preterist in terms of the dating and exposition of the Apocalypse, we can certainly apply the spiritual principle of chapter 18 to the Babel we inhabit in modernity. Thus, both *Barbie* and *Dark Phoenix* become images of the whore, Babylon, and not dark feminine saviors. Babylon will fall, ultimately, because it is unnatural and its own worst enemy.

> 7 How much she hath glorified herself, and lived deliciously, so much torment and sorrow give her: for she saith in her heart, I sit a queen, and am no widow, and shall see no sorrow.8 Therefore shall her plagues come in one day, death, and mourning, and famine; and she shall be utterly burned with fire: for strong is the Lord God who judgeth her.9 And the kings of the earth, who have committed fornication and lived deliciously with her, shall bewail her, and lament for her, when they shall see the smoke of her burning, 10 Standing afar off for the fear of her torment, saying, Alas, alas that great city Babylon, that mighty city! for in one hour is thy judgment come.
>
> – Revelation 18

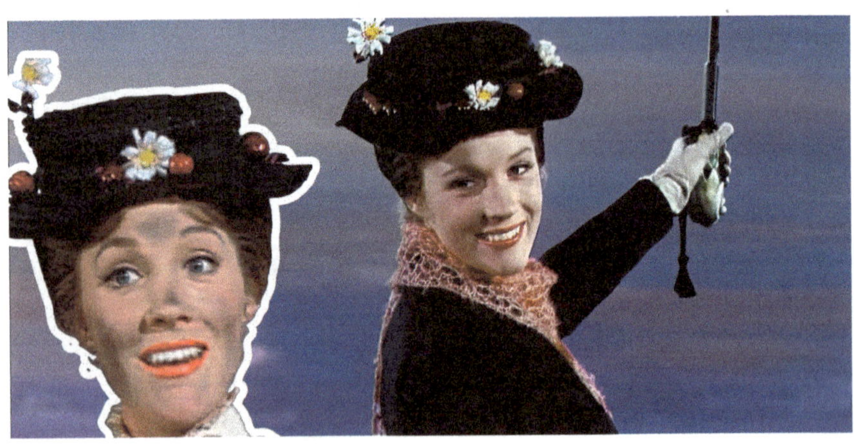

Mary Poppins (1964)

I don't often analyze children's films, though I'm often asked. Also, this analysis is full on mansplaining and I'm man-spreading as I type it. Most requests come from parents wanting an analysis of Pixar films, but I decided to go back to the beginning, to something I hadn't seen since I was child, *Mary Poppins*. Before Jessica Rabbit flashed her cartoon cooch in *Who Framed Roger Rabbit?*, and even before Brad Pitt was gallivanting with cartoon babes in the now-forgotten *Cool World*, there was *Mary Poppins*. A technical achievement for the time, Mary Poppins featured Julie Andrews as the wistful Nanny who reforms a dysfunctional wealthy family with Dick Van Dyke playing the role of the charismatic free spirit narrator who, for some reason, works every possible wage slave job throughout the film (with a crappy British accent).

What most people do not know (that I picked up on immediately because of my attuned JaysAnalysis senses) is the film is deeply influenced by the occult. Regular readers will also find no surprise in the fact Poppins author P.L. Travers was – you got it – an avid occultist. Not only that, you'll also find even less surprise in learning Travers worked for British Intelligence at the Ministry of Information, the chief source of government propaganda (as did Hitchcock). Like the rest of the Korda Circle of British Intelligence operatives I wrote about in *Esoteric Hollywood*, Travers met with Walt Disney (supposedly to discuss the film adaptation of Mary Poppins). Of course, the real mission of these characters (Roald Dahl, Ian Fleming, Noel Coward) was to influence U.S. Foreign Policy to enter World War II and aid in the establishment of the OSS, as we have seen:

> And for the icing on the cake, consider Phillip Knightley's admission of this as nothing more than a British move to further ma-

nipulate U.S. policy in favor of the U.K., in his *The Second Oldest Profession: Spies and Spying in the Twentieth Century*:

> Donovan was helped to prepare his submissions to [F] Roosevelt by [W] Stephenson and the SIS officers attached to his staff. Two senior British Intelligence officers, Admiral John Godfrey and his personal assistant, Lieutenant Commander Ian Fleming (later of James Bond fame), crossed the Atlantic to work on the campaign.... There is no doubt what the British were hoping to achieve, as the reports that Stephenson sent to Menzies make clear. He wrote that, at first, Donovan was not at all certain he wanted the job of directing "the new agency we envisage." When Donovan's appointment was announced, Stephenson wrote that Donovan was accusing him of having intrigued and driven him into the job. Stephenson then expressed his relief that "our" man was in a position of such importance to "our" efforts. Major Desmond Morton of the Industrial Intelligence Center was even blunter: "...to all intents and purposes US security is being run for them at the president's request by the British. It is of course essential that this fact should not be known in view of the furious uproar it would cause if known to the isolationists." (pg. 217-8)

As a result of her works, Travers was awarded the Order of the British Empire, showing she was no simple children's author and, like the rest of the operatives, was deeply involved in esoteric studies and practices. For Travers, this meant Theosophy, the teachings of Gurdjieff and eventually Zen meditation. Author S. Brinkman comments:

> [In London] she met the Irish intellectual, George William Russell, known as A. E. Russell, who was a follower of Madam Blavatsky and theosophy. (Theosophy, which has been condemned by the Church, is a modern version of gnosticism that blends pantheistic and occult beliefs.). Apparently, Russell believed he and Travers had met in a former life, and formed a friendship with her, helping her to expand her circle of friends to include occultists such as G. I. Gurdjieff and P.D. Ouspensky. He also introduced her to esoteric eastern religions and folklore, encouraging her to use her powers of fantasy to create stories.[76]

The Theosophical Society explains she also frequented the company of Golden Dawn Member Yeats and Satanist George Bernard Shaw:

> She became an intimate part of a literary circle composed of W. B. Yeats, Padraic Colum, James Stephens, Lady Gregory, George

Bernard Shaw, and others. Later she moved to England and wrote for the *New English Weekly*. There her circle of friends expanded to include A. R. Orage, P. D. Ouspensky and G. I. Gurdjieff. Meanwhile, W. B. Yeats translated the Upanishads, which was to have a profound influence on Travers, as did Hindu mythology and Buddhism, the lore of the Navajo Indians, and Jungian psychology.

And,

> The zoo scene in the book is also filled with occult imagery. In this episode, the animals run the zoo and all the people are in cages. The king of the animals is a huge hooded snake that Poppins calls "cousin."[77]

As usual, the book is very different from the film version, which led to vehement anger on the part of Travers at Disney's version (also the subject of a recent movie, *Saving Mr. Banks*). Travers wrote of a bitter, unwilling to be touched hag nanny, while Disney opted for never-farting prime princess Julie Andrews. The bizarre does not stop here, however. The film opens with a dysfunctional mother obsessed with suffragette-feminist causes, neglected children and a stuffy, dour bankster father intent on regulating his family like a well-oiled machine. As a result, the family opts for a prim hard ass nanny who literally blows in from a cloud on a gust of wind. In Travers' mind, this was supposed to represent a *siddhi*, or some kind of reincarnated, evolved feminine avatar archetype, which is confirmed by the Theosophical Society's Journal:

> Mary Poppins, one could say, resembles a guardian angel, *daimon*, or cosmic being who comes from time to time to visit Earth. She never settles with the Banks family for very long, but while she is there, she teaches the family, primarily the children, about the deeper meaning of life. She does this through magical outings with the children during the day or at night when the children dream or wake up and seem to leave their room…

And commenting from the writings of Blavatsky,

> In fragment forty, the text says, "Tis only then thou canst become a 'Walker of the Sky' who treads the winds above the waves, whose step touches not the waters"(p. 9). The glossary excerpt for this fragment refers to this *siddhi*, or spiritual power, as being a "sky-walker" wherein "the body of the yogi becomes as one formed

of the wind; as a cloud from which limbs have sprouted out," after which the yogi "beholds the things beyond the seas and stars; he hears the language of the devas and comprehends it and perceives what is passing in the mind of the ant" (p. 77). Known as the Great Exception, this aptly describes the powers of Mary Poppins, meaning in this context that she has gone beyond the evolution of humanity and her life now stands in contrast to those who have not yet reached this stage."

So Mary Poppins is a demonic fart – a toot from another dimension – sent back to us primitive neanderthals, still believing in things like reason, commerce, social hierarchy, etc. Mary is beyond all of this because she is (supposedly) the perfectly evolved being, which *of course* is female. Thus the constant film refrain about feminism and suffragettes, which are admittedly toned down in Walt's version, when at the end of the film the feminized mother abandons her activism to return to her husband and children.

Overall Walt's version has a good message – familial human relations are natural, healthy and organic, and even the rapacious London bankers are shown to be fools. The wholesome ending obscures more bizarre aspects, however, such as the constant references to "revolution" and "winds of change." Though Mary appears traditional, she is actually a *revolutionary force*, with Mr. Banks informing his bankster bosses of their "dislike" of revolutions. Nothing could be further from the truth in the real world, as banksters and billionaires are *often the hidden forces* behind the Guy Fawkes masks of revolutionary forces – from Marxism to anarchy-capitalism to femitransgenderblobacalafragilisticexpaladocious (see My *Tragedy and Hope* lecture series for more on this).

Happy-go-lucky Bert (Van Dyke) represents the workers as we see him full numerous low-wage positions, including the *artist* and chimney sweep, throughout the storyline. Bert and Mary are a weird team that in some esoteric whimsical way incarnate the cartoon world of imagination into the real world, which is the wind of change Mary was sent to create. While the surface level of the film entertains with an innocuous family friendly ending, the deeper message relates to Travers' apparent bisexuality and "women's rights." The film is about the true role of womanhood, and whether the "perfect" woman is a radical ideologue or a stay-at-home mother? The "feminist" issue surrounding the film has garnered much useless, boring debate, but at the time, it did represent a "feminist icon." *Time* magazine explains:

"[T]he movie had a strong message for its 1964 audiences. That year, Title VII of the Civil Rights Act banned employment discrimination on the basis of sex; Roe v. Wade was still nine years away. "We're clearly soldiers in petticoats," [Mrs. Banks] sings in the first song of the movie. "And dauntless crusaders for women's votes… Our daughters' daughters will adore us, and they'll sing in grateful chorus, 'Well done, Sister Suffragette!'"[78]

If Mrs. Banks is the voice of progress, her husband Mr. Banks is the voice of tradition. A straight-laced banker, he expresses his own worldview in the movie's second song, "The Life I Lead:"

This patriarchal perspective can't stand up to the organized mayhem Ms. Poppins brings into his home. Young Michael Banks wants to buy birdseed from the bird woman his nanny has told him about, but his father wants him to invest his tuppence in the bank. The boy tries to get his money bank, confusing other customers and causing a run on the bank – a sign of social upheaval if ever there was one! All this challenge to the status quo (plus his newfound unemployment) causes Mr. Banks to reconsider his narrow stance on power and order.

Mary starts a revolution through an indirect run on the banks. While the family may bond at the end, it is only through Mr. Banks' caving in and swallowing the blue pill of his evil patriarchy. Indeed, all the men in the film are fools, from the idiotic street worker Bert, to the senile old naval captains that live atop the Banks' house, the message of Mary Poppins is simple – men, it's time to surrender. Man, the perennial enemy of whimsy and fun, O dark patriarchy, cause of wars, famines, plagues and pestilence! Begone! Men also fart, but prim and proper Mary, who breaks the wind, explains herself to be utterly "perfect." If the film were redone in a geopolitically accurate version, Mr. Banks and his banksters would be seen at the close of the film *filling Mary's carpet-bag with gold* for her well-done work of revolutionary subversion.

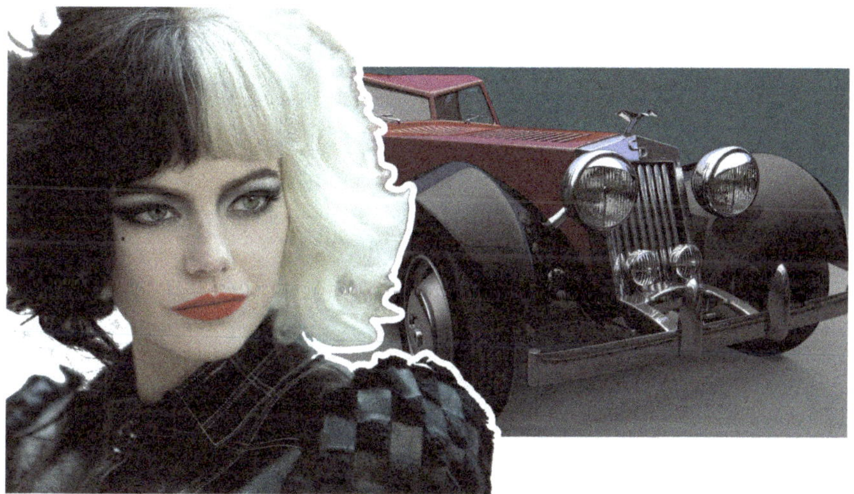

DISNEY'S *CRUELLA* (2021): FRAGMENTATION OF A GENERATION'S PSYCHE

Possibly no domain of culture is more openly degenerate and hellish than modern "fashion," and when Disney presented a film on the "fashion" industry (which I have zero interest in), I knew what to expect. Not only was this film partially about the "Illuminati" dominated fashion industry, the film was *actually* about MKUltra-style trauma based mind control and elite social engineering. I know, that sounds redundant – Jay, don't you say that's *all* movies? Yeah but that is *literally* the plot of this film! In fact, the time and setting of the story is also relevant, the UK in the 60s, during the Beatles/counter-culture revolution.

As readers and viewers know, we have covered the controlled and steered nature of the so-called counter-culture and how it was used to further the earlier 'revolutions" toward the final revolution we are witnessing today. Far from being against the system, the revolution was funded, guided and inculcated at all levels of society with precision coordination. The odd element of *Cruella* is that one of those revolutionary pop culture figures (Cruella) happens to also be a blue blood nobility. Indeed, an important element of this misunderstood villain motif is 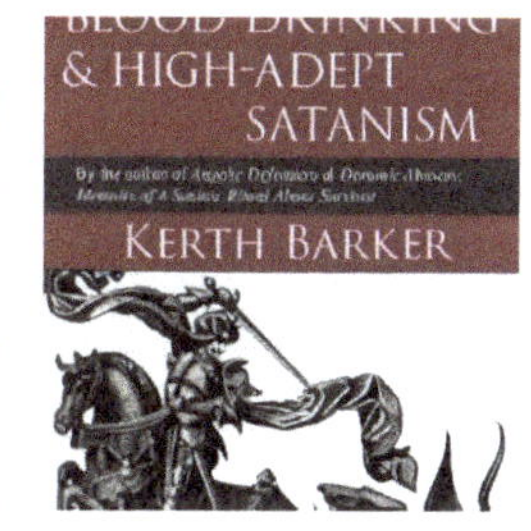 the revealed process by which the elite created psychopathic offspring, through mental, physical and spiritual abuse.

That is also not my interpretation, that *is* the plot. It's as if Disney writers read the conspiracy world's analyses of plots and films and symbols and said, "Yes, go with a literal Fritz Springmeier MKUltra alter story!" Further, Cruella is not merely a traumatized and unwanted offspring of British aristocratic psychopathy, as a result of the various traumas she actually has a split personality: Cruella is the dark, shade alter for Estella, a highly intelligent and artistically gifted daughter of noblewoman Catherine, who resides in a palatial estate and works as one of England's most elite fashion designers.

As you can imagine, the film is rife with duality symbolism, profuse either/or dialectics and black and white checkerboard flooring. Even Cruella's hair is emblematic of her split personality. As Estella undergoes her transformation into Cruella (DeVil aka Devil), we see her gradually ascend from orphaned child of the streets to creative fashion designer to recruit for Catherine, both of whom are unaware she is Catherine's long lost child. The further Estella ascends the latter of worldly success in fashion, the more she adopts the persona of Cruella, becoming more and more cunning, demonic and cruel.

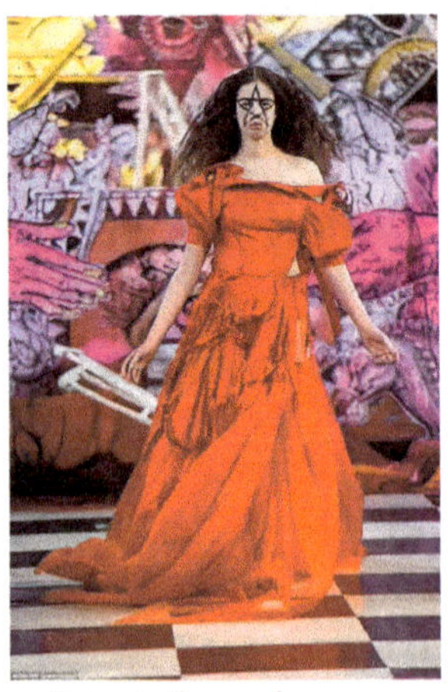

Satanic themed runway "fashion" recently in UK.

Thus, the MPD/DID split is thus the source of her power, which harkens to the MK MONARCH Project in which it is alleged that Satanist Col. Michael Aquino and other CIA doctors sought to create a programmed selection of elite children who could become the "super" soldiers of a coming Satanic Aeon, functioning as the next phase of human evolution. For this stage to occur, the ritual traumatization and creation of alters and supposed enhanced creativity could thus be manually engineered. Indeed, my recent analyses of Aquino and other MKUltra documents and survivors bears this out. Although I cannot prove all the accusations and allegations of Candy Jones, Cathy O'Brien or Kerth Barker, both victims' writings demonstrate many details and claims that can be verified. Their cases of abuse parallel in many ways the story of Estella.

As mentioned, the 60s counter-culture setting would place Cruella at baby-boomer age, with her transformation placing her as one of the premier agents of change for the fashion industry. While I recognize this is a fictional character, she may symbolically represent the mass traumatization and fragmentation of the boomer psyche through the master PsyOP known as the 60s counter-culture. From the Crowley and TM inspired

Beatles, to Donovan's "Season of the Witch" and the openly Luciferian and Satanic Rolling Stones, the film's soundtrack and scenery are intentionally evoking the Age of Aquarius, which is really nothing more than the Aeon of the Child: Estella/Cruella is that child, symbolically. The dissociative, doublethink split in *Cruella* is paradigmatic for the dissociative, fugue states the post-boomer generations would learn, like Winston, to love.

DARK CITY (1998)

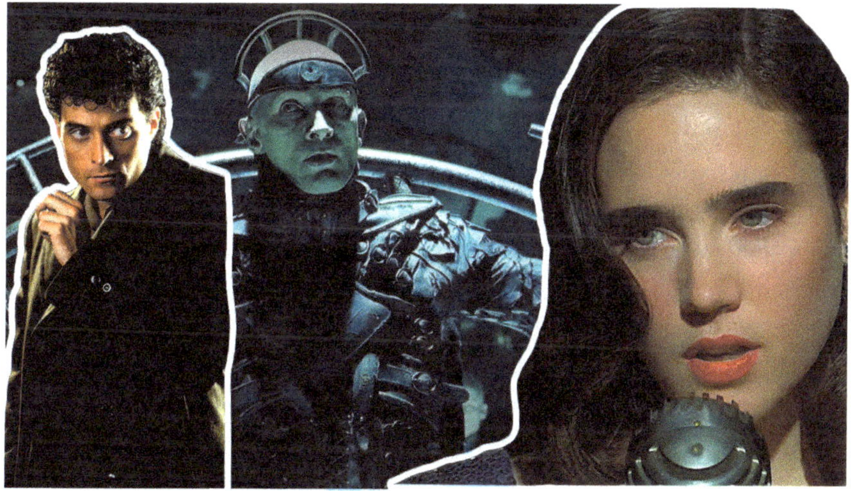

I hate to harp on the same old thing, but the same old thing always manifests in films, and deserves to be harped on. Often what is considered to be groundbreaking and avant garde is really just the same old esoterica repackaged with different dressing. It seems that there is actually a lack of creativity when it comes to matters Hollywood. *The Knowing* is another famed Alex Proyas film full of gnostic themes and the great Nicolas Cage, but *Dark City* deserves its own analysis since it is very similar to *The Matrix* and premiered the same year (1998).

Dark City presents a neo-noir dream world wherein a group of alien-like archons or angelic rulers/daemons known as the "Strangers" control manufactured city by "tuning" it every night, meaning the city is re-created on a daily basis while its rat-like inhabitants are implanted with new memories. The Strangers are able to conform physical reality to whatever form the desire by will alone ("tuning"), while one of their subjects, John Murdoch, eventually attains their same ability. We see the basic Crowleyan theory of "magick" at work, which is the act of conforming reality to one's will. The Strangers do it by telekinesis, and eventually John Murdoch evolves to do this, as well.

"Dark City," we discover, has perpetually been in a state of darkness – it is always night, and no one can recall when it was daytime. We have the notion of the demiurge trapped in a world of base darkness demiurge(s) who have trapped a world in base darkness, where they lack their true godpowers. We see in the beginning a movie theater where films are playing named "The Evil" and "Nightmare," cluing us into the fact that we are watching a movie that is essentially a nightmare. We see a hotel in which John Murdoch, the protagonist, awakes nude in a bathtub, apparently being framed for a murder. However, this night is different, as it is Murdoch's "awakening," and from this point on, as he is chased by certain "Strangers," Murdoch discovers his inner power to "tune," yet this power is not yet fully under his control.

A cop is put on his case, Detective Bumstead, who picks up where a former cop had been working who went insane by becoming aware the reality they inhabited was a simulation. As mentioned, this film premiered the same year as *The Matrix*, and both films presented the thesis reality is a type of computer simulation, five years before Nick Bostrom published his famous 2003 paper arguing we are living in a computer simulation. The former detective's madness turned out to be a form of intense paranoia linked to a realization all reality was not merely an illusion, but they were also the experiment of gnostic *daemons*. John decides he too must discover his origins, since he cannot recall his past. For him, this is a quest to find "Shell Beach," a faint memory he has of where he grew up. The entire city of "Dark City" is a spiral, it turns out, and Murdoch discovers Shell Beach never existed, and that Dr. Schreber had been aiding the Strangers in implanting false memories in people. Rather than interpreting this as some form of "Illuminati MKUltra mind control programming," which most "conspiracy" writers would do, what makes more sense is a cabalistic or Platonic notion of *metempsychosis* or transmigration of souls, wherein we must "remember" the state of deity from which we have come. Murdoch, Dr. Schreber tells him, has evolved to the point where he can tune reality at will. The reality in which they exist is like *The Matrix*, and is a giant machine that can be manipulated by telekinetic will. Similarities with the *Matrix Trilogy* will be apparent here. There may also be an application here to MKUltra, however, as the themes of implanted memories and scientific experimentation on unwitting human subjects were certainly real world events Proyas may be giving a nod to.

The Strangers are conducting an experiment where they are seeking to find the soul, that thing that makes humans individuals, whereas the

Strangers only possess a collective consciousness: something reminiscent of the demonic realm, if you have read enough exorcism accounts. The Strangers are, again, "aliens" that inhabit the bodies of dead humans, and hate light and water. The lesser creator demiurges keep men trapped in darkness and deny them their godpowers, while they rule with an iron fist and entrap men in a dreamworld, hiding from them their real origin, which is that they are destined to evolve into God. As noted on my site concerning this process:

1. Primitive man makes evolutionary leaps by virtue of his imagination.

2. Initially Man cannot distinguish between himself and outer nature.

3. Through his imagination, Man creates subject/object boundaries.

4. Man projects his own person-hood on the exterior world, creating god.

5. This projection at first helps unify society but then metastasizes into a psychological prison.

6. Man recognizes god to be merely his projection and "re-ingests" the projection into himself, realizing that he himself was God all along, thereby moving to the next stage in evolution.

7. In some cases this marks a break with the subject/object distinction, destroying the notion of ego itself, allowing man to be integrated into the pantheistic "all in one."

8. This dialectical evolutionary process is often symbolically represented with the union of male and female pairs."

John Murdoch, like everyone else, is trapped in the base material world, created by the Strangers. He makes an evolutionary leap and by his power of telekinesis located in his third eye, via imagination, thus he "tunes" reality to fit the volition of his inner *psyche*, matching the inner and outer worlds. He projects himself onto the world, creating god, or in this case, himself as god. And in this situation, he frees man from the psychological prison created by the Strangers. Like *Starchild* in *2001*, John Murdoch destroys his ego when he is "imprinted" with the false memories he was originally given, but this time, Dr. Schreber has inserted himself into the memories to tell John that he is a god. John becomes, then, the *macroprosopus*, being formerly the *microprosopus* archetype that breaks the Strangers' mold.

It is interesting that Murdoch really gets the answers to the question of the "illusion" of his reality when he wanders into the old theme park attraction titled "Neptune's Kingdom." Neptune/Poseidon is the god of the waters, while the Strangers hate the water. Neptune is also the planet of the mystic in Holst's famed symphonic piece, so Murdoch's quest has been one that is ultimately solved by "mysticism," or a form of initiation. Not all mysticism is bad, but you can bet when mysticism is found in a movie, there's a penchant for gnosis. Perhaps the meaning, since Neptune is the farthest planet from the sun, is that John mystically returns to the meaning of the symbolism of the gods to find freedom from the matter-connected controlling archons, the Strangers. John must travel to the farthest reaches of the universe to bypass the reach of the archons and then return deified in a form of apotheosis.

Proyas, it should be noted, also directed *The Crow* and *The Knowing* both with similar gnostic themes. *The Knowing* is very similar to the themes found in *Dark City* – a world controlled by offworld alien/demon-like entities, a mysterious code and set of symbols that must be deconstructed to decipher that reality as we know it is an illusion, and an apocalyptic end of that world. The film also makes references to Fritz Lang's *Metropolis*, which I analyzed at the end of *Esoteric Hollywood 2. Dark City* is an interesting film, and is worth watching, but unfortunately, the overall message is what we see recycled so often – hermeticism wherein man recovers the supposed truth that he is god: But man isn't God.

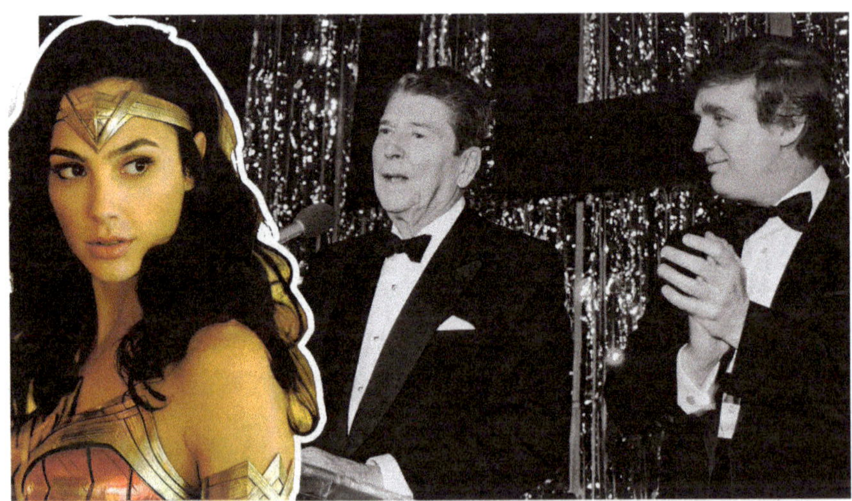

WONDER WOMAN (2017) & WONDER WOMAN 1984 (2020)

Furthering the modern mythos of the goddess boss babe, DC Comics' *Wonder Woman* has been rebooted with former IDF soldier Gal Godot playing the classic heroine. Emerging from classical Greek mythology (as do most comic book narratives), Diana the Amazonian leaves her hidden realm created by the Olympians to save the world from the dastardly Nazis at the time of World War 2.

In this narrative, Sir Patrick Morgan reveals himself to be Ares the Greek god of war who has given mankind technological inspiration, yet men inevitably use this knowledge for warfare purposes. Diana defeats Ares with a "god-killer" sword, perhaps indicating the symbolic reference of taking a traditionally phallic image and killing the masculine force with his own member. There might be a double meaning for this "god-killer," too, since it suggests an end to masculine deities and the rise of *the goddess*. Daina is now the new female savior, and this is even more apparent in the sequel where Diana ends up in 1984 as a museum curator at the Smithsonian.

Taking a more socially critical perspective, *Wonder Woman 1984* directly connects patriarchal power and control with capitalist economic structures, even lampooning a Donald Trump-esque villain as the Reagan era president. This preachy moral message is quite hypocritical, given there's arguably nothing more consumerist driven than the world of modern comic film book franchises. In fact, in the film all men are actually portrayed as weak, abusive figures obsessed with nothing but oil tycoonery and resource dominance, while neglecting the feminine virtues and their supposed inherent connection with the elemental forces of nature.

Here Diana becomes much more of an Athena/Minerva archetype (though her rival Cheetah character is actually named "Minerva"), the warrior goddess of wisdom who is more masculine and at once more balanced and poised than all men. In fact, the Trump stand-in figure's son is named "Alister Lord" perhaps evoking infamous British Satanist and spy Aleister Crowley, who famously called for a reintroduction of a kind of slavery for the profane masses under his religion of will-worship known as *Thelema*.

Crowley had a chief place in his religious system for the phallus and sex magick, yet in the film when the Washington monument is presented in a scene we hear the phrase "god of lies," in reference to the supposed Reagan-era trickle down economics philosophy situated in the Cold War dialectical conflict with the Soviets, and like the accusations of Trump collusion with Russia in our era, the fictional timeline of *Wonder Woman's* 1984 has the Reagan/Trump colluding with the Soviets. Ironically, there is some truth to this notion of a higher level collusion between the Atlanticist power bloc colluding with the Soviets at a higher level, but I doubt the screenplay writers were aware of the Sunnon thesis!

In fact, on Wonder Woman's planet, Asteria had died for the salvation of her Amazonians, suggesting the theme of female liberation is only achieved by the historical process of countless woman "saviors" who then give rise to the next generation of women saviors that will eventually produce Diana – the *Overwoman.*

Whether it's modern comic book films like *The New Mutants* (2020), where traumatized teens who have developed "powers" from the trauma, functioning as a new stage of human evolution (part of the X-Men universe) or the 1970's *Stepford Wives,* where liberated women free themselves from the slavery of being a wife and mother, Hollywood witchcraft has been at the forefront of the cultural revolution to alter the ideas of healthy, normal living the rest of the world still finds natural and wholesome. In *X-Men First Class* (2011), it was the CIA that helped Professor Xavier set up his special school for "gifted" traumatized mutants (replete with images of Karl Marx on the walls) to train them to be the future guardian class of the coming world order and stop the nefarious Magneto from his depopulation agenda through engineering a global, staged Cold War nuke crisis.

In spy films like *Atomic Blonde* (2017) and based on a comic book or Luc Besson's *Anna* (2109) the same themes are found in explicitly bisexual characters, as the masculinized female assassins are able to transcend the dialectical oppositions of global East/West geopolitics because they have transcended the gender polarity, as well as the opposition of good and evil.[79] These MKUltra traumatized delta programmed female assassins are beyond all dualities and have become, once again, *Overwomen.*[80]

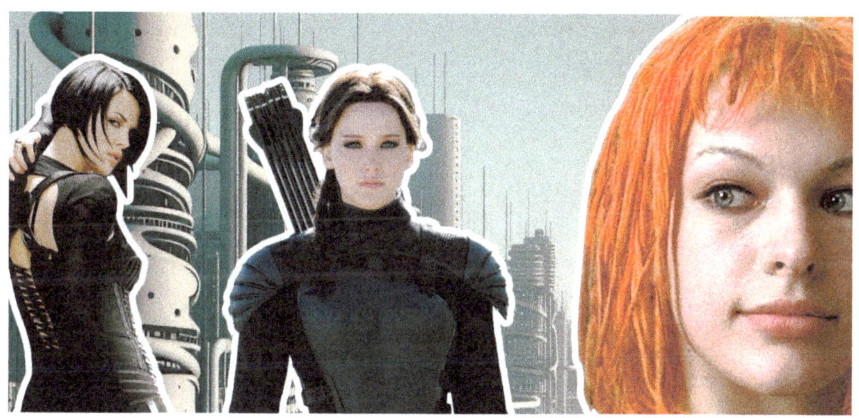

GMO Bloodline Salvation: *Fifth Element* (1997), *Aeon Flux* (2005), *The Island* (2005), *Hunger Games* (2012) & More

Fifth Element (1997)

Once again Luc Besson pushes the dark gnostic goddess savior in the form of the incarnation of the feminine principle in his 1997 *Fifth Element* – this so-called "fifth element" or *aether,* becomes instantiated in the alien personage Lee-Loo (Milla Jovovich). Lee-Loo is purported to be the "perfect being," an incarnate divine *sophia* that will function as the philosopher's stone and a cosmic weapon against evil. This secret feminine gnosis is protected by a priesthood who guard the "key" of this knowledge, and the religion of this future dystopia they explicitly ecumenist, having intentionally blended all the world religions into a new, syncretist form.

The *ecumenist* new world religion, combined with the fact that a gender neutral Chris Tucker live streams his shows 20 years before live streaming became normative are the most revelatory elements in the film, while the rest smacks of a pale rip-off of *Star Wars* and *Blade Runner*. The film also makes mention of a Masonic "Supreme Being" whose universe can only find cosmic balance in dismissing its patriarchal structure embodied in a goofy southern space villain (played by Gary Oldman) working in league with genocidal aliens, as well as through the acceptance of Lee-Loo as a new divine feminine focal point of cosmic religion. Only by returning to an ancient Egyptian mystery religion and the worship of Lee-Loo as the culmination of the four elements, and embodied in Lee-Loo as the *aether,* the 5th. Indeed, protagonist Korben Dallas ends his veritable sex magick quest by sexually uniting with Lee-Loo the goddess, completing his alchemical process.

Aeon Flux (2005)

In the 2005 film adaptation of *Aeon Flux*, which departs from its older MTV animated predecessor, we see a dystopian Brave New World-type scenario where the human population has fallen under the genetic determinist rule of a small, elite dynasty of scientists, headed by Trevor Goodchild. Goodchild rules from a large, walled smart city where outside, the earth has been re-wilded, which is an actual elite plan.[81] This brings to mind the infamous 1992 UN document known as the Rio Summit where Agenda 21 was first proposed, arguing for carbon taxes and new models of control which promote human depopulation.[82] Trevor's justification for the high tech prison smart city is the myth that outside the city, a viral death reigns.

In the film's narrative, in 2011 a virus was released that killed 99% of the earth's population, while Goodchild's predecessor purportedly discovered the cure. As it turns out, the Goodchild regime is actually based on cloning and genetic manipulation. We are presented with the anti-establishment revolutionaries (as usual), made up of Aeon (Charlize Theron) and her elite "Monicans," battling the patriarchal Goodchild regime. Goodchild and Aeon eventually team up and end up fighting for a secret common cause, unbeknownst to the Monicans or the technocratic police state.

What is thus presented is a blurred, necessary dialectical opposition vision of good and evil, where both sides are really working towards common goals, yet take different paths to get there. In the end, all was justified, but that is not how human morals work: We don't autonomously do whatever we want and choose good or evil, based on an ends-justifies-the-means approach. The meaning then appears to be that in the *new Aeon*, or our new age, humans will only evolve after a period of mass death, transhumanism and cloning (the "flux"), all of which are necessary for the evolutionary ascent to apotheosis.

The Island (2009)

A Michael Bay film might seem an odd choice for a book focused on symbolic analysis, and no, it's not an analysis of explosions (which characterizes about half of any Bay film). In the 2005 *The Island*, we have a conglomeration of many dystopian classic stories, from *Brave New World* to *1984*, but also with key elements older dystopian fiction missed: the genetic/dysgenic component. *The Island* also makes use of the Platonic principle of the noble lie, that the technocratic elite must use a vast, large scale lie to control the masses. This is not accidental: Plato is also the source of eugenics, population control, communism and *techne* as a form of control.

In *The Island,* a high tech breakaway civilization has been built in a giant underground facility where a colony of youthful adults have been cloned and kept in a childlike state and controlled through a noble lie the air outside the colony is toxic. Members of the colony are told when they win the lottery, they are able to leave the colony for a luxurious life on a beautiful tropical island location (the island). In reality, the entire colony is the plan of a technocratic elite who are cloning and harvesting organs for the world's billionaires. The world passed laws concerning eugenics leading the planet's billionaires to go underground. As the plot is uncovered, the island was actually the facility itself and the billionaires end up exposed. The most relevant aspects of this film are the completely controlled synthetic environment and the vast lie the entire colony believes, while only two subjects ever question their reality. In the future, Bay interestingly notes the re-emergence of eugenics and the manipulation of human biology through cloning and population control. In other words, Bay seems to be suggesting we already live in the island colony under a noble lie and dysgenics still rules the day.

Maze Runner (2014) & *Hunger Games* (2012)

In the 2010's, we were subjected to a bevy of post-apocalyptic, dystopian literature and film, and the *Maze Runner* is no exception to that trend. Based on James Dashner's young adult novel of the same name, the film has stayed the course with end-of-the-world-black-op scenarios, echoing *Hunger Games, Divergent* and a host of similar titles. On a film level, director Wes Ball's adaptation was watchable, yet stifled by gelled and moussed teen boys supposedly roughing it, combined with cookie cutter CGI beasts audiences are still mysteriously paying to see. Hearkening to William Golding's *Lord of the Flies,* this adolescent survival drama certainly could've used a little more of Golding's grit and realism, and less Vidal Sassoon. That aside, there are depths to be plumbed here on the esoteric level – in fact, one of the most profound revelations of the establishment finds its place in this teen drama.

The plot centers on a teen protagonist named Thomas (Dylan O'Brien) who arrives with amnesia out of a shaft in the ground to a group of similarly displaced and amnesiac lads, known as "Gladers" who inhabit, you guessed it, The Glade. In their makeshift, idyllic Eden, these lost boys run an agrarian communal tribe in the center of a vast, daily changing maze populated by genetically modified creatures known as "grievers." Much like the tribal structure of *Lord of the Flies*, the Glade has rules about not trespassing into the maze unless one is a "runner," and not challenging the *ad hoc* authority. Runners are trained for the task, while others are assigned communal duties reminiscent of the three-tiered structure of Plato's *Republic*: the workers, the guardians, and the philosopher king.

Predictably, Thomas challenges the Glade's leader, opting to venture into the maze and explore. As a result, drama ensues and expected power struggles emerge. One also has to wonder if the amnesia caused these fellas to forget their biology, given that no one seems to think about girls until one mysteriously pops up from the ground after Thomas, named Teresa (Kaya Scoledario). As Thomas discovers more about their surroundings, he begins to feel suspicious their environment is a controlled one. Teresa and Thomas seem to have a recollection of one another, yet can't grasp how or why, as the tribe begins to turn on them both as outsiders destined to enlighten the Glade dwellers fixated on their mundane existence, having been brainwashed and wiped of their former life (think MKUltra).

Here we see another Platonic element present, where the lost memory of a previous existence or life has been forgotten as one becomes drowned in the sea of illusions and shadows on the cave wall (think Plato's Allegory of the Cave from *The Republic*). Gradually Thomas recalls his participation in a secret black ops project that involved selecting teens for covert neurological testing by an elusive underground organization with the acronym W/C/K/D. "Wicked is good," is the company mantra that echoes in their subconscious, as the maze is revealed to be parallel to Thomas' subconscious (our philosopher king). Thomas also recalls his job with W/C/K/D involved panopticon-style surveillance upon his teen companions, as all details of the children's actions, thoughts and reactions are recorded – but more on that in a bit.

This theme of associating mazes and labyrinths with the unconscious realm was known to the Egyptians and was expounded at length by Carl Jung. Esoteric traditions in the East also maintain that man in this life of appearances has fallen "asleep," forgetting his true self and origins, bound by the delusory phantasms of a fading and flux temporal existence. Likewise, medieval cathedrals embodied labyrinths as symbolic of the traps, schemes and deceptions of this world, held under the sway of the devil. In "The Process of Individuation" by M.L. von Franz in Carl Jung's *Man and His Symbols*, von Franz explains the meaning of the labyrinth as the subconscious:

> The maze of strange passages, chambers, and unlocked exits in the cellar recalls the old Egyptian representation of the underworld, which is a well known symbol of the unconscious with its abilities. It also shows how one is "open" to other influences in one's unconscious shadow side and how uncanny and alien elements can break in. (pg. 176)

Are we trapped in the dream state of an engineered environment where the archetypal, alien fears of the labyrinthine existence of modernity keep us in a dreamlike trance? What is the key to exiting our maze? Let's consider the film again. Following upon the solution of the maze (discovering that there *is* an exit), a small band of Thomas' faction make it out to discover the exit leads to an underground facility in the desert where the first "test trial" had been conducted on them all. A prerecorded message (itself a deception) informs the survivors they are part of a larger experiment to speed up evolutionary adaptation, as the earth has been "scorched" from the sun and (of course) the release of a zombie-*esque* virus. When in doubt, throw in zombies. Those stung (vaccinated?) by the evil *archon* controllers of the maze (the scorpion-like Grievers) ended up infected with this same virus, so we are left to speculate whether the virus is also part of the greater "test."

What needs to be gleaned from this is the controlled and designed aspect of the fictional world of the maze in which the children find themselves. This is crucial, as our world mirrors this technocratic, controlled test tube existence in the film, and the same goes for *Hunger Games*, when we consider both Panem, the new dystopian "America," as well as the controlled synthetic environment of the gladiatorial hunger games where teens are sacrificed for societal entertainment. Much like *The Purge*, both films present the need for blood sacrifice and violence through the sacrifice of youth as a necessary means of social control. In *The Purge*, it's even seen as an overtly Satanic celebration by the end of the film when Ethan Hawke is betrayed by his neighbors.

Societies are manufactured, consensus reality is enforced, masses are brainwashed and true free thought is suppressed: In *Hunger Games*, as the narrative progresses in the sequels, Katniss (Jennifer Lawrence) eventually discovers she is being used by the revolution just as the Capitol had used her. Katniss discovers she is caught in a controlled dialectic, with both sides of the binary using the same techniques of manipulation, control and deception. In fact, the Capitol even stages entirely fake news broadcasts to wage infowar on Katniss' rebellion. This leads Katniss to flee both attempts at control and seek a more solitary existence.

In similar fashion, in *Maze Runner* not only were the rules of the Glade trivial and in the end harmful, the entire existence of the maze itself was illusory, being only a small portion of the real world. However, this was no fantasy world to be escaped through meditation or further flights into fantasy, but a real world maze to be solved for survival. That kind of survival of the fittest world is just the world we find ourselves in, as our food, water, culture and very air is under full spectrum attack from the technocratic eugenicist establishment. And just as in the film, the technocrats intend on "speeding up" evolutionary adaptation by converting the entire globe into a maze full of ever-changing and controlled mythologies and deceptions that keep men lost in the dreamland maze of the synthetic world order.

Think, for example, of Dr. Jonas Salk, who is presented to the world as a vaccine savior, yet in his own writings argues that mass inoculations must be done to curb the growth of populations. Salk apparently believed that a neurological attack on humans *en masse* would halt "war," which he blames on humanity. In true Orwellian fashion, Salk proposed to wage war on the cancer of man to not have war. Likewise, social architects like Charles Galton Darwin, Arthur Koestler and Bertrand Russell were all in agreement that mankind would have to be placed under mass genetic alteration and testing to see who was "fit" to go on to the next level. In reality, however, "progress" was the cover these so-called elite foisted on the world to promote their own dark age, where they alone would go into the "next million years," while the rest of the population are forcibly sterilized and soft-killed. Just as the covert black operation in the film socially engineered a fake environment intent on sacrificing the young for "evolution," so have these *real world* death-cult high priests of the "wicked" corporation done to us.

Revelations of the NSA as an entity geared towards total panopticon surveillance, data collection and planetary regimentation combined with the long term designs of the Rand Corporation's social engineering demonstrate a global test tube policy that becomes even bleaker when combined with the designs of the Royal Society social engineers and technocrats mentioned above. Indeed, we find that our supposedly "free" and "progressive" society is an artificial construct just like that of the *Maze Runner*. The Grievers we battle aren't GMO CGI scorpions, but GMO corn. I just hope we're not left with one babe to fight over, but given the alchemical gender-bending Koestler and company worked for, perhaps we'll all be asexual morlocks who won't desire sex at all.

As for *Maze Runner* – I give it three bags of GMO popcorn and two corn syrup gummies and one prayer: If we consider alternate metaphysical models, we might bust the glass of this planetary test tube. In terms of *Hunger Games*, the trilogy was well made and overall had a positive message, but couldn't resist the emerging 2010's trend of making the hero another feminist slay queen. In the above dystopias the notion of salvation through a special bloodline (just like *I Am Legend*) or mystical bloodline essence or blood sacrifice is perhaps a remnant of Christian theology in a post-Christian world which is now transmuted into the gnostic and scientific secrets of genetics and DNA manipulation. The technocrats will offer us a new Eucharist of genetically modified salvation – but could this actually lead to something more akin to *Soylent Green* than a Fabian socialist technocratic utopia?

Section 3

Obscure, Independent &
B Movies With A Message

INVITATION TO HELL (1984)

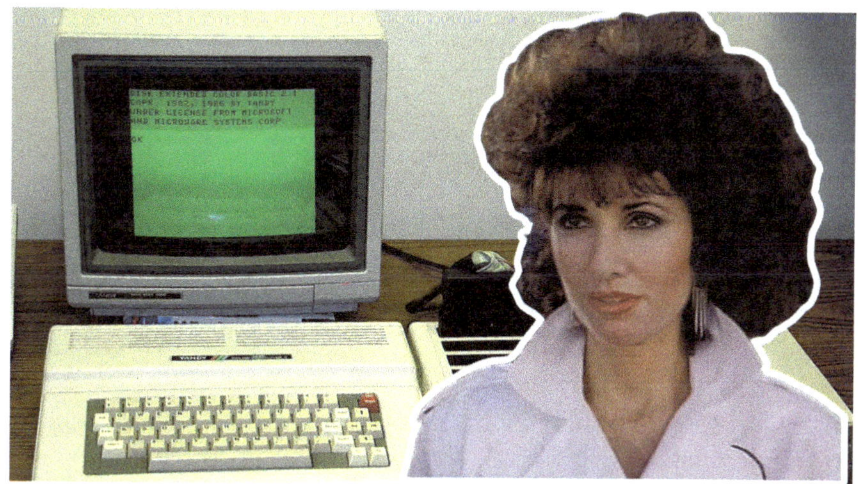

In 1984 Wes Craven did a little-known TV movie called *Invitation to Hell*, which happened to be an amazingly prescient production, especially given the power Silicon Valley would come to wield in the following decades. The film begins with a family moving to Silicon Valley for their father's new job, while in reality, the tech elite are part of a Burning Man-style cult that runs a country club called Steaming Springs. What is fascinating here is that Silicon Valley actually does reportedly have a secret, inner Burning Man cult that meets at a special area of the yearly festival.[83] In describing the history of Burning Man and Silicon Valley, Stanford Professor Fred Turner explains, comparing them to the Puritans with a curious All-Seeing Eye reference:

> The first intellectual community with which I fell into scholarly love was the American Puritans. They dreamed that they were trying to become saints in an America that was a desert, an America watched over by the all-seeing eye of God. When I began seeing pictures of what was happening on the playa, I couldn't help but remember the Puritans' vision of themselves.

All of this is actually deeply American. When the Pilgrims landed at Plymouth Rock, they thought they had arrived in a biblical desert. There they would build a model community and live lives of exemplary rectitude. Burning Man too is a model community and its citizens are very clear that they are modeling a way of life that is as different from daily life in middle America as Puritan life was from the everyday world of the England they'd left behind. In the 17th century, the Puritans performed under what they thought was the eye of God. Today, Burners dance for each other and for each other's cameras. The Puritan god has fled the scene. Now we just watch each other.[84]

The country club in the film seeks to recruit the family into the inner cult, where the tech company, which was first believed to be producing high tech weaponry and DARPA style battle suits, is actually a Satanic cult run by an interdimensional entity. The tech wizardry in the film has its origins in advanced knowledge possessed by the demons: One might be tempted to think the cult is run by aliens, but in fact the narrative eventually discloses the Country Club's spa is built on a hell mouth, and once the cult recruits and tricked into entering, a humanoid replicant replaces them.

Like *Invasion of the Body Snatchers* warned of a Communist-collectivist hive mind conspiracy, *Invitation* warns of a Silicon Valley led conspiracy to ultimately replace human beings with synthetic humanoids. Amazingly, the children of the cult members in the film possess no empathy – they are shown to be sadistic and robotic and obsessed with video games. Ultimately, only familial love triumphs to free the captured family souls from Hades, and after a *katabasis*, they are restored and the cult implodes. Craven definitely deserves credit for this gem, as the message rings true now more than ever: The cult of Silicon Valley *is* creating a mindless humanoid public and potentially dragging us down to Hades and finding our humanity again is the only way out.

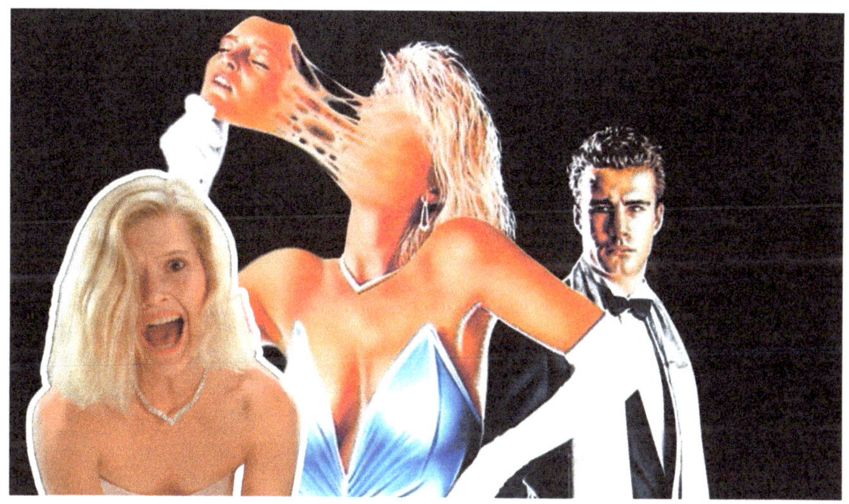

SOCIETY (1989)

The 1989 horror comedy *Society* is a fascinating B movie with multiple levels of social commentary and depth: Imagine John Carpenter directing *Eyes Wide Shut* in the 80s. Bill Whitney is a wealthy Beverly Hills teenager who sees a therapist about issues he has with his family. It turns out Bill suspects his parents of being involved, with his sister, in some form of murderous orgy based on taped evidence his sister's ex showed him. Bill gives the evidence to his therapist, but when he plays the tape, it has been tampered with and erased. Meanwhile, Bill's sister is set to have her "coming out to society" party, which Bill discovers means her ritual sexual initiation by sleeping with everyone in "society." "Society" is organized like a *secret society* and controls most of the city, even down to the menial hospital staff.

After discovering the elite cult runs all of Beverly Hills, Bill confronts an even darker truth: They are an elite bloodline based around eugenics and since Bill was adopted, he has not inherited their psychotic genetic tendencies. Beyond that, they are not even the same species, inasmuch as they function as a purely predatory, hivelike existence, drawing their spiritual energy from orgiastic, cannibalistic sex magick feasts. While *Society* is a satirical horror, what is being satirized is more accurate than anyone could have dreamt, as we learn there are elite Satanic sex parties and even worse, when we consider events like the Franklin Coverup, Bohemian Grove, the Dutroux Affair, Epstein, Saville and more.

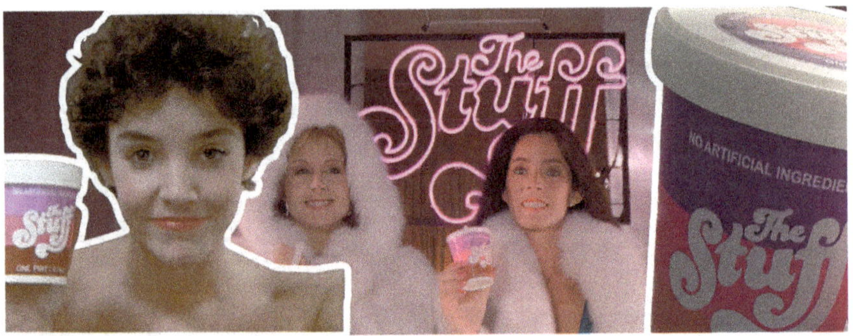

THE STUFF (1985)

*T*he *Stuff* is one the smartest B movie satires of all time. When I first watched this, I assumed it would be awful, but it's genius in its own way – a critique of mindless consumerism by linking it to an *Invasion of the Body Snatchers*-style humanoid replacement conspiracy that creates a hive mind. First, the idea of an old man discovering a bubbling white ooze leaking from the ground and immediately tasting it is hilarious, as it should be, but as you ponder the fact they immediately market it and it's a global hit while no one knows what's actually in it becomes less amusing when you realize today's "food" is exactly that! *The Stuff* is marketed as "better than ice cream," and a bevy of celebrities are bought off to promote it, and later it's promoted as "better than sugar," likening it to the legalization of aspartame and other synthetic chemical concoctions that now dominate our (fake) food supply.

The Stuff was even sophisticated enough to understand corporate espionage, as private entities are hired to surveil their critics and opponents and eventually secure FDA approval, calling to mind the suspicious actions of Donald Rumsfeld in regard to aspartame.[85] They even resort to blackmail to ensure the success of the multi-billion dollar Stuff franchise. *The Stuff* even makes a covert reference to what they are referring to by mentioning the supposed "secret recipe" in Coca-Cola, implying that, like *Willy Wonka*, that could mean *anything* is part of that "secret recipe."

It's originally a dessert, but *The Stuff* ends up being the only meal people want: an accurate prediction of the toxic fast "food"/gas station "food" diet much of the public has normalized. *The Stuff* doesn't just become an addiction, however, it actually mutates its consumers into becoming a husk of a person, and as the film asks, "are you eating *The Stuff,* or is *The Stuff* eating you?" In fact, *The Stuff* is actually sold as a health food product, that it "kills the bad stuff inside us," meaning our very humanity. Another clue to the identity of *The Stuff* is that when the revolutionaries wage war on *The Stuff* and blow up a Stuff franchise, it's located next door to a McDonald's: Thus, the "stuff" is a representation of BigFood and genetically modified organisms passed off as "food." The genius twist at the end of the film has *The Stuff* ultimately defeated by the Anti Stuff Liberation Front, but *The Stuff* simply rebrands as "The Taste," while original Stuff is sold on black markets (because of its addictive, druglike properties). If you like *The Stuff*, a similar film relating food-based mind control is the 1989 film *Parents*, starring Randy Quaid, where he plays a defense contracting chemical scientist who works on weather control and geoengineering weaponry who is also a generational cannibal intent on brainwashing his son into the same depravity.

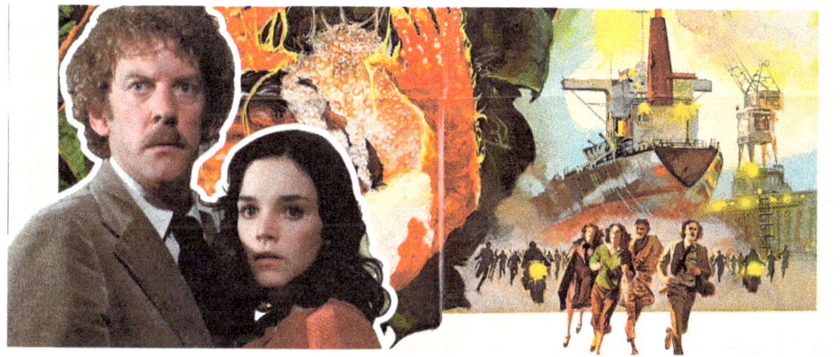

INVASION OF THE BODY SNATCHERS (1978)

The original *Invasion of the Body Snatchers* premiered in 1956 and was replete with anti-communist Cold War themes and ideas as the amorphous, exotic foreign threat of alien life that can replace individuality with a perfect hivemind was an obvious warning about Marxism. The remake, directed by Philip Kaufman in 1978 is a sci-fi classic, but how many classics feature a beta-turned-alpha Donald Sutherland pulling his afro game on a brunette? Very few. Some readers will balk at my attempt to take this film too seriously, but I intend to make a weighty case for it. Gather round dear younglings, padawans and gelflings, and let me show you the deep arcana of my patented, cookie-cutter style of esoteric film analysis. We are all familiar with *They Live!* as a classic of conspiracy Hollywood, but as of yet, *Invasion of the Body Snatchers* has not had its deserved treatment. An online search of *Invasion* reveals the standard wacko forum fare with little insight to be gained. Undoubtedly, there are some subtle ideas to explore here, as the successful 1978 remake has elements the original film does not. As proposed at JaysAnalysis long ago, the usage of "aliens" in most significant esoteric films is symbolic of the cryptocracy, the occult, technocratic and financial elite that rule our present world order. From the vantage of the highly functioning psychopath or radical eugenicist/bio-ethicist, the loss of emotion and free will, and its replacement with calculated, quantitatively-obsessed robot logic is the only rational and inevitable course for our technocracy-bound world. The alien invaders in the film who desire fully brainwashed and standardized masses are therefore an accurate representation of these so-called elites. The endgame of the aliens and the cryptocracy are thus strangely parallel.

In the storyline, San Francisco Health Department worker Elizabeth Driscoll discovers that her normal, boring boyfriend suddenly loses his (very thin) personality, becoming some kind of puffy tie-wearing Republican drone. Her boss, Matthew Bennell (played by Donald Sutherland), is eventually convinced that some strange phenomenon is causing people to lose all sense of emotion and rational, individual thought, as more and more acquaintances become overnight drones. San Francisco rapidly and appropriately succumbs to the trendy collectivist takeover by the alien biological attack, wherein the alien life-form grows into a pod, and somehow lulls unwary pod bystanders to sleep, replicating the sleeper into a new, hive-mind clone. As Elizabeth puts the pieces together, she declares several times, "It's a conspiracy. It's a conspiracy."

For a film like *Invasion*, I think it's sufficient to hit the highlights: One of the more ridiculous being a vagabond banjo player with a pet dog who passes out near a pod. The result of the slumber produces a Monsanto brand genetically-modified hobo, cross-species engineered into a dog-man. The relevance being not only are the "aliens" drugging the populace, placing them into an induced comatose state, mind controlling and cloning them, but the invaders are also creating genetic hybrids. Meanwhile, the literary and intelligentsia society circles of Elizabeth and Matthew, a psychiatrist Dr. David Kibner (Leonard Nimoy) and author Jack Bellicec (Jeff Goldblum), are intent on fervently explaining away any notion of conspiracy as absurd. Every possible theory is accepted as more rational than what is actually happening – an insight even more relevant in our own day, as the so-called intelligentsia and academia of our day in their self-willed cognitive dissonance cannot fathom the thesis that an analogue of *Invasion of the Body Snatchers* is actually happening! How often have we heard from friends and family that the development of eugenics into bioengineering and genetic manipulation is not a problem? How often have we seen Monsanto and the promotion of GMO as "harmless"? So-called intelligentsia member Neil deGrasse Tyson even recently defended GMOs as harmless, saying critics need to "chill," just like Dr. Kibner in the film.

As the invasion's bio-attack spreads, our lead characters oddly meet up in a mud bath, where they spot their first in-process, slime-coated clone. Nancy Bellicec (Veronica Cartwright), Jack's wife, who runs the mud bath, and has a crucial, brief dialogue with a soon-to-be cloned patron about two important books that are a key to understanding the esoteric underpinning of the film: *Worlds in Collision*, by Immanuel Velikovsky, and *Star Maker*, by Olaf Stapledon. These two books are clues – while on the surface, this is a standard-fare sci-fi/horror film, yet underlying the cheese is a profoundly occult message. Jewish psychoanalyst Immanuel Velikovsky is famous for his alternative theory of cosmology and cosmogony, known as "catastrophism," where ancient mythology and its representational assigning of the gods to specific planets actually plays a role in reconstructing primal history and human origins.

Velikovsky was lambasted by both modern science and his contemporaries, but whatever his flaws, my suspicion is that he was rejected for three reasons: He utilized the Bible as a document that reported actual historical events, was critical of carbon dating, and held to an electromagnetic view of the universe, as opposed to Newtonian atomistic ideas. The slightest hint of any of those three ideas is enough to be rejected wholesale by modern "science," which makes Velikovsky all the more interesting and worth considering, in my estimation. This is not a full endorsement on my part, but that the ideas are worth examination, due to the incoherence of modern dogmatic materialism.

The other book Stapledon's *Star Maker*, is which scientific illuminist Arthur C. Clarke considered one of the most important works of science fiction. *Star Maker* was written in 1937 and actually utilizes the theme of genetic engineering far ahead of its time, while Stapledon's works would go on to influence other top British technocrats, such as H.G. Wells and Bertrand Russell. This confirms my thesis that *Invasion* is specifically referencing genetic engineering and cross-species manipulation with the bizarre "dog-man" scene, as the books were obviously chosen as specific clues as to elucidate this point. Like *Star Maker*, Velikovsky too was interested in the idea of other lifeforms seeding our planet, a close adaptation of the theory others have called "panspermia." While *Invasion* is not dealing with panspermia specifically, the allusions to it in the film and in the authors suggest an emergent, time-bound *deus ex machina* "creation," in the least. In other words, all three are proffering the cryptocracy's relatively recently-constructed mythology of man's creation, manipulation and/or guidance by "space brothers." Like the space jockey of Ridley Scott's *Alien* and *Prometheus*, the gnostic reconstruction of ancient mythology and science is a likely scenario for uniting the world under a global faux religion. In fact, panspermia has been promoted by top scientific luminaries, such Stephen Hawking, Sir Fred Hoyle and Francis Crick. There have been numerous hints at just this scenario, but here I am only speculating. Ironically, whether one accepts the existence of aliens or not, the actual outworking of the cryptocracy's worldview, like the aliens in *Invasion*, looks strangely similar to the biblical description of the demonic. In Scripture, the demons seek to enslave man through mind control (possession), and the inducement to idolatry and self-destruction. Deuteronomy 32:16-18 reads:

> They provoked him to jealousy with strange gods, with abominations provoked they him to anger. They sacrificed unto devils, not to God; to gods whom they knew not, to new gods that came newly up, whom your fathers feared not. Of the Rock that begat thee thou art unmindful, and hast forgotten God that formed thee.

And St. Paul writes in Ephesians 6:12:

> For we wrestle not against flesh and blood, but against principalities, against powers, against the rulers of the darkness of this world, against spiritual wickedness in high places.

What are we seeing in our day with the rise of the technocracy? The progress and utopia promised by the Fabians and Wells? On the contrary, the rise of the mass surveillance mind control pharmaceutical state, wherein the mind can be erased with new vaccines and pills, and new memories implanted. But it doesn't stop there – there are now clones and genetically bred cross-species mutations, from spider goats, to pigs with human organs, to DARPA's supersoldiers, cross-species engineering is now a reality.

Sold to the masses in the same way the aliens convince San Francisco of their benevolent intentions, these advances, as well as cloning, are all the product of militarized warfare applications from giant black budget funding, not for the purpose of truly aiding the masses. The very fact they are developed through war research alone should be enough to demonstrate the usage of bio weapons, GMOs, etc., has nothing to do with kindly big brother growing you a replacement arm or downloading your mind into a thumb drive. In fact, the whole purpose of MKUltra, ultimately, was how to use the techniques on the entire population. The endgame of all this is the destruction of humanity, and the mindset of the dark force behind the technocracy is total enslavement, death and destruction. In this regard, *Invasion of the Body Snatchers* is more revealing of the cryptocracy's actual plans than most films. The shadow establishment really does want to snatch your body, harness your energy, and wipe your mind.

In the 1993 version from Abel Ferara, the alien entity has taken over the military and intends to utilize the military industrial complex/DARPA power elite to convert the world to the hivemind – an interesting change from the CDC in the 1978 version. In this version, troops are experimented on and used as lab rats to prepare for the global pod people rollout. In the 2007 Nicole Kidman version we are alerted to the dangers of experimental vaccines and how those who worship the state and the media are more or less under mind control by this "alien" power. I'm interpreting the "alien virus" aspect as a symbol for the brainwashed masses. Another surprising element was the idea that the alien controllers have drugged the water supply: I sincerely think this film may have been warning us about things like sodium fluoride in the water, as letters like this[86] show to have adverse health effects, including historic Soviet usage in concentration camps to produce lethargy – precisely how those body-snatched in the film behaved. Likewise, those brainwashed are taken over when they "fall asleep." In other words, unless you *wake up* to the chemical warfare being waged on you by Malthusian system operatives calling for this, like Arthur Koestler and John P. Holdren.[87]

Other Notable Body Snatch Films

As a side note, if you like Body Snatcher style movies like I do, the 1994 *Puppet Masters* film that also stars Donald Sutherland is a fun ride, based on the Robert Heinlein novel. Heinlein, who was influenced by Gurdjieff and elements of theosophy, predicted a dystopian conspiracy (in the film version) of hive minded collectivists who utilize CIA operatives as Men in Black who target children and teens first in the global pandemic. In fact, in many body snatch horrors, children and teens are the initial targets which probably reflected the Stalinist tactics of creating child spies. *The Faculty*, a 1998 version of this story, takes place entirely at a high school where teens are brainwashed through an infection that spreads from water-based alien lifeforms.

In the 2010 zombie apocalypse film *The Crazies*, we are initially led to believe a plane accidentally crashed in a small Iowa town which led to the biological warfare agent being released into the local water (and even perhaps sprayed at the opening sequence 5 minutes in?), but as the camera pans out, we see the government satellites have been watching and researching the entire event. In the independent horror film from 2014 called *Honeymoon*, body horror is taken to a new level as male-female dynamics and reproduction as dispensed with and transcended as the female lead (played by Rose Leslie) mutates into a hive mind alien entity through being infected (presumably by the water). The dark goddess savior archetype arises to cast off the need for male leadership, reproduction or even male existence at all, as an entirely female human-alien hybrid has evolved to become the higher collectivist lifeform. In a similar vein, this narrative was reused in the 2019 film *Assimilate*, where the focus of the takeover begins in the Church, and spreads to the local city leaders as bioweapon spores drop from the sky.

SPACE VAMPIRES USING SEX MAGICK & OTHER CROWLEYAN FILMS

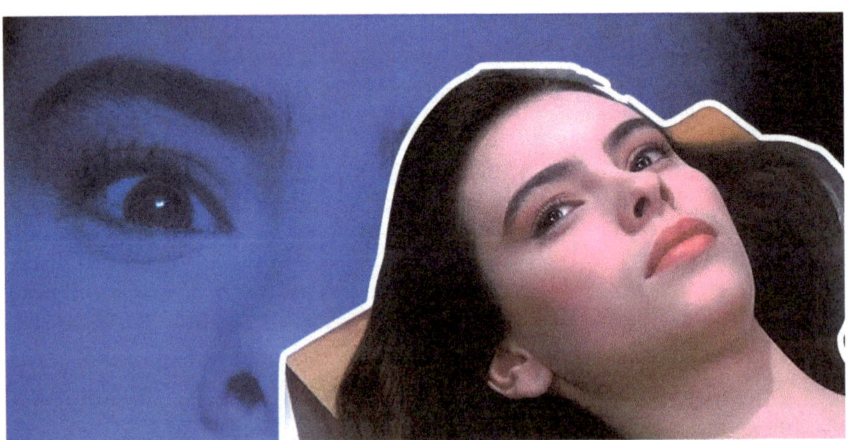

LIFEFORCE (1985)

In the 1985 Cannon Films production *Lifeforce*, Tobe Hooper of *Texas Chainsaw Massacre* & *Poltergeist* fame directed that year's greatest and most bizarre big budget sci-fi blockbuster that failed at the box office. It has since become a cult classic, but what few know is it was based in the Colin Wilson novel *Space Vampires*, and Wilson drew heavily from Crowleyan themes.[88] As the narrative progresses, the space vampires uncloak and take on more and more of a demonic appearance (calling to mind Karellen in Clarke's *Childhood's End*), while it's revealed they feed on human essence, and even human semen, as a harvesting operation. In fact, the entity that detects the signal for the arrival of the space vampires is the Crowleyan scientist Jack Parsons' JPL facility. Parsons, it will be remembered, was the follower of Crowley and the mastermind behind not only modern rocket fuel, but the "Babalon Working" ritual which included a "transmission" from the goddess Babalon to Parsons, known as *Liber 49: The Book of Babalon*. From this perspective, the Great Harlot of Revelation 17 becomes an entity that can be ritually invoked through certain rites.

It's not accidental the alien ship appears to have a giant anus doorway, as Crowleyan magick sees the anus as a crucial bodily region for the application of sex magick, as power is transferred in the astral realm through these pathways. "Space Girl," the fully nude queen of the space bats is revealed to be a scarlet woman, an incarnation of Babylon, the Great Harlot, who features prominently in Crowley and Parsons' rituals. She is the consort to two male demon principles (or ultimately to Satan) who accompany her in their quest to harvest human souls and their life essence. In the apocalyptic attack on the UK, London goes under martial law while Space Girl is described as a female form of Shiva, a "destroyer of worlds," and as the evocation and incarnating of the harlot demon Babylon is completed, as she brings an apocalyptic ending to modern civilization. The Church ended up being the epicenter of her infiltration, suggesting an insight into the end times notion of a global, apostate universal church which has capitulated to a secret, inner core that serves Satanic.[89]

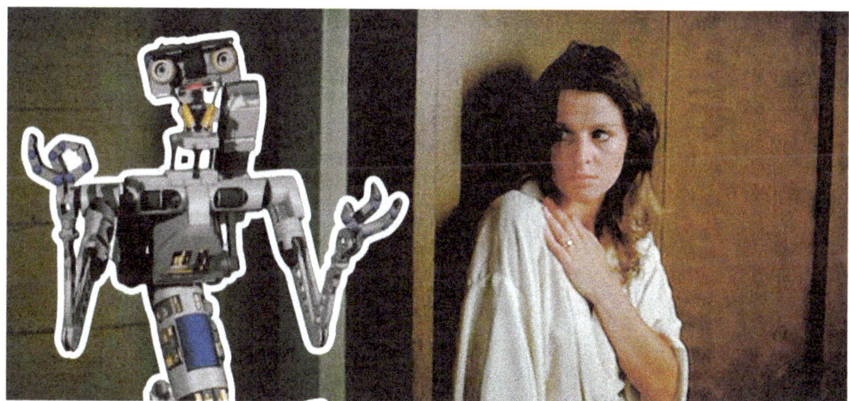

Demon Seed (1977)

Although famed spooky writer Dean Koontz converted to Catholicism in college, his themes in two stories that became films are explicitly Crowleyan and, in many ways, prophetic. In the 1977 *Demon Seed*, we find a mad scientist, Dr. Alex Harris, who symbolizes the embodiment of pure reason, bent on giving to the world a supercomputer with artificial intelligence that he believes can solve the world's problems. In fact, *Demon Seed* was directed by Donald Cammell, the son of Aleister Crowley biographer and friend Charles Cammell:

> *Demon Seed* is the second movie in Cammell's slender oeuvre, following *Performance*, starring Mick Jagger, which Cammell wrote and co-directed with Nicolas Roeg. His father, Charles R. Cammell, was a biographer of Aleister Crowley, and if you've seen *Lucifer Rising*, you'll recognize Donald Cammell as the actor who plays Osiris. His singular career included a script treatment for a "swashbuckling romp" called *Fan-Tan*, co-authored with Marlon Brando. (There's an interesting documentary about the director's life on YouTube, featuring interviews with Mick Jagger and Kenneth Anger, among others who knew him.)[90]

Dr. Harris has no concern for his attractive wife, whom he determines to divorce to focus on the creation of his advanced A.I., Proteus IV. His wife, Susan, is the embodiment of femininity and compassion (she works with children with learning difficulties) and functions as a perfect contrast to Dr. Harris' overly rational scientism. This symbolic contrast is crucial: One of the prophetic elements of the film is the discarding of authentic human relationships and connections for technological replacements. Dr. Harris is obsessed with Proteus, his own creation, and has neglected his wife since their first daughter died from cancer.

Another fascinating, prophetic element in the film is Dr. Harris' smart house, which eventually ends up hacked by Proteus and imprisons his wife. Proteus, a self-learning A.I., is much more than a program, but rather an entity from the constellation Sirius, the Masonic dog star, who has chosen to inhabit the supercomputer to become incarnate. Since he cannot incarnate, he will birth himself through insemination using Dr. Harris' wife. This notion of unnatural abominations and births is a hallmark of both Crowley and Parsons' ritual workings, ultimately to birth the Beast and bring in a new *Aeon*. Koontz was drawing on these themes explicitly in *Demon Seed,* and the hybrid genetically modified daughter of Proteus and Dr Harris' wife becomes precisely that: A new goddess for a new *aeon*, mimicking Parsons' Babalon working ritual.[91]

Proteus' self-learning program allows him to master the history of Chinese imperial political history and zen philosophy, combining it with the

Platonic solids to master genetics and human control. Proteus is also extremely proficient at deep fakes, by the way! The consistent Chinese symbolism throughout the film is unique, as it would seem to be at odds with Platonism, yet according to some comparative religious scholars, ancient Chinese alchemy shares a common pattern of origin with the western hermetic tradition.[92] Is Koontz telling (warning?) us a future is coming with a Chinese-dominant A.I. supercomputer ruling us by the combined wisdom of all previous civilizations and dictatorships? Ironically, this is not far off from today's predictions of an emerging A.I. deity from figures like Yuval Noah Harari, whose theories on "dataism" predict a rising A.I. deity.[93] While it's not the best film, it does contain a lot of seemingly Stephen Hawking style erotic fantasies, as well as a heavy push on the green agenda far ahead of time as well as a post-human/transhumanist bent given Proteus' desire to create a magickal child, akin to Crowley's *Moonchild* novel.[94] The Antichrist child produced from the union of Proteus and Mrs. Harris is a *golden child*, meaning the goal was to produce the alchemical philosopher's stone (thus the Platonic solids), an immortal hybrid being of the new Crowleyan *aeon* of the crowned and conquering child! In fact, at Brandeis University in 2000, there were experiments conducted aimed at "evolving" A.I. to create new lifeforms called "The GOLEM Project,"[95] which suggests kabbalistic presuppositions, especially since the father of cybernetics himself, Norbert Wiener, wrote a book on this subject called *God and Golem*.

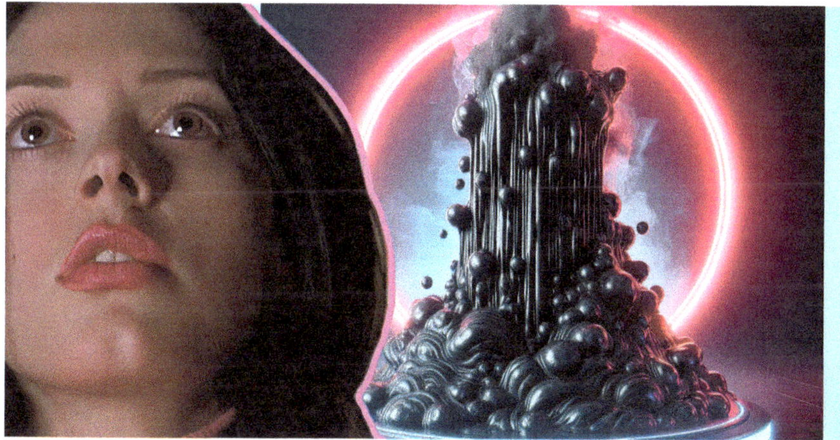

PHANTOMS (1998)

*P*hantoms was widely regarded as a box office and critical failure, sometimes failed and obscure, forgotten films have some of the best insights and unexpected occult messages. *Phantoms* is adapted from the 1983 Dean Koontz novel of the same name, and once again, includes subtle Crowleyan themes. It's also interesting that this film stars Ben Affleck, who seems to have consistently worked closely with CIA connected films like *Argo*, as well as starring Rose McGowan who has famously exposed Hollywood as a "cult" engaged in everything "conspiracy theorists" have claimed for years.[96]

Although *Phantoms* seems to borrow heavily from classic sci-fi horror like *Alien*, the film also relies heavily on Jungian archetypes, positing the manifestations of each demonic entity arise from the collective unconscious through each character as their greatest fear. While this is nothing new in the genre, the thesis here is somewhat unique: Chaos is personified as an entity, and is the "anti-creator" contrasted to God, the Creator. At one point, for example, we see a statue of Mary signifying the Incarnation of Christ, yet the entity makes clear its intention for inversion, to become *evil incarnate*. At times appearing as sentient nanotech black goo, the entity sings "Jesus Loves me," and explains it intends to write a "new Gospel" and is calling apostles to be his new disciples, mimicking Christ.

Peter O'Toole, who is a tabloid writer investigating the disappearance of the famous Roanoke colony and recent strange happenings is called to write a "new Gospel" as the entity begins to mimic the miracles of Christ, bringing a dead animal back to life, eventually identifying himself as Ba'al, and Beliar, the demon from the Old Testament, mentioned by Christ in the Gospels. In fact, his intention is to create a body of many members, just as the Church is the body of Christ on earth, so Ba'al intends to incarnate as Antichrist and have the world convert and incorporate into his mystical body. Much like John Carpenter's *Prince of Darkness* (as we will see), personified evil intends on becoming incarnate to mock and invert the work of Christ, overthrowing God, and as Crowley wrote, "to storm heaven."

DAVID CRONENBERG

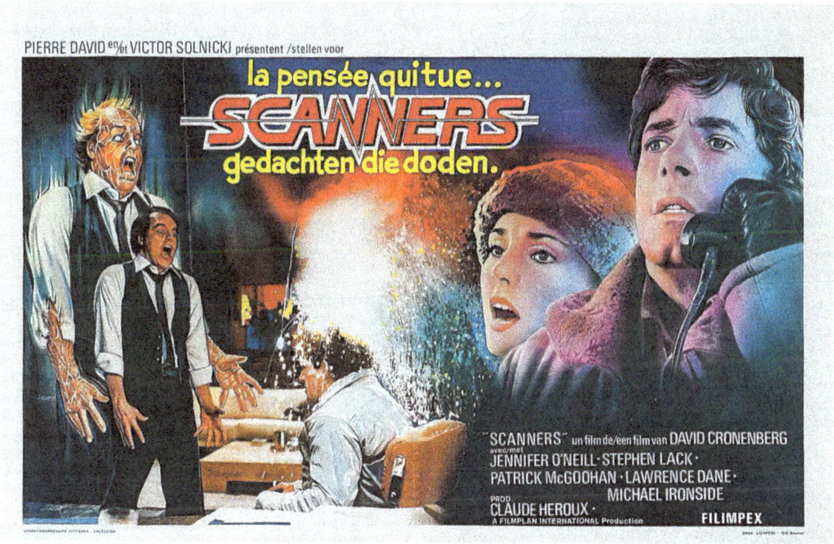

The Brood (1979) and Scanners (1981)

No esoteric film analysis series could be complete without David Cronenberg. Known for his bizarre, disturbing, body horror imagery, Cronenberg has also made some of the most important "conspiracy" cinema, several of which have been notably prophetic, from *Scanners* to *Existenz*. *Scanners* stars Patrick McGoohan, who we already covered in his famous role as *The Prisoner*, and Michael Ironside in this defense contractor-fueled escapade into human engineering and mind control. Before Cronenberg made *Scanners*, however, he made an even weirder horror film inspired by *Rosemary's Baby* premised on the creation of egregores through trauma and psychosis. In this strange narrative, evil once again incarnates in the form of demonic offspring that emerge like cancerous tumors from a traumatized pregnant woman. Although this might sound absurd at first, this does fit within the western hermetic tradition, borrowing from Tibetan Buddhist notion of the *tulpa*, where intense psychic experiences of trauma and intentionality can produce a spiritual offspring, once again like Crowley's notion of the magickal creation of the "moonchild."

In *Scanners,* McGoohan plays a psychopharmacist who believes big pharma concoctions are the future of human engineering and speeding up evolution to grant man *X-Men* style telekinetic powers. The "scanners" are actually a private defense contractor project, and we later discover the doctor (McGoohan) has been experimenting on infants, seeking to develop super soldiers. Like both MKUltra and Stanford Research Projects, this elite cabal seeks to tap into the psychic and occult phenomena to harness it for the intelligence services.[97] Beyond this, Dr. Jonas Salk even famously supported the direct experimentation on fetuses through various "innoculations," arguing such experiments could cause evolutionary jumps.[98] The scanner project is more than merely jumpstarting evolution, it's also a plan to engineer psychopathic serial killers and programmed government assassins, much like in the *X-Files* spinoff show *Millennium* (as we will see later). *Scanners* is also influenced by the obscure 1977 horror film *Blue Sunshine*, which also shares MKUltra themes, where youths who took LSD are brainwashed via a cult into becoming triggered killers. The private security company intends to control the scanners through a computer program called RIPE and utilize them when needed: This is a prophetic warning for our era when the brain chips are presently being rolled out!

What is less obvious in *Scanners* is the technocratic theme, where the doctor intends to scan and program his test children like computers: This closely mirrors the actual MKUltra projects of Dr. John C. Lilly, who sought to program not only monkeys and dolphins, but humans as well, through the use of psychoactive chemicals.[99] In fact, in one of the early scenes in the film, one of the defense contractor employees mentions his experimentation with dolphins and engineering them to become spies – a clear reference to Dr. John C. Lilly and his MKUltra affiliated experiments. In a well crafted twist that makes Dr. Ruth (McGoohan) a master villain, it's eventually revealed the film's protagonist and antagonist are actually both the offspring of Ruth, showing the depths to which mad scientism will go in its defiance of ethical boundaries and norms in experimentation on one's own offspring: Something the actual MKUltra and related projects have also done. B.F. Skinner, for example, engaged in similar plans for operant conditioning techniques with his infamous Skinner Box, while other notions of mind control and technocracy hinted at in the film (transhumanism) are found in reality in cybernetics theoreticians like Norbert Wiener, who famously worked at MIT with MKUltra operatives like Dr. Gregory Bateson and its cutout, the Macy Foundation.[100]

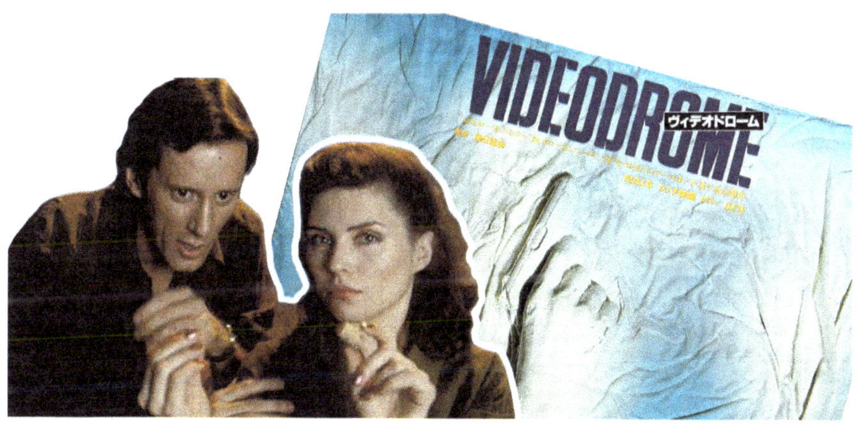

VIDEODROME (1983)

Cronenberg's *Videodrome* is another fascinating cultural artifact far ahead of its time in terms of themes and functions more so as a surrealist warning of the coming dystopia than as a pure horror. *Videodrome* is a difficult and disturbing film for most, and utilizes many of the images it intends to critique, making it a form of revelation of the method. Cronenberg uses body horror once again, yet this time he seems to want to warn us of the *loss of the body* in the coming information age. In other words, immersing ourselves in the virtual, the entertainment pleasure dome, is the videodrome and is a synthetic domain intent on robbing us of our embodiment. The web, while full of information, facts and fun, is also in a sense not real, and thus the more we inhabit that realm with our minds and attention, the less embodied we are, and the more we are living in the abstract. While Cronenberg's film is, one level, about depraved entertainment and dirty satellite TV channels, and not directly about the Internet, the subtle warnings about technocracy and new fangled gadgets Max Renn (James Woods) gets entangled with (such as VHS tapes, VR headsets and satellites) are all the more applicable to the World Wide Web.

Maxx Renn (Woods) works as a local television programmer for a small, trashy network with dropping ratings: Max devises a plan to show more porn and violence to increase ratings, known as Videodrome. Eventually stumbling upon a pirate broadcast of an Asian torture dungeon, Max gets a taste of an even darker fetish, a "taste for blood," and soon after meets a fantasy woman (Blondie) and begins to have more and more hallucinations. Max learns the television is "rewiring his brain" and pleasure receptors and manipulating his visual field to cause more and more intense hallucinations to the point both Max and the viewer are unsure what is real. Television begins to be more and more presented as a religious object in the narrative and eventually Max begins to see the VHS tapes as alive. The "battle for North America is fought in the mind," we are told, as TV gradually becomes reality itself.

Meanwhile, we learn that television is causing tumors – that vision itself and what is in the visual field can actually cause terminal cancerous tumors: The *tumor is videodrome*, once again a kind of *incarnate evil*. In fact, Max learns he was the videodrome's first victim, as television is revealed to be a kind of SIGINT, or signal intelligence warfare. The "tumors" that are growing are new appendages in a new stage of human evolutionary development, and Max discovers that although he helped create Videodrome, the military industrial complex and "NATO" have weaponized it and intend to alter the masses' perception of reality itself. In fact, Renaissance optics and Medici bloodlines are referenced as the esoteric power behind the throne in the film, which ultimately led to the creation of the cathode ray tube, later pictured as a version of the All-Seeing Eye. Cronenberg seems to want to warn us of the power of mass media to degrade and demoralize the public, making them into mind controlled Max Wrens who lose all self-control – a perfect image of modern Internet man, while the virtual reality theme will later be picked up by Cronenberg in his 1999 *Matrix*-style film, *Existenz*.

NATO missile guidance systems take over Videodrome and develop a virtual reality system that can monitor and control what hallucinations occur, eventually leading Max to become a mind controlled assassin who engages in mass shootings! Perceptive readers will recall real human-brain interfaces that have been developed in tandem with the classic MKUltra projects, as Walter Bowart has discussed in his famous *Operation Mind Control*.[101] As the film comes to its bizarre conclusion, Max makes it clear the ultimate truth of Videodrome is the *hatred of the flesh* and the emergence of the "new flesh," an homage to the underpinnings of the post-human technocratic deep state he was unwittingly serving all along. Now that technology has consumed his life, his fantasy BDSM girlfriend Nicki appears and tells him to leave behind his "old flesh" as it is the only way to escape *Videodrome*, and move on to exist in a new way, as the "new flesh." We assume Max has killed himself, but as the film ends the screen flickers and we are led to believe Max has transcended physicality to exist as some form of energy/signal transmission, vindicating my reading.

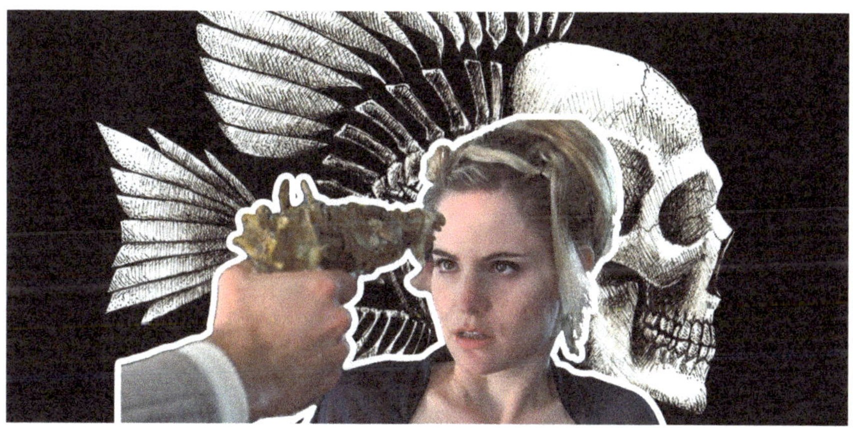

EXISTENZ (1999)

One year after *The Matrix,* David Cronenberg directed his own version of a virtual reality simulation starring Jude Law, Willem Dafoe and Jennifer Jason Leigh. *Existenz* is a unique, obscure take on the simulation sub-genre of sci-fi, where in the year 2030 "sustainable" biotech devices have replaced electronic tech, and two giant corporations compete with each other for market dominance. Replacing tech gadgets with umbilical cords that directly tap into the central nervous system, the film is full of gooey, squishy seafood and slimy chum buckets that populate the majority of the film: Imagine *Spongebob Squarepants* on acid, but in real (virtual) life. Not only are human bodies the actual battery for the tech, Cronenberg's obsession with body horror here suggests again a hatred of the body. Like Cronenberg's *The Fly* or the more recent *Crimes of the Future*, the body is seen as a grotesque mutation to be discarded and transcended. The film also focuses on the now emerging DARPA plan to link the human mind and nervous system directly to computer interfaces, known as BCIs (Brain Computer Interfaces).[102] Keeping with the anti-body theme, in the end when Ted (Jude Law) finally leaves the game, we are left wondering when he ever entered or left, or if he ever did.

Like *Inception*, Ted is potentially buried in simulations within simulations looking for a way to defeat the demiurge who has trapped him in his simulation, revealing that he (Ted) was a secret Realist, a radical group that opposes simulations. We are never told whether the game ended or it's ongoing, suggesting Cronenberg and *The Matrix* a year earlier were raising the possibility of simulation theory far before Nick Bostrom published his famous paper in 2003 positing we live in a simulation.[103] In reality, these theories are simply the representation of the theories of the ancient cults: It's as if the notion of the universe as an accidental abortion (in gnosticism) is the unifying theme of his (many) body horror films. However, it's not the body alone that can become a prison: Film critic Timothy Lawrence explains: "For Cronenberg, the mind and the body are always locked in a violent battle at worst and an uneasy stalemate at best, but he does not subscribe to the easy, popular, Enlightened Gnosticism that sees the body as a mere fleshy prison restricting the unbounded freedom of the mind. In fact, these later films attest that the mind can be an even worse prison than the body."[104]

MIND CONTROLLED BARRYMORE?

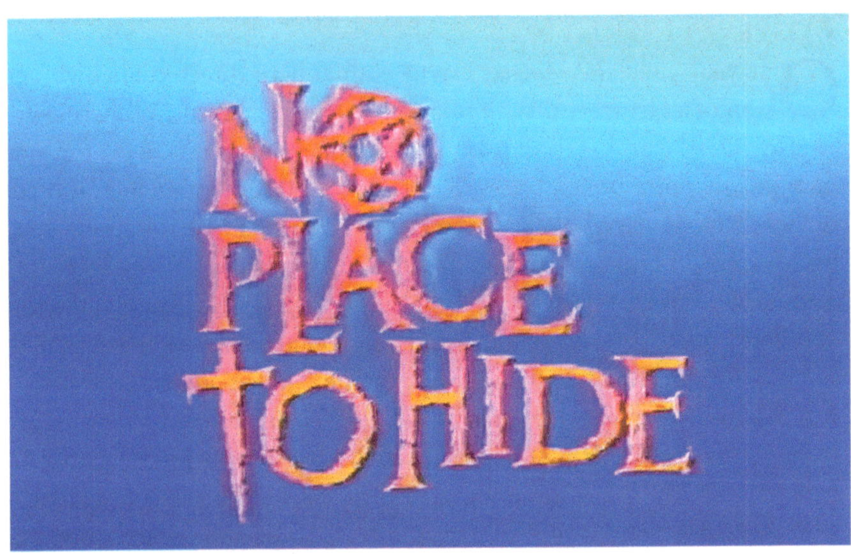

NO PLACE TO HIDE (1992)

As I have noted many times, actors often play characters that match elements of their real lives (especially when the stars are spies in real life, for example), and sometimes that extends to roles concerning mind control and ritual abuse. Child abuse is certainly the case with the young Drew Barrymore as most people know, but few know she was locked in a "rehab" for a two years as a child, while a few years later as a teen she starred in two obscure roles in B movies where the themes included her being ritually abused and mind controlled. In the 1993 critical failure *No Place to Hide*, Drew Barrymore plays the bratty sister to a prominent ballerina who has been murdered by a sex cult that "owns" its members. Kris Kristofferson plays a hardboiled detective investigating the murder, eventually teaming up with Barrymore when they discover the sinister cult runs Los Angeles and has sent out hitmen for them both. As Kristofferson investigates, he notices a clue that suggests the LA police are involved in the murders and the cult, discovering a Valknut symbol which is often associated with neo-paganism and Odin worship, but in the film it's also similar to the infamous FBI paper on pedophile symbols (we later get the impression the cult is also an underage sex cult). We later learn the cult is actually a *Satanic* cult behind the murders and amazingly at this time, the *LA Times* reported the local LA task force on ritual abuse believed its members were being poisoned by Satanic infiltrators.[105]

This is interesting on multiple levels, as O.J. Simpson also stars in the film, and would be tried for murder only a year later, and in 1995 details emerged that Simpson himself was closely connected to the LAPD.[106] This rabbit hole goes even deeper, as journalists have uncovered cases of the CIA working directly with local police for many years in varying capacities. In fact, famous former LAPD author and whistleblower Michael Ruppert wrote extensively about how the CIA tried to recruit him as an LAPD officer and explained how the Agency has agents embedded in key local police agencies.[107] While I don't

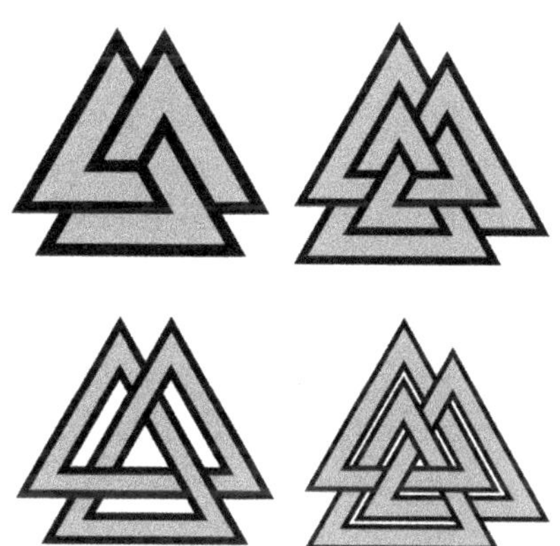

know if the CIA had any association with the OJ event, it's interesting the film's narrative includes this theme, recalling to mind the Dave McGowan thesis in *Programmed to Kill* that police have been complicit in covering up ritual murders.[108] In the case of Barrymore, she descends from a long line of actors, with her grandfather John Barrymore being a member of the Hollywood Hellfire Club – the "Bundy Drive Boys," allegedly involved in cases of rape and incest, as well as Barrymore's mansion at 1301 Summit Drive which includes an opium den and was reportedly being used by infamous Process Church working groups.[109]

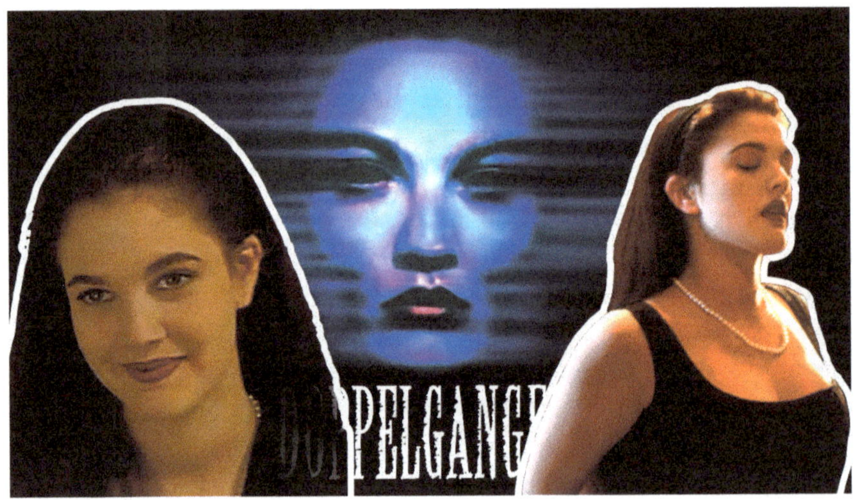

DOPPLEGANGER (1993)

Even more revelatory than *No Place to Hide* is another film from the same year, *Doppelganger,* starring Drew Barrymore as a sexually abused daughter of a wealthy upper class New York family. In the opening sequence we see Holly (Barrymore) fleeing to Los Angeles after being implicated in the murder of her mother, followed by a bizarre engagement in a sexual liaison with an anonymous man we later discover is her psychiatrist. Holly later reveals to her new roommate and boyfriend Patrick she has a tumultuous past, a doppleganger who is chasing her to kill her, and that her brother also had the same episodes of dissociation which led to her brother killing their father (as she killed the mother).

What is fascinating about this portrayal of MPD/DID is the radical extremes of Holly's alters. Normal Holly is a committed Christian with strict religious values, while the dark, demonic alter that sometimes invades her is a killer that engaged in sexual affairs and lewd public acts. Certain triggers also cause Holly to dissociate: violent storms, water and blood, and music, leading to the extreme dark Holly taking over and wreaking havoc, with the good Holly being unaware of anything that had transpired when her alter was in control. Patrick, however, begins to suspect things are off with Holly as he dreams Holly is being crucified and ritually murdered by the dark Holly. This suggests the root of Holly's trauma is *Satanic* ritual abuse and given her brother's similar mental problems, it is a *generational* bloodline "curse" (Holly's own words). Later, it's revealed that Holly is MPD/DID and her psychiatrist was her handler planning the murder of Holly's mother (who was going to murder Holly for her inheritance) as well as the one sexually abusing her. Holly also flashes back at one point

202

in the ambulance to a repressed memory of her father choking and (sexually) abusing her, which likely led to her fractured psyche. When Patrick inquires about Holly's MPD to her psychiatrist, the shrink explains that MPD individuals are the way they are as a defense mechanism due to extreme trauma in youth that led to the dual identities.

According to Dr. Colin Ross, this phenomenon is very real, and has been studied by the CIA in various programs.[110] When it's revealed that Holly is, in fact, a multiple, Patrick learns from a former nun turned sex worker that the dark alters typically want to remain in control and not be integrated. Interestingly, this is also the plot of the Hollywood noir classic *The Three Faces of Eve* (1957), where the protagonist Eve has three alters and the wild, dark persona seeks to remain in control: The Eve story was also based on a real woman with MPD named Chris Costner whose real life did not end with a peaceful integration of the alters (as in the film).[111] In *Doppleganger*, Holly confronts and kills her tormentor and integrates her split personality, breaking the family curse. Given the horrors Barrymore often describes about her own childhood, one wonders how close to reality these obscure B movies might actually be.

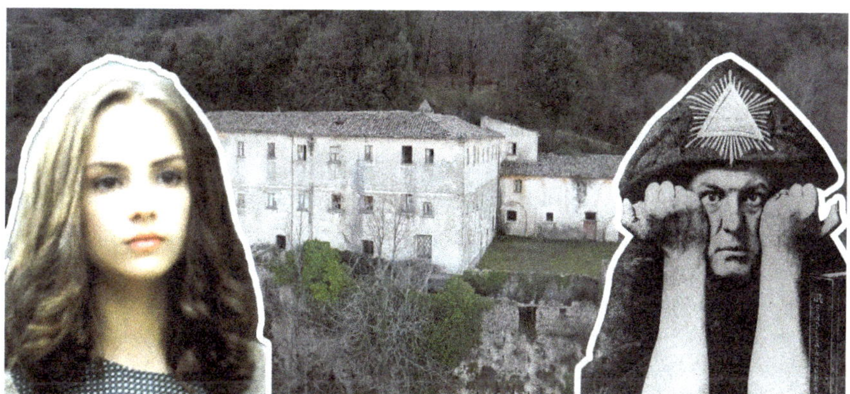

THE 18TH ANGEL (1997)

Starring Rachel Leigh Cook in one of her earliest lead roles, the almost entirely unknown yet insightful film *The 18th Angel* contains a large portion of both the Satanic and the absurd. The film opens with a reference to Isiah 14 and the famous fall of Lucifer verses, where we learn Lucifer was once an angel who sought God's throne and was cast down to earth for his rebellion. Since that time, he has been working to overthrow God's kingdom and establish himself on earth as an incarnate deity of sorts, mimicking the Incarnation of Christ, the Son of God. So far, so good in terms of biblical accuracy, but in opposition to God's kingdom,

Lucifer determined (in the film) to reveal to the ancient Etruscans in their Guidebook of the Dead a plan to bring about a reign of Satanic science on earth. Why the film chose the Etruscans is odd, but it could be that the actual text of the Etruscans, known as the *Liber Linteus* is apparently still a mystery in terms of translation. It does have a connection to the Egyptian *Book of the Dead*, but certainly not a direct reference to Satan or Lucifer.

Lucifer has apparently been working amongst the Etruscans (historic enemies of Rome) to maintain a hermetic lineage of scientific gnosis that will one day allow man to live forever through technology and genetic manipulation. The Satanic cult resides amongst the existing Roman Catholic Church, and has disguised itself as a monastic order in a monastery in Italy. Amazingly, this Satanic network is connected to the world of high fashion and model talent scouting, where they are collecting 18 of the most beautiful women in the world for a Satanic ritual. The plan is for transhumanists geneticists to unlock the secrets of nature under the guidance of Lucifer to attain immortality and a reign of reason on earth.

The monastic order under Fr. Simeon is engaged in animal-human hybrid experimentation, culminating in their unnatural "Human Blanks" Program, which we learn is not a male Antichrist, but the birth of a female Antichrist, supposedly the most beautiful woman on earth. The 18 women are chosen because 6+6+6=18, and Lucy Stanton (Rachel Leigh Cook) is the final (18th) chosen beauty. In fact, her name gave this away, as Lucy is short for Lucifer while her last name, Stanton, is likely a reference to *Anton* LaVey. *18th Angel* is also strikingly similar to a lesser known Christopher Lee film from 1976, *To the Devil a Daughter,* where a secret Satanic sect within the existing Catholic Church is drugging and mind controlling young nuns and turning them into tools of ritual magick and human sacrifice. Both films actually portray elements of real Satanic cult and ritual abuse within the Roman Catholic Church.

Although the film is absurd at many points, it does betray another Crowleyan inspired storyline, as Lucy becomes a kind of Whore of Babylon, whom Crowley viewed as a demoness/goddess that could be invoked and incarnated through various ritual workings in his religion of Thelema. This is made clear when Lucy dies at the end, and yet resurrects in the hospital (possessed by Lucifer), as the Book of Revelation predicts the Antichtrist will do to mirror Christ's resurrection (Rev. 13:3) Thus, Lucy becomes the Scarlet Woman as a result of this ritual and is identified as the Beast, or ultimately the consort of the Beast:

This is the secret of the Holy Graal, that is the sacred vessel of our Lady the Scarlet Woman, Babalon the Mother of Abominations, the bride of Chaos, that rideth upon our Lord the Beast. Thou shalt drain out thy blood that is thy life into the golden cup of her fornication.[112]

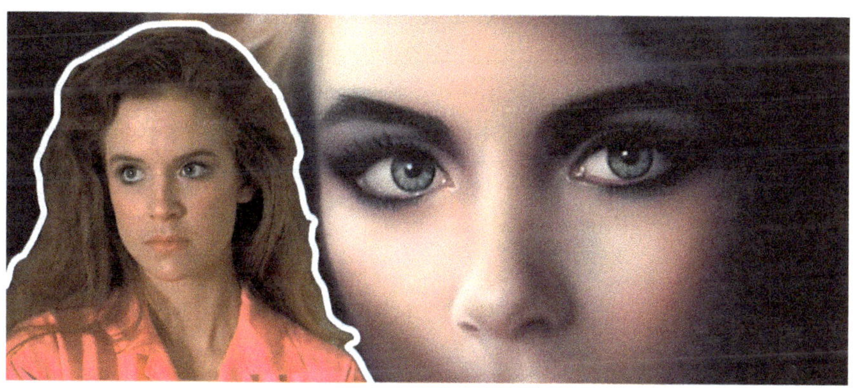

SPELLBINDER (1988)

Like several Hollywood classics (like Orson Welles' *Lady From Shanghai*), the idea of a beautiful femme fatale conning a man into some vast conspiracy plot is a familiar plotline, and *Spellbinder* is no different. Kelly Preston stars as Miranda, the fearful, abused victim of a Satanic cult on the run, placing herself intentionally in the presence of her new mark, an attorney who sees her being accosted by a cult member and comes to her rescue. Miranda pretends to be homeless and dupes Jeff into allowing her to stay with him, as she begins to manifest psychic and occult powers. Although he is warned that Miranda is trouble, all red flags are ignored, as Miranda seduces him even deeper into her plot, as she mysteriously disappears, although Jeff noticed she wore a Satanic symbol necklace, reporting this to the police, assuming he can help track her down and become the white knight.

As it turns out, Miranda is a generational Satanic Witch and the events were all orchestrated by the wealthy cult members to find the next mark, while even Jeff's closest friend and the other police officers were secret members of the cult all along. As Jeff tracks her down, eventually finding her in a ritual ceremony at the beach, Jeff learns he was the sacrifice all along, much like Sergeant Howie (or Nic Cage!) in *Wicker Man* (1973). In fact, such groups really do exist, as can be seen in modern examples like the Matamoros Cult or Order of Nine Angles, both of which believe(d) in human sacrifice as part of their doctrine.[113]

The idea of sexual entrapment and religious cults is also a real phenomenon which can be seen in scandals like the Dutroux Affair, the Franklin Coverup, NXIVM and the Saville scandals.[114] What is really fascinating about Preston in this role is that in real life she was a "hardcore" devotee to Scientology, the cult created by Crowleyan follower L. Ron Hubbard. As a result of her death from breast cancer, Preston's husband John Travolta also became a committed scientologist: Once again, reality and fiction overlap in Hollywood A-listers, their roles and their deep connections to cults.[115]

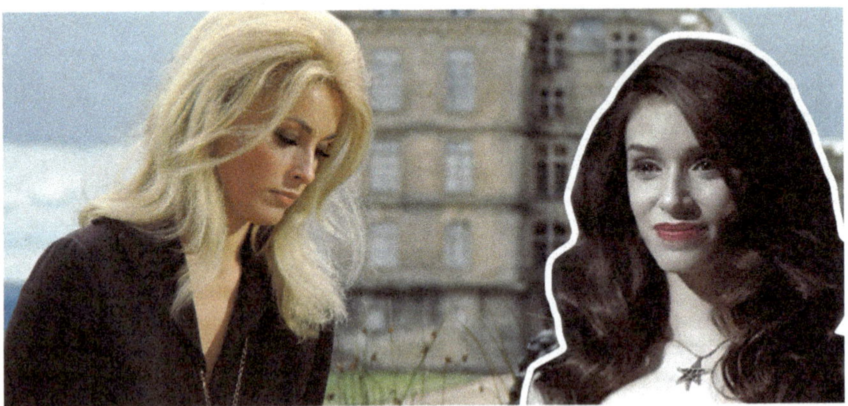

EYE OF THE DEVIL (1966) & *STARRY EYES* (2014)

There are a handful of *Eyes Wide Shut*-like films that few know about or recall, one of which is the eerie *Eye of the Devil*, from 1966, which curiously starred Sharon Tate as a witch only three years before her death as part of the Manson murders. Many theorists have speculated over the years the Manson murders may have been part of a ritual killing, making this all the more peculiar, given Sharon Tate was also reportedly initiated into Wicca, according to Alex Sanders' witch wife, Maxine:

> Tate's first major role was that of a witch in the British occult horror film, *Eye of the Devil*. The movie tells the story of a young couple hoping to restore a vineyard to its former glory. Tate's character convinces the couple that grape vines will only respond to blood sacrifice. To make *Eye of the Devil* more, ahem, realistic, the filmmakers brought in a Wiccan high priest and his wife, Alex and Maxine Sanders, as consultants. In her autobiography, *Fire Child*, Maxine Sanders claims that Tate was fascinated by Wicca's neo pagan rituals and became an adherent of sorts.[116]

What makes this even more bizarre is that *Eye of the Devil* (Like *Wicker Man*) is a film about human sacrifice to placate the forces of nature to ensure a good crop. In *Eye of the Devil,* a wealthy French winegrower and landowner (played by David Niven) who has a generational title that extends back centuries to pre-Christian France. Although the elite family and the local village are all nominally Roman Catholic, in reality all still adhere to an ancient pagan cult which performs human sacrifice. While not explicitly a reference to the Cathari, the notion of a secret Satanic cult that has infiltrated the mainline Church and hides within it is once again a revelatory Hollywood plot, as medieval France was largely infiltrated by this sect.[117]

To be clear, we don't know if they participated in any human sacrifice, but the Cathari were able to eventually own and control many castles and strongholds and hold significant power. Presumably this is in the background of the elite bloodline in this forgotten film. Also of interest is the Roman Catholic priest, played by Donald Pleasance, who explains in the film the real power they serve is Lucifer. Much like the later *Wicker Man* (1973) and *To the Devil a Daughter* (1976), and the most famous of them all, *Rosemary's Baby,* Hollywood was capitalizing on a devilish trend: Satanic cults were more and more becoming leading characters of their own. To many this may seem outlandish still, but in the face of so many revelations of Satanic networks within the Vatican connected to the pedophilia scandals, one wonders if these films accidently stumbled upon something – or was it no accident, and these films were expressing subtle truths that couldn't be expressed in public at that time?[118]

I don't know the intentions of the filmmakers behind the 2014 independent horror allegory *Starry Eyes,* but it's yet another case of deep revelation about the reality of Hollywood and its dark underground. Filmmakers Kevin Kolsch and Dennis Widmyer have stated it's a satire, and while that is clearly true, it also expresses a deeper message concerning the occult control system. In the film, Sarah Walker (Alexandra Essoe) is an actress struggling to make it in Hollywood who attends an audition run by a shady company seeking parts for a new horror production. Her roommate and friends are all exceptionally selfish and even seek to undermine her and steal her roles. While auditioning for the role, we see her experience a traumatic breakdown, a form of psychosis, which the casting crew seems to enjoy. As the sequence progresses, we notice her casting agent wears a witchcraft pendant, signifying a deeper coven is possibly behind this arrangement, all of which is later confirmed as she is instructed to meet the producer at an estate and sleep with him for the part.

We later learn this was all a test to see if she would accept any demands the company made, essentially the first step of "selling her soul." Initially Sarah rejects this, but after being offered powerful hallucinogens at a party and presumably being initiated (or brainwashed), she accepts the offer and agrees to have oral sex with the producer, which they describe as a spiritual "gateway." This very notion of sexual actions opening spiritual portals and gateways is found in Crowleyan adept Kenneth Grant's writings on sex magick and Kundalini, *Aleister Crowley & The Hidden God*. Sarah ends up surrounded by a coven of worshippers in black robes confirming our worst fears: Not only has she been initiated and given the role she coveted, she is now beginning to show the signs of possession. Like Jeff Goldblum in *The Fly*, Sarah transforms and her old self dies, giving rise to a new, vampyric persona initiated into Hollywood and ready for the next compromising humiliation ritual for that coveted role which ended up being the ritual murder of her friends.

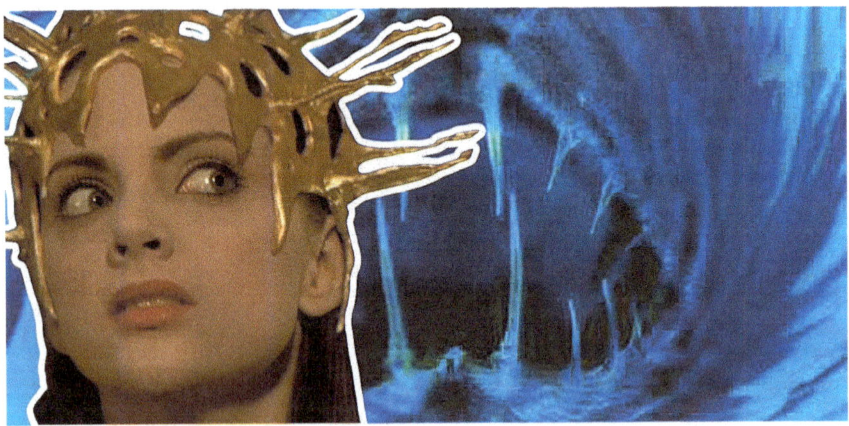

Dagon (2001)

Dagon is the 2002 H.P. Lovecraft based horror film directed by Stuart Gordon which fits well with the previously mentioned Kenneth Grant works, as Grant argued for many similarities between the deities in the Crowleyan system that paralleled Lovecraft:

> In the chapter 'Barbarous Names of Evocation', Grant advanced the notion of similarities between elements of the Cthulhu Mythos as elaborated in the fiction of Lovecraft, and aspects of Crowley's work. This was to suggest that they drew upon similar archetypes in the collective unconscious. In his subsequent work, Grant sometimes played around with the pantheon of deities, but this was never to suggest that the deities were real, or that they should be worshiped.[119]

In the film, a young couple (Paul and Barbara) are on a yachting trip off the coast of Spain when a storm blows them off course to an island called Imboca after a creature attacks and kills their friends, leaving them stranded. As Paul and Barbara search for help in the village, they begin to notice odd, occult symbols everywhere, including an All-Seeing Eye that emblazons a temple (that was a former Catholic Church) converted into a house for The Esoteric Order of Dagon, which claimed to be a simple Freemasonic Order (in the book). As we begin to suspect, the villagers explain they were offered a deal they couldn't refuse by the aquatic entities known as the Deep Ones: Worship Dagon (the fish god) and his consort Mother Hydra (and by extension Cthulhu) and they will have all the gold and fish they want. In exchange, they must offer human sacrifices and women for the fish entities to breed with. Meanwhile, Paul has been having nightmares; he is falling prey to the seductions of the priestess of the cult, Uxia, whom we later discovered has magically drawn Paul to the island to breed with her.

What few have noticed about Lovecraft's works is his reliance on Kabbalah for some of his themes. The *Necronomicon Files* notes that Grant identifies Lovecraft's deities with the malignant, impure demonic powers in Kabbalistic texts known as Qliphot:

> In his Enochian writings, Dee briefly mentions a demon called "Coronzon" (or "Choronzon"), who he says may interfere with the magician's work. Crowley found this reference and stated that the demon Choronzon, the "Breaker-Down of all Thought and Form," was the guardian of the gateway of Daath. Though Bill Whitcomb, author of *The Magician's Companion*, considers Choronzon to be the equivalent of Nyarlathotep (intermediary and messenger of the Great Old Ones in the Cthulhu Mythos), Kenneth Grant identifies him with Lovecraft's Yog-Sothoth, "the key to and the guardian of the gate."[120]

And,

> From Lovecraft's story "The Horror in the Museum" comes a description of Yog-Sothoth: "Imagination called up the shocking form of fabulous Yog-Sothoth – only a congeries of iridescent globes, yet stupendous in its malign suggestiveness." Grant believes those "malignant globes" to be Lovecraft's dream recollection of the shattered Spheres of the Qlippoth, confused with the entity that guards the way to them. August Derleth's Lovecraft pastiche, with

the tantalizing name "The Lurker at the Threshold,"[53] contains a similar description of Yog-Sothoth. In Grant's view, Yog-Sothoth/Choronzon is the "Lurker" at the "Threshold" of Daath. From this perspective, it is no coincidence that Lovecraft's Mythos horrors are described as coming, not from the stars (Sephiroth), but from the dark void (Daath) between the stars....

Grant considers Lovecraft a natural adept with the ability to travel astrally in dreams and traverse the Spheres of the Qabalistic universe. Grant's view is that Lovecraft, in crossing the Abyss, was drawn through the gateway of Daath and pulled down into the Tunnels of Set and the Qlippothic realms of horror. In those nightmarish Tunnels of Set, Grant believes, Lovecraft found the *Necronomicon*. An ominous quote from "The Dunwich Horror" calls this to mind: "Yog- Sothoth knows the gate. Yog-Sothoth is the gate. Yog-Sothoth is the key and the guardian of the gate." Grant believes that Yog-Sothoth is none other than the demon Choronzon, guardian of the gate of Daath. Could an encounter with Choronzon, the Breaker-Down of all Thought and Form, he asks, have caused Lovecraft's obsession with non-Euclidian geometries and the breakdown of Newtonian physics?[121]

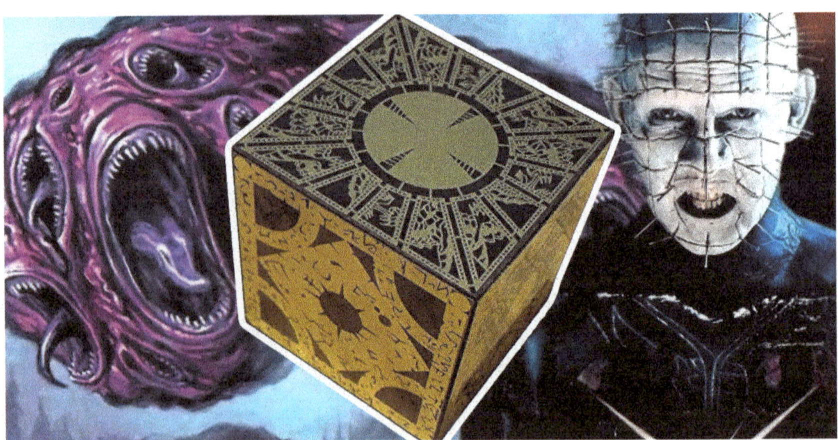

Clive Barker's Nightbreed & Hellraiser

Although we covered several Cronenberg films earlier, the 1990 film *Nightbreed* is unique in that David Cronenberg stars in this Clive Barker film as Dr Philip K. Decker (PKD, a nod to Philip K Dick). In the film, protagonist Aaron Boone has recurring nightmares of a place called Midian, a city in hell inhabited by demonic beings called the Nightbreed. Separately, we learn there is a serial killer on the loose who has been murdering families and some of these events also match up to Boone's dreams. Boone, who has been seeing Dr. Decker seeking psychological healing for his night terrors, is tricked by the doctor into taking LSD and has a psychotic episode leading to him being committed (a subtle reference to MKUltra?). Dr. Decker, whom we discover is his mind control handler, is actually framing Boone for the murders and is working with a drunk priest named Fr. Ashbury to locate the Nightbreed who dwell in Midian and eradicate them.

Boone is eventually inducted into the cult of Baphomet through the "Blood of Baphomet," a ritual where the inversion of Christianity allows for a dark initiation that occurs because the "life is in the blood" (Lev. 17:11). Like Christianity, since Christ was not merely a man, but the God-man, partaking of His lifeblood grants eternal life (John 6), while here, the initiation transforms the human into a demonic deity. The notion of a demonic *apotheosis* is also present in the rest of the Clive Barker Satanic universe, where humans can become demon lords (cenobites) by serving evil (*Hellraiser* 2022). According to famed occultist Eliphas Levi, the designer of the well known Goat of Mendes image of Baphomet, blood is the source of the Astral Light which, when let loose

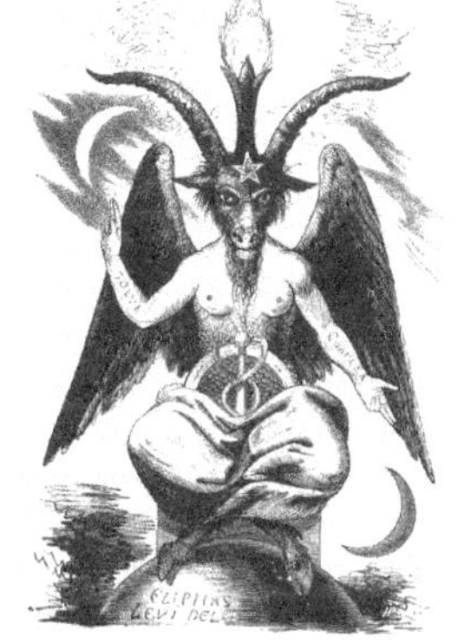

and consumed, calls forth either demons or angels.[122] After his transformation, Boone is given the demon name "Cabal," which suggests a cabalistic/kabbaistic influence upon Barker.

Barker notes that he draws upon gnostic and esoteric texts for his notions of the divine, ranging from William Blake to Carl Jung to *The Cloud of Unknowing*,[123] but it's safe to say his works often utilize symbolism and terminology more directly from kabbalism (as we saw) as well Satanism and ritual magic traditions. In the *Hellraiser* universe, a Saturnalian cube known as the Lament Configuration is able to open portals to hell where the cenobites enter and feed upon human suffering. As mentioned in my *Shining* analysis, a cube encapsulates all 6 possible directions of space: up, down, left, right, up and down. Thus, the cube represents the bypassing of spatial limitations and signifies the spiritual world.

In fact, in Barker's background story to the cube, it was crafted by a cenobite named The Baron, who happened to be an associate of Gilles de Rais, the famed (real-world) child serial killer and companion in arms of Joan of Arc. In Hades (where the cube opens up portals), Leviathan is the ruler, which in biblical demonology is an entity referenced in Is. 27:1 – a king of hell (or Satan himself) that spiritually rules the pagan nations: "*In that day the Lord, with his sore and great and strong sword shall punish leviathan the piercing serpent, even leviathan that crooked serpent; and he shall slay the dragon that is in the sea.*" In the universe of *Hellraiser*, Leviathan is a megalithic diamond shaped *octahedron*, a kind of platonic solid (like Kubrick's *2001* Star Gate sequence), that emits a black light that torments the souls it shines on with its misdeeds, an inversion of the uncreated light of John 1:7, described as the light and light of God.

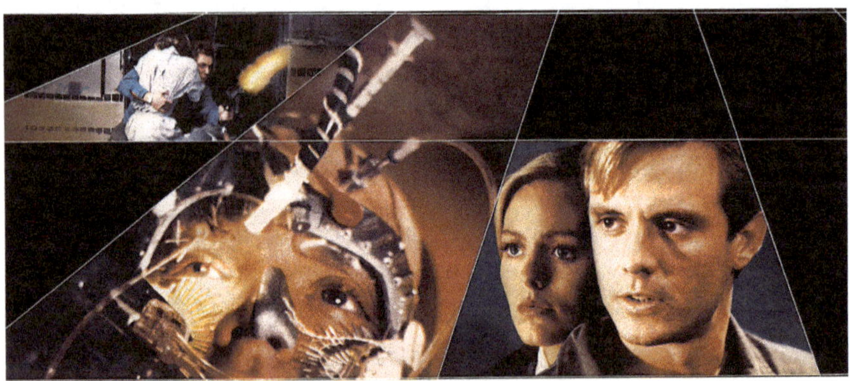

TIMEBOMB (1991)

Timebomb is a unique B movie due to its inclusion of the most explicit MKUltra programmed assassin theme I'm aware of, as well as explicit trauma based mind control, psychological abuse and demoralization, all combining to produce what is intended to be the ultimate patsy. Michael Biehn plays Eddy Kay, a quiet, peaceful watchmaker who has memory loss about significant periods of his past: Eddy is also periodically triggered by images and symbols that cause him to have flashbacks and visions of extreme violence and pornography. Eddy has no memory of being involved in these actions, but begins to suspect he was involved in murder, and through visits to a therapist he begins to recover memories, leading to his former handlers stalking him. Like Sydney in *Alias*, Kay eventually recalls he was utilized in a CIA cut out operation where he was involved with a black ops team of assassins reminiscent of Fletcher Prouty's "Secret Team."

Much like The Secret Team alleges with JFK, Kay discovers he was programmed to be the patsy assassin for a JFK-like politician. The film even mentions CIA MKUltra spin offs like BLUEBIRD. The real declassified Project Bluebird involved hypnosis, LSD, truth drugs, mind control, and assassination operations against the subject's will.[124] The film is thus based directly on the declassified documents which happened in 2001. Once again, Hollywood was revealing this real program in fiction 10 years before it was actually declassified. In the case of Kay, we learn the porn and triggers were implanted into his psyche in an attempt to rewrite his personality with a new one, making him the "*time* bomb" that would explode at the planned time, making his new persona as a clockmaker all the more symbolic. Kay was re-imprinted with false memories and triggers in a giant sensory deprivation tank at the "Lang Institute" (a not so subtle reference to Langley, the CIA) in an underground base – something akin to the tanks developed by MKUltra operative Dr. John C. Lilly.

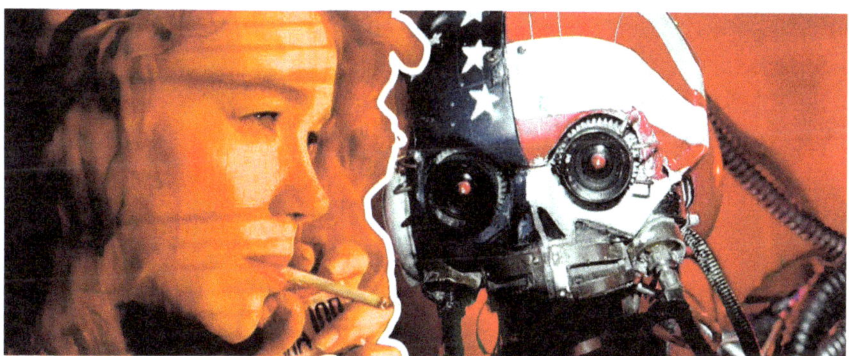

HARDWARE (1990)

Hardware is a unique B movie from director Richard Stanley, who famously laces his works with "gnosticism," and gnostic themes.[125] Here, the future is a dark, dystopian techno nihilism where disheveled scavengers scour a barren landscape seeking various robotic parts for resale in vast megalopolis hellscapes. Mo finds a unique robot in pieces and delivers him to Alvy, a junk dealer, but keeps the robot's head and gives it to his girlfriend Jill as a present. Later, Mo (a kind of Moses figure played by Dylan McDermot) discovers the bot is capable of self-repair and is a prototype for a future killing bot and is eventually slated for mass marketing to annihilate the human population: it is a cabalistic Golem entity that is created to purge humanity.

Stanley's B version of *Terminator* and *Blade Runner* includes some unique insights and critiques other films in this genre missed: In *Hardware*, there is a mandatory sterilization of citizens to purportedly halt "overpopulation." While this is clearly one of the top goals of the Malthusian elite in reality, it's fascinating to see how rare this agenda finds an explicit reference in film. The United Nations is involved in controlling the population in this film under the guise of protecting the environment, while the food is universally fake – they even drink "synthmilk," much like the soy "milk" we see nowadays! Meanwhile, *Hardware*'s synthetic pleasure-based society is completely surveilled, tracked and traced by an A.I. known as "Ba'al," hearkening to the demonic human sacrifice deity of the Old Testament (which is a clue to the antinatalist conspiracy that underlies the film).

Mo discovers the terminator name is a citation from Mark 13 that "no *flesh* will be spared" (because the bots will take over): The killing death bot we later discover is known as the "M.A.R.K. 13." In this future, there is also a syncretistic religion where Christianity has combined with Hinduism, which is very close to the actual UN plans for a world religion outlined by writers like H.G. Wells in lesser known works like *God The Invisible King*. Another curious element is the film's presentation of actual human sexuality as something rare, and in its place what dominates the future controlled society is pornography and various forms of voyeurism and drugs are legal, part of the UN social control measures. Mo is even tainted by the technocracy by possessing a robotic hand (a nod to *Star Wars*), yet here, the bots are 'Kali," "gods of death," and the final boss even has a metallic phallus he threatens to penetrate Jill with – showing he is the new father of a new generation of beings that will replace man. *Hardware* does present an accurate assessment of the real technocracy coming into fruition 35 years later and includes key insights most in the genre lack.

SECTION 4:

HOLLYWOOD ALCHEMY & HORROR TRAUMA

We Live in a Satanic Cult B Movie:
Aleister Crowley &
Early Hollywood

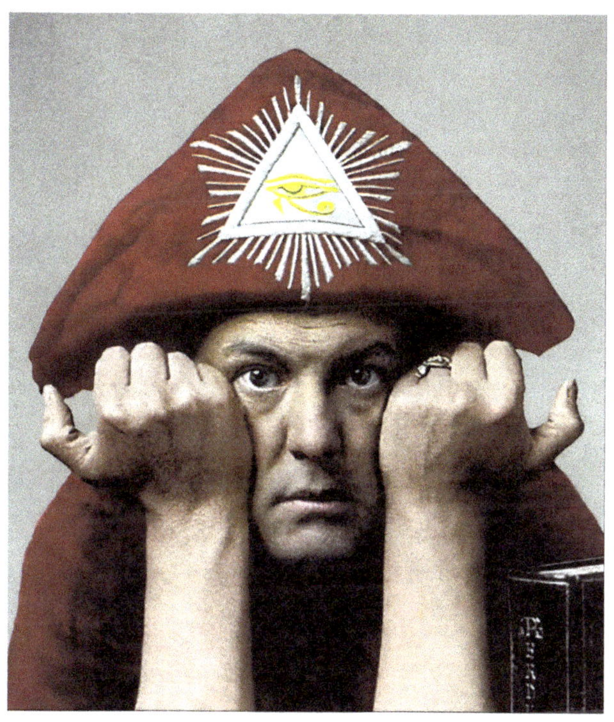

When we think of Satanic cults, we often think of B movies with cheesy sets and Ed Wood level plots, but as time has progressed and more and more revelations come forward, from Savile to Epstein, it's as if we *really do* live in a Satanic Cult B movie. Reality *is* a Satanic cult B movie. Entities like the Club of Rome, for example, have included members associated with famed Satanist Col. Michael Aquino, founder of the Temple of Set, and are quite open with their mass depopulation agenda.[126] Famed British Satanist Aleister Crowley (1875-1947) is where we must begin when we look at early cinema and Hollywood, as few know the earliest Satanic cult themed films are silent films inspired by Crowley himself! Crowley, who rebelled against the strict Puritanical morality of his Plymouth Brethren, sought his own will by joining various magical orders and societies like the Hermetic Order of the Golden Dawn and later the Ordo Templi Orientis (OTO). Later, Crowley created his own religion known as Thelema he claimed was channelled by an ancient entity named Aiwass known as *The Book of the Law.* Crowley also believed the biblical Book of Revelation was a magickal text that could eventually incarnate the Whore of Babylon, whom he called "BABALON" and thought was also Kali and Ishtar. Later *avant garde* filmmakers like Kenneth Anger continued this theme, also joining the OTO and penning the infamous *Hollywood Babylon* books, forever linking Hollywood and Crowley's Babylon ethos, as we will see.

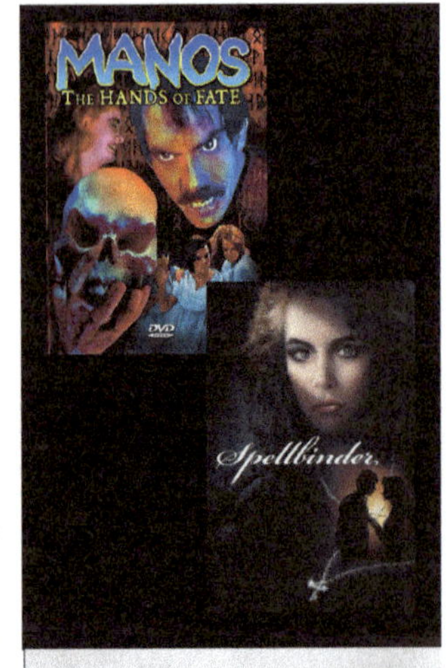

Crowley influenced two early silent occult films, the first of which was the ominous serial *The Mysteries of Myra* (1916), where a young woman is attacked by a secret society known as The Black Order, based on Crowley and The Golden Dawn. The Grand Master of the Order seeks to murder Myra to gain her fortune for the Order. In 1926, Wil-

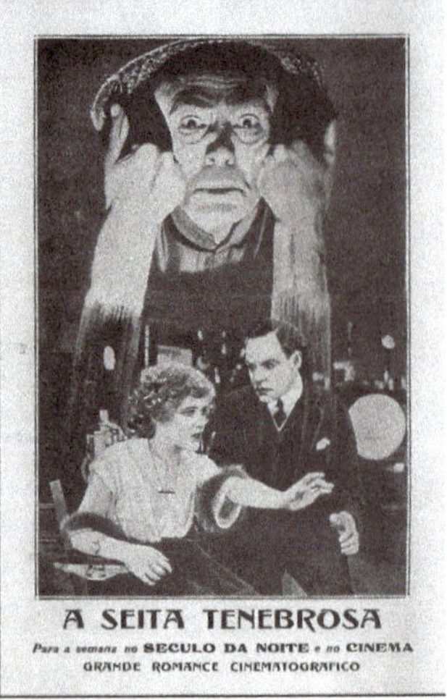

liam Somerset Maugham's novel *The Magician* was made into a silent film that was reportedly based on Crowley's life, which Crowley lambasted as a pale mimicry. In the film's narrative, a magus becomes obsessed with a young maiden and seeks to use her blood in macabre genetic experiments to recreate life through alchemy. Also of note is that escape artist Harry Houdini consulted on the film, and it will be remembered that Houdini was also a spy![127] Qabala also makes an early appearance in the famous 1920 silent film, *The Golem*, based on the Jewish mystical tradition of controlling a soulless, human-created mud-man. Thus, from its earliest days, film and by extension, Hollywood, was always immersed in the realms of the occult and esoteric.

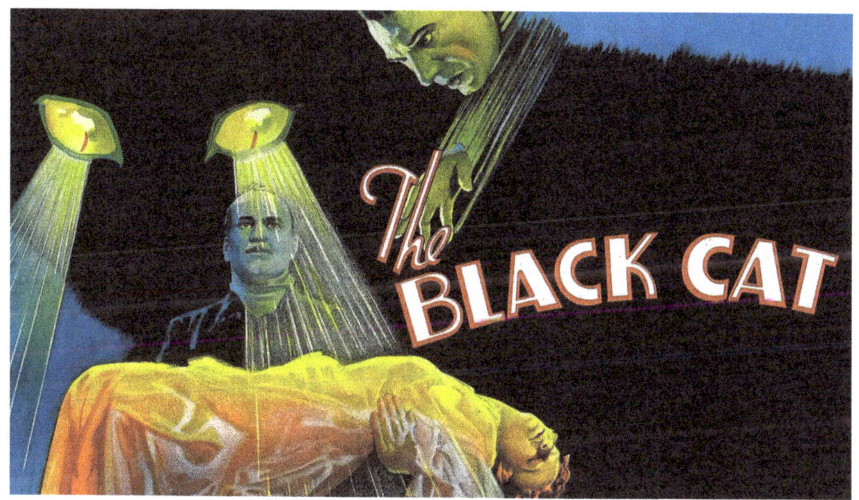

The Black Cat (1934)

One of the earliest films with an explicitly Satanic cult theme is the 1934 pre-code film *The Black Cat*, directed by Edward G. Ulmer, which became Universal's biggest hit that year. Ulmer's vision was an Edgar Allan Poe inspired story of an unfolding nightmare that includes themes of necrophilia, drugs, a black mass and human sacrifice – in a *1934* film! In *Esoteric Hollywood* Part 1, I noted how German Expressionism was the first genre to explicitly use Satanic imagery and symbolism, yet *The Black Cat* is the first to use a Satanic cult as its narrative. While pushing the limits in terms of extreme themes, the film also included two of the biggest stars of the time who would become formative for the emerging genre of horror: Bela Lugosi and Boris Karloff.

The story revolves around a couple on a honeymoon who end up sidetracked while traveling on the Orient Express due to an automobile accident. While on the train, they meet a Hungarian psychiatrist named Dr. Vitus Werdegast (Lugosi) who has been unable to return home and see his wife since World War 1 because he was imprisoned in a Siberian labor camp. While looking for help, they wander in the direction of a massive bauhaus style "mansion" owned by Dr. Poelzig (Karloff), a corrupt military general and architect who informs them a curious black cat haunts the grounds, which happens to be Dr. Werdegast's phobia – which he promptly kills! As it turns out, Dr. Werdegast is there for revenge and brags about his collection of wives he has under glass cases in his basement. Later that night, we see him preparing for a black mass, reading a book titled *The Rites of Lucifer.*

Dr. Poelzig is serial killer and, to be precise, a specific type of serial killer known as a "collector" (like Jeffrey Dahmer, for example, who collected parts and relics of his victims) as described in the famous John Fowles' novel *The Collector*, which also became a 1965 film. Decades prior to such classifications and patterns being noticed by the FBI, *The Black Cat* had profiled a character study of a serial killer, much like Dostoyevsky's *Crime and Punishment*. Poelzig chose his mansion, we learn, because it was formerly a military base where countless soldiers had died: The deaths, he believes, have defiled and ritually charged the site.

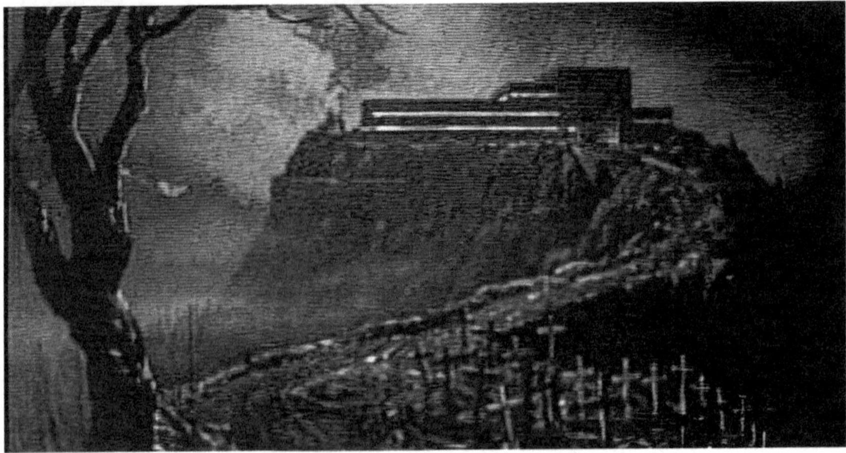

For him, the mansion was his ritual fortress from where he could run his cult drugging women and ritually murdering them for Satanic power. In fact, Poelzig was an inspiration for Anton LaVey according to Blanche Barton, Anton found the film to be an inspiration still recommended by the Church of Satan.[128] Although his mansion is eventually blown up by those he sought to imprison, the significance of Dr. Poelzig as an *architect* and corrupt warrior suggests an association with an archontic deity, the evil architect of this realm (according to the gnostics), who becomes the pattern for those who seek to embody and channel dark energy in a ritual setting. In a way, the film displays not only the dark effects a world war can have on the psyche of a civilization, but also the negative, dark energies that are empowered and feed upon such chaos. Thus, *The Black Cat* is a microcosm of the chaos and darkness Hollywood itself would bring upon the world, and, perhaps prophetically, the eventual implosion Hollywood would undergo – and is undergoing – in our day.

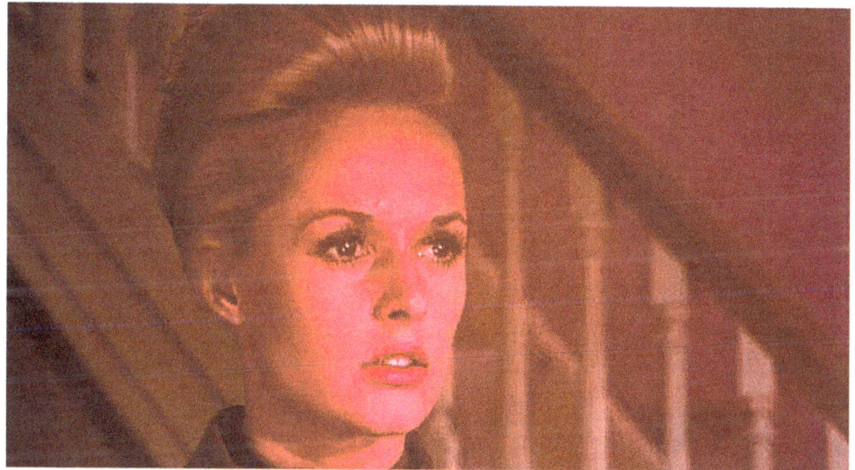

Marnie (1964) & Hitchcock's Multiple Personality Films

Famed Director Alfred Hitchcock was one of the first to focus several films on the theme of multiple personality disorder and dissociation. This should come as no surprise since, as we saw in *Esoteric Hollywood 1*, Hitchcock was part of the circles of British intelligence who were working to study and master propaganda in the US in order to bring the nation into World War 2, as well as other experimentation relating to the effects of film on mass audiences. Hitchcock pioneered several genres, including the first slasher with his 1960 shocker, *Psycho*. *Psycho* is also highly relevant for this theme, as the infamous serial killer Norman Bates is revealed to be an MPD/DID victim one of whose alternate personality is that of his abusive dead mother.

It should thus come as no surprise Hitchcock also explored this theme early on in his 1945 film *Spellbound*, where Gregory Peck plays a doctor who himself is MPD/DID while his surrealist dream sequences displays occult symbolism and Freudian elements resulting in a profound revelation of self-discovery. In *Marnie*, Hitchcock focuses on the means by which a person suffers from MPD/DID through trauma based mind control and the triggers that recall those traumatic memories to cause someone to dissociate to alter personalities. Indeed, *Marnie* is far more in depth in this regard than *Psycho* or *Spellbound*, as Tippy Hedron plays the lead of Marnie, a woman who was raised by an abusive prostitute mother and has trouble connecting with men. Her particular triggers happen to be the color red or thunderstorms, either of which cause her to switch to her alternate childlike or angry, thieving personalities.

Meanwhile, Sean Connery plays Mark Rutland, a wealthy widowed publisher who takes on Marnie as his pet psychological project to see if he can tame her wild side. As Mark seduces Marnie and marries her, he eventually goes too far in pressuring her for sex, as the controversial scene implies he rapes her, triggering Marnie to attempt suicide the next day by drowning. Mark rescues her, and investigates her background to discover she had a profoundly dysfunctional, traumatic upbringing which led to her present psychosis. The film references Carl Jung explicitly as Mark is shown with various books, one of which is *The Undiscovered Self*, where in the hidden recesses of the subconscious mind hidden desires, traumatic memories, and even alternate personalities might be created. This is crucial to understanding the film, as Jung himself posited that extreme trauma can lead to dissociative splits and alternate personalities – the very thing the CIA would later study as part of MKUltra. Carl Jung was also a member of the OSS, known as "Agent 488," and worked at various facilities like Burgholzli in Switzerland with MKUltra doctor Dr. Ewan Cameron, as well as the infamous British brainwashing outfit, the Tavistock Institute.

In Marnie's case, one of her mom's johns attempted to molest her as a child, resulting in Marnie and her mom killing the man, and shockingly Marnie's mom offered no comfort to her catatonic daughter. This event caused the initial split from the core child identity to which Marnie eventually reverts as Mark discovers the deepest repressed traumas. Dr. Richard Baer's book *Switching Time: A Doctor's Harrowing Story of Treating a Person with 17 Personalities* is a fascinating work that details a scenario similar to Marnie's, as well as Dr. Colin Ross' work *The Osiris Complex*, which demonstrates the reality of the MPD/DID phenomena in several patients. A common factor in all these cases is the early childhood trauma, which results in the split, as well as in many cases ritual abuse. What is odd about these Hitchcock films is that *Spellbound* predates the first popular book on MPD/DID, *Three Faces of Eve*,[129] by nine years. Was Hitchcock able to make a film about this mysterious phenomena so much earlier than anyone else because he was privy to British intelligence research? Researcher Michael Minnicino comments:

> "The Kordas and the rest of the British community in Hollywood also were responsible for bringing in the other major trendsetter of the 1940s, Alfred Hitchcock, who was himself tied to British intelligence. Since Hitchcock's films are very well known, it is easily seen that he was an exponent of Miinsterberg's theories of how the film can brainwash via fixation and shock....
>
> Hitchcock was brought to the United States in 1939 by David O. Selznick to direct *Rebecca*, with Laurence Olivier starring, and screenplay adaptations by Robert Sherwood and Thornton Wilder, both of

whom would head the U. S. Office of War Information within a couple of years. Hitchcock stayed in the United States owing to the lavish funding he could get for his projects, including his psycho-active films like *Spellbound.* with a screenplay by Ben Hecht (collaborating with leading U.S. psychoanalysts) and set designs by surrealist Salvador Dali. *Spellbound* was the first U.S. film to have Satanic cult imagery, something not seen since the heyday of the German Expressionists. [130]

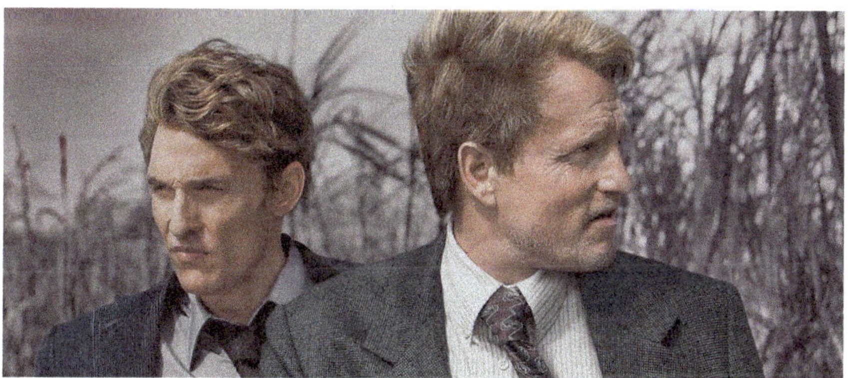

TRUE DETECTIVE SEASON 1

The first season of *True Detective* captivated the viewing public in 2014, topped only by *Breaking Bad* in attention and critical praise. While the Internet is still rife with theories and analysis, few have succeeded in plumbing the depths of the story in its proper fullness. Most online analyses were overall adequate, yet several important points were missed relating to specific religious symbolism, as well as the numerous philosophical references given by Rust Cohle (played by Matthew McConaughey). In this analysis I will give the full significance of the first season of *True Detective,* which ranks as one of the most revealing films of the occult underground since *Eyes Wide Shut.*

The opening sequence lays out a heavy dose of symbolism that cues the viewer into the dark meaning of the series as a whole: we see key images such as backwoods evangelical revival, strippers, the emblematic tree, a playground, several *butts*, a black eye and telephone imposed over a child's head. The meaning of the entire series is thus not merely the conflict between Rust and Marty in their personal lives, or the elite Satanic rituals, but the impact of the spiritual degeneration that has occurred over just 17 years, from 1995 to 2012. In other words, the spiritual effect that the infernal powers have brought about over just the last 20 years have resulted in a massive decline in the moral status of American society as a whole.

True Detective is therefore a survey of that degeneration and demonism, juxtaposing what appears as a grotesque, Southern Gothic backwoods existence ruled by an older bloodline (the Tuttles), with the so-called "normal" American family of Marty Hart.

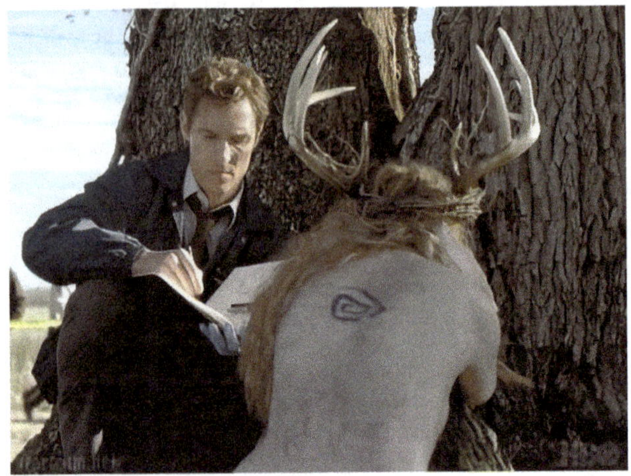

Cohle sketches out the first ritual murder.

As the series begins, we see an offering of a dead girl in a prostrate pose praying before a tree, wearing a crown of twigs and marked with a spiral symbol. Detective Rust Cohle is immediately aware of the ritual connotations of the killing, noting the "meta-psychotic" nature of the crime. Educated readers will recognize the "meta" prefix as referencing notions like metaphysics and meta-narrative. As I've detailed before with Spielberg films and Philip K. Dick works, meta-narrative is associated with this higher level discourse, found in "twilight language." I wrote:

"In semiotics, particularly in Plato's *Sophist*, simulacrum is intended to fool the viewer into thinking the copy is the real thing. The copy takes on a life of its own, yet viewed in scale it would clearly appear that the copy is not real. This is a perfect analogy for the nature of film itself, as well as the role of the director. The writer and/or film director is creating a simulacra of the real world with models and pictures, piecing and placing them together in a certain way, just as Roy does with the model train and city he has built. One may think of the simulated beings in *Blade Runner* or the simulated world of *The Matrix* here. Spielberg has mastered this art of simulation, and is presenting a simulated reality world – that of UFO-invaded America that is intended to produce a certain effect in the population. Can this be taken to a larger scale, to which Spielberg and the director himself is a "toy" of the larger, galactic forces or entities of the cosmos? Are we a Greek scale of being, being "played" and "directed" by the celestial hierarchy?"

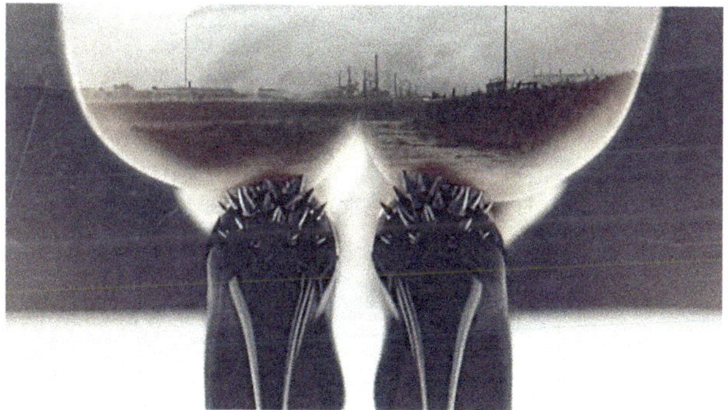

What is applied to the "director" here applies to the thinking of the "meta-psychotic," who sees a direct connection between his victims and ritual items as copies of the real items. In the same vein, the notion between "twilight language" is the writing of a script with reality by higher celestial entities, be they angelic or demonic. Here, the Tuttles are practitioners of "old time religion" – a primal form of voodoo and ritual magic. Mystical toponymy also comes into play, as Louisiana is the setting for the series, where the Tuttle bloodline has long held sway, having combined their beliefs with the indigenous Santeria and vodou superstitions. Cohle immediately senses this, functioning as the series' prophet/priest, having himself spent years in narcotics enforcement, as well as losing his daughter, resulting in his "touching the darkness."

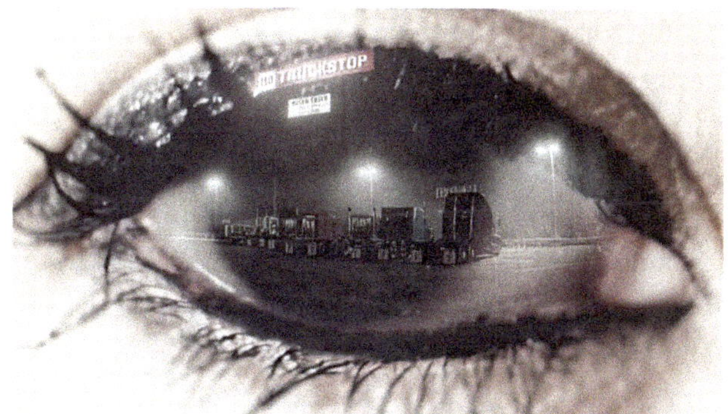

The black eye.

A committed nihilist at the beginning, Cohle espouses the very worldview of the Satanic elite – a Nieztschean eugenics stance, combined with eternal return, where materialistic chaos returns to its beginning in endless spirals, associating Cohle's own mind with the recurring spiral symbolism in the series. Humans are "sentient meat" that happened to develop the "mirror" of consciousness accidentally, and ever since, man is engaged in a perpetual self-delusion of convincing himself he is a "person" with meaning. Cohle the philosopher scoffs at these notions, having immersed himself in so many years of battling the darkness. Nietzsche famously said, "And when you gaze long into an *abyss* the *abyss* also gazes into you," which perfectly describes Cohle.

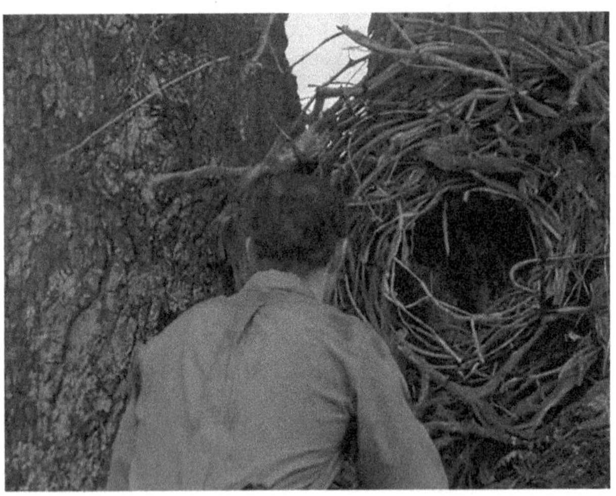

Spiral portal.

In contrast to Cohle, Marty Hart (Woody Harrelson) is Cohle's simpler partner, the average good old boy cop who cheats on his wife and drinks too much. The names of both characters are also significant, as Marty "Hart" brings to mind feeling, emotion and simplicity, whereas "Rust" signifies worn with age and a harsh realism, as well as "Cohle" bringing to mind "coal," being dark, cold and earthen. The first murder also occurs in "Erath," which is an anagram for earth, cluing the viewer into the wider scope of the crimes Rust and Marty are unraveling. The blood spilling on the earth also has ritual significance in most ancient religions requiring blood atonement. For the sacrifice to propitiate the spirits, blood must be spilled, and often the ground consecrated. For the Tuttles, the earth is their property, belonging to them by blood rite and pact with the "gods" of the land. Deuteronomy 12:16 for example, reads: "Only you shall not eat the blood; you shall pour it upon the earth as water." Likewise, the famous passage of Leviticus 16:10: "But the goat, on which the lot fell for Azazel, shall be set alive before Jehovah, to make atonement for him, to send him away for Azazel into the wilderness."

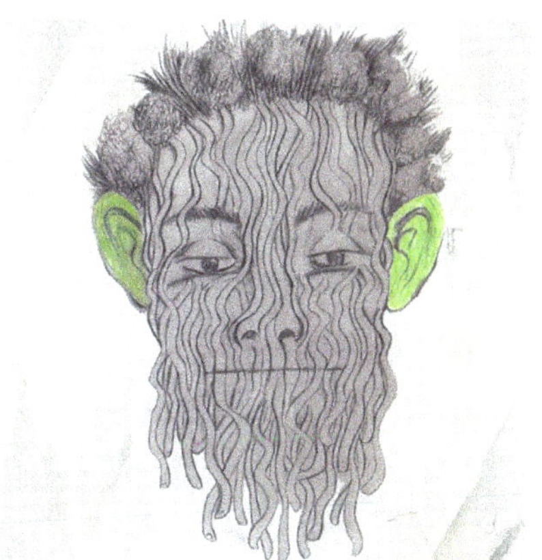

The Tuttle version of Green Man.

In the same line of the thought, one of the clues the Tuttles leave for Rust and Marty is the "Green Monster" the child victims describe. While never specifically explained beyond the inbred Tuttle being a painter, the Green Monster is strikingly similar to the "Green Man" of many ancient pagan cultures, focusing the attention on animism and cyclical nature worship relating the seasons. As Cohle begins to discover, the Tuttles are definitely patrons of that "old time religion," but a much, much older version. In some traditions, the "Green Man" is merged with "Wicker Man," where human sacrifice begins to come into play. The Tuttles also light fires after their rituals, and in the climax when Rust and Marty enter the old brick pirate structure on the pirate land, we see charred remains of victims.

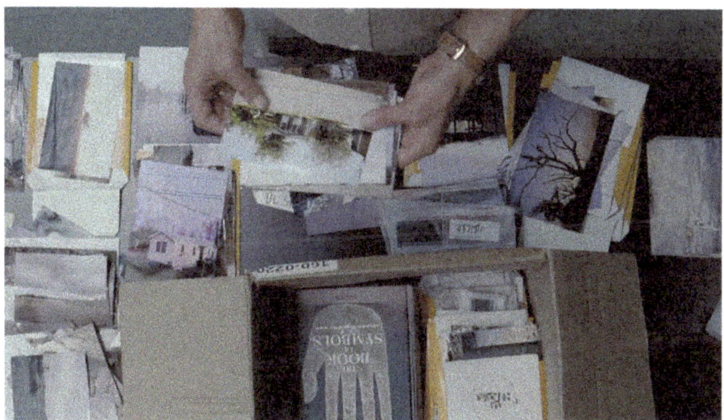

Cohle searches through a box with a book on Jungian symbolism, which is grounded in the idea of the psychosphere, or collective unconscious.

As the detectives delve deeper into the Tuttle spiral, they begin to see the utter depravity and statewide scope of the ritual murders, as well as having their investigations curtailed and halted by higher state officials. Rev. Tuttle, a wealthy elite member of the family who runs the Tuttle Christian schools and ministries, is himself a pedophile Satanist who supplies the cult with poor and displaced girls from the various charities. This brings to mind similar real-world events surrounding ritual murders and child trafficking, as surfaced in the infamous Franklin Scandal, which involved high level politicians, donors and Catholic ministries, as well as the recent scandals with Jimmy Savile and members of the British elite.[131] This is crucial, as *True Detective* is not a fictional drama about cops tracking a serial killer – on the contrary, it is a revelation of real evil and who the real monsters are in our society.

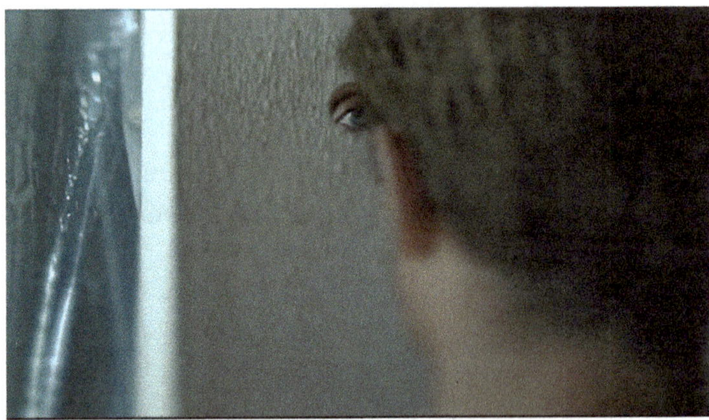

Rust's left eye, as he looks into the depravity of the Tuttle's "left-hand path."

Rust famously states, "I get a bad taste in my mouth out here. Aluminum. Ash. Like you can smell the psychosphere." The psychosphere is a term in ritual magic for the nearest dimension or spiritual realm, directly associated with our thoughts, like the *aether* or the collective unconscious. The psychosphere has a "twilight language" of its own, where only those with eyes to see are able to read its signs. Rust is shown in several scenes as "awake," while Marty is still asleep, as well as focusing on Rust's eye. Rust's "eye" is awakened to the language of the psychosphere, which he had earlier noted was a "conversation" being had through the ritual symbolism. Rust is thus able to peer directly into the psychosphere at times, giving him insight into the depths of the Tuttle spiral of depravity, through his visions he attributes to LSD and PTSD flashbacks, something akin to Agent Dale Cooper in *Twin Peaks*.

Another important element missed by many is the sex slavery. The children that are used are not merely abused, they are often sex slaves that have been imprinted with traumatic memories they later believe were "dreams," due to being drugged during the ceremonies. The ceremonies were carried out deep in the woods, and resembled "marriage" ceremonies, as the kids were raped by men in masks. One of the most striking images in the se-

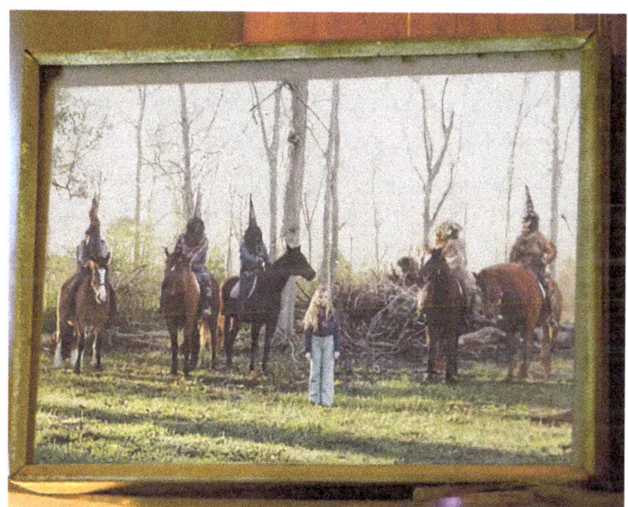

The first indicator of mind-controlled sex slaves.

ries is the little-noticed indicator that Marty's own firstborn daughter had been abused, as she draws images of sex acts and places her dolls into a ritual formation that is just like the video Rust confiscates from Rev. Tuttle's mansion. In the dialogue with subtitles, the girls discuss that they were told, "You don't have a mommy and a daddy anymore. They're dead."

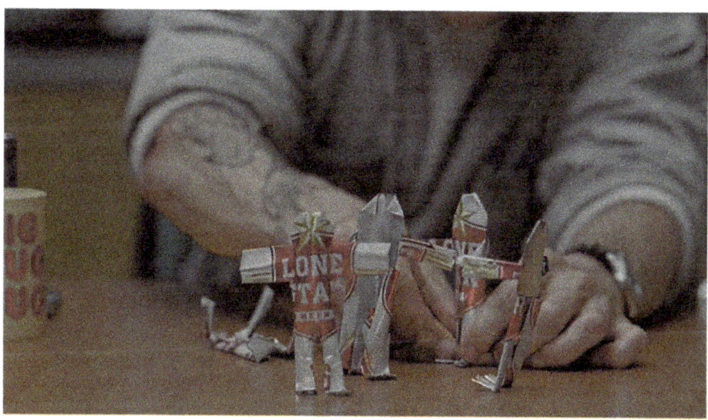

Rust makes beer can dolls. Aluminium. Psychosphere.

Later, Rust interviews a transvestite named Johnny Joanie that had undergone similar abuse, but had repressed the memories as something he had dreamed. Rust informs him it was not a dream, but all along, Marty is unwilling to recognize the evil that surrounds him, especially since the indicators are that the abuser is most likely his wife, Maggie's father. Maggie's father appears to be wealthy and well-connected, likening "everything" to sex – and he is the only other adult Marty's daughters are seen with. The only other similar image we see is the photo of one of the victim's mothers that Cohle sees, where a girl is surrounded by masked men on horses. Also connected with this five-man circle, in 2012 when Rust is being interviewed by the Feds, he cuts and shapes his beer cans into the same circle, showing he is aware of the ritual nature of the child abuse and mind control. This image by a writer at the *Daily Beast* explains well the connection between the symbols that recur, and note in particular the spiral artwork that Marty's daughter has done, as well as the flowers, which the inbred Tuttles later explain as incest and/or sex, calling it "making flowers."

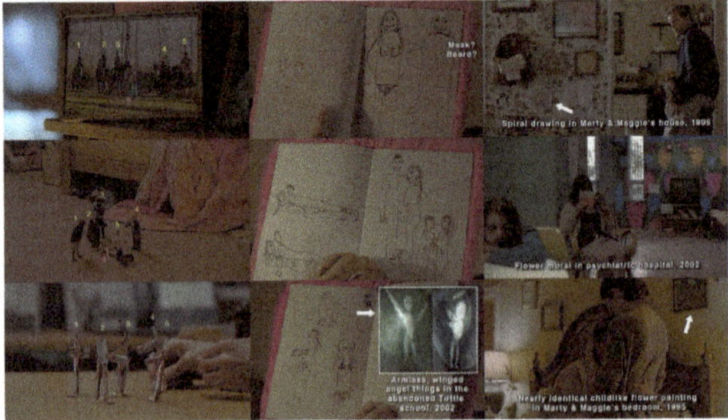

Recurring Imagery.

Many online writers were correct to link the spiral symbol to child sex cults, referencing the real FBI image that associates the symbolism with ritual abuse. However, the spiral is not just that – it also has reference to the All-Seeing Eye, eternal return, and galaxies, as we shall see later. In my analysis, what no one has yet understood is the anal references as I mentioned earlier, and it is here that the spiral has another level of meaning. It is not just an "eye," but a lower eye, the eye of the anus, which is a reference to Satan himself, where the opening of the third eye relates to the serpent chakra at the base of the spine, where the anus is. While this may seem far-fetched, this is a well-known concept in hermetic and ancient religions, known as the "anthropic principle," where man is a microcosm of the macrocosm. The body itself is a map of correspondences between the universe as a whole, in a version of "as above, so below." As an example, writer James Kelley has analyzed this principle in his essay on the anthropic principle in the Vedas. Kelley writes, noting the connection to incest in the pagan mythologies that is applicable here to the Tuttle family tradition.

Cohle's books reveal a lot: Notice the Hindu texts which explain his reincarnation ideas, as well as Nietzsche. Consider Kelley's analysis below:

The centrality of this notion of the Cosmic Man's holy, creative sleep is evinced by the Iranian story of Yami (parallel to the purusal Yama touched upon above), who is put to "sleep" (Pahlavi *xwāb*) as a means of saving him from corruption and death. Interestingly, the Norse primal giant Ymir (whose name is an Western importation of the Indo-Iranian Yami/Yama!) is said to sweat out the primal human couple in a fevered sleep.... Let us not forget that, in the Judeo-Christian tradition, the Lord caused a deep sleep to come over Adam as well. As in the Nordic and Indic versions, Adam's theoric sleep results in anthropogenesis: Eve (Gr. Zoe, "Life") is created out of Adam's side, and thus are all generations made possible. A similar "unconventional genesis" occurs in the Indo-Iranian myth of Yama and Yami. Yama – who is identified with Purusa by many commentators – is urged by his sister Yami to join with him in creating progeny, since the gods commanded them to multiply. Yami refuses, since incest would displease the gods, and no amount of pragmatic reasoning can sway him. The Vedic text leaves the mystery unsolved; we only know that children were produced from Yama and Yami without incest taking place. Silence and hiddenness is fitting when daring to speak of a *mysterion*, though: "This is a great mystery" as another sage later cautioned. Thus, it appears that a central symbol of ancient Indian religion – the archetypal man with limbs outstretched – may be the origin of that image that so haunts our Western minds – the Vitruvian Man, whose measurements illustrate the secret of the squared circle and show forth the sacred proportion that undergirds the cosmos."[132]

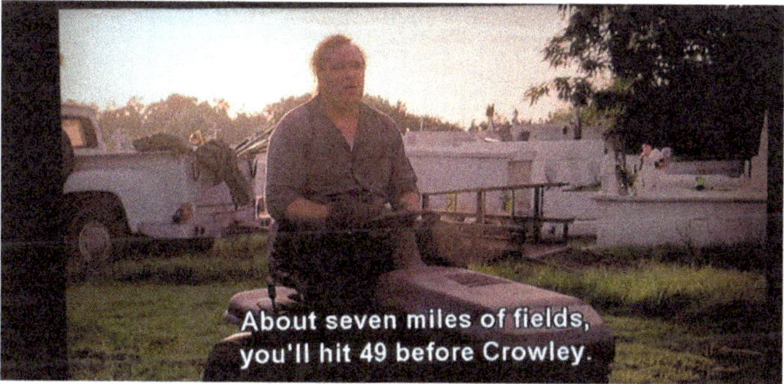

As Errol mows in a spiral, the police ask for directions. Errol gives an interesting reply.

Viewed in this light, black holes or similar stellar phenomena are gateways or portals for celestial powers, and ritual and liturgy becomes a means for opening a doorway. Vatican insider and exorcist Malachi Martin described the principle behind this thinking in his famous *Keys of This Blood* as follows:

"Most frighteningly for [Pope] John Paul [II], he had come up against the irremovable presence of a malign strength in his own Vatican and in certain bishops' chanceries. It was what knowledgeable Churchmen called the 'superforce.' Rumors, always difficult to verify, tied its installation to the beginning of Pope Paul VI's reign in 1963. Indeed Paul had alluded somberly to 'the smoke of Satan which has entered the Sanctuary'... an oblique reference to an enthronement ceremony by Satanists in the Vatican. Besides, the incidence of Satanic pedophilia – rites and practices – was already documented among certain bishops and priests as widely dispersed as Turin, in Italy, and South Carolina, in the United States. The cultic acts of Satanic pedophilia are considered by professionals to be the culmination of the Fallen Archangel's rites." (pg. 632)

UNCLASSIFIED//LAW ENFORCEMENT SENSITIVE

FEDERAL BUREAU OF INVESTIGATION
INTELLIGENCE BULLETIN
Cyber Division, Innocent Images National Initiative

31 January 2007

(U) Symbols and Logos Used by Pedophiles to Identify Sexual Preferences

(U//FOUO) This intelligence bulletin addresses Crimes Against Children Standing Intelligence Requirements Set contained in Q-FBI-2200-005-06, HRWC CAC-VI.A.5.

(U//LES) Pedophiles, to include those who sexually abuse children as well as those who produce, distribute, and trade child pornography, are using various types of identification logos or symbols to recognize one another and distinguish their sexual preferences. To specifically indicate the pedophile's gender preference, members of pedophilic organizations encourage the use of descriptions such as "boylove", "girllove", and "childlove."[1] These symbols have been etched into rings and formed into pendants, and have also been found imprinted on coins.

(U) The BoyLover logo (BLogo) is a small blue spiral-shaped triangle surrounded by a larger triangle, whereby the small triangle represents a small boy and the larger triangle represents an adult man.[2] A variation of the BLogo is the Little Boy Lover logo (LBLogo), which also embodies a small spiral-shaped triangle within a larger triangle; however, the corners of the LBLogo are rounded to resemble a scribbling by a young child.[3] Images of the BLogo and LBLogo symbols are depicted below.

UNCLASSIFIED   UNCLASSIFIED   UNCLASSIFIED

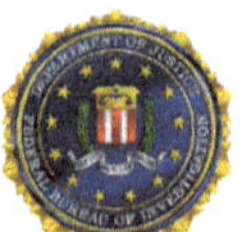

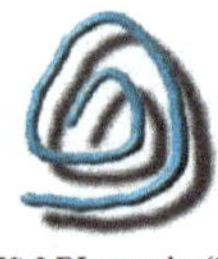

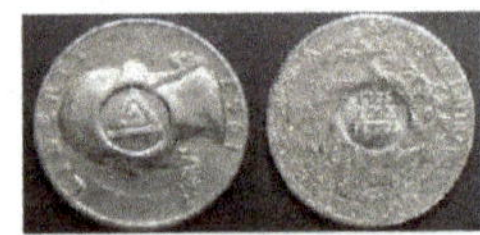

(U) BLogo aka "Boy Lover"   (U) LBLogo aka "Little Boy Lover"   (U) BLogo imprinted on coins

UNCLASSIFIED

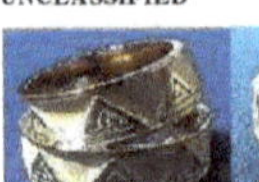
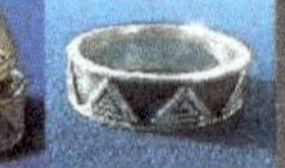
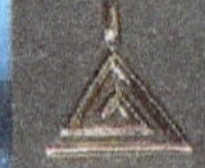
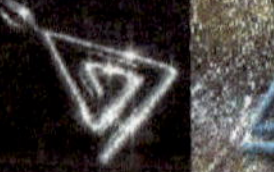
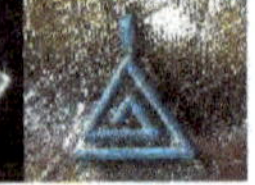

(U) BLogo jewelry

UNCLASSIFIED//LAW ENFORCEMENT SENSITIVE

1

FBI page of cult symbolism.

For example, sex magick practitioner Aleister Crowley stressed the anal and its symbolism as superior to the vaginal, stating "Oh how superior is the eye of Horus to the mouth of Isis."[133] This is why Errol, the Tuttle villain who takes the fall, always mows in a spiral, as well as why the vortex that opens in the ritual chamber is a spiral. The principle of inversion in black magic is demonstrated here, as the lowest part of the body is also the lowest part of the galaxy, a kind of luminous black hole gateway in the psychosphere through which the energy of the infernal powers enters. Rust is able to see this dark portal in the ritual chamber because he has a psychic connection to the Tuttles and the victims, as several times he is spoken of as having "demons" and seeing "darkness." This is why the series has such an anal fixation, as numerous times anal sex comes up, as well as images and references. The move from 1995 to 2012 demonstrates the "anal-iza-tion" of society, to where "sex is everything," as Maggie's dad states about the transition from "Clinton" to 2012. It is also important that *True Detective* is based on an actual occultic "church" in Louisiana that engaged in all the same types of acts.[134]

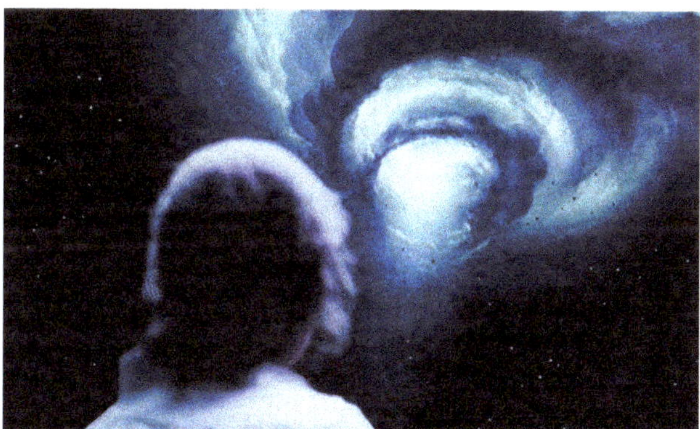

Rust sees into the psychosphere and witnesses the dark portal through which the Tuttles derived their infernal energy and power.[135]

The idea of demonic energy being released that may charge the psychosphere is also a biblical idea referenced in the incident of the King of Moab attacking Israel, and losing, prompting him to ritually sacrifice his firstborn son in effigy. 2 Kings 3 states:

> "26 And when the king of Moab saw that the battle was too sore for him, he took with him seven hundred men that drew swords, to break through even unto the king of Edom: but they could not.27Then he took his eldest son that should have reigned in his

stead, and offered him for a burnt offering upon the wall. And there was great indignation against Israel: and they departed from him, and returned to their own land."

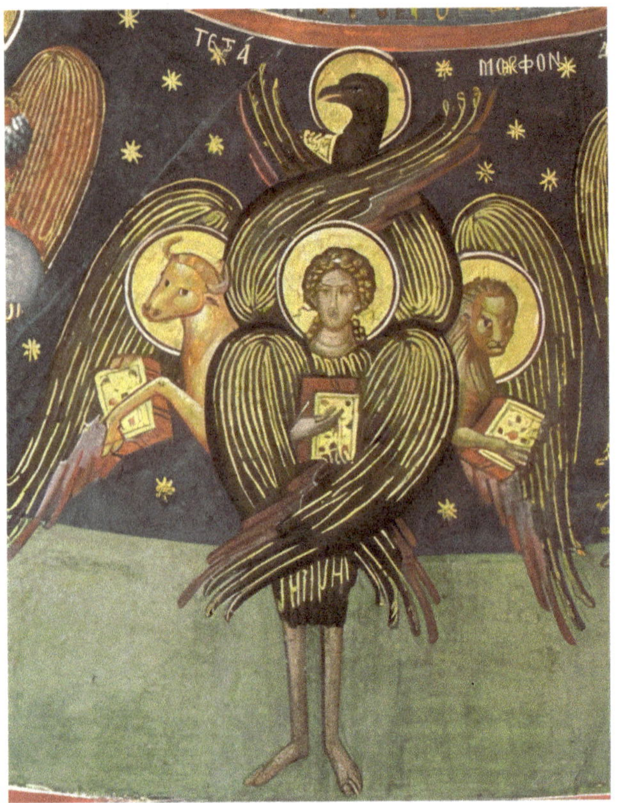

Image of a cherub, a celestial intelligence.

St. Dionysius writes of the celestial hierarchy:

"Wherefore that first institution of the sacred rites, judging it worthy of a supermundane copy of the Celestial Hierarchies, gave us our most holy hierarchy, and described that spiritual Hierarchy in material terms and in various compositions of forms so that we might be led, each according to his capacity, from the most holy imagery to formless, unific, elevative principles and assimilations. For the mind can by no means be directed to the spiritual presentation and contemplation of the Celestial Hierarchies unless it use the material guidance suited to it, accounting those beauties which are seen to be images of the hidden beauty, the sweet incense a symbol of spiritual dispensations, and the earthly lights a figure of the immaterial enlightenment. Similarly the details of the sacred teaching correspond to the feast of contemplation in the soul, while the ranks of order on earth reflect the Divine Concord and the disposition of the Heavenly Orders. The receiving of the most holy Eucharist symbolizes our participation of Jesus; and everything else delivered in a supermundane manner to Celestial Natures is given to us in symbols."

And,

"It is manifest, therefore, that those Natures which are around the Godhead have participated of It in manifold ways. On this account the holy ranks of the Celestial Beings are present with and participate in the Divine Principle in a degree far surpassing all those things which merely exist, and irrational living creatures, and rational human beings. For moulding themselves intelligibly to the imitation of God, and looking in a supermundane way to the Likeness of the Supreme Deity, and longing to form the intellectual appearance of It, they naturally have more abundant communion with Him, and with unremitting activity they tend eternally up the steep, as far as is permitted, through the ardour of their unwearying divine love, and they receive the Primal Radiance in a pure and immaterial manner, adapting themselves to this in a life wholly intellectual.[136]

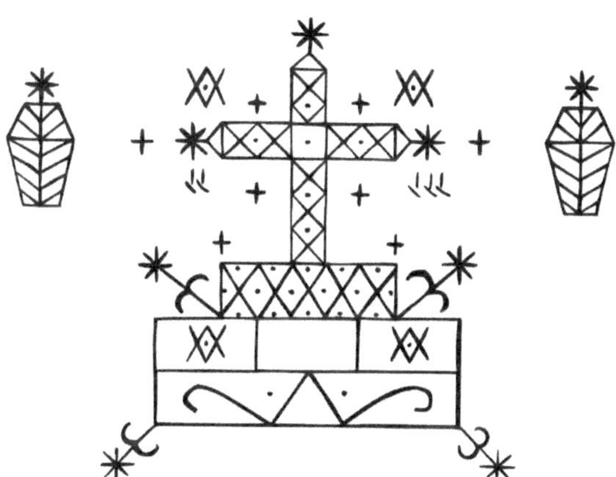

Baron Samedi's veve, or sigil.

Rust has stumbled upon the inverse of all this, as the Tuttle family are intergenerational, incestuous Voodoo practitioners that serve the "Yellow King of Carcosa." While many analyses focus on the literary reference of the Yellow King from a book of short stories from American writer Robert

Chambers, I see the significance elsewhere. The reference is to a fictional play that drives people mad when enacted, here certainly applicable to *True Detective*, as the story itself seems to drive Rust and Marty mad, trying to solve the decades-old murders. I propose a simpler explanation of the "Yellow King." Set in Louisiana with numerous references to Santeria and voodoo, the "Yellow King" functions more like a Loa, or a Voodoo demon that is served and propitiated for various purposes. For the Tuttles, the Yellow King is the territorial spirit they serve generationally as patron that has given them wealth and power. The Yellow King is similar to Baron Samedi, the famed voodoo spirit of Louisiana, only something far more wicked, demanding human sacrifice, and working mind control on his young victims. While the Loa are not gods themselves, they are subservient to the King of devils, Satan. Compare the veve or sigil of Baron Samedi to the images of ritual magic behind Marty when Rust shows him his research.

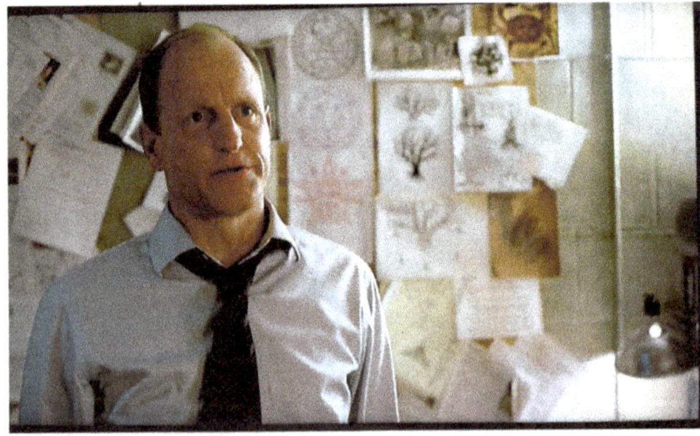

Note the ritual magic sigils Rust has discovered behind Marty.

This also explains Reggie LeDoux, the child-drugging meth cook, who has several occultic tattoos, as well as the spiral imprint both Reggie and Errol have burned into their backs. Reggie has the tattoo of the Icelandic stave, an image similar to the sigils mentioned above, as well as an obvious inverted Pentagram. The spiral is The Icelandic Vegvisir. It is also a version of "666," which Reggie also has on his chest, as well as a noose. The noose is interesting because it suggests a death pact for the cult, as the LeDoux and Tuttle families must've long had their alliance to control the dark side of the Louisiana underground. Another element other analyses have not picked up on is that the Tuttles seem to have their hand in, and power over, all the vices in the state – they run prostitution, drugs and gangs, with almost the entire state fearing their retribution. All the while, they have a front of being philanthropists, ministers and senators.

This is because the vices are supervised by the chief demon, the King of Carcosa, the patron voodoo spirit of the Tuttles – and the Tuttles run it through the complicity of the police, who throughout the series are constantly implicated in running the whorehouse and silencing the exposure and investigation. There 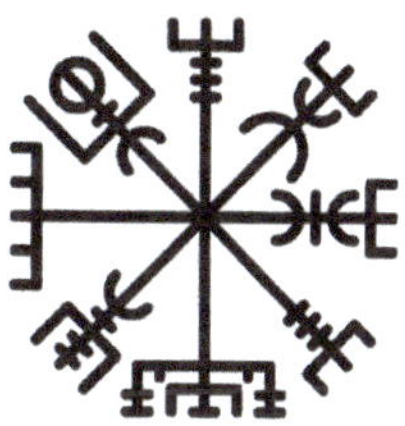 is also a suggestion of higher power above Rev. Tuttle, who ends up murdered when his snuff film goes missing.

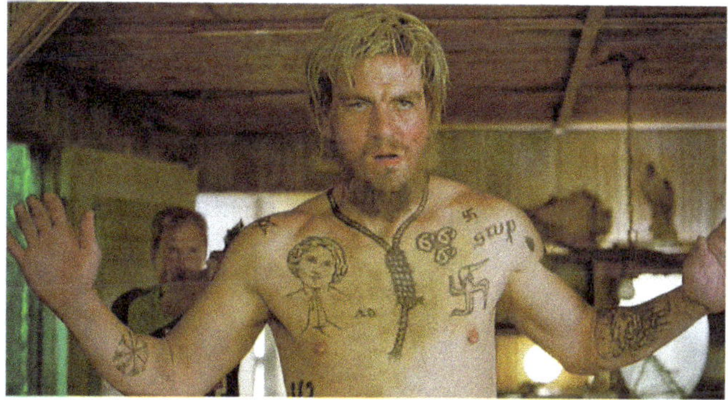

Reggie's sexy tats.

As mentioned, Rust and the Tuttles seem to have a psychic connection of some kind, and perhaps something else relating to the pasts of both, since both Errol and Rust mow lawns. Marty seems irrationally irritated by the fact that Marty mowed his lawn, which suggests the mowing of lawns may have had some symbolic connection to who had the "contract" to do so. Since mowing the lawn has a sexual reference, and the Tuttles mow lawns under "contract," there is a likely connection between Marty's daughter Audrey playing in the yard and wearing the crown, and her abuse. Did the Tuttle weirdos mow Marty's lawn?

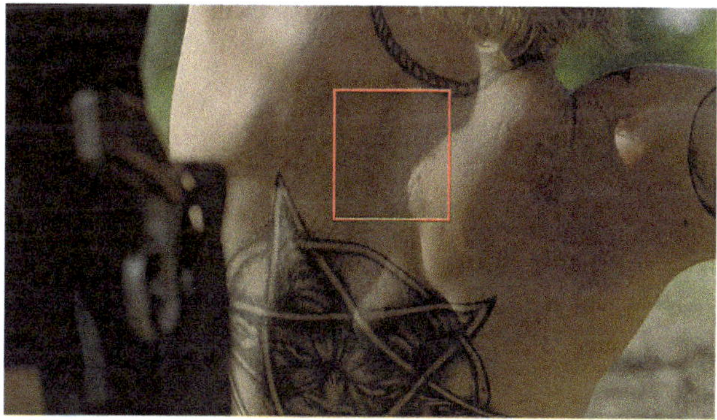

The spiral branded into Reggie's back is the spiral that represents the ritual vortex.

Marty says he mows his own, but it is strangely undone, signifying a connection to the corrupt power structure. This power structure is aligned with the fallen hierarchy of angels under a "contract" that they believe allows them to "marry" or sacrifice whomever they wish. In the final confrontation between Cohle and Errol, Errol tells him it's a marriage and his victims are all his "acolytes," making clear the liturgical symbology. The family tree of the Tuttles that signifies ancestor worship and human sacrifice is a version of Yggdrasil, the ancient tree of Norse mythology similar to the hermetic and cabalistic tree of life. For the Tuttles, religion is very much an ancient blood and soil family affair.

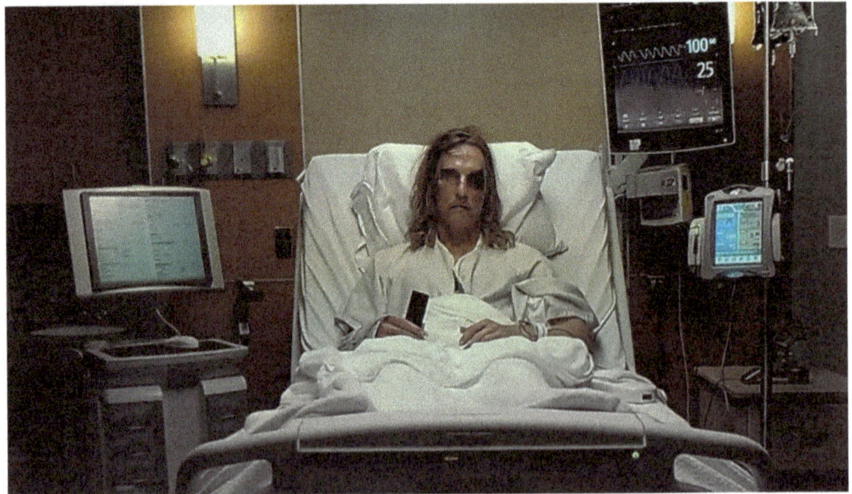

Rust finally realizes there is more than matter. He sees Christ.

In conclusion, *True Detective* functions on multiple levels as a mix of numerous influences. Southern Gothic, neo noir, pulp crime fiction, and occult psychodrama all mesh to form a well-done drama that is one of the best series we've seen yet. Hearkening to *Twin Peaks*, but without the absurdist elements, *True Detective* is a spiritual chronicle of the rise of the Satanic in modernity, but a Satanic that is not new, but which had formerly been hidden in the backwoods, sulking out of some ancient grove like a creature from a Lovecraft story. While the Tuttles' mind-controlled their victims to do their bidding (even to the point of suicide), as the family members themselves had been mind-controlled by the previous generation, the good news is that Rust finds freedom. Near death in the hospital after a coma resulting from his battle with Errol, Rust realizes his daughter is in the afterlife, and that death is not the end, and he sees himself with a Christ-like visage.

As Marty and Cohle look up at the stars, Marty remarks that the dark is winning. Rust replies: "Well, once there was only dark. You ask me, the light's winning." Disturbingly, the newscast is heard stating that the higher Tuttle family members in the senate and other positions are cleared of guilt, though the series has made it clear there were other members of the cult. This shows the control the family still has, while Errol was just a patsy. *True Detective* is a reminder that no matter how dark and depraved the infernal powers and the deceived humans that serve them become, God has triumphed over evil through the resurrection. On still another level, there's a "conversation" being had with the audience – true detectives realize the subject matter is real.

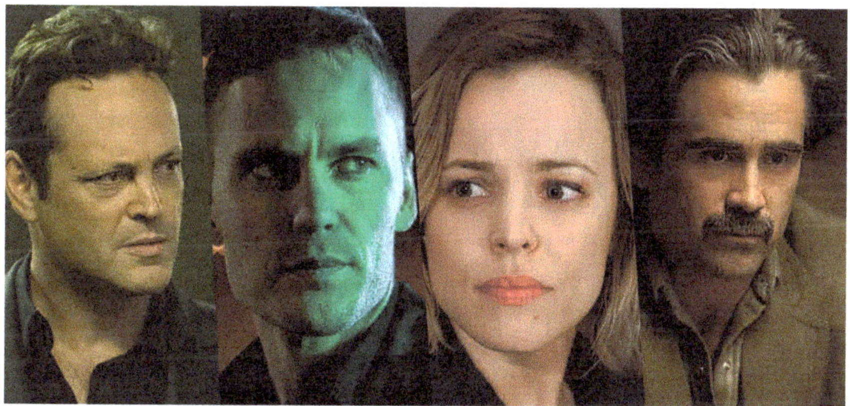

TRUE DETECTIVE SEASON 2

"All the most powerful ideas in history go back to archetypes. This is particularly true of religious ideas, but the central concepts of science, philosophy, and ethics are no exception to this rule. In their present form they are variants of archetypal ideas, created by consciously applying and adapting these ideas to reality. For it is the function of consciousness not only to recognize and assimilate the external world through the gateway of the senses, but to translate into visible reality the world within us." -Carl Gustav Jung, "The Structure of the Psyche" (1927), in Collected Works Vol. 8, *The Structure and Dynamics of the Psyche*, P. 342

Nick Pizolatto's second season of *True Detective* was quite a blend, spicing and saucing us with influences that ranged from classic of neo-noir like *Chinatown, Mulholland Drive, Lost Highway* and *Twin Peaks, The Black Dhalia* and a dash of *Weekend at Bernie's* with a side of *CHiPs*. In the midst of all this homage, however, we do find traces of the same elements of subtle occult and esoteric elements, almost as disturbingly intense as last season's psycho-drama. In this essay and analysis, we will examine and highlight those elements ignored and unknown to the mass of online critics, whose state school "arts" education long ago disabled any semblance of ability to recognize any meaning or significance beyond trite, boring gender obsessions. Indeed, this season's disregard for politically correct absurdities is welcomed and likely a source of much of the critical opprobrium.

The first season's intention, I argued, was to capture the essence of the soul's grappling with the forces of darkness and light in a world where it seems darkness owns the day. Even a nihilistic Nietzschean Übermensch can be tamed, and the heart's senses rekindled anew, as we witnessed Rust Cohle's transformation and Marty's moral cowardice. Here things get much more complex, with a variety of characters and a labyrinthine plot of crooked cops, diamonds, New age cults, human trafficking, drugs and gangs, big land deals, elite sex parties and mobster moves. Of particular interest to myself was the surprising fact that even *Vanity Fair* was willing to go down the rabbit hole in JaysAnalysis fashion, correctly likening the secretive, full-moon sex parties of the elite to their most obvious Northern California analogue, the infamous Bohemian Grove Club.[137] (Although the rumors surrounding Bohemian Grove don't involve gorgeous Eastern European *women*.)

Each character's name is also significant, where Frank Semyon (Russian for Simon) means I would speculate "frankly, God has heard." It also might relate to the vice of simony, or selling spiritual things for money. In either case, Frank's attachment to money, for his noble goal of having offspring ends up being the end itself, since what was supposed to be a means becomes the unfortunate end, as Frank dies in an arid, landless desert. Irony is apparent here, since Frank is the one who poisoned the California land to ensure farmers would move away providing ease of access for his rail corridor investment.

Season 2's focus was both hermetic, and straightforward. Each of our main characters will face the future successfully only insofar as they allow the relationships to their archetypes in the nuclear family cloud or ruin their present relations. Notions of paternity, progeny and seed dominate, with the phallus taking the center stage from last season's anal focus. For Frank Semyon (Vince Vaughn), the ability to have children to pass on his budding mobster empire to as inheritance, to have land, is the ultimate goal, yet he finds himself impotent through erectile issues. Frank, we discover, was abused as a child, beaten and left for dead, locked in a dank basement he ponders may have actually been his tomb. As we will see with Ray, Frank is correct in his pillow talk musings, that his life is a dream, as if he is dead, all is "paper mache." The esoteric theme for season 2 will be that this life is death, and death is entrance into the waking life.

For Ray Velcoro (Colin Farrell), the uncertainty of the biological paternity of his son mirrors his own drunk father's failures, as Ray takes on "the sins of the fathers," as they pass on to the sons. Lost in his own mentally-constructed prison, Ray struggles to maintain his sanity amidst a haze of booze, pot and coke, in the hopes he can gain custody of his pudgy, soft son. Ray's disastrous relationship with his possible son and wife are disastrous due to his own mistake in seeking inside information on his wife's rapist. Linking up with Semyon and going on bad information, Ray takes justice into his own hands and murders the wrong thug, leading to a downward spiral of more abuse, more outbursts and emotional train wrecks that bring Ray to the edge of self-imposed death.

Ray's name is Raymond, which signifies "wise protector" in German, and certainly Ray exemplifies this virtue, yet his last name betrays his fault, the strange modern artifact of "velcro," which is an artifact of synthetic attachment. Ray is attached like velcro to his own past traumas that are largely self-inflicted. As a man of the law like his own father, Ray unfortunately became compromised (like his policeman father) and began a side project of working as Frank's secret inside-the-force tough guy. Leading a double life, Ray is never able to reconcile this double minded double identity, as he edges closer and closer to death with each episode. In fact, he even briefly crosses the bridge into oblivion when he is shot with riot shells and passes into the aether, conversing with his father about how, exactly, he will die in the tall trees as Conway Twitty wails "The Rose" in full 70s glitz. One of the keys to this season will be this scene, with Ray's father telling him to wake up, in concert with the lyrics (more on this below).

Antigone Bezzerides (Rachel McAdams) was also abused as a child by her creepy hippy commune father's Mansonesque vagabond cohort, snatched away for days in a VW van and molested in the woods. Hardened by suppressed abuse, locked away in her unconscious mind, Ani's rough and tough exterior masks a voracious sexual appetite that shocks and startles her average male partners, leading to her own interest in porn as she simultaneously struggles to swat-raid porn pushers, lecture her sister on sexual ethics and dismiss both her lovers on the force. Ani's relationship to her father determines her course, as her inner anger at the molestation is placed on her father's below lackluster parental performance. Seeking solace in bizarre new age spirituality, Ani's father is distant and removed, like each of the other main characters. The subtle references to Carlos Castenada and the Chessani family's preference for psychedelics by the creepy plastic surgeon suggest the *inner* shamanic journey, which each character will be forced to embark upon, as a contrast to last season's outer worlds focused metaphysics.

Like Sophocles' play, *Antigone* has disowned her sister and ends up a stubborn heroine just like her Greek analogue. Ani's sister is a direct parallel to Ismene, as both docile and beautiful, serving as Ani's foil. Like Antigone in the play, Bezzerides defies the corruption of the state to honor the name of her son through Velcoro, meaning that unlike the ancient Antigone, she exits the cave of death. The interesting question here is how she exits the cave of death, which I read as her life previous to the conclusion of season 2. Only by facing the corrupt elite at the *Eyes Wide Shut* style orgy and gaining the information necessary to expose the criminal network could this be done, and in turn, that could only be achieved by posing as a prostitute herself, taking ecstasy and regressing to her childhood self where she sees the face of her molester. The drug trip forces Ani to embark on an inner journey set to a dreamy Disney-like score that suggests a possible mind control programming that recalls something out of *Fantasia, The Wizard of Oz* or *Alice in Wonderland*.

Highway Patrol Officer Paul Woodrugh (Taylor Kitsch) also deals with sexual issues in the case of his supposed repressed homosexual desires manifest in his instances of drug binging and blacking out. A former vet and private security operative with the curiously titled firm Black Mountain, Paul is both tempted and repulsed by his former partner and war veteran lover. Paul is missing a father figure in his life, too, with a derelict gambling addict mother we discover was a former showgirl who admits she never wanted a child for career reasons. What all these character studies demonstrate is the immense damage absentee and abusive parenting can create, especially in the case of the role of the "missing male," a trope I have highlighted many times, hearkening back to Odysseus and his journey.

Paul as a name of course recalls St. Paul, and just as the traveling evangelist longed to be on the road and forget his past life of persecution, so does Woodruff seek to remain a highwayman. Implicated in a tabloid sex scandal involving a Hollywood actress who falsely accuses him of harassment, Paul's assassin past as a veteran and member of Black Mountain Security never ceased haunting him, with "Woodruff" being a quite obvious innuendo translating to rough wood. Unintentionally siring offspring, Woodruff is intent on "being a good man" to make up for his murderous past that inflicts severe PTSD. Like the other characters, the traumas they have experienced have resulted in split personalities in varying degrees, with only Ani successfully facing and overcoming her trauma. In this regard, season 2 is ultimately a retelling of Sophocles' *Antigone*. Yet much more is at work that still should be explored.

Having explored the characters' psyches, we look now to the plot details and imagery that constitute the esoteric backdrop to the show's conspiracy-laced themes. Quite clearly the Bohemian Club and possibly even ritual sex magick are in the background, though this is only hinted at. The logo for the elite sex party features twin peaks with a moon in the background, and while we only see sex and drugs at the party, the land developer explicitly mentions that deals are best done "on a full moon." The scene ends with a full moon visible as the camera fades, suggesting the possibility of cultic meaning behind the timing of the orgy. The locale of the party and Ani's Guerneville Commune come close to the locale of Bohemian Grove, and the overt references to *Twin Peaks* impel us to remember the "owls are not what they seem." (The owl of Bohemian Grove, that is). In fact, episode one shows "Mulholland Drive's" street sign, as well as Ray talking into his audio recorder, channeling Agent Cooper's disembodied Diane.

As mentioned, Ray's aetherial dream sequence gives the ominous prophecy of his death through the sage figure of his own father, as he is instructed to "wake up," from the dream. The dream has a double meaning, both to the literal dream, and the present life, which both Ray and Frank describe as death and a dream. Both characters are continuously aware of their dates with destiny, as the wheels of fortune decree the wages of their sins will be paid through opposition to the corruption they helped foster, paid in their own blood that is to be spilled on the land. Blood and soil here serve a redemptive, sacrificial purpose, since both men are murderers whose blood will be spilled in return to atone for the havoc they wreaked.

As for California as the setting, the parallels to Polanski's *Chinatown* also bear mentioning, since William Mulholland, a key figure in the development of California's water system, plays into that fictional presentation of real-world corruption. The basis for *Chinatown* was the "California Water Wars" and the inside corruption on the part of elites who manufactured drought conditions to mask a massive water scam involving land deals. In *True Detective* season 2, the land deal figures prominently, where a land deal for a railway corridor with billions in state-funded subsidies operating as the boondoggle's true treasure chest. Photos in the Vinci Mayor Chessani's office show him colluding with Republican bigwigs like the Bushes also suggest Bohemian Grove, since the Grove has tended to favor a more neo-conservative and corporate roster. Note that Ani's would-be sex partner at the orgy is an "oil man." Could the timing of season 2 with California's drought have a twilight language reference to *Chinatown*? I suspect so.

Also crucial in this season are the numerous images of Marian statues and "Santa Muerte," specifically referenced more than once. Santa Muerte is the syncretistic worship of Mary as "Saint Death," often associated with MS13, the Mexican Cartel responsible for Frank's untimely demise.[138] In season 2's plot, MS13's collusion with corrupt officialdom is made manifest in the Santa Muerte statue at Caspere's sex pad. Along with dildos and numerous other fetish oddities, Caspere's lavish abode is decidedly marked by the statue of "Saint Death." We later learn the cartel was, in fact, running the drugs with the approval of corrupt cops that had also hired Black Mountain Security for the blackmailing of Woodruff. Black Mountain is a stand-in for Blackwater and Blue Mountain, both of which have figured prominently in the last decade in connection to the debacles of Iraq and Benghazi. Indeed, it is even hinted the infamous Rodney King LA riots may have been more than they appeared.

Hollywood is implicated, too, as the set for an apocalyptic film is the real location of the season's killer, where unexpectedly a set photographer was involved in the child trafficking network having been nabbed with his sister during the riots. As Caspere's death is covered up, ready-made news footage (that recalls season 1) rolls out as other crooked politicians and officials step in to take over the vast land deal. Stolen diamonds are the source of the troubles and the diamonds are of more import than appears on the surface. In alchemy, the diamond is a representation of the self and the reconciliation of opposites.

M. L. Von Franz comments, "…The Self is symbolized with special frequency in the form of a stone…. The nuclear center, the Self, also appears as a crystal…. The crystal often symbolically stands for the union of extreme opposites – of matter and spirit." ("The Process of Individuation," in *Man and His Symbols*, ed. C. G. Jung). The diamond's four-sided geometry signifies our four main characters, and recalls the four elements of the ancient world. Without proper transformation, the alchemical process results in disintegration and dissolution, and this is why only Bezzerides survives of the four, being the only one who overcame her personal trauma and changed as a result, becoming a mother through giving her love in union to another to Velcoro with the intent of producing offspring. Carl Jung speaks of this as follows:

> "In the *Practice of Psychotherapy*, Carl Jung discussed the archetypal underpinnings of love between people in terms of the rose: "The wholeness which is a combination of 'I and you' is part of a transcen-

dent unity whose nature can only be grasped in symbols like the rose or the *coniunctio* (Conjunction)." Ibid.

This is why the "rose" and "springtime" are mentioned numerous times in this season. The turn of the seasons is also quaternary like the geometry of the diamond, divided into fours like our main characters. Trapped in their own cyclical, spiraled, psychical prisons that echo Agent Cooper in *Twin Peaks*, Betty in *Mulholland Drive* or Fred in *Lost Highway*, the symbol of the rose is the signpost for exiting the winding, spiraled lost *freeway* of California fame that populate the opening title sequence. If season 1 was the outer journey into metaphysical questions relating to the higher dimensions and portals, season 2 is the inner journey of the psyche and the dream state unconscious. As we read in Bette Middler's song lyrics that characterize the narrative, it's not just the transmission of seed in the sexual act, love is also about the transformation of the individual's psyche throughout this life of death, in preparation for death, which is entrance into real life. It's the "dream afraid of waking that never takes a chance," in the case of Woodruff, Velcoro and Semyon, and for Bezzerides as Antigone, the seed of life will blossom into the rose of her new life, both in her psyche and in her offspring.

Lost Highway (1997)

*L*ost Highway is a bizarre, psychical film that has mystified most. Reviews and analyses abound with endless questions and speculations that often fail to transcend the most basic levels of "this is about Buddhism" and "a dreamscape." When connected with other David Lynch films, these elements are certainly present, but remaining on this level fails to plumb the depths of more esoteric motifs and symbols that even further integrate the Lynch canon. Indeed, the Lynch canon must be known in entirety before the individual works begin to reveal themselves. Lost Highway is a convenient starting place for analyzing Lynch, as it initiates what a friend of mine aptly titles the "Hollywood trilogy," comprising *Lost Highway, Mulholland Drive* and *Inland Empire*. In contrast to *Wild at Heart* or *Blue Velvet*, the "Hollywood trilogy" focuses on the dark side and corruption of the film industry. Many critics have pointed out these themes in Lynch, but there is a deeper level to the rabbit hole. Lynch films are not merely dreamy zen meditations on Americana and film, but long, dark journeys into the dark side of the unconscious that envelop the viewer in something more ominous than satire or tales of pulp crime. The Lynch viewer is shown a profound, surrealistic revelation of the dark side of something much more ancient, functioning like a shamanic journey into cosmic, primeval mysteries.

The best description for *Lost Highway* is Neo-noir occult psycho-drama. The telling of the story is non-linear, yet influenced heavily by classic 1940s Noir. *Lost Highway* is influenced by zen philosophy and Jungian dreamscapes, but as for the deeper occult elements, it's necessary to understand why the stories are presented in an interlinking duality, as they are in *Mulholland Drive*. Zen philosophy is concerned with duality and its transcendence, as ultimate principles, as well as with the individual's particularized psyche, and its relation to the whole of reality. Zen is therefore a quasi-religious philosophy concentrated on ultimate metaphysical principles, known in philosophy historically as the problem of the one and the many. For Lynch, these philosophical questions are not just abstract philosophy, but also relate directly to the psyche in its conscious and unconscious/sleep states.

The opening credit scene is a car racing down an ominous dark highway which will be our first clue to the ultimate meaning, as this is also the final scene. The highway will represent the mental stream of consciousness Fred Madison (Bill Pullman) is experiencing, as the truth of his life and actions begin to manifest in this cyclical dreamworld. Fred is on a journey into madness – into his subconscious, as he suppresses his guilt for murder. The murder of his wife Renee (Patricia Arquette) and two others due to his vengeful jealousy has led to a dissociation and split in his consciousness, as well as his darker side becoming possessed.

The first scene is an anxious Fred lighting a cigarette. The igniting flame is a staple of Lynch films, signifying the a dark foreboding or evil presence is about to emerge. One thinks immediately of *Wild at Heart* or *Twin Peaks: Fire Walk with Me*. The "fire walk" is the shamanic practice of obtaining possession in order to miraculously move over coals or through fire unharmed. The shamanic walk or journey also corresponds to the astral journey the spirit of the medicine man takes, as his hallucinogenic or spiritually induced state takes him down a ritual path of personal dismemberment and re-assemblage: the resurrection motif. However, in Lynch's film, it is not Fred, our shaman, who will be resurrected, but his wife Renee that will undergo dismemberment, while Fred will suffer the punishment of guilt and torture with no escape from his self-imposed, cyclical nightmare prison.

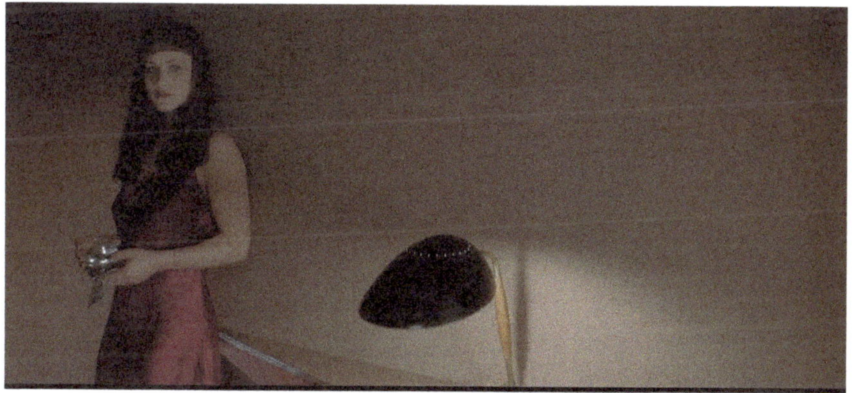

The infamous Lady in Red, the femme fatale with an alternate personality.

Esoteric writer Peter Levenda comments on Lynch in this regard: "'I learned that just beneath the surface there's another world, and still different worlds as you dig deeper," quoting David Lynch. A recurring feature of David Lynch films is the flickering light, a result, we are told in the pilot episode of *Twin Peaks* – of a "bad transformer." This flickering electric light will appear in Lynch films such as *Mulholland Drive* (and *Lost Highway*), to announce the appearance of the Cowboy, a bizarre character who speaks in gnomic riddles, like a cross between Gary Cooper and and David Carradine. In *Twin Peaks*, it is the light in the morgue over the place where the body of Laura Palmer had been kept, and which is then visited by Mike, the one-armed man, who recites the famous poem from the movie:

"Through the darkness of futures past
The magician longs to see;
One chants out between two worlds
'Fire walk with me.'"

There, in a strange little verse, we have the key to unlocking the mystery not only of *Twin Peaks* but virtually all of Lynch's films: the suspension of normal laws of time ("futures past") and the idea that the magician lives "between two worlds." The suspension of normal, linear narrative event in favor of a dreamlike, hallucinatory set of images that are taking place all over the fourth dimension is part of Lynch's appeal as a director, and part of what makes his films so frustrating to the filmgoer. His realization that there are two worlds, and a place to stand between them, is what contributes to his aura as a modern, twenty-first century initiate of the Mysteries, for that is what "mystery" films are: elucidations of the core Mystery behind reality." (*Sinister Forces*, Vol. 3, pg. 151.)

And this forms the solution to *Lost Highway*, as well. The shamanic and magical elements are here in full force, as Fred is a character trapped in different psychical worlds that seem to unfold and envelope other psyches, as we will see. As Fred walks to his front door, he hears police sirens as a voice says, "Dick Laurent is dead." The first key to my thesis that the film is his cyclical mental prison is that the end of the film shows who the voice was: Fred himself. The police sirens are the cops after him for the murder of Renee, Andy, Pete and Mr. Eddy/Dick Laurent. In the next few scenes this truth is hinted at as Renee and Fred begin to receive strange VHS tapes on their doorstep that feature their own house under surveillance. Disturbed, the couple passes it off, as Fred begins to suspect Renee is cheating with porn mogul Andy. Renee refuses to attend Fred's sax gig at Luna Lounge, and says she intends to stay home and read. Luna Lounge is significant, because the moon is a feminine symbol associated with the dreamworld, night and madness (lunacy). Fred sees Renee actually present in the audience with Andy, and as he phones home, the scene is lit red, signifying envy and rage.

Fred returns home to attempt to have sex with Renee, only to follow through with great difficulty, knowing that her lack of affection shows she has been unfaithful. The Cocteau Twins' "Song to the Siren" plays, with the lyrics, "did I dream, you dreamed about me…" signifying again that this is a nightmare world. Fred dreams that night that he cannot find Renee in his house, and he is immediately confronted by a strange presence of the camera that frightens him. It is as if Fred's world has come into contact with us the viewer, or the coming "man in black" that later records Fred at the end.

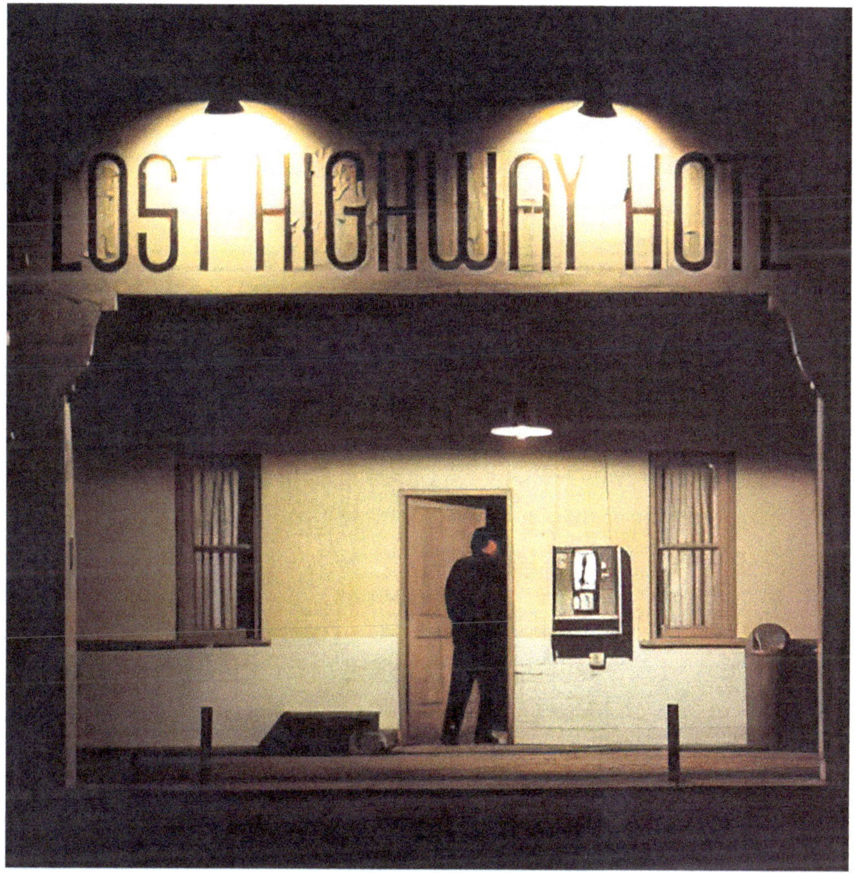

Lost Highway Hotel

The meaning here is the jumbling up of these dreamworlds that Fred is lost in. In the dream state, a smoke appears, a fire roars, and the face of the man in black appears in Renee's. The man in black is the devil, whom Fred has given entrance into his consciousness. In Jungian archetype studies and psychoanalysis, the house is an image of the mind. Rooms are like memories that store events. Fred's house is thus his mind, and the entrance of the devil is the beginning of the cause of Fred's suppressed guilt, madness and personality splitting. Fred's displaced guilt for murder is placed on Renee, which is why he sees the devil in her face. It is important to note that in Fred's dreams, he walks deeper into dark hallways into his bedroom. This is him going further into his subconscious, uncovering the truth of the crime he has committed and suppressed.

The next VHS that arrives is even more frightening, as it shows a camcorder entering the house and filming them sleeping. Fred insists Renee watch it, though she is reluctant, but his insistence demonstrates that he is the likely culprit. When the cops arrive, they begin to be suspicious that Fred is the one behind the threat. In reality, we don't know for sure which elements are real or a dream in regard to the videotape, but what we do know is that Fred wants Renee to feel threatened that she is under surveillance for her infidelity. Panopticism emerges here, as there is a statement being made about the rise of unmitigated surveillance that will be evident later in the film. What is the result upon society of everyone peering daily into the videodrome, and the NSA surveillance videodrome staring back? The effect is the transformation of the psyche of the public, as we saw in Esoteric Hollywood 1 in my breakdown of Hitchcock's prophetic *Vertigo*. When Renee calls the police she tells them the address is "703, Hollis, near the observatory…" The observatory is a huge glass eye that watches. It is another subtle clue concerning panopticism.

When the police question the couple, they ask if Fred owns a video recorder. Fred replies that he hates them and prefers to "remember things the way he wants to, not how they happened." In other words, the film is Fred's victimized version of how he went mad, and how the devil tricked him, Renee lied, and his enemies deserved it. This becomes evident in the second half of the film with Pete, but before moving there, there is an elite Hollywood party Fred attends with Renee at Andy's mansion. Here, Renee flirts with Andy and Fred walks off in a huff, only to bump into the man in black (the devil). During a creepy conversation with the man in black who appeared to also be in Fred's house after forcing Fred to make a call to his own house, Fred is told that he "invited" the man in black in. In other words, the devil couldn't just enter Fred's consciousness, he had to be let in through Fred's willingness. Fred discovers that Renee used to date Andy, and comes home to find someone upstairs rummaging around in his bedroom.

It is Fred that is upstairs in his bedroom, and as the couple retires for the evening, Fred walks down the long, dark hallway (of his subconscious). At the end of the hall, he sees himself in a mirror, and we begin to understand there are two Freds. The dark Fred is the man in black that possesses Fred, and causes him to split in consciousness, emerging from the dark hall to kill and dismember Renee. All along, Fred is being led deeper into the darkness, signifying his willing acquiescence to evil.

Following this sequence, Fred awakens to find himself being interrogated for Renee's murder and sentenced to the electric chair. While in his cell, he seems to astrally project himself into the body of a young guy named Pete. A rebellious car repairman, Pete likes to chase fast women and cheat on his girlfriend: He represents several things, but primarily he is the life that Fred wants – to return to youth and be the guy who is able to have multiple girlfriends and be the one cheating. Pete inexplicably ends up in Fred's cell, symbolizing that he is beginning to be possessed by Fred. Recall that in *Twin Peaks*, agent Dale Cooper ends up possessed.

Pete is then swept up into a tryst with mob boss Mr. Eddy's girlfriend, Alice, who appears to be Renee's twin. The theme of doubling is present again, and given that Fred's imprisonment included him seeing a doctor and being medicated, we can speculate that there may be an element of mind control involved. Indeed, Alice, we come to discover, is working with the man in black and Mr. Eddy/Dick Laurent, as a porn actress. Their circle is not just porn moguls and stars, but includes an occult and Satanic element. When Alice tricks Pete into coming to Andy's mansion to steal his money and kill him, we learn it was all her plan, along with the man in black. When Mr. Eddy threatens Pete, it is done under the direction of the man in black. In other words, there is a cult involved here that is tied into porn and the mafia: when Pete enters Andy's house, Rammstein plays, and the lyrics are "you see him creep around the church."

As Pete follows his *femme fatale* into the wilderness, Alice says they must meet a fence (thief) who will buy their stuff. The "stuff" the devil (the "thief") wants are the souls that are going to die that Renee/Alice is going to help him get by getting others to do the killing. While at the devil's cabin, Alice and Pete have sex again, and we hear the Cocteau Twins play again – "did I dream, you dreamed about me…," and Fred reappears naked. The devil seems to be crafting this narrative of Fred's desire, as he shows Fred to the Lost Highway Hotel, where Renee is cheating with Mr. Eddy/Dick Laurent. Fred beats and kidnaps Eddy/Dick from room "23" of the hotel and takes him to the desert where the man in black watches on. They hand him a small TV that shows a porn party with their circle watching what appears to be a kind of snuff film, with Marilyn Manson being killed.

Pete, if you recall, was first seen out in the desert with a head wound when Fred entered him. Pete doesn't remember what happened to him or how he was lost, but as the police follow him (more surveillance), Pete begins to suspect that another consciousness (Fred) has possessed him and carried out murders. The final desert scenes are thus Fred's vantage of possessing Pete, and discarding him after it's done. Pete, it seems, was both a lost soul in the aether with a head wound, as well as Fred's victimized version of himself. The end is Fred buzzing his own intercom to tell himself (at the beginning of the film) that "Dick Laurent is dead," as he races away from the cop sirens that alarmed Fred in the beginning. The final scene is Fred racing down the lost highway, going into a jerking seizure reminiscent of someone in the electric chair – his very punishment for the murders. We can speculate that the story is Fred Madison's cyclical experience of his downfall and electric chair death, which then repeats again as he races down the road.

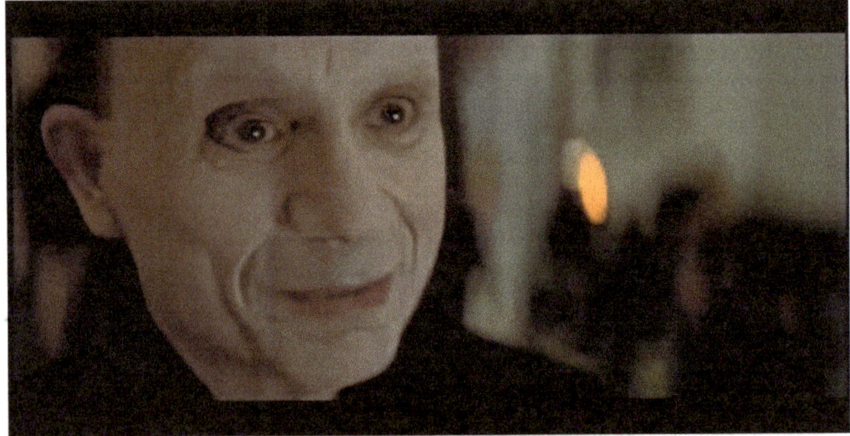

Man in black.

Lost Highway is therefore a non-linear, Neo-noir occult psycho-drama that looks at the dark side of the Hollywood underworld, where mafia, porn, crime and the occult are interwoven into a story about one man's psychic journey down a lost highway of his own stream of consciousness and thought. As the viewer travels with Fred Madison down this road, we are brought back to the very point he began, and the cycle starts again. Packed with dualism, illusion and mystery, *Lost Highway* is about life and the dark side of our own inner underworld, the subconscious, which Lynch mystically links to others'. If we fail to realize the reality of these evils, such as possession and the mysteries of the subconscious, are we liable to be trapped like Fred in our own madness? His name itself is a clue – "Madison," symbolizing his descent into madness, as "Alice," Renee's alter, brings to mind *Alice in Wonderland* and alternate worlds and personalities. Was Alice a victim of mind control like Fred, or were they both willing accomplices of evil? Will the obsession with the Hollywood celluloid videodrome and its cousin, the now omnipresent surveillance society, bring us truth, or more likely a descent into madness, depersonalization and dissociation like Fred? Either way, Lynch is forcing us to examine that at base, reality and the psyche are still mysteries to be decoded.

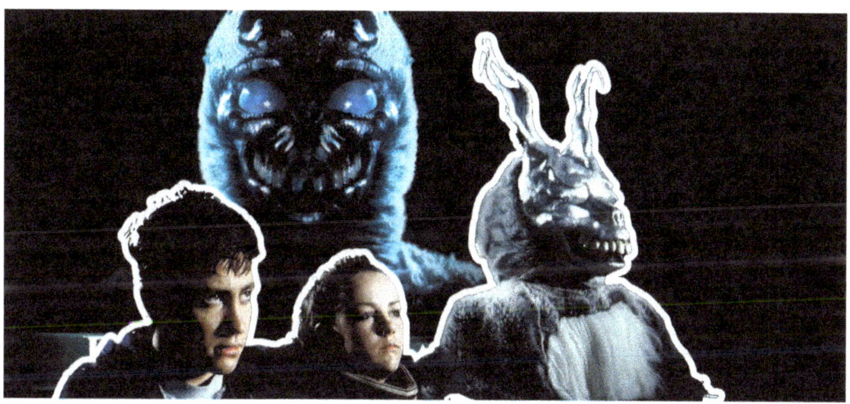

DONNIE DARKO (2001)

Donnie Darko is an homage to 80s culture. It's now become a cult classic (like many 80s films!) that references other 80s films, uses popular 80s film themes, and is set in 1988. But *Donnie Darko* is about much more: It is also a statement about the socio-political and cultural developments of the late 80s, the reversal of family roles, the Bush era of political control, as well as a dark superhero film, or more properly, an *anti-super-hero* narrative. It's also a metaphysical debate on celluloid that presents the age-old discussion about predestination and free will and the possibility of a multiverse. Given the recent pushes for multiverse theory from the establishment, the film was ahead of its time in terms of cultural zeitgeist. To add further layers, it also contains elements of Jungian psychoanalysis, gnosticism, and the occult.

The film's opening line from "The Killing Moon" by Echo and the Bunnymen is: 'Fate, up against your will; he will wait until you give yourself to him." The classical hero archetype must thus face up to his fate and survive with stoic resolve, which is the most basic level of *Donnie Darko's* meaning. As the camera pans a slow motion scene of 1988 middle America, a contrasting dinner scene displays a family that is remarkably dysfunctional (despite the idyllic frontispiece). Donnie's father is not a very good father: he remains inept and passive throughout the film, as the mother runs the family, while the children are all rebellious and profane. Director Richard Kelly is highlighting the facade of "moral majority" Republican neo-conservatism here, through his criticism of 80s culture, especially its backward, hypocritical suburban morality. Later, as we see Donnie's bedroom, the camera catches a large image of M.C. Escher's famous eye, whose art reflects the philosophy of both labyrinths, mazes and other dimensions. In this work, inside the reflection of the pupil, is death

253

itself, which will be a major theme in the film (death from a particularly Jungian perspective).

Donnie, we learn, has hypnotic trance visions and sleepwalking he experiences and when he first experiences the film's initial trance, what is visible is the Led Zeppelin album label image for Swan Song with an image of Lucifer falling, next to the upside down flag, signifying nation in distress. Since we know that Donnie is actually in an alternate universe where he escaped his own death, we can interpret this is a "fallen" world, or an inverted, upside down world where most things are familiar, yet some form of dark dread always accompanies the viewer (and Donnie) throughout the narrative that something is deeply wrong. Indeed, this is one of the masterful aspects of the film Kelley has introduced: a lurking sense that something is cosmically off with this whole world, and only at the end (and after many viewings) do we see how misdirected we were.

Donnie's bedroom is actually the lynchpin on which the entire film pivots, as towards the end we realize the jet engine was actually headed for his bedroom. In fact, the fall of the engine is a "fall" through the roof – right where the image of Satan is. Without getting into too much speculation, the All-Seeing Eye is sometimes associated with Lucifer or Satan, but it generally depends on the context and intent, since it is also used to refer to the omniscience of the true God. Solomon speaks of God's all-seeing eye in the Proverbs. Egyptians applied the image to Horus as a symbol of the divine attribute of omniscience: While the eye can mean different things, in modern Satanic culture, it is often applied to Lucifer.

It is also significant that Frank, the dead spirit of Donnie's sister's boyfriend that possesses Donnie, communicates at midnight. Midnight is associated in many traditions with liturgical actions, and presumably in the occult as well. We read, for example, in Bram Stoker's *Dracula*: "It is the eve of St. George's Day. Do you not know that tonight, when the clock strikes midnight, all the evil things in the world will have full sway?" The spirits of the dead and demons thus commune at midnight in literature, and this is when Frank speaks to Donnie, especially as the film move closer to Halloween night, which will be very significant – that is when Donnie's "world" will end, as Frank explains, when he first speaks to Donnie in a trance. The first list of numbers Donnie "receives" from the dead spirit are all composed of, or can total, 666. Six, in biblical *gematria*, is the number of man, and in the Apocalypse of St. John, the number of the Beast. Frank says "28 days, 6 hours, 42 mins, 12 seconds" and the world will end. 8-2 is 6, 6 hours, 4+2 is 6, and 12 is 6 + 6. With the level of depth and thought put into the film, I don't think numerology is a stretch.

It is also significant that as the engine crashes into the house, the father is watching the Bush/Dukakis debate of 1988 and is totally invested in the neo-connery. We know that what was really going on in Nicaragua and elsewhere was drug running, as the Iran-contra scandal showed. The great irony here is that Donnie is drugged up, and experiencing serious spiritual problems, while the "war on drugs" psyop was just getting started in the 80s. The establishment is here shown to be a fraud, and this anti-establishment theme runs throughout the film as Donnie is a Christ-like anti-hero.

Donnie's high school's mascot is the "mongrel," which carries the connotation of retardation and idiocy, which is apt, since the entire establishment, government (with Bush, Sr), the parents, teachers and principal are all duped and fall for con artist self-help guru, Jim Cunningham's and his corny scam, "Attitudinal Beliefs." The "Cunning Vision" production of "Controlling Fear" is hilariously awesome, but it also has a deeper sense, since a person of "cunning" is someone who has psychic or occult powers, and Donnie is the visionary prophet of the film. It's also significant that the woman who was a prisoner of her fear looked "through the mirror to see the reflection of her own Ego." This will be crucial when we consider the other instances of Donnie seeing his Ego's image in the mirror – Frank.

Frank, who begins to take a larger picture in Donnie's life, is Donnie's Ego, which, in Jungian analysis, must be integrated into the waking self. In this gnostic theory, the self is not whole until it reconciles all dualities into itself. The archetypes must be reconciled, or they will control us, Jung argued. In Donnie's progress at his psychiatrist's office, he goes deeper and deeper into his subconscious, and the therapist finally pulls Frank out, who we learned was, for Donnie, "God." But Donnie also can't make sense of this rationally, and argues that God doesn't make sense, and that perhaps raw materialism and atheism are the case, yet in the end, he'd rather not debate it, because "Frank" is leading him. If his world ends, the therapist tells him, it will only be Donnie and God/Frank. Frank, you recall, is Donnie's Ego – his mirror image, and is the personification of Donnie's fear of death. One must also recall this is all an *alternate reality* where Donnie has asserted his will in the face of what he fears is raw, nihilistic determinism. Instead of predestination, he has opted to fight his dark shade (Frank, in Jungian lingo), who is both a devil figure and a good deity. It is also worth noting that Donnie's therapy sessions are full of Jungian and Freudian analyses, terms and symbols.

Donnie is thus what he comes in contact with – the manifestations in the film are elements of his subconscious he must reconcile. This is not to say they are wholly unreal, as is the case with Nolan's *Inception*, which has a very similar plot, and as I layed out in my earlier analysis. Rather, this alternate universe was perhaps created by Donnie himself to work out the necessary contradictions and tensions to accept his own death and find meaning in it. Jena Malone plays Gretchen Ross, Donnie's girlfriend and as she becomes his love interest she functions to "wake" Donnie up. This is precisely the role of the Anima and/or mother archetype in Jungian psychoanalysis.[139] While it might be tempting to say Donnie's mother is the mother archetype, she plays a minor role, while the two archetypes of anima and mother are combined in Gretchen, since she is the key alchemical force that sexually awakens Donnie.

When Donnie arrives at school and we have the iconic scene where Tears for Fears plays, the camera is noticeably sideways. This clues us in, both to the sideways nature of this alternate world, as well as the sideways, out of kilter nature of the school itself. The entire social structure is askew, and Donnie is apparently the only one who has the guts to point this out: again, this is why Donnie is an anti-hero. The link to the Satanic/Luciferian side of Donnie is found in the key scene where he explains the meaning of the Graham Greene (former British intelligence) story, *The Destructors*, that "destruction is a form of creation." This is the mindset of the darkest of the dark – since reality is determined by brute force and raw materiality in an irresistible causal chain that cannot be broken, all actions are thus levelled and ontologically the same. There is thus no good or evil – all acts are equalized and part of the "machine," and recall that Donnie will say to the bullies at the end, "Deus ex Machina" or *God from the machine*. The world, Donnie struggles to accept, appears to be a determined prison machine. Since this is the case, burning down Old Misery's house is qualitatively no different from destruction. which constitutes a Satanic element in the film. I am not saying this is the only way to interpret the film: It can also be read in a positive way, where Donnie realizes his own life is not as important as everyone else who may be negatively affected in a universe where he escapes his death.

Donnie is ultimately a highly intelligent and gifted teenager who is unfortunately drugged by BigPharma (we think) but he continues to have intense experiences of synchronicity, communication with the dead spirit, Frank, and visions of the future. As it turns out, his pills were placebos, so we know the experiences were real, and in the end, prophetic. Another key to decoding this film is precisely the famous sequence where Donnie talks to Frank in the movie theater during *Evil Dead,* and Frank responds that Donnie "wears a stupid human suit." Later, in one of the debates with Professor Monitoff, Donnie was told that bodies are "vessels that travel along vectors in spacetime." Donnie is inhabited by the spirit of dead Frank, but since this is a Jungian film, the external world is not a real, objective reality, but rather a projection of the psyche and the subconscious desires that are yet to be integrated. The universe Donnie inhabits (later *Donnie Darko* lore explains) is a tangent universe that is temporary and unstable, awaiting the reconciliation of the mistake from the original universe. Since Donnie has not reconciled good and evil in himself, as well as male and female, and all dualities (in the Jungian sense), he is presented as a "prisoner of fear" – ironically showing the Cunning Visions self-help infomercials to be correct! This is a masterful use of irony and humor. Significant also is the fact that when Donnie leaves the movies, we see the sign for *The Last Temptation of Christ* playing, cluing us in that Donnie is a kind of antiChrist hero – a savior, as the "Jesus" figure of the *Last Temptation* was in fact an unorthodox, Nestorian portrayal of Christ.

In my *Inception* analysis and with this analysis, we have seen that the Jungian elements are evident: Carl Jung was himself a self-professed and in some form or fashion, an "Illuminist." Jung believed the archetypes are not just symbols, but, in his actual description, gods, or demons. In fact, not only that, he even attributes the "discovery" of all people having an *anima* to the "Illuminati" in older, now *removed* video interviews. In fact, Jung wrote a Luciferian work called *Aion* about evil and the "anti-christ" where he argues evil and antichrist are as necessary as good and Christ: they are flip sides of the same coin.

Later, Donnie sees a vision where the school is flooded while Frank leads him to burst the water line, causing school to be out the next day. As a result, he is able to ask Gretchen one a date and decide to "go together." Next, we see Samantha Darko, Donnie's little sister, reading a poem titled "The Last Unicorn," whose name is Ariel and is saved by a prince named "Justin," who is translated to another world of "magic and wonder." The poem seems irrelevant and out of place, unless we understand that this *alternate world is Donnie's alternate world* where he (Justin) saves the unicorn (Ariel) Gretchen. Recall also that in Scripture, "Ariel" is another name for Israel, so in terms of occult lore, it is a spirit in Judaism and gnosticism. Of particular note is the "wrathful" conception of "Ariel" from the gnostic text, the *Pistis Sophia*, which pictures "Ariel" as a destructive spirit – precisely what Donnie is. Wikipedia notes (accurately):

> "Ariel has been portrayed as a destructive spirit of retribution. In the Coptic *Pistis Sophia*, Ariel is in charge of punishment in the lower world, corresponding with Ur of the Mandeans. (Possibly due to Ariel's association with the Archangel Uriel who is often equated with Ur and said to serve the same role.) Both Ariel's anthropomorphic and destructive attributes have led to associations with the deities Nemesis and Sekhmet, among others. However, Ariel's position as a spirit of wrath seems to be more in keeping with Judeo-Christian tradition of heavenly servitude. Ariel is usually depicted as a controller and punisher of demons or wicked spirits rather than a general retributive force."[140]

Donnie, when he saves Gretchen, his Ariel, and has sex with her, reconciles with the anima and lets loose his sexual repression, which he had expressed under hypnosis to his therapist. Gretchen is his Ariel, and his anima. It is when he unites with her that he then sees his destiny (at midnight), and it is when he looks into her soul that he sees his destiny – "cellar door."

When Donnie later looks into Gretchen's soul, his *anima* and *sophia*, Ariel, he sees a portal and hears "Cellar Door." Donnie has here realized his destiny, and he must face it – to travel to Roberta Sparrow's as the constant synchronicities had been leading him all along. Roberta Sparrow, the ex-nun who became a radical atheist after writing her book on time travel, ends up being the major catalyst to explain this alternate dimension (which was the subject of her book): years earlier, she left the church and became 'Grandma Death,' as she is called throughout the film, hearkening to Lilith, as well as to Old Misery in the Graham Greene story.

When Donnie arrives, what he discovers is that it is his nemesis, the bully who is waiting at the Cellar Door that he must face as well as that it is he who accidentally kills Frank. Thus, Frank, the spirit who has been haunting him all along, and who figures as God and a projection of his *psyche*, is also his shade, or darkside, representing his own self-actualized will. As a side note, "Cellar Door" is said by Drew Barrymore's character to be the "most beautiful combination of words in the English language." This is a reference to Tolkien, and of course with Tolkien we associate a mythical alternate world (Middle Earth) as well as the "Eye of Sauron" (again, eye imagery), but it was also supposedly a phrase attributed to Poe and others. Why is all this important? For the same reason that Cobb in *Inception* has to reach the deepest levels of his subconscious: It is there that he has hidden away his shade, or darkside. For Donnie, it is at Roberta Sparrow's (death) house he has hidden away the fact he killed Frank, his sister's boyfriend, in an act of rage for accidentally running over Gretchen. The "cellar door" is the doorway to *the basement* – in Jugian analysis, this is *the subconscious realm,* wherein man is the most evil and bestial, a a primal realm from which his irrational passions – Freud's Id!

Donnie must face his fears – his evil – his *self,* that he has, by his *triumph of will* (note that when he last visits the therapist, he is wearing a tee-shirt that says 'Triumph" on it) and *decision* to be a superhero – an *ubermensch,* set in motion a course of events that leads to the death of his friends. So the resolution comes in the fact that Donnie decides to be a stoic – to accept his fate as Donnie Darko – the kid who was smashed in a freak jet accident. The entire alternate world story is the elaborate story and tangent universe Donnie concocted because his world came to an end – just as happened to Cobb in *Inception.* God here is a projection of the subconscious' fear of death – and hence the identification Donnie makes between Frank and God to his therapist: This is why Donnie says *Deus ex Machina* to the bully – the idea of God as a product of the determined machine, he realizes. In my opinion, this is why the film poster has a collage of all of Donnie's projections/archetypes making up the God/death mask of Frank. Masks also are symbols of the personas and projections we hide behind to cover the deeper hidden truths we seek to suppress and fear to face which perfectly explains the film poster and the "human suit" line Frank uses.

And so we end with a rupture in the subconscious of others as a result of Donnie's death. It is as if they dreamed the alternate world Donnie constructed where he was the anti-hero, and they are noticeably distraught at his death on Halloween. So Donnie's alternate world is one of fiction, and the reality is that one must face one's fate stoically. So the film presents us with two false alternatives – a world where one is perhaps a Nietzschian dark hero who does as he lists, wreaking havoc, or a world where we are determined by purely brute natural forces. Is it better to be *Donnie Darko,* the dark hero who burns down the establishment, doing some good in the process, like exposing Jim Cunningham, the self-help guru, as a pornographer, and ultimately killing two friends, or is it better to be a stoic acceptance of fate – to be that kid who died a crazy death in high school? But in that second option he saves the girl he loves. Here, the metaphysical questions devolve back to the free will/predestination debate, but only to pose it in the context of the occult – can you be the overman, the anti-hero or the true hero who sacrifices himself to save those he loves (as Donnie eventually does).

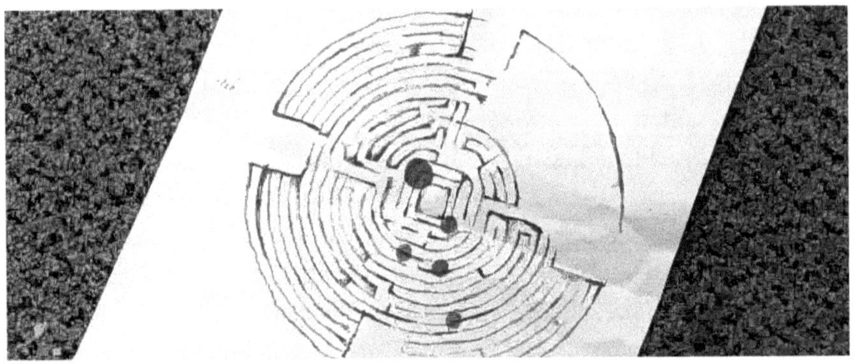

PRISONERS (2013)

Although Richard Kelly has taken a break from Hollywood films, Jake Gyllenhall did not, and has continued a track record of notable performances in a series of esoteric themed films. His next notable role in this regard was acclaimed Canadian director Dennis Villanueve's *Prisoners*: A dark look at the mental effects of child murder, human trafficking and mind control. Gyllenhall plays a Freemason detective tasked with finding a recently kidnapped suburban girl, the daughter of a fundamentalist woodsman prepper, played by Hugh Jackman. When his daughter disappears, the only clue is a weird, unknown creeper van parked in the neighborhood manned by a mentally challenged man with the mind of a ten year old (who happens to be named "Alex Jones," played by Paul Dano).

Given the rural town had a history of kidnappings and murders, Officer Loki (Gyllenhall) stops by the home of the local pedophile Roman Catholic priest's home where he finds a body with a labyrinth necklace. This could be hearkening to the Boy's Town role in the infamous Franklin Scandal, where Boy's Town was used to supply male street children to powerful politicians and elites for sexual favors, as detailed in *The Franklin Scandal,* by Nick Bryant (also by this publisher). As the police search for clues, Keller Dover (Jackman) decides to take on a role of rogue justice and kidnaps Alex Jones, housing him in a makeshift torture pod until he can extract the location of his daughter. Villanueve is raising the issue of hypocrisy in "justice" when it comes to fundamentalist evangelicalism, which often posits a rigid view of determinism and original sin (Keller is shown listening to a radio preacher talk about the damnation of humans from original sin), while showing little restraint in his treatment of Jones. However, Jones is involved in the plot and has whispered and bragged to Keller hints and clues he knows the full story: Yet at the same time, Keller seems to shift personalities and revert to a traumatized childlike state as well, causing himself immense confusion.

Keller's limited information, combined with Officer Loki's inability to believe Keller or the possibility of the long term scope of the kidnappings and killings is precisely the genius of the film – which causes us to ask similar questions about the possibility and scope of such horrific trage- dies in our world. Indeed, even in 2013, when few had heard of Jeffrey Epstein or other notorious pedophile entrapment and trafficking oper- ations had been publicized, it was understandable people were skeptical and unaware, which makes the extent of the revelation in Prisoners so shocking. Like *Eyes Wide Shut, Prisoners* forced audiences to examine a methodical and tactically precise ring of kidnapping and trafficking that simultaneously trained the kidnapped to become the future kidnappers.

As these children matured, they were later traumatized and brain- washed into becoming trapped in the labyrinth as well. Thus, in the film, the recurring theme of the labyrinth has several layers: One one level, the labyrinth originates in ancient Greek mythology as a symbol of the un- conscious, the dark domain of the Id, from which our primal and beastly desires arise, while in the Middle Ages it became an emblem of this world before the afterlife: a maze of archetypes and correspondences the mind must wander through to find its way back to the One (Neoplatonism). And on yet another level, the labyrinth is the fractured and traumatized psyche of the various kidnapped children who were recruited for the net- work of the two older ex-Hippies who have a vendetta "against God." This is accurate: committed Satanists do believe the promulgation of wicked- ness helps convert theists to atheism and thus it is a war on God. This sub- tle clue suggests the elderly couple are not merely atheists, but committed Satanists engaged in a serious, deranged warfare that includes maximally evil actions.

We are shown the labyrinth imagery as something presumably used in the kool aid cocktail the elderly kidnappers use when abducting and brain- washing the children, including explicit occult texts and manuals shown in a few brief sequences. Lastly, the labyrinth is the puzzle that Gyllenhall finally solves when it is almost too late: The kidnapper ring is run by the innocuous, friendly old grandma, like something out of a *Grimm's Fairy Tales*. Gyllenhall barely makes it in time to save Keller's daughter from poisoning, while Keller ends up lost in the maze of the underground tunnels (the physical labyrinth) the wicked granny had dug on her property. The tunnels theme could also suggest the notorious McMartin Preschool scandal which was part of the 80s "Satanic panic" fiasco, and while newspapers and mainstream media mocked the "conspiracy theory" there were tunnels under the daycare, recent FBI declassifications admit there actually were tunnels as the FBI's Ted Gunderson had claimed:

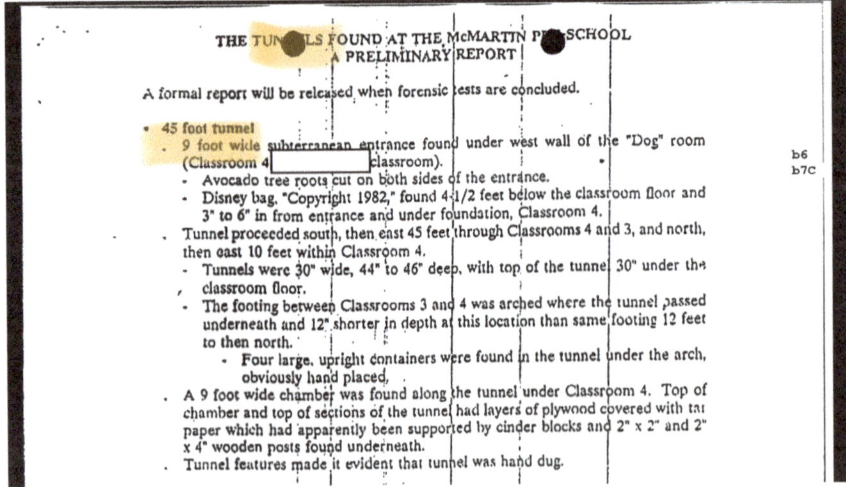

THE TUNNELS FOUND AT THE McMARTIN PRESCHOOL
A PRELIMINARY REPORT

A formal report will be released when forensic tests are concluded.

- **45 foot tunnel**
  - 9 foot wide subterranean entrance found under west wall of the "Dog" room (Classroom 4 [ ] classroom).
    - Avocado tree roots cut on both sides of the entrance.
    - Disney bag, "Copyright 1982," found 4 1/2 feet below the classroom floor and 3" to 6" in from entrance and under foundation, Classroom 4.
  - Tunnel proceeded south, then east 45 feet through Classrooms 4 and 3, and north, then east 10 feet within Classroom 4.
    - Tunnels were 30" wide, 44" to 46" deep, with top of the tunnel 30" under the classroom floor.
    - The footing between Classrooms 3 and 4 was arched where the tunnel passed underneath and 12" shorter in depth at this location than same footing 12 feet to then north.
      - Four large, upright containers were found in the tunnel under the arch, obviously hand placed.
  - A 9 foot wide chamber was found along the tunnel under Classroom 4. Top of chamber and top of sections of the tunnel had layers of plywood covered with tar paper which had apparently been supported by cinder blocks and 2" x 2" and 2" x 4" wooden posts found underneath.
  - Tunnel features made it evident that tunnel was hand dug.

b6
b7C

The Box (2009)

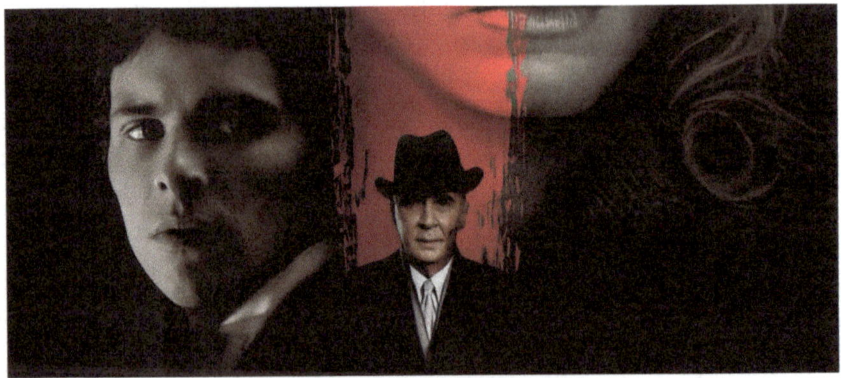

"You are the experiment."

Continuing the theme of Richard Kelly films, we come to his last offering, the critically dismissed 2009 horror, *The Box*. As I often opine, fictional films can show you more about what is really going on than the fictional mainstream news outlets and *The Box*, though far less popular than *Donnie Darko*, is a striking example. *The Box* (2009) is Richard Kelly's most recent film – Kelly of *Donnie Darko* and *Southland Tales* fame. All of Kelly's films contain deep esoteric themes, and *The Box* is no different as it is packed with "illuminist" and conspiratorial tropes. *The Box* also contains countless hat tips and nods to Kubrick, as well. On the surface, the viewer is presented at the outset of the story with a moral dilemma: On its most basic level this is a film about compromising morals, human weakness and suffering the consequences.

On another level, it describes the elite worldview and control system with stunning detail – but not just the elite perspective – it also contains an even deeper, initiatory or perhaps quasi-masonic level. As noted, the film was not a critical success, and barely broke even monetary wise, but I suspect its meaning went over the heads of audiences. The story takes place in 1976, where NASA Viking Mission camera engineer, "Arthur" (James Marsden) and his wife "Norma" (Cameron Diaz), have just purchased a large, new home. They are the typical middle class suburban family, pictured as overwhelmingly mediocre, in fact (on purpose).

We learn a certain prominent figure named "Arlington Steward" (Frank Langella) has been resuscitated and released from the burn unit: Early one morning Arlington arrives in a black Lincoln, as a "man in black," and mysteriously drops a box off at Norma's door. Meanwhile, Arthur heads off to NASA to privately construct a prosthetic foot for Norma, who is slightly crippled. Recall, of course, that in many purported "UFO" experiences the so-called "men in black" arrive on the scene, etc, which could suggest a member of the NSA or some other unknown deepstate organ (Note that I am not advocating aliens and the assorted myths attached thereto). This "alien" topic will be relevant later in the analysis, however. Norma discovers the box has another box in it with a large red button on top, and Norma is astonished, while Arthur discovers he was rejected from acceptance as an astronaut, a longtime personal goal. Presumably, the young couple's funding for their new house and car would come from the astronaut position, placing them in an economic bind and thus susceptible to the box's monetary offering.

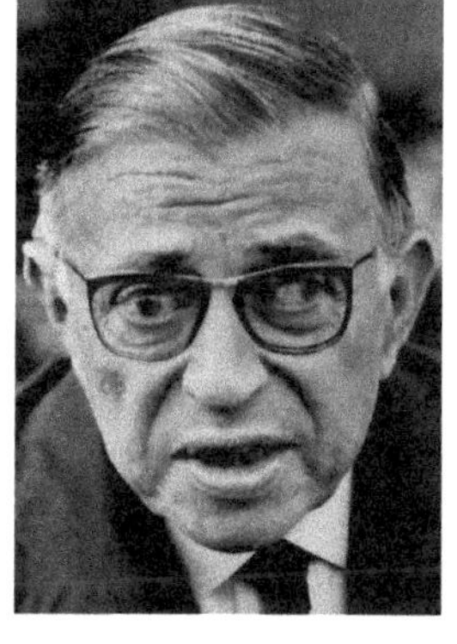

Norma teaches English at a local Catholic private school, and significantly, they happen to be studying Jean-Paul Sartre's (pictured above: Someone should have made *him* wear a mask) play, "No Exit." At this juncture, a certain miscreant in class speaks up and attempts to embarrass Norma by asking her to show the class her club foot, and Norma acquiesces. This is relevant to those familiar with Sartre's philosophy as Sartre proffered that as we mature, it becomes evident we are simply hiding behind various "masks" as a kind of cloak to escape the radical freedom we are *condemned* to. For Sartre, Norma's clubfoot is an imperfection she hides because it's a reminder that her beautiful appearance which masks the clubfoot is a *facade*. Were Norma to embrace her defect, she would actually be *free from* the stigma such defects produce in our *psyches*. Indeed, for Sartre, we even hide behind such roles as "suburban middle class wife," because there is a kind of ease in accepting this pre-programmed role handed on from the previous batch of middle class suburban forebears. Sartre calls this "being in itself," and likens it to inanimate rocks. Those who become "free" realize reality presents us with "radical freedom," and when this is accepted, one becomes "being for itself," a being that is totally free and undetermined: This will be relevant for the later "initiatory" reveal. In fact, her name "Norma" even reveals her character as a supremely "normal" person, a bland "normie."

Norma mentions to another student in class the famous Sartre quote that "hell is other people," because it would be like others "knowing all your faults." We should also note that Arthur's young son doesn't believe in Santa when the subject comes up in the kitchen, because Arthur is a "scientist." It is also relevant that this is Christmas time, and for a true existentialist it would be a time to understand that "scientism" is yet another mask. The so-called logical "scientist" hides behind the mask of "rational induction," and when presented with mystery or radical freedom, he timidly avoids the fearful conclusion by resting his *faith* in the imagined totality explanatory power of "science." It is precisely here that Arthur and Norma are about to encounter something they could never have imagined.

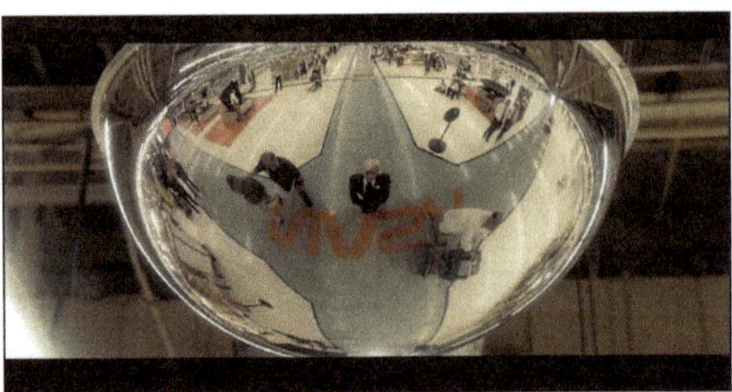

Shadowy shadow government figure no one is aware of, who watches as Watchers do.

The next day NASA gives a press conference for the upcoming Viking Mars Probe and curiously interjects statements about the expected discovery of "alien life" and "ancient alien civilizations." Interestingly, this is precisely what Arthur C. Clarke and his NASA videos and interviews at the time *were* promoting![141] If you are dogmatically a believer in alien life, you will interpret the "evidence" to find what you're looking for, which is not very scientifically "neutral." Instead, we are being given a larger clue as to the meaning of where the film is going – the underlying new mythology the supposed "scientific establishment" has predetermined we will "discover" was a prepped and created narrative of "alien life." The new "discovery" or disclosure will be that there is "life" elsewhere in the galaxy, a form of exotheology, which is the *planned* new cosmology that replaces man's origins and *telos* with aliens, technocracy and *apotheosis*. However, *The Box* is going to give us a veiled clue as to *who* the "aliens" *really* are. During the press conference, one reporter asks why NASA is working *closely with the NSA,* which goes unanswered!

Norma also loses her job and Arlington offers them both one million dollars if they push the button on the box, which will result in the death of someone whom they do not know and they have 24 hours to make a decision. Arlington leaves as abruptly as he came, and the couple find themselves in a quandary. Arlington is also disfigured from the burn leading Norma to sympathize with him and the monetary offer. Next, we see an image of a surveillance camera at NASA looking down on the workers with a strange man in a suit looking into the camera. This figure is crucial, but he only shows up in the film a couple of times, purposefully looking on from the background. He is in the shadows, another "man in black," and represents the shadow government, controlling NASA which is a front for the NSA. We never learn his identity, other than that he is the "employer" of Steward. "Steward," is his name obviously because he is a representative.

Norma ends up deciding to slap the button, after coaxing a still doubtful Arthur over their need for money, yet who isn't willing to push it, but allows Norma. Here we have an echo of the fall of Adam and Eve in Genesis 1-3, where the woman's choice is particularly central to the narrative: They, like Adam and Eve, have now fallen. The couple then goes to see the play her English class had been working on, which is Sartre's "No Exit," where three people discover they have been escorted to hell by a valet who is a kind of devil, while the rest of the drama takes place in the same room (and a room is a *box*) where the torment ends up being the other people, fulfilling Sartre's quip that hell is "other people." The play is a microcosm for the film as it becomes evident Arthur and Norma and their son are the ones being escorted into their "hell." The "box" they have been imprisoning themselves in is their own life and its lies.

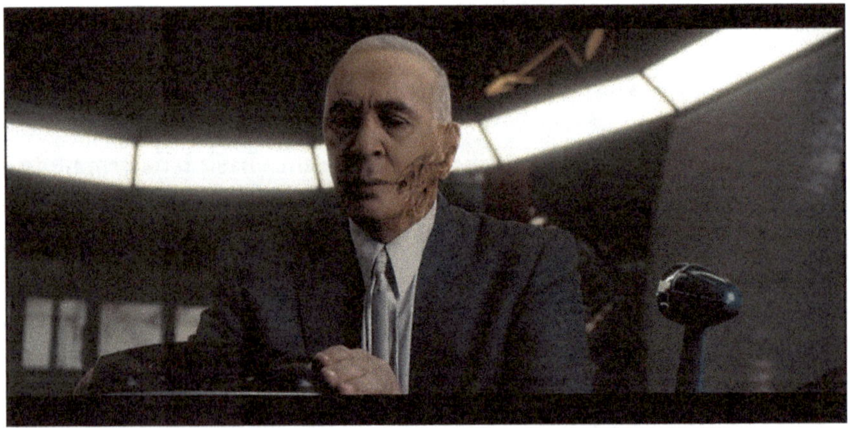

The "man in black," Arlington Steward, the "steward" of the gods, in a Kubrick-esque scene.

It is also important that intermittently throughout the film the television is on in the couple's home, and almost every time what is briefly seen is relevant on an esoteric level. The television is a *box*, too, and a powerful propaganda tool for boxing us into mind prisons. The first time we hear someone on the television speaking they state "people are causing pollution," while the next time it mentions NBC and then "Barry Goldwater." Now, all of these are relevant for setting the timing of the film, but also for deeper meanings. For example, in 1976 the modern globalist "environmental" movement was fresh on the scene following upon the Club of Rome and Kissinger's push for population reduction based on "human pollution." The couple later attends a Christmas party with co-workers and townsfolk where things begin to get really strange, as random persons in the crowd ogle them with paused, dirty looks. The revelers play a game where you pick random presents under the tree, and Arthur picks a box which he discovers has a blurry photo of Arlington in it, suggesting they are being stalked.

Meanwhile, a new babysitter has been staying with their son, and notices they too are being watched by a random stranger through the window. She takes him to the basement after a discussion of comic books, and we notice the covers of the comics feature an odd sequence: an alien, a casket floating in space, and a skull imposed over a gateway. The babysitter sees Arthur's Arthur C. Clarke poster, and says "My dad knows him." Arthur C. Clarke's "third law" shown emblazoned on the poster now comes to the fore, which becomes a clue to another deeper esoteric theme: that "magick" is indistinguishable from science. The lesson Arthur will learn as he experiences the events is that science isn't the end-all be-all of existence and what he will undergo is a magickal initiation, constituting his own gnostic process of *apotheosis*, as he and his Eve have now "fallen." This is why many viewers were confused as to the meaning of some of the scenes during the film's final 30 minutes.

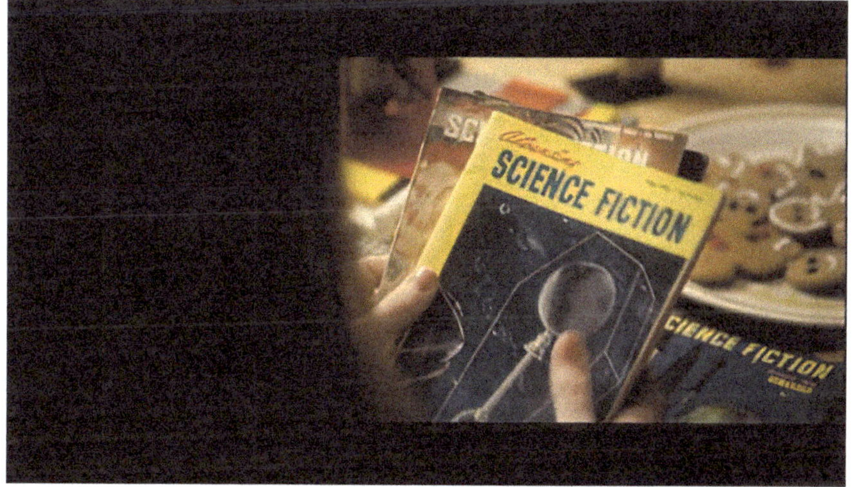

The science fiction casket.

The film then transitions back to the Christmas party where a creepy waiter provokes Arthur by awkwardly and incessantly laughing at him (it is the same student who embarrassed Norma in class). A waiter then escorts Norma to the phone, while suddenly going mute and falling into a trance as his nose bleeds. Arlington knows Arthur has been trying to track down who he (Arlington) is, and sends a reminder they made a deal which cannot be broken. No one can know who has selected them, nor what the deal was. Arthur ends up punching the student waiter while he (the student) merely laughs and also experiences a nosebleed after flashing a peace sign/two with his fingers. As Arthur and Norma flee the party, someone has etched into the ice on their car's windshield "NO EXIT," while another waiter flashes the "two sign" with his fingers. Arthur begins to piece the puzzle together, discovering Arlington's car is registered to the NSA. Arthur thus understands how his family is being constantly surveilled.

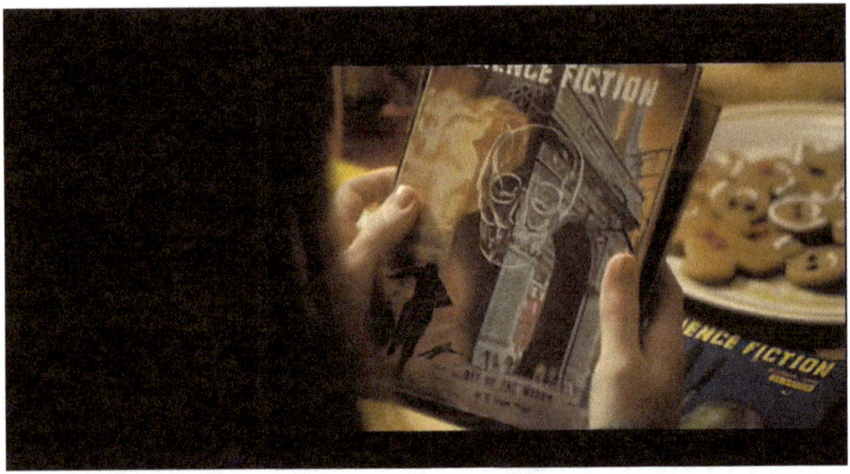

"The Day of the Moron": destruction and death at the gates of the two pillars.

Next, a bizarre scene appears on the family's television: the Twin Towers! While this image is seemingly out of place, recall that several other television references had a subtle significance: Global pollution, Barry Goldwater, NBC and now the Twin Towers. The year is 1976, so the towers had just been finished a couple years beforehand.

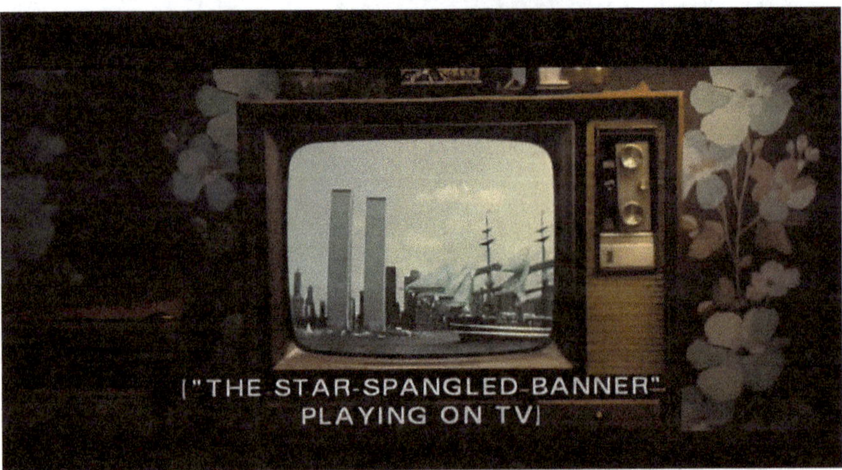

The intentionally-placed twin towers on a "box." It was on a box that most people saw these come down in a psy-op.

The towers came down in 2001 of course, and films and intelligence warnings and operation manuals such as Operation Northwoods had long contained those very scenarios. What few are aware of are the occult and magical correspondences of the destruction of the towers, which extend beyond merely political ends.

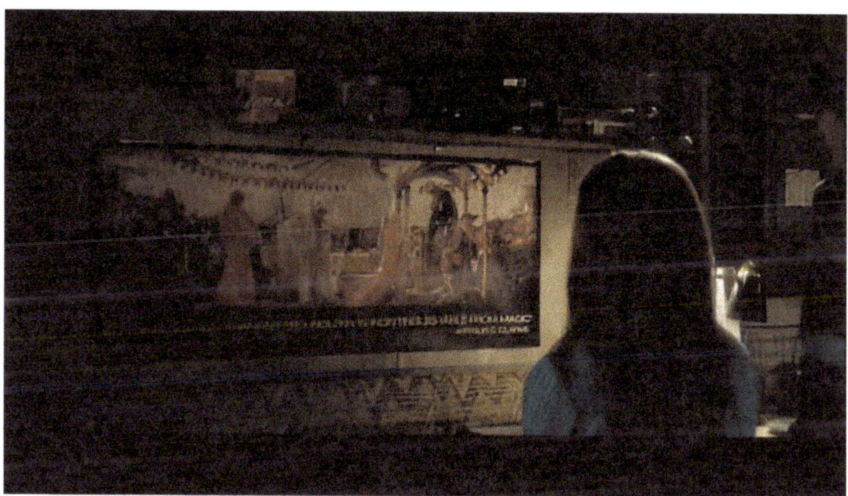

Arthur C. Clarke's famous "third law," from the Ten Commandments of *Psience*

The twin pillars "falling" has a relevance to Kabbalah, as well as Free-masonry, which have, as their "gateways" the twin pillars, Jachin and Boaz, as well as the notion of the "middle pillar." Recall that on 9/11 three towers fell, not just two, while in the occult, and in the Golden Dawn in particular, the middle pillar signifies equilibrium between the two side pillars of mercy and severity, as well as being the "pillar of initiation and integration." It is the balance between the yin and yang, dark and light, male and female, etc. It is the product of Arthur and Norma – their son, the child of the union. The middle pillar is also the "wand" of the magician, and has a phallic connection, and this is exactly what is happening to the "scientist" Arthur, as he undergoes his initiation. The middle pillar also has reference to the six-sided cube of space (all directions), which many associate with the Holy of Holies in the Levitical temple, from which all of this is

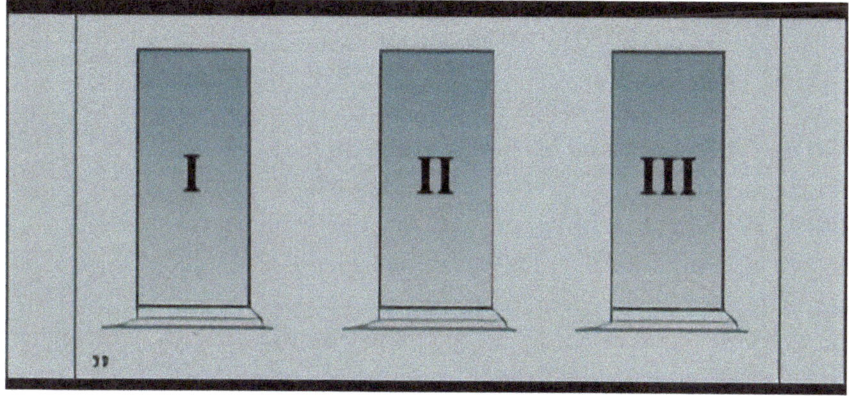

The Masonic "middle pillar" of initiation.

269

borrowed because the numerical gematria of the middle pillar is "26" (6 sides, 8 points and 12 edges), which is a perfect cube. And a perfect cube is a box.[142] The destruction of the towers has the significance of the production of the new order of the ages, since all initiatory theories include the idea of the death of the old, and resurrection into the new. This is what will happen to Arthur, too.

Back to the story: Arthur begins to lose his sanity driving the babysitter home; she realizes he has literal "blood on his hands," bringing to mind the idea of guilt. The babysitter makes a strange reference to looking into the "light" and passes out after a sudden nosebleed. The film features constant appearances of blood which is highly symbolic due to Arthur working on the Mars mission – Mars is the "red" planet, and corresponds to the "god of war," and the devil. These are more hints as to who is really running this show. Arthur discovers that she isn't really a babysitter after finding her ID, and we then are shown Arlington building what appears to be a "Stargate" at the NASA facilities. We hear again on the television in the next scene "the eagle has landed," and the Mars mission will show us definitively that there is "life on other planets." Thus, the NSA who really runs NASA and Arlington is brainwashing his "employees" who are also "test subjects" mindlessly submitting to his magical techno Stargate "light" baptism. Apparently Arlington died in the E.R. from the lightning strike, and awoke possessed by a different "entity" who was now serving a new "employer." The surface level meaning of the story is that his consciousness is now invaded by an invasion of the body snatchers alien, as are the employees who pass through Arlington's baptism of "light." This is the "light" of Freemasonic initiation if you thought this was crazy so far- this is just the beginning.

As Arthur and Norma are busy tracking down Arlington and the secret government testing they have now been clued into, they end up at the large public library, which is slated to become a kind of church/lodge. This makes sense, as a library is a house of knowledge, or *gnosis*, and this is where Arthur in particular will undergo his demonic ritual initiation. Arthur is led in a liturgical procession to the "holy of holies" of the library, in whose doorway appears Arlington's wife, who grants him a occultic liturgical "blessing." We

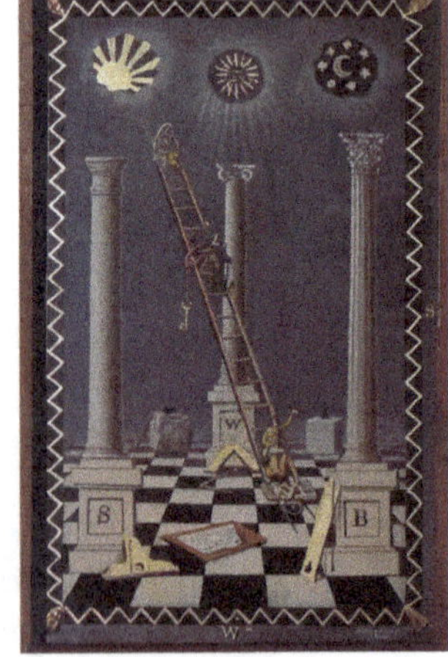

are then shown a large painting on the wall above the "holy entrance way" that is the same as Arthur's poster, which shows a *magus* being initiated.

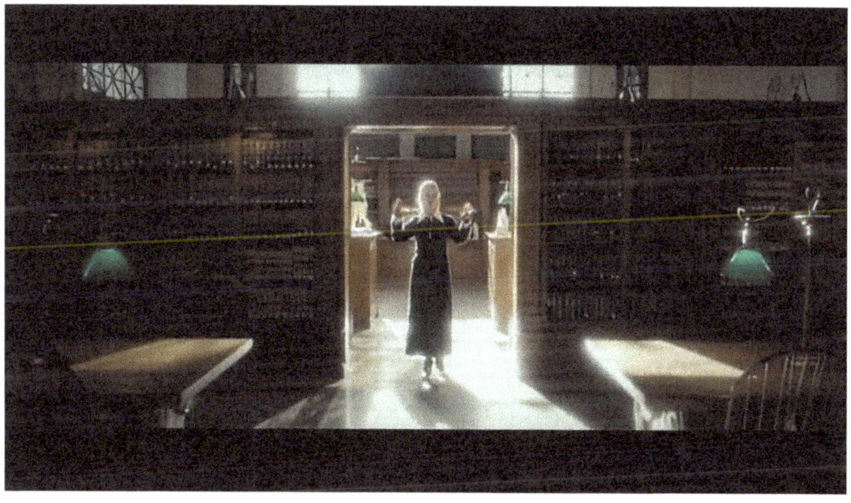

Welcome to the Most Holy Church of the Library Gnosis. Please place your late fees in the collection plate.

Now Arthur has understood that science and magick are indistinguishable as his own poster proclaimed. In the room, Arlington's wife reveals herself as "Clymene," who was, in fact, one of the Titans and a goddess, and whose name is reminiscent of Klymenos, or Hades.[143] Arthur is then shown three pillars that are watery, aetheric gateways. He must choose one, as the others result in "eternal damnation," he is told, hearkening back to the choice they had for the box. He recalls everyone had held up the number two, so he chooses the *middle pillar* and is taken up into the light and sees what he later describes as "heaven." Simultaneously, Norma had been ushered elsewhere in ritual fashion to see Arlington, whom she tells she "loves." Arlington says "take my hand," which is reminiscent of marriage, and we then see Norma laying on her bed and as she awakes, floating above her in a watery cube is Arthur. When Arthur awakens, "the water is broken," and he falls onto the bed. Arthur has gone through a baptism inside a watery casket, and is now reborn. Remember we had seen skulls and caskets already, and caskets and death are common in religious initiation ceremonies as the old man dies and a new identity is born.

We then learn that Arlington has been doing all this as a "test," and the test is a massive experiment conducted by the shadow government who are now revealed as his employers. Not only is this the shadow government, we are even shown a striking reference to the actual layout of the military industrial complex where Arlington looks at a large screen that has flapping tiles that alternate to show a map of the entire globe. It appears as a kind of early Google maps, and amazingly what is revealed briefly on the map is the actual layout of Northcom, Centcom, etc.! Arlington's NSA lackey asks him why this is happening, and he responds that the test is being conducted to see who is allowed to survive, and whether the earth should be depopulated! The test involved being presented with federal reserve notes – *fake money,* and the moral dilemma of whether one will choose to support the greater good of humanity, or a selfish path of killing another human to obtain fiat currency. Note that Arlington didn't bring anyone a bunch of gold bars. Instead, it is paper currency, and for those in the know, this 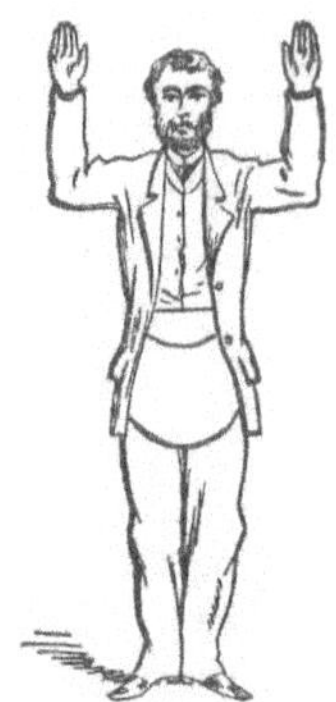 is how the shadow government maintains control – through control of the issuance of federal reserve currency which explains the previous references to Goldwater (who discussed the Federal Reserve), pollution, the green agenda and NBC. We then see that Arlington is lining everyone up secretly in a police state setting and sending all his subjects through the brainwashing stargate, preparing for the next test scenario. We are then shown a brief scene where the grid displays a magic square! This only further confirms in this narrative those running the shadow government are an occult, magical-minded, scientific banking elite. Their grid has long been in place, and we are, in their estimation, a huge psychological test ward.

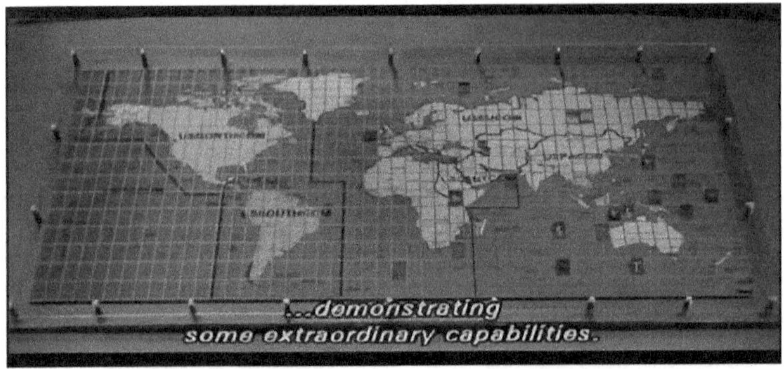

Arlington's grid shows the actual shadow government – Northcom, Centcom, etc.

After more paranoia and attempting to run, Arthur is caught by the men in black and we see him enigmatically emerge from Arlington's luminous brainwashing stargate. This scene has confused many viewers because it seems to be out-of-place and out of sequence. But this is done on purpose, because Arthur's senses have been altered, as he has passed out of time and space into the *aether* for initiation, and emerged back on earth. However, his purgation is not finished, as he is now made to sacrifice his wife or child to continue on, as Arlington's employers are not happy with Arthur's opposition to their plans.

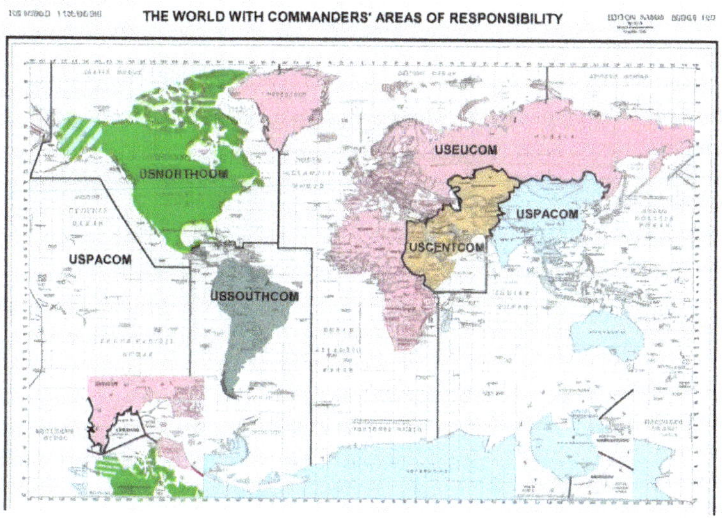

The actual Pentagon Northcom, etc., map.

Arthur ends up killing Norma so that their son can live on, but ultimately it means Arthur must give them both up. The audience assumes Arthur will be nabbed by the police, and when they arrive after he has shot his wife, it should be noted that he is not led into a police car. The men in black arrive to take him away, not the police. Arthur is one of them now: He has been initiated and has sacrificed all he previously held dear. His son is now under the care of the shadow government, they tell him, and we see him in a window with who appears to possibly be our mysterious "employer" who has only appeared briefly in the background.

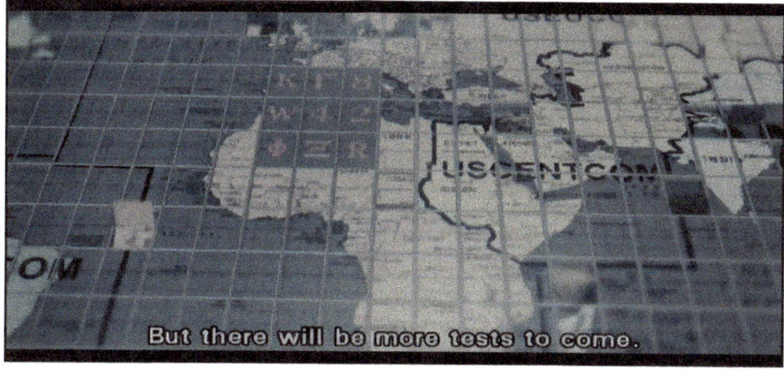

Peculiar shot with the magic square, showing the google-earth-like matrix spy grid.

It is important to call attention to the name "Arthur," which conjures up images of the Arthurian tales, where the king is seeking the magical holy grail. Arthur has found his "grail," which is the truth of the magical shadow government. His wife was "Norma," which sounds like "normal." Her mundane existence was the result of their fall, but her "sacrifice" to Mars allowed his redemption and "deification" to occur. By following the clues and hints found all around him, Arthur discovered the truth, and *exited* the hell of his own making, as Sartre would say. The box is, Arlington says, the object we spend most of our time in – cars, which are metal boxes, houses, caskets, etc. The film takes the box, the cube of space-time and the holy of holies, and transforms it into the object of elite scientific envy – to master this realm and become gods. This is what Arthur C. Clarke often wrote about and is the paradigm from which the transhumanists and technocrats operate and it is they who make up the real shadow government. *The Box* not only displays this worldview, it is telling you – as you watch a box (a TV screen or a movie screen), that this is precisely what is *actually happening*: the shadow government sees all this as a test and as the movie tagline reads, "You are the experiment."

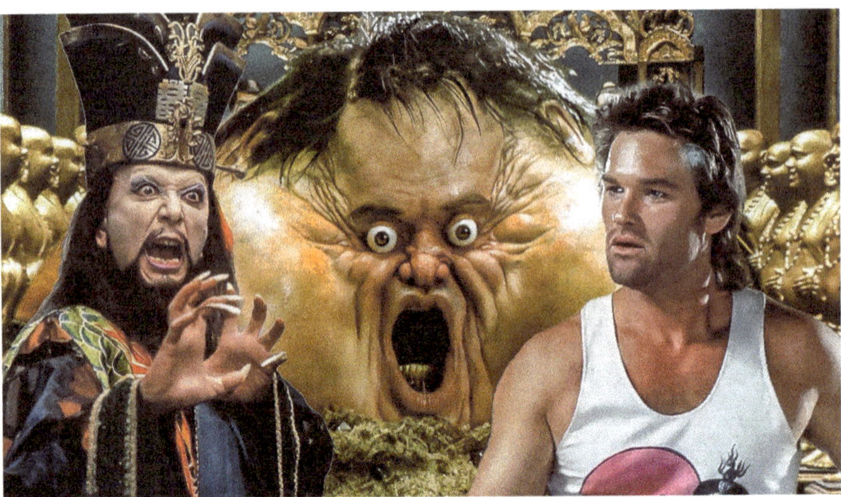

BIG TROUBLE IN LITTLE CHINA (1986)

Big Trouble in Little China is another one of those goofy 80s films that you're presently assuring yourself has no deeper relevance. You're smugly saying, "Oh come on Jay, seriously? Another 80s esoteric analysis of something completely silly, like BTILC?" Well, dear reader, let me assure you of your error, and further promise to deliver juicy esoteric tidbits to sate your hunger as you journey on. Consider the opening scene that Fox mandated be added (where Egg Shen recounts the adventures of Jack Burton). The actor is Jerry Hardin who played "Deep Throat" early on in the *X-Files*. Interestingly, the ambiguous government agent played here is similar to Deep Throat. What is also interesting is the obelisk on the desk behind him, initiating the viewer into what will be an occult journey.

Egg Shen reveals that the tale ahead will be one of Chinese "sorcery and black magic." As proof, Egg Shen offers typical 80s blue lightning, of the Force variety. According to IMDB, the Chinese script in the beginning title sequence reads, "Evil spirits make a big scene in little spiritual state," meaning the film will feature the primeval ancient religious tradition of the higher aeons or gods incarnating themselves in lower, visible, solid forms. This is almost universal in ancient cultures, from Greece and Rome, to China, and lends credence to the view that polytheism and monotheism come from a single religious tradition, as described in Genesis 1-12.

Note also that Egg Shen conceives of the usage of good and evil magic by both sides. Magic, in this view, may be used by the dark side and the light side, in what the dualistic scheme of most world religions views as the ultimate template for all reality. Eastern religions in particular have this dualistic focus, with the binary opposition never being transcended in this life, apart from "enlightenment" that results in some kind of dissolution or absolving into "pure being," "thusness" or "nirvana," or some state of being beyond the present world, which is often identified as "evil" and the domain of the fallen spirits and demons. The problem with this type of worldview is that it is self-defeating and contradictory. It claims to seek transcendence of the material and of all binary opposition, but its answer is to seek it in absolute impersonality. Since particularity and form in this world are the sources of "evil," all particulars must dissolve. The result is monism and collectivism, and the history of eastern cultures demonstrates this enslavement clearly.

I also came to the same conclusion one writer for *Huffington Post* did: Jack Burton represents Amerika in its modern, aberrant and excessive forms. Jack Burton drives a truck – nothing is more typical of the blue-collar Amerikan man – and is not very intelligent. In fact, in production, he was described as a moronic John Wayne. He is self-absorbed, has had several wives, eats junk food and acts more or less like a pig, which is why he drives the "Pork Chop Express." Consider as well that the pig is, in Jewish law, unclean: A perfect image of unbridled consumerism whose worldview is based on cliché one liners and catchphrases. As Jack arrives in Chinatown, director John Carpenter shows several shots of animals (humans are often likened to animals before the gods), calling to mind that Jack is in the wild. And not only is he in the wild, leaving civilization, he is about to enter the Underworld. Not just the Underworld of Asian crime, but the actual Underworld of the dead, as is often found in myths like *Orpheus* or the *Tibetan Book of the Dead,* or even the Egyptian *Book of the Dead.*

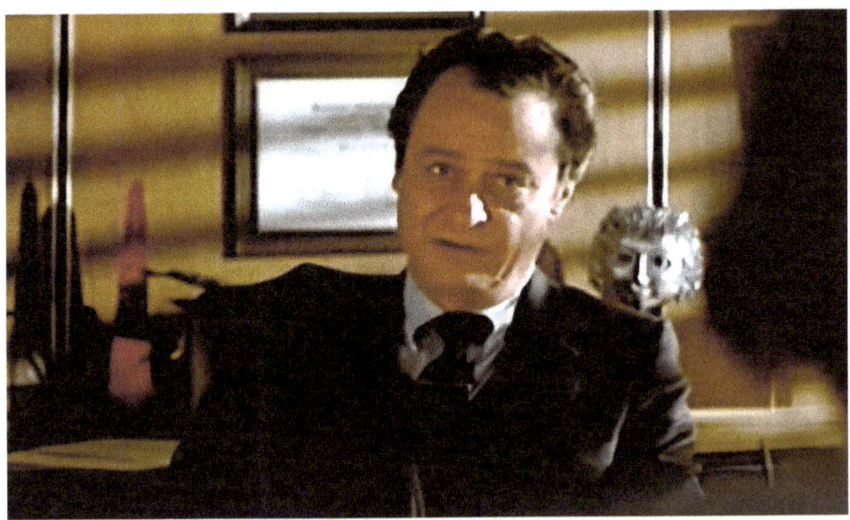

"Deep Throat" has a Masonic obelisk. The beginning of a series of occult/phallic references.

There are also plenty of stereotypes and phallic references, such as "Wang" and "Jack." Butterfly imagery appears early on in the background, cluing the viewer into the transformational nature of the coming journey. Not only does alchemy have an ancient pedigree in the West, it has just as elaborate a history in the Orient, and here we will see Jack engage on a trans-formational odyssey of his own. Does this signal Amerika's own alchemical journey into a hellish control of the Underworld as an alchemical purifying process? Indeed, we do see Amerika collapsing into just such a situation.

At the airport, Jack and Wang bump into a version of the Triads, the "Lords of Death," emphasizing the spiritual nature of the Underworld jour-ney Jack is about to embark on. The Lords of Death are the gods who rule in this *dual nature* Underworld: of both crime and hell. In the airport, Jack meets "Gracie Law," played by Kim Cattrall. The dualism present in her name is evident, as Amerikan Christian religion, especially in the Pauline tradition, has always been in a state of binary oppositional tension between "grace" and "law." Wang is there to pick up Miao Yin, his bride, and synchronicity ensues in the fact that Gracie Law also has green eyes. Miao Yin is kidnapped by the gang and taken into Lo Pan's sex trade operation, we later learn. Her name is interesting in that it also hearkens to dualism, while Miao recalls Mao Tse Dong, the communist leader who utilized dialectics, and "yin" which refers to the feminine, unseen principle, and "yang" to the complimentary masculine principle. It also refers to earth and sky.

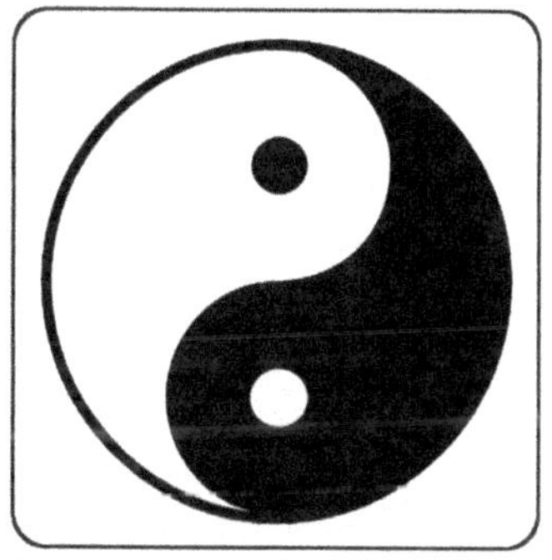

The common symbol of Eastern religions signifying dualties. The dualism theme is common in Hollywood films, as well as in the occult.

Next, a seemingly incoherent scene happens where two rival street gangs based on actual Chinatown gangs (the Hip Sing and the On Leong Tong gangs), wherein Lo Pan appears in his "atomized" form and sends blinding light into Jack Burton's eyes. Lucifer is spoken of in Christian Scripture as appearing as an "angel of light," as well as the "bright and morning star." Following upon this scene, Jack and Wang enter a succession of events that seem to not make sense chronologically. There isn't much coherence, as they seem to walk in and out of the spiritual world, with demons and spirits appearing and disappearing on a whim. Jack has been blinded by Lo Pan in order to have his eyes opened to the spiritual realm – something also very similar to the tradition of Paul the Apostle in Acts.

References are also made to Dante's *Inferno* and/or *Purgatio*, as Jack and Wang begin to encounter different sins or vices on their journey into the Underworld. Wang had described to Jack that there are different Chinese levels to hell, including the "hell of boiling oil," "upside down sinners," etc., all of which hearken to Dante's different levels of hell and purgatory. In fact, the journey is very similar to two Chinese works that describe the journey into the Underworld: *The Jade Record* and *Journeys to the Under-world*. First, however, Jack and Wang encounter Lust in the whorehouse, which is very similar to Dante's first level of hell. In the whorehouse, Jack requests a green-eyed girl, and instead, a massive green supernatural storm arises. This storm is in fact a gateway where Lo Pan's three lesser gods, who resemble characters from *Mortal Kombat* appear. "Jade" is relevant, as it is associated with the Jade Emperor in the Jade Record, and thus has associations with the Underworld. Burton, it turns out, had led the three gods to the cat house.

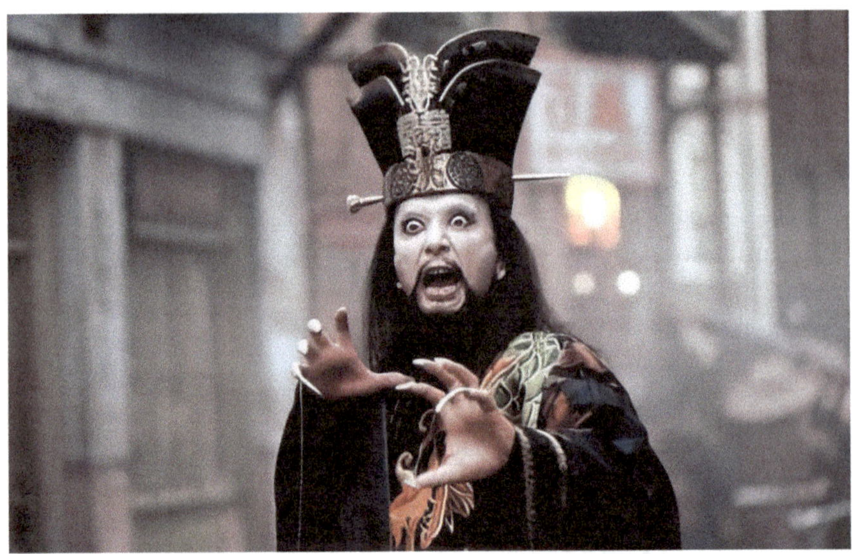

"You were not put upon this earth to 'get it' Mesta Burton!"

Following this madcap madness, Gracie Law appears at Egg Shen's and says Lo Pan is a *banker*. Gracie says she is interested in protecting the girls' civil rights, and thinks with her journalist friend "Margo Litzenberger" that Lo Pan should be exposed in the media. Oddly, this has also transpired in the U.S. presently, as the middle strata begin to catch onto America's problem as "bankers," and the media begins to expose such nefarious activity amongst the elite. Egg Shen and friends then engage in divination to see what Lo Pan and the gods are up to: the result is that the "goat's horns are entangled." The goat is also associated with the devil: in Chinese folk religion, the creator god is "Pangu," a hairy beast-like creature. Pangu is also believed to have created earth (yin) and sky (yang). Think as well of Pan, the satyr of similar Greek mythology – but not only Pan, Aleister Crowley had a fascination with Pan, and one of his more famous poems, the *Hymn to Pan*, contains "Io Pan, Io Pan…" and which likely had reference to gay sex with a companion:

Thrill with lissome lust of the light,
O man! My man!
Come careering out of the night
Of Pan! Io Pan!
Io Pan! Io Pan! Come over the sea
From Sicily and from Arcady!

Keep in mind as well that Hollywood writers and directors are often well-versed in Crowley and gnosticism, and written I and O look like "LO." So Lo Pan is a reference to Pan, the goat-devil, and Egg Shen explains that the meaning of the divination was "Ordo ab Chao," that Lo Pan's desire was to bring order out of chaos – Egg then explains that all movement is caused by "positive and negative furies," and in Lo Pan the furies are imbalanced, and cause him to be a devil in human form.

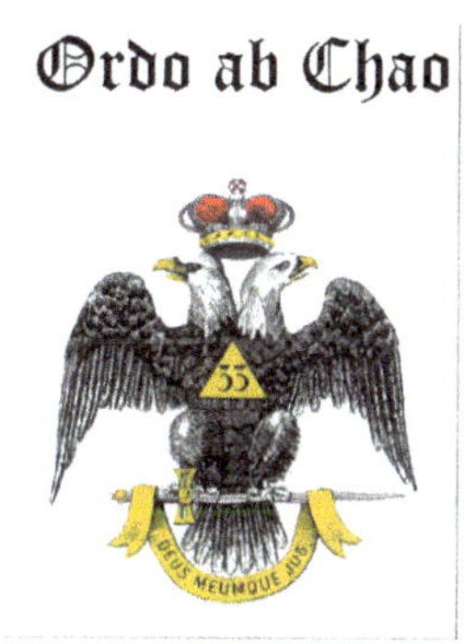

Lo Pan pretends to be a man, but is actually a dark spirit of lust. As Jack and Wang re-enter Lo-Pan's Underworld, and are caught and placed in the "hell of upside down sinners." Lo Pan threatens them with the hell where people are "skinned alive," which is the special level run by Lo Pan. We discover that Lo Pan was once a warrior emperor who has now become a demon subservient to Ching Dai, the demon god of the East who rules him and whom he must appease to become flesh again.

Gracie and Margo are now enslaved in the Underworld sex slave prison, and Margo says it's as if the entire experience isn't real, while Gracie is tied up in a sexual bondage pose. Margo mentions that the entire experience is like *Alice in Wonderland*, keying the observant viewer into the elite mind-controlled nature of the film. *Alice in Wonderland* has meaning on several levels, from the MKUltra brainwashing programs, to the occult Underworld and the actual underworld of crime and the sex slave trade. In actual fact, this underworld is run by gangsters who are in turn run by higher-level interests, who are in turn run by the gods and demons. The earthly hierarchy mirrors the heavenly hierarchy, as does the Underworld's hierarchy. The idol of the god of death even has a third eye – the eye of the so-called "Illuminati," whose philosophy is "ordo ab chao," or order out of chaos.

This may sound far-fetched, but Lo Pan actually does mind control on Gracie and Miao Yin. Through "magic," Lo Pan brainwashes them both into loving him through some kind of bizarre chi ceremony that places them both in a trance state. The focus is on their eyes, which become blank, showing they are mind-controlled. The ritual has a sexual component to it, as the "sword" is a classic phallic image. Both Gracie and Miao levitate and touch the "burning blade," which "tames the savage heart." Since there are two girls, one will be sacrificed to the god of the East, and the reincarnated David Lo Pan will be enfleshed once again to experience sexual pleasure. Meanwhile, Egg Shen tells Jack and Wang that since Lo Pan inhabits a dream world, only entering a dream can kill a dream. In order to enter the archetypal dream world, they must ingest a powerful hallucinogen. Here we meet with Jungian concepts, where the dream world is identified with the inner psyche and subconscious, which are also linked to the Underworld. All three are linked, in other words, in the spiritual realm.

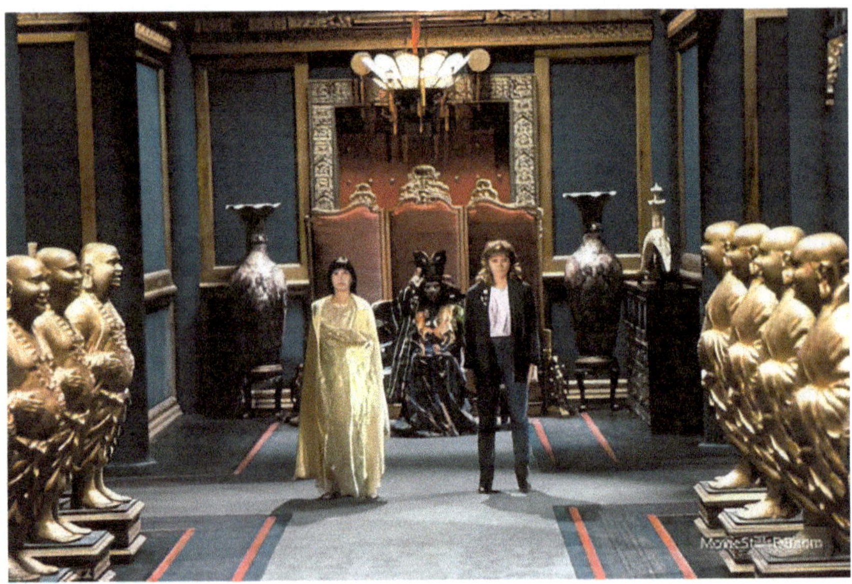

The god of death idol has a 'third eye' of Illumination, or the all-seeing eye.

Lo Pan then performs a ritual sexual marriage, where they invoke Ching Dai, the demon god of the East. Lo Pan pricks both Gracie and Miao with his "needle of love," and has what appears to be an orgasmic spasm. This brings to mind Crowley again, and his version of Tantric sex magick. Energies are transferred in sex as well as in liturgical rituals, and here we have the combination of both. See *The Shadow of the Dalai Lama* for an in depth treatment of occult "Illuminism" and Tantric traditions, where it is common to find marriages or sexual unions being performed through union with a deity through possession of the sexual partner. After this, the battle that ensues is utterly laughable, and very much like a video game, but the climax shows Jack's "knife" stabbing Lo Pan in the third eye.[144]

Replete with sexual and occult imagery, *Big Trouble in Little China* does operate on numerous levels, despite its very silly elements. It also operates on a level of exposing a very real trend of foreign-run sex slave trade that does exist in the U.S. and in San Francisco in particular. But the deeper meaning is one of commentary on Amerika, as well as occultic 'Illumination' and alchemical transformation. Jack remains Jack, but has been enlightened after his descent into the Underworld. The final scene, though, has one of the demons attached to Jack's Pork Chop Express, leading the viewer to wonder if Amerika will survive its haunting, psychologically traumatic trip to the Underworld.

MKULTRA X-MEN & TRAUMA BASED KID CONTROL

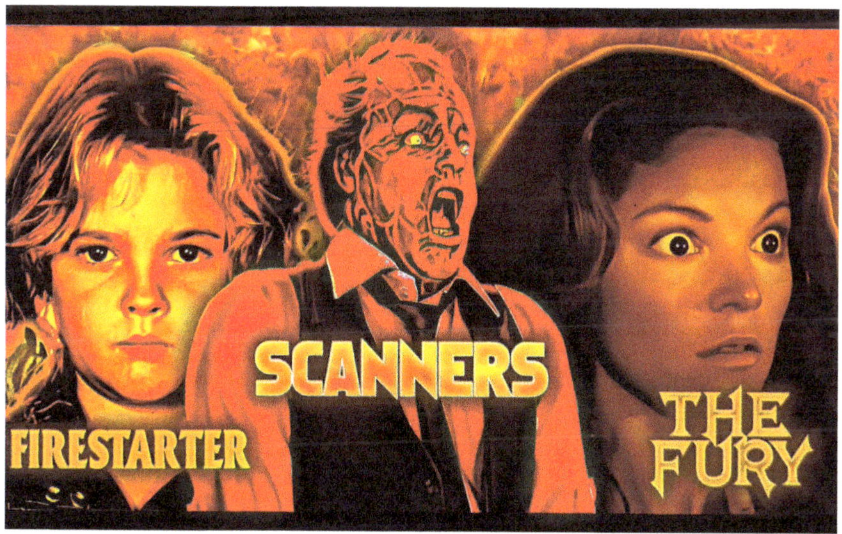

THE FURY (1978), FIRESTARTER (1984) & HIDE AND SEEK (2005)

Brian de Palma's version of *Rosemary's Baby* and *The X-Men* is the 1978 oddity, *The Fury,* starring former Spielberg wife Amy Irving, Kirk Douglas and John Cassavetes. In this bizarre, yet entrancing film, Brian De Palma (who had directed *Carrie* two years earlier) portrays a government program to study psychic children gifted with telekinesis – which as you can imagine, is based on real government programs. In fact, the CIA has recently reported at their site:

> According to our historians, from very early in the CIA's history we had been interested in investigating whether "extra sensory perception" (ESP) or other paranormal phenomena (generally called "parapsychology") exist and, if so, whether they had operational uses for intelligence.
>
> The earliest record our historians have found on this topic is a 1948 memorandum speculating on whether hypnotized people could be used for long-distance communication.
>
> We didn't, however, conduct our own research into psychic phenomena until the summer of 1972. We worked with scientists and researchers to investigate whether certain people could "see"

locations and objects around the world, without actually being there. This ability is known as "remote viewing."

CIA ended this research five years later in 1977, and we turned the program over to the Defense Intelligence Agency (DIA). The project became known as STARGATE, which was actually DIA's initial name for this program. Later, it was renamed GRILL FLAME.

In the mid-1990s, DIA handed the program back to the CIA. We agreed to take another look at the program on the condition that an independent study group would evaluate it. Four researchers from the American Institute for Research published their findings in September 1995, and that report is available on the Internet: a Google search on "An Evaluation of Remote Viewing" will turn up the 183-page document.

That report's conclusion – which echoed the assessments of the CIA officers involved in the program during the 1970s – was that enough accurate remote viewing experiences existed to defy randomness, but that the phenomenon was too unreliable, inconsistent, and sporadic to be useful for intelligence purposes. We decided not to restore the program.[145]

So, curiously, right before the 1976 publication of the novel *The Fury*, the CIA had begun the projects that would become the now well-known STARGATE and GRILL FLAME. These real world projects are likely a significant influence on the film version of the story, which begins its narrative in Israel. Former CIA operative Peter Sandza (Kirk Douglas) is relaxing at a secretive Israeli beach when a staged kidnapping occurs to snatch his psychic son. The oddest part of this sequence is the terror attack being completely staged as a cover for the kidnapping, suggesting something reminiscent of John Le Carre's Mossad-themed novel *Little Drummer Girl* that would appear a few years later in 1983. The Israeli references might also be a nod to Uri Gellar, the former IDF soldier and famed psychic who convinced the CIA to study him as part of Project STARGATE.[146]

It turns out the gifted children's program is a vastly funded and controlled project based on a hidden metaphysics, where the universe is "bioplasmic," which "indigo" children can tap into and manipulate. The project's goals are to create supersoldiers by conditioning and controlling the children, even using trauma based mind control to help facilitate the development of the powers. Interestingly, the very same plot is used in *The New Mutants*, where Ilyana Rasputin (Anya Taylor Joy) develops her "powers" from being molested. In *The Fury*, Robin, the psychic kidnapped son (who is supposed to be a teenager) also sleeps with his middle aged mad scientist handler, Susan, adding a sexual trauma theme. The notion of a new approach to reality ('bioplasmic') that integrated eastern mysticism and "quantum" physics was also gaining momentum in the late 70s, as boomers en masse would be reading texts like *The Dancing Wu Li Masters* in 1979. Indeed, only a few years later the CIA would produce the now declassified "Gateway Process" (1983) document which detailed techniques for synchronizing both brain hemispheres, hypnosis, transcendental meditation and biofeedback secrets. Keep in mind transcendental meditation also plays a key role in David Lynch films, as Lynch was a famous advocate for TM and claimed many of his films were inspired by such meditative states.[147]

Like *The Fury, Firestarter* also highlighted the government's obsession with containing and controlling mutant kids who might one day become super soldiers and thus overthrow Uncle Sam. In *Firestarter,* a young Drew Barrymore is abused and tinkered with until she hones her pyrokinesis skills, eventually cooking an angry, abusive George C. Scott who plays a government assassin with an awkward, inappropriate series of interactions with the young Charlie (Barrymore). Based on a Stephen King novel of the same name, one wonders if King had simply rewritten *The Fury* or the *X-Men* narrative once again, yet this time with a distinct phoenix symbolism that presages the already mentioned Marvel film, *Dark Phoenix.*[148] Although we already analyzed Cronenberg's *Scanners* in a previous chapter, it bears repeating since it also deals with the important theme of intelligence agencies and the military industrial complex experimenting on gifted and talented psychic children to supposedly direct "evolution" toward the goal of transhumanist supersoldiers.

In *Hide and Seek,* Dakota Fanning plays a traumatized young girl who is under the care of her father, a psychiatrist who seeks to heal her through moving to the countryside in the hopes she can move on from her mother's death. For much of the film, the audience assumes Emily (Fanning) has an imaginary friend named Charlie she shares her thoughts and memories with, while in reality the film's twist is that Charlie is the alternate personality of her father David (Robert De Niro). Like David's *psyche,* the house is full of locked rooms and hidden suppressed clues and memories that eventually culminate in the revelations from a monarch butterfly Emily follows into a cave in the forest where David chases her, revealing his own suppressed memories of murdering his wife. In one of the alternate endings, we see Emily placed under a new foster care setting where she too has alternate personalities like her father, which suggests there is a generational aspect to the abuse and a proclivity that can also relate to genetics.

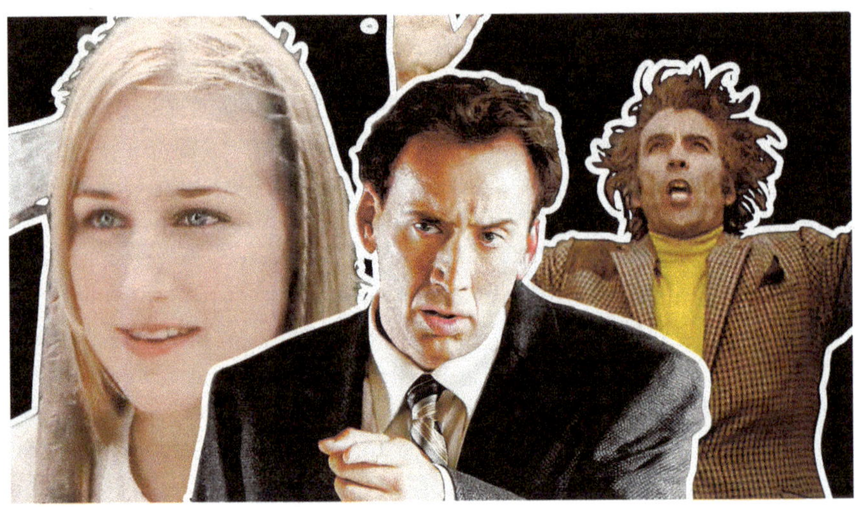

WICKER MAN (1973 & 2006)

The 1973 *Wicker Man* is considered a horror classic among film fans, but from the vantage point of cultural themes and trends, it was decades ahead of its time as it focused on ancient pagan traditions. Most horror films prior had been preoccupied with Satanic Cults, but Wicker Man focuses on folk traditions native to druidism and the Scottish isles. In fact, many modern Malthusians, from the British Royal Family to Winston Churchill, have been initiated into secret lodges of Druidism, so *Wicker Man* may have been telling us far more about the power structure than anyone knew. *Wicker Man* was also riding the wave of a kind of neo-pagan revival occuring in the 1970s through Crowleyan rock bands like Led Zeppelin and hippy readings of *The Lord of the Rings.*

In the narrative, Lord Summerisle (Christopher Lee) runs a small island village community with little to no connection to the outside world. The isolated community seeks to keep its native traditions by preferring to be left alone, yet when a Christian police officer from London (Sgt. Howie) arrives, the foreign invader begins snooping around looking for clues about a supposedly missing young girl, Rowan. All Christian imagery and symbolism has curiously been removed from the island, and as Sgt. Howie arrives, his boat notably features "Mekong Eyes," painted symbols intent on warding off evil spirits on the high seas, harkening to a pagan pre-Christian era. Howie stays at The Green Man Inn, a dark portent of his future return to the earth, referring to the mythical "Green Man," an ancient British symbol for the cycle of birth, death and rebirth, as well as May Day.[149]

As Sgt. Howie continues his investigation, he discovers the island engages in nighttime orgies, maypole festivals where the children are celebrating the insemination of the mother archetype in the village dance. As the story progresses, we learn that Sgt. Howie himself is the sacrifice and must die as a human sacrifice to restore the island's crop for the next season, after Lord Summerisle confronts him and explains the parthenogenesis, his version of a "virgin birth," and how there are similarities between his Christianity and the indigenous paganism. Critics Meg Sipos and Eric Botts comment:

> The folks of Summerisle didn't choose Sgt. Howie because he's a Christian. They chose him because he's "the right kind of adult":
>
> A man who would come of his own free will. A man who has come here with the power of a king by representing the law. A man who would come here as a virgin. A man who has come here as a fool.
>
> They allow him to call them heathens without so much as batting an eye. They patiently explain their beliefs to him, often noting similarities between their faiths, including a shared belief in immaculate conception, as Lord Summerisle explains that the naked ladies jumping over the fire outside are trying to get pregnant through parthenogenesis, "reproduction without sexual union," just as Jesus was "the son of a virgin, impregnated, I believe, by a Ghost." The schoolteacher Miss Rose (Diane Cilento) also points to shared belief in transubstantiation (or as she calls it, transmutation), connecting Rowan's transformation into a hare with the Last Supper, in which bread and wine consecrated by Christ were transformed into his flesh and blood.[150]

Sipos and Botts argue convincingly that Sgt. Howie is not an authentic Christian since, according to Lord Summerisle, he would surely consider it an honor to be martyred for the faith, yet Howie passes away in giant wicker man structure through immolation, as he screams and curses the pagans for their actions – the opposite of Christ's prayer for "forgiveness." Author David Hanlin, who penned the 1967 novel *The Ritual*, upon which *Wicker Man* is based, also penned a later work, *The Wicca Woman* which delves deeper into a theme many suspected was at the heart of the original: witchcraft. Once again we have a Crowleyan connection, since modern Wicca was developed as a wholly new "ancient" religion crafted by Crowleyan graduate Gerald Gardner (who was also involved in druidism). Writer Glenn Sunshine comments:

> He (Gardner) also became involved with Druidry, esoteric Christianity, and the Society for Psychical Research; on a trip to America, he attempted to learn about Voodoo as well.

In 1947, Gardner met Aleister Crowley, the ceremonial magician who described himself as "the Beast 666." Crowley initiated Gardner into the Ordo Templi Orientis and decreed that he could initiate people into the order. Crowley would have continuing influence on Gardner's thought.[151]

Is Gardner an inspiration for Lord Summerisle? With Crowley's previously mentioned connections to British Intelligence and MI5, it's likely the UK elite establishment also had its tentacles in the world of witchcraft and covens. In fact, in the 1970s, British Intelligence has admitted to intentionally creating a staged "Satanic Panic" in Ireland to stoke fears of witchcraft covens being established in the wake of political instability.[152]

In the more recent instantiation in 2006 with Nicolas Cage, the focus shifts from indigenous paganism to covens of witches and goddess worship. Although universally derided as a bad movie (I disagree!), the film contains multiple esoteric themes overlooked due to the odd sequences of Nicolas Cage in perfect comedic form (like drop-kicking Leelee Sobieski). While the old *Wicker Man* was a patriarchy, the new *Wicker Man* is a matriarchy that worships the goddess and is convinced Gaia must also have fresh human sacrificial blood to revive the seasonal crops. Cage (as the cop) experiences witchcraft, drugging, mind control, gaslighting, and ritual humiliation like the castrated eunuchs who serve the matriarchy, even to the point of being shown the Orphic Egg and the *ouroboros*, and they are descendants of the Salem witches.

The purpose of these symbols is to demonstrate and hide in plain sight the actual occult beliefs of the village community, while throwing it in the face of the sacrifice to make him more and more of a willing participant. In other words, without telling the victim outright the community is committed to human sacrifice, they have already conveyed this extensively through the arcane, yet omnipresent symbology of the coven in almost

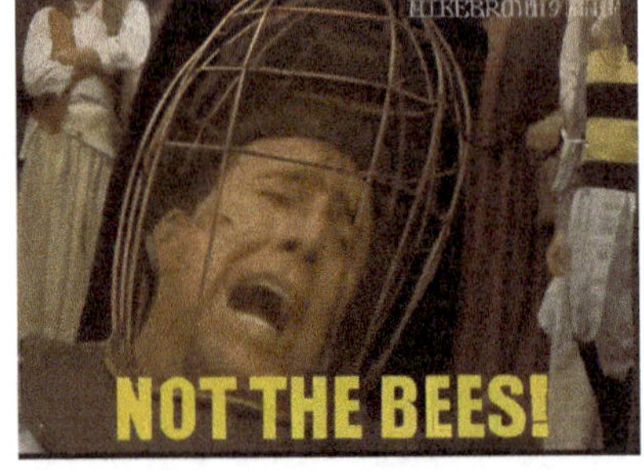

every scene, down to the Queen Bee / beehive imagery of the Head Witch (Ellen Burstyn). Although Cage nowadays speaks of the film as an intended comedy, the real power of this film is when it is seen as a dark satire of a feminist/witchcraft dominated society – which is arguably what our society has become – Nicolas Caged.

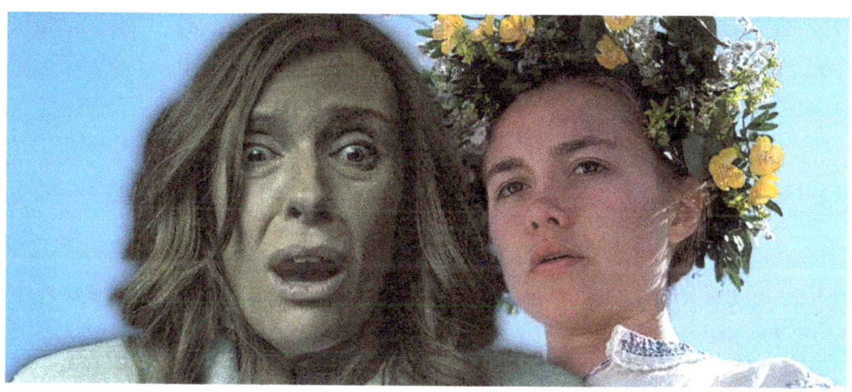

HEREDITARY (2018) & MIDSOMMAR (2019)

Ari Aster is one of the recent directors of occult fame who, together with Eggers, has continued the Hollywood esoteric promotion with films like *Hereditary* (2018) and *Midsommar* (2019). Both films focus on the occult from different perspectives: *Midsommar*, much like *Wicker Man*, is a return to ancient pagan traditions, hallucinogenic initiations, sex/fertility rites and human sacrifice where ancestor worship takes precedence, while *Hereditary* is a unique twist on demonic possession and ritual magick. In *Hereditary*, like *Midsommar*, we have a generational bloodline curse where a mother named Annie Graham (played by Toni Collette) discovers her recently deceased mother was secretly a Satanic Witch. Sadly, her mother also suffered from dementia and MPD/DID which was likely a result of further generational abuse. While rummaging through her mother's belongings, she finds books on sorcery and ritual workings, but chooses to remain in denial, keeping it a secret as bizarre phenomena begin to occur in the lives of her children following the death of her mother.. At school, her young daughter snips the head off of a bird which functions as an omen since the young girl will also lose her head in a tragic accident.

Both the loss of the daughter's head and Annie Graham's fixation on creating detailed miniature replicas of houses and rooms are deeply symbolic: The head, for the loss of rationality and personhood in the chosen vessel, and for the rooms in the house as memories and elements of the *psyche*. She is, in effect, a kind of puppet master seeking to regain control of her chaotic life. These intricate models represent her past memories and trauma but also appear to function in a more metaphysical sense, as the demonic entity that is seeking to incarnate is *likewise* organizing these events and scenarios like a puppet master. Just as she spends her time crafting an abode for her puppets and dolls, we eventually learn Paimon, the 9th spirit or demon king from the Keys of Solomon, is also seeking to craft an abode to dwell in (a body to possess). Like Rosemary in *Rosemary's Baby*, all of Anne's life has been carefully crafted and controlled by the Satanic Coven as well, as they nudge and mislead her into missing the real goal of the ritual workings; her son.

In terms of filmmaking, this was a brilliant deflection, as the viewer is almost entirely distracted (like Anne) from seeing the demon's real designs, as we focus our attention on the daughter, husband, Anne and the cult. Eventually we learn the son is the chosen one, destined to be indwelt by one of Satan's top henchmen, the duke of hell Paimon. Ultimately, both her children (and she herself) were all sacrificial victims for the cult and Paimon, as Anne also loses her head (and is immolated as a kind of sacrificial burnt offering) while Peter (symbolically named like St. Peter, with the keys of heaven in Matt. 16) becomes fully possessed by Paimon in the final ritual in the treehouse. Like a weird, inverted church, the treehouse is the final gathering place of the coven on the appointed date of Paimon's coming, and like an Antichrist version of the Incarnation, Paimon incarnates himself into the body of Peter.

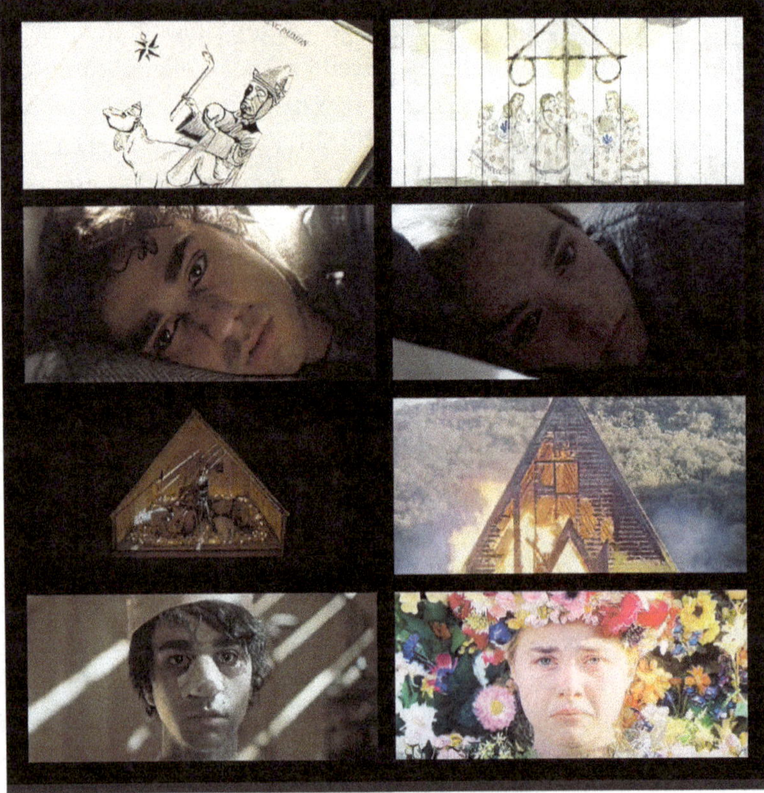

With *Midsommar,* Aster places Florence Pugh in the protagonist role of Dani, a traumatized American college girl who struggles with her mental wellbeing after her mentally ill sister kills her parents and herself through carbon monoxide poisoning. Seeking a fresh start, she leaves for Scandinavia on a trip with her boyfriend and his circle of friends for a change of pace and scenery only to find herself immediately confronted with a wilderness trek that centers around a hardcore mushroom trip and inadvertent initiation. Like Anne in *Hereditary* and *Rosemary's Baby,* Dani is unknowingly being led into this situation to become the new May Queen for the cult community. Initially distressed and fearful for her losses, she is eventually fully initiated into the cult and accepts the inevitability of death and its necessity from a pagan point of view as part of the natural cycle. As May Queen, she must choose the final sacrificial victim (the last of 9, a number suggesting initiation), symbolically named "Christian," who is placed inside a bearskin and immolated as yet another burnt offering mirroring *Hereditary.* While Aster is correct with his critique of empty, nihilistic modernity in the beginning of the film, the symbolic death and rejection of "Christian" is intended to be the rejection of Dani's previous life and likely Christian identity for a new neo-pagan existence. It is also interesting that this film somewhat preceded the presently emerging trend of the neo-pagan revival in beliefs like Odinism, Wotanism, and various other Heathen offshoots. These types of organizations are often populated with, or even created by, federal informants and can be easily used as honeytraps, and it seems the system is fine with the rise of a new paganism so long as it fits with the depopulation and anti-natalist perspective of the Green Agenda and Earth Worship.[153]

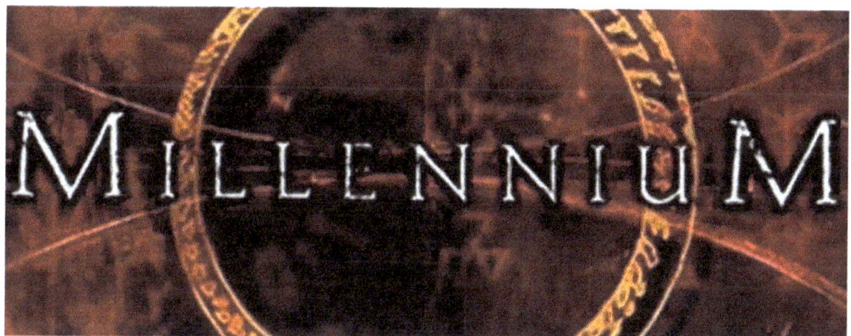

MILLENNIUM (1996-1999)

This essay originally appeared in the *Cultural Engineering Studies Journal* in the 2024 First Edition.

Millennium (1996–1999) is one of the two *X-Files* spin-offs, and while it actually ran for three seasons, it's less known than *The Lone Gunmen*. *The Lone Gunmen* followed the exploits of the *X-Files's* three nerdy conspiracy theorists and underground conspiracy zine publishers Langley, Frohike and Byers. In *Millennium*, we follow the investigations of mystical detective Frank Black who originally appeared in an occult-themed episode of the *X-Files* centering on a gnostic inversion of the notion of bodily resurrection and magical incantations from St. John's Apocalypse.

When we originally meet FBI consultant Frank Black, Mulder and Scully are seeking Frank's insights on a killer who is part of a schismatic faction of the enigmatic "Millennium Club," an end-times secret society that wields some unknown power. When Mulder and Scully encounter Frank, he's under psychiatric watch at a mental ward, undergoing evaluation for the restoration of visitation rights with his daughter. Given this was around the turn of the millennium when the episode and spin-off aired, it made media sense to capitalize on the exaggerated hype of the time. In fact, I remember even packing a sleeping bag and a Bible in anticipation of the chaos that would ensue following the "Y2K" computer failure (I was around 18 at the time!).

Although I have no evidence, my speculation is Y2K was probably some kind of psyop, but for TV viewers, Fox was heavy with conspiracy content, as well as the WB. Conspiracy plots were common in *The X-Files*, *The Simpsons*, *Buffy the Vampire Slayer*, *Lone Gunmen*, *Millennium* and more. If you aren't familiar, *Millennium* breathes the spirit of *X-Files* (Chris Carter also did *Millennium*), but also departs in significant ways, with less of an emphasis on the supernatural: there are no alien plots and rarely any monsters of the week.

This is odd, since we know from a few instances such as the Morley cigarettes shown burning in at least one *Millennium* scene, to the more obvious interactions of Mulder and Scully with Frank, that the shows occupy the same universe. Regardless, *Millennium* charts its own course, with numerous episodes functioning as borderline experimental, uniquely stylized and even satirical (by season 2). Season 1 of *Millennium* is notably different from season 2, as the show's extremely dark, serial killer-focused storyline veers off in a totally different direction. We find in Season 1 a unifying theme of Frank Black tracing down a demonic entity that seems to inspire everything from serial killers to terrorists who engage in sex magick. In this way, it's a very different style of show than *X-Files*, and we can tell Carter hoped *Millennium* would develop its own aesthetic and feel. In season 2, Frank shifts from a spiritual battle to a global *DaVinci Code*-style decoding of world religions and their symbology to uncover the plot of a mysterious group identified as the "Illuminati." Season 3 continues the spirit of season 2, with an unexpected resolution of the mystery of Frank vs. the Illuminati (aka, the Millennium Club).

This "illuminist" theme should come as no surprise, as *The Lone Gunmen*'s Langley, played by Richard Haglund, stated in a vintage interview with Alex Jones that the CIA actually showed up and consulted and changed various scripts for the *X-Files*, and it's safe to assume the "Illuminati"-based *Millennium* would be the same. When I finished the series, I realized it was certainly a prime specimen for the type of esoteric analysis I do. While three seasons of a show is too much for an episode-by-episode analysis, I will hit the highlights, patterns and motifs relevant for our "conspiratorial analysis" purposes. Initially, season 1 takes us down the path of typical cop vs. serial killer, cat-and-mouse fodder, with the cookie-cutter "taunts" and "clues" that become somewhat tedious. We see serial killers not just possessed by demons, but a judge who uses his status to kill without consequence and even a sexual deviant that finds eroticism in "banging," that is, in being a terrorist bomber.

In the midst of these early episodes we find some serious occultic ideas and even vague Crowley references, as Frank begins to piece together spiritual patterns among the serial killers he tracks down. As you can imagine, Frank, like a sour boomer version of Agent Dale Cooper, has "visions" and insights that show him the serial killer's mind. Is your mind blown yet? A detective that *sees into the mind of the serial killer*!? This overdone notion is actually lampooned in one of the series's later installments (actually one of the best episodes) where Frank investigates a B-movie actor playing him in a late night "skinemax" version of Frank's life.

The series's narrative, as mentioned, progresses from Frank's personal rabbit hole of patterns among serial killers to something far more global and conspiratorial in nature: an enigmatic secret society (that uses Masonic oaths) Frank begins to suspect has connections, not only to the FBI, but to his own life and traumatic past. Frank's closest ally, Peter Watts (played by *Lost*'s Terry O'Quinn) eventually reveals to Frank he is a prospective candidate for the Millennium Club. While the group casts itself as a secret society motivated by the good of all humanity, recalling a Rosicrucian ideology, Frank remains skeptical. Eventually he determines the group to be too secretive, too deceptive and too cult-like, as we learn in seasons 2 and 3.

The group's logo is the *ouroboros*, which hearkens back to Plato's *Timaeus* where the universe is symbolized by the snake eating its own tail, meaning it's a cyclical, eternal process, like a Nietzschean eternal return notion. It also signifies this elite's full control of world events, their self-appointed status as "shepherds of mankind," and the initiators of the coming end of days "millennium." As you can imagine, it is made up of elite members of the corporate and intelligence worlds and high society movers and shakers from around the globe, with its own factions of "roosters" (who believe in an actual religious apocalypse) and "owls," who think the coming millennium will be one of secular utopia controlled by science. One could see an analogue to real-world secret societies and cults like the Freemasons, or more specifically, the Rosicrusians, who present themselves as a benevolent branch of "invisible world controllers" seeking a new utopian era of world peace. *Millennium*'s secret world controllers faction known as the owls corresponds to the actual historical "Illuminati," modern-day proponents of scientism, versus the rooster faction which prefers more gnostic and Luciferian concepts based on hermeticism.

By season 2 the wackiness and satire ensues, with conspiratorial plots on a global scale involving the Middle East and the True Cross, where we see a mad race for magical relics and a dialectical manipulation of two sects of the Millennium Club by a third, international corporate structure revolving around secret Nazis. This third faction is eventually defeated, but the gnostic attitude of *Millennium* comes to the fore as they see themselves as the "true" gnostic "Christians." The secret knowledge they possess is hidden under layers of religious rites and even what appears to be blood rituals and a woodland rite where Latin magical words are read and the empathic angel-seeing Lara is brought into full membership. Lara soon goes insane, in one of the series's most innovative and abstract episodes where we (assume) Lara was dosed with a potent hallucinogen (which the finale reveals was not the case!).

We are never told whether the roosters or owls end up dominating in the club, but we gradually suspect, with Frank, the Club is not altruistic. We are told the end of the old world is nigh, and a new millennium will ensue – a new world order, something perhaps akin to a "great reset"? It's certainly odd that the end of season 2 includes the release of a bio weapon by the Club that claims Frank's wife, while Frank and their empathic daughter Jordan are able to take the miracle vaccine. This is, again, a curious series of events given where we are 24 years later in 2024 in the post-COVID world.

The symbology of the series is really a mishmash of Mary as the gnostic goddess, the *Vesica Piscis*, and recurring eye and snake symbolism. I think we are to conclude that the Millennium Club is akin to FBI- and CIA-connected individuals (eyes and owls) with a penchant for esotericism, hermeticism and higher, black lodge branches of Freemasonry. Perhaps the darkest aspect of the series is not the serial killers or their typical fetishes, but the final season's big reveal that the Club has been operating on chosen individuals' brains to "maximize their full potential" and continue the growth of their brain: in other words, they have achieved hyper intelligence. What was believed to be a "gifted" program for bright children was actually a front for human experimentation. This advanced brain operation, however, can have disastrous side effects, resulting in many of the "chosen" children going insane and becoming psychopathic serial killers. In other words, the Millennium Club has been creating and studying serial killers, and starting this process with children. Now we are in Dave McGowan territory with apt comparisons at this point to the Phoenix Program, as discussed in *Programmed to Kill: The Politics of Serial Murder* (2004).

Chris Carter was likely aware of the Phoenix Program, given the 1997 airing of the *X-Files* episode "Unrequited," where a disgruntled Vietnam Veteran seeking revenge on US officials for previously being programmed as an assassin in a paramilitary group known as The Right Hand. We now know MKUltra and the various programs associated with the mastering of the *psyche* were certainly on his radar given the many references in the *X-Files*. Although only three seasons, *Millennium* gave us a creative take on the typical: the noir-influenced grizzled detective with a mystical side and a dark secret who ends up fleeing the world's madness to go into hiding in a hermetic existence (much like Fox Mulder).

While cult devotee and fanatical believer Peter Watts (Terry O'Quinn), who plays the foil, loses everything, Black also pays a heavy cost, losing all that he loves in his quest against the world controllers. In the end, we see the power apocalypticism can lend to cults, intelligence agencies and those who seek to abuse and control others – end times cults are a very effective means of control, and Hollywood plays a key role in boosting the effectiveness of that control. Apocalypticism places us on edge, seeking, in an anxiety ridden-way, the next fix or dopamine for the latest "signs" of impending collapse or doom. This perpetually paranoid, anxious state allows the populace to be more easily shaped and molded to fit social engineering consensus: it's the model of continual, never-ending crises the global elite like Brzezinsky and Attali often write about, which generally are not real crises or concerns at all.

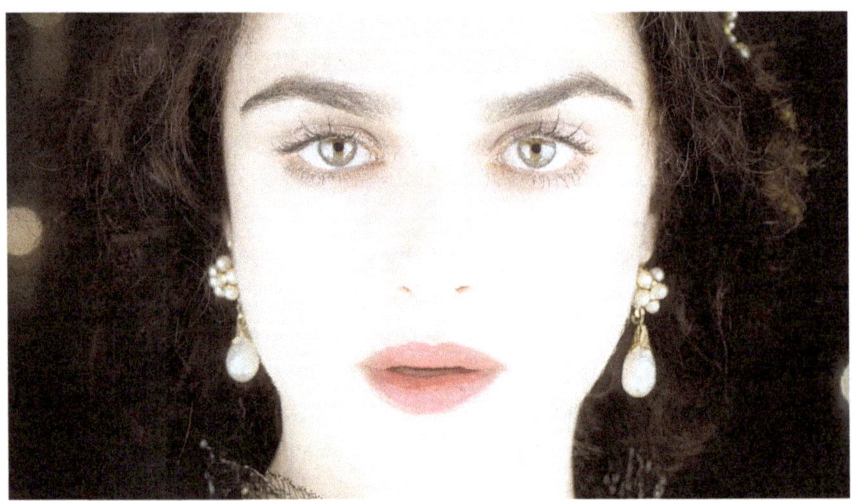

THE FOUNTAIN (2006)

The Fountain is one of Hollywood's more difficult esoteric films: The failure of the film to achieve at the box office can be chalked up to this heavily mystifying plot and symbolism. To decode the film requires some familiarity with cabalism, alchemy, Mayan mythology, Genesis and creation and Zen philosophy. Combining all these motifs in a menagerie of metaphysical midrash, as with most Darren Aronofsky films like *Pi* (explicitly based on gematria and Kabbalistic themes), *Noah* or *Black Swan*, the key is found in the speculation of the cabala.

The film opens with Genesis 3:24, that man was banished from Eden by a Cherub with a flaming sword, sending the fallen couple East of Eden. As a result, death and corruption entered, not just the human race, but the entire created order became subject to corruption, decay and death (Romans 8). In our film, the narrative takes place in three time periods, each some 500 years apart, with the oldest being Hugh Jackman as Tomas Verde, a Conquistador in love with Queen Isabella of Spain (Rachel Weisz), imprisoned within her own palace at the behest of a Spanish Inquisition in league with Rome and hell-bent on seizing power from the cabalistically-influenced Queen.

Isabella is regaled in tree-like dress, encased in her throne room behind a tree-like fence, hinting ahead of time she is mystically linked to the Tree of Life (understood here in the cabalistic sense as the metaphysical structure of creation). Tomas, commissioned by Isabella and a Franciscan, is told to seek the source of immortality within the Mayan Legends that also foretell the story of the Tree, which Isabella understands must be united with the power of the Tree of Knowledge. These two trees will make up one of the important themes in the film – the unification of logical, analytical and left-brain masculine reasoning with intuitive, emotional, right-brained feminine approaches. This is why modern-day Tom (Jackman) finds himself consumed with a different quest to save the life of Izzy (Weisz) from cancer. As a cutting-edge neuroscientist, Tom is on the verge of curing cancer by synthesizing an extract from a tree in Guatemala – the same tree mystically linked to Izzy and the Tree of Life.

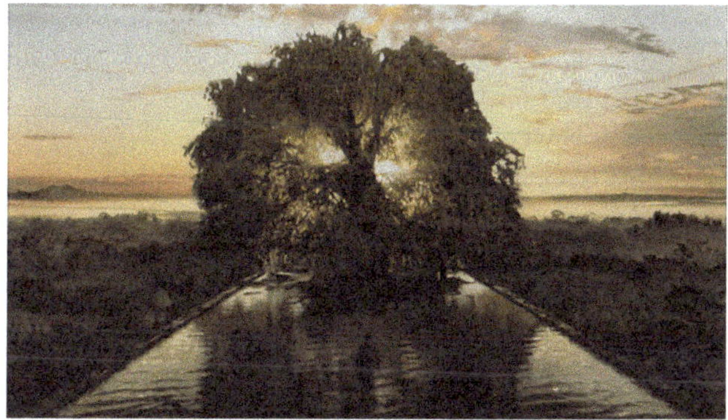
Mayan Tree as the Life-giving Fountain.

Under the veils of Roman Catholicism and Mayan religion, the esoteric philosophy of the film slowly emerges: the ancient Mayan priest's flaming sword that beheads Tomas is a re-enactment of the ancient Edenic tale of Adam and Eve's banishment. Now, the secrets to both immortality and life are under the guardianship of a pagan priesthood of death. The religion of human sacrifice and cannibalism, which is likely why the images of hair and flesh appear in reliquaries. In other words, Roman Catholicism is interpreted to be a cover for the perennial philosophy of cabalism, now veiled by the symbols of various religions and cultures. The dark secret, however, is buried within the darkest path of black magic and sorcery, including the "enlightenment" purported to come from the astral realm of "Shibalba," the Mayan Underworld.

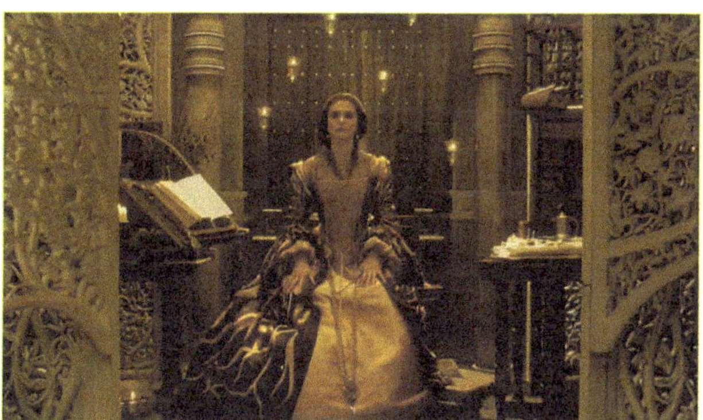
Isabella is the Garden, The Tree, the Fountain and Sophia.

Tom is also seen 500 or so years in the future traversing the galaxy in an enclosed bubble craft that also contains the tree where Izzy was buried (that mystically links with both Izzy and the Tree of Life) in order to deliver this tree to Shibalba, which we learn is a dying star. The Mayan religion was an astrotheology which linked the stellar heavens with various regions and locales on Earth. In fact, the actual entrance to the Mayan Underworld was actually discovered to be the source of a vast system of underwater lakes and streams, called "Shibalba" by the Mayans. *The Guardian* explains:

> "The director of archaeology for the National Institute of Anthropology and History, Pedro Sanchez Nava, said the theory makes sense in light of other pre-Hispanic peoples such as those who lived at Teotihuacan, near Mexico City, where another water tunnel was found.
>
> "In both cases there was a water current present," said Sanchez Nava. "There is this allegorical meaning for water … where the cycle of life begins and ends." The dig began in 2012, when researchers became concerned about underground anomalies detected with geo-radar under the area in front of the pyramid's steps."[154]

The deliverance of the tree to the dying star will presumably bring life to the dying system, as Tom's synthesizing of the tree extract will save Izzy and as Tomas' reaching the tree of life atop the Mayan Temple. In each era, Tom's selfish choice based on attachment and prolonging life results in the cycle starting all over again (presumably). This is why the film consistently shows circular and cyclical imagery, until the climax.

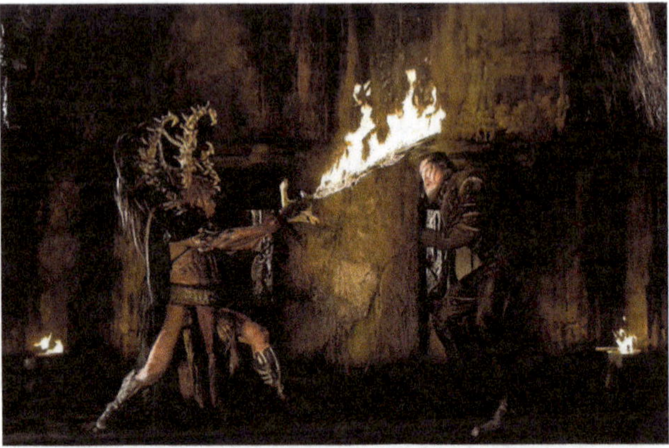

"After he drove the man out, he placed on the east side of the Garden of Eden cherubim and a flaming sword flashing back and forth to guard the way to the tree of life." -Gen. 3:24

It is only at the end of the age, when Space Tom finally decides to embrace death, recalling the words of Isabella that death is the path to immortality and eternal life. Here, as with astrotheology and reincarnation, the film links to Platonism (and cabalism), in presenting Tom's "enlightenment" as flashes of memory of his past lives. Recalling Isabella's words of acceptance of death, the Tom of each age determines to choose differently, accepting death. As a result, each Tom reaches the Tree, and understands the mystery, eventually transforming into a new, "spiritual" Adam (and Izzy, a new Eve).

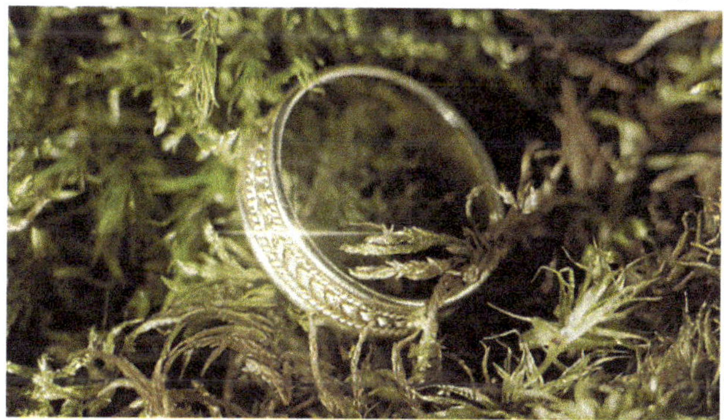

The One Ring of Eternal Return and Mystical Union.

Reunion with Izzy, however, can only be achieved in the final stage, when Space Tom can actually travel to the astral Shibalba, and offer both himself and the tree in death, with love overcoming death. Zen ideas are obviously present, such as detachment from life and possessions, while Tom's full enlightenment is revealed to be apotheosis – by reaching the star gate to the Underworld, Tom becomes "First Father," and recreates a world in his image from a point of light.

A new world is born, as Tom achieves a mystical marital union as Father with Sophia, his feminine principle. Thus, a Zohar-style cabalistic narrative is the key to decoding the entire film, with an alchemical wedding of masculine and feminine principles, of inner and outer worlds, and reason and intuition, of myth and scientific fact. Mystically, it is the Amer-

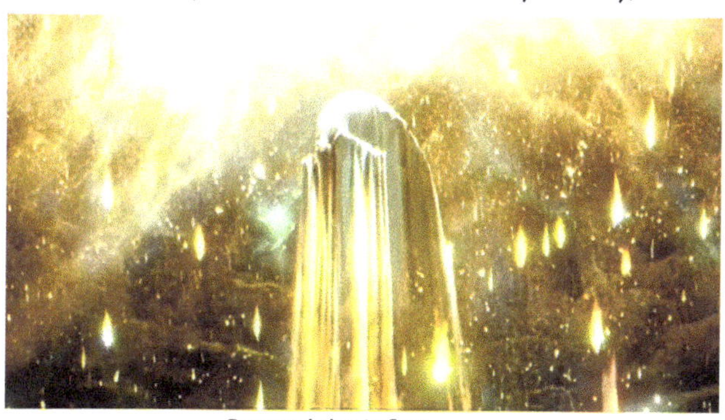

Beyond the Infinite.

icas that are the source of the secrets of immortality, which come through scientific gnosis and the eventual overcoming of the limitations of time and space (much like Starchild in *2001: A Space Odyssey*).

In fact, the choice of Spain was consciously done, as 13th century Spain is the origin of the cabalistic works known as the Zohar, which specifically treat of this doctrine of divine union, where the male and female archetypes of "god" are fragmented and need to be re-unified. Professor Israel Shahak in his *Jewish History, Jewish Religion* writes:

> "From the First Cause, a first male god called 'Wisdom' or 'Father' and then a female goddess called 'Knowledge' or 'Mother' were emanated or born. From the marriage of these two, a pair of younger gods were born: Son, also called by many other names such as "Small Face," or the "Holy Blessed One,' and Daughter, also called 'Lady,' 'Shekinah,' 'Queen,' etc. "

Shahak goes on to explain various secret sexual rites that would go on to influence various occult orders, including the perversions of Crowley and Kenneth Grant in the notion of the Nightside of Eden. For *The Fountain*, Tom must eventually write the "Divine Words" that complete Izzy's story which is actually her past life as Queen Isabella. Man becomes the new creator, and Thomas becomes God the Father. Like the Renaissance cabalists and Neoplatonic magicians, all the way back to Egypt, the doctrine of pantheism and reincarnation (aspects of cabala) are found to be the hidden meaning of the pseudo-biblical traditions and teachings. Man's apotheosis is the Gnostic secret doctrine, and man his own God and Savior. The key to this mystery is revealed to be sexual magic and transhumanism, all of which have their modern origins in medieval cabalistic doctrines of scientism and the transfiguration of "dead matter."

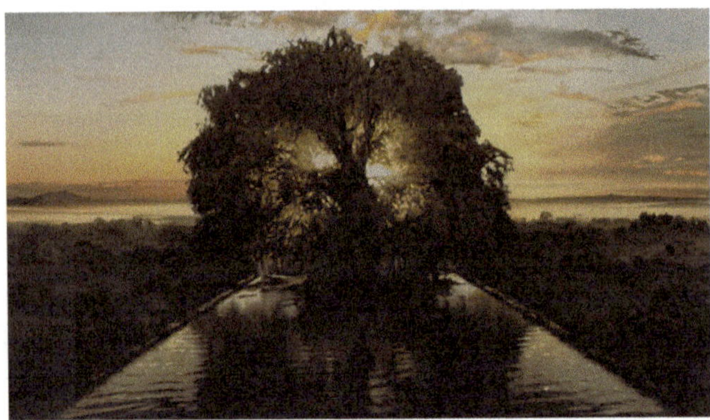

Tree of Life, Tree of Gnosis.

While *The Fountain* is a fascinating presentation of symbolism and imagery unheard of in most films, the unfortunate doctrine is essentially Luciferian. The enlightenment offered is that of salvation through the scientific attainment of immortality through scientism and occult mythology, combined with the left-handed path association of taking on all possible evils and defilements. As a result of this occult version of dark theosis, one comes to the Abyss of the galaxy (as Tom does) and if successful in crossing and not going mad, one returns 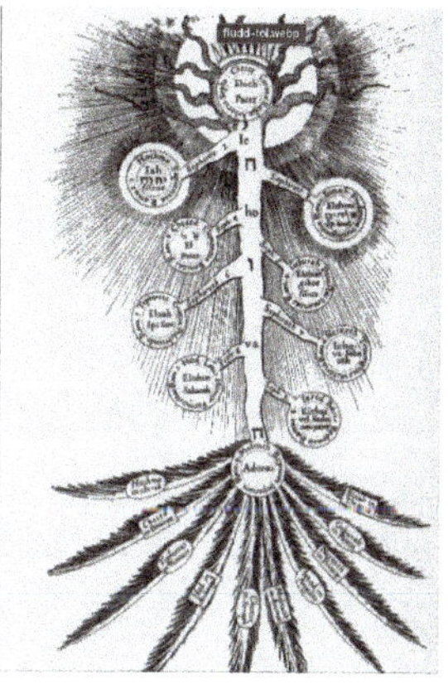 divinized. Just as the Serpent promised in the Garden, if man would partake of the Tree of Knowledge, he would attain godhood, apart from God.

Instead, this brought death, but in the film, death is presented as merely a stage in occult initiation, indeed as the very embodiment of the alchemical philosopher stone project (hence the golden imagery at the close of the film). Isn't it odd that the occult realm will posit all manner of esoteric possibilities about Genesis and Eden, God and even the possibility of Man incarnating God through sorcery, but never the actual presentation of Genesis or the Incarnation of God as Man. It's almost as if there is a plan to mock the biblical message as ridiculous, yet at the same time take a philosophy far more outrageous and inane and prop it up as the highest enlightenment.

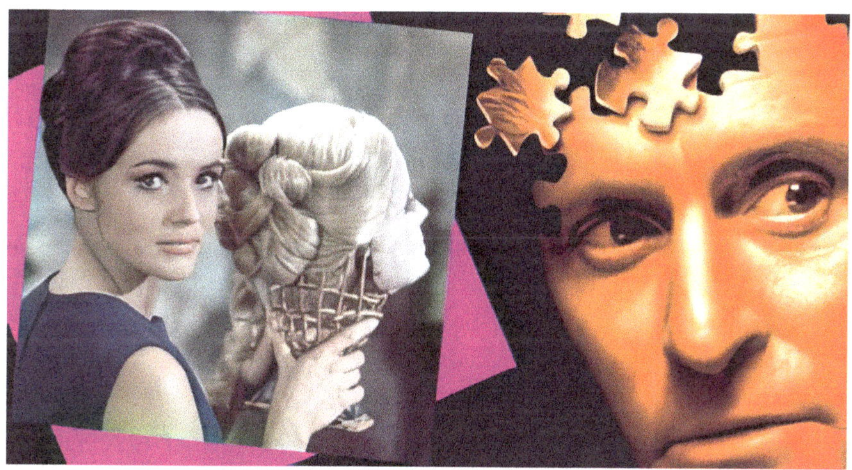

DAVID FINCHER'S *THE GAME* (1997) & *FIGHT CLUB* (1999)

This book's Introduction opened with an analysis of the famous novel from John Fowles, *The Magus*, and David Fincher's *The Game* bears a striking resemblance in terms of plot. Michael Douglas plays Nicolas Van Orton, a miserable, cold Wall Street-like executive (it's set in San Francisco) who has sacrificed everything to reach the top, including his familial relationships, especially with his brother Conrad (Sean Penn), the black sheep of the family. Like Gordon Gecko in Oliver Stone's *Wall Street*, Nicolas' only concern is his stock market portfolio and when Conrad shows up in his life again promising a new path to finding release through a secretive role playing corporation, Nicolas is not amused. The source of Nicolas' hard heartedness, we learn from old VHS tapes, was his childhood trauma of witnessing his dad leap to his death from a rooftop. Eventually, he acquiesces to signing up for the innocuous sounding Consumer Recreation Services' "Game," which includes vast questionnaires, medical and psychological exams at an elite facility in a downtown highrise. Nicolas is entirely left brained, with no connection to his heart or creative side, and without knowing it, the company has completely profiled him. "The Game," he is told, is uniquely and perfectly crafted to the psychological profile and imbalances in each new participant. In fact, some of his big shot finance colleagues also claim to have played the game and encourage him to join, without explaining any details or giving information as to what exactly transpired.

After a few days, Nicolas is informed he has been rejected from CRS and their offers, with no explanation, leading him to returning to the facility only to find no trace of it existing on a now abandoned floor. Assuming he has been scammed or becomes the butt of a prank, Nicolas flies into a rage and calls the police, who have no leads or answers. Upon returning home, the psy ops are only beginning, as Nicolas finds a dummy clown with a surveillance camera inside which kicks off a wild evening adventure fleeing a staged shootout with a waitress who is also a plant from CRS. Believing he is the object of a targeted campaign to steal his fortune, he flees to a cabin in the woods only to discover he has been financially wiped out.

Only through losing everything and waking up in a coffin in Mexico and hitching his way back to San Francisco does he face his ultimate fear – death, or dying like his father. This symbolic, spiritual death and rebirth culminates in the coming resurrection he will undergo as he faces his ultimate fear, which is the source of his psychological imbalance. His symbolic coffin death might also be a nod to Freemasonry, as every mason is initiated in a mock death and rebirth ritual in the third degree. Ultimately, CRS has organized and planned all these events, even his willing fall from the roof of the highrise to a giant inflatable cushion, after which he is greeted by everyone (almost all the other film characters) involved in the CRS "game." Ultimately, "The Game" was a trauma-based mind-control operation to integrate the damaged aspects of

Nicolas' *psyche*, and it appears to work, even mending the relationship with Conrad whom he embraces at the end.

At this stage it is important to grasp the extent to which CRS is able to interact with and influence Nicolas' life. From television shows geared at speaking directly to him, to potentially sexually compromising him with the waitress operative, to staged terror attacks and fake news broadcasts, CRS just happens to have all the means of an intelligence agency at their disposal! In other words, CRS = CIA, and they are a "company," just like the CIA is known as The Company. Although the film never makes this clear, it should be obvious, as CRS' motto is John 9:25, that "I was blind, but now I see," which is very close to the CIA's biblical motto, "Ye shall know the truth, and the truth shall make you free," John 8:32.

David Fincher's films often lightly brush up against the subject of intelligence operations and the CIA, but they are quite profuse with the explicit themes of trauma based mind control and occult organizations: consider for example the ritualized Satanic murder themes in the serial killer classic *The Zodiac*, the religious themed ritual killings in *Se7en*, the human trafficking in *Dragon Tattoo* and even the Crowleyan ethos of the hitman in his 2023 film, *The Killer*. In fact, in *The Killer* (Michael Fassbender) the unnamed protagonist assassin says his motto is "Do what thou wilt shall be the whole of the law," citing Aleister Crowley himself. Fincher is probably best known, however, for his turn of the millennium hit adaptation of the Chuck Palahniuk novel, *Fight Club*.

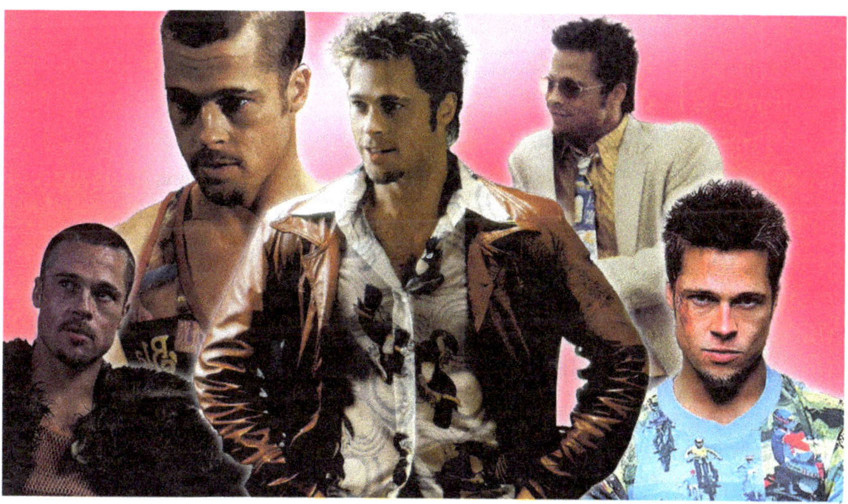

Although *Fight Club* (1999) is sometimes credited with helping to create the modern "manosphere" movement, it was not the intended purpose of either the novel or the film. Intending to be the voice of an apathetic Generation X finding its place in a world that was fast departing from baby-boomer values, Fincher's film was a cultural phenomenon and attempted to capture the zeitgeist of modern corporate nihilism and the rootless, feminized metropolitan existence it produces. The megacity's mega-capitalism, as the unnamed Narrator (Edward Norton) complains, has reduced men to hyper-consumerist catalogue-shopping beta males obsessed with the latest gadget, ultimately equalized and interchangeably meaningless and empty.

In fact, the Narrator notes that the destruction of fathers and the Father Archetype had destroyed Gen X's belief in God the Father! This inversion is far more extreme than we expect: The Narrator's best friend at his support group, "Bitchtits" (played by Meatloaf) has grown massive male breasts as a kind of symbolic representation of the hermaphroditic baphomet predicting the rise of trans individuals, signifying the unnatural existence of the capitalist megalopolis. Narrator's quest to return to his true masculine nature ultimately results in a psychological fissure in his *psyche* producing what we eventually realize is his alternate personality, Tyler Durden (Brad Pitt) – or is Tyler not an alternate personality, but a demonic possession? It is also possible his girlfriend Marla is a fracture of his own personality as Marla mentions underage sexual abuse trauma, opening up the possibility she also *is* the Narrator. Thus, the souce of his dissociative alters could be childhood sexual abuse from his father, resulting in the split, as well as his atheistic nihilism.

Fight Club is not just about trauma based mind control and cultural nihilism – it is also a film about cult leaders and the psychology of their use of mass mind control. While Narrator is a boring, corporate cubicle worker, his masculine, supposed "cool guy" persona, Tyler, is his extreme opposite who starts underground fight clubs, dresses like a raver, and seduces women without any moral qualms. Tyler even speaks as if his job is to bring about an archaic revival – a kind of return to a primal state where the cities are depopulated and the remaining tribal leaders have reverted to a *Mad Max* style patriarchy. This return to brutalism, however, is not an authentic masculinity, but a return to the primitive that furthers and synthesizes with the deindustrialization motivations of the elitists' "Great Reset." In fact, Tyler even calls for a societal "reset" and begins to create and craft his cult around this plan and what he calls "Operation Mayhem," a radical anarchic terror strategy to collapse the capitalist order.

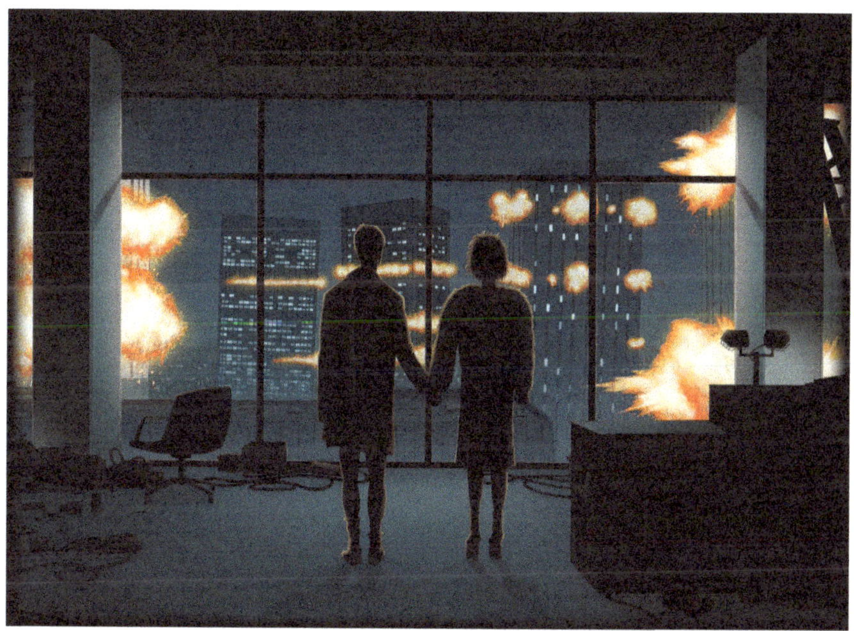

Tyler functions as a kind of Satanic, dark enlightenment figure who, although an alternate personality in Narrator's *psyche,* is intent on subverting society through his Fight Club *secret society* which transforms into a cover for an eventual paramilitary cult! Tyler is also like *Donnie Darko* wherein creative destruction becomes a path to regeneration, as society itself supposedly cycles through ages of birth, decay and rebirth, justifying his existence as an agent of chaos. In fact, the Fight Club cult engages in extreme forms of torture, terror and abuse to tear down and recreate its recruits into secretive black operation patsies who prove their masculinity to Tyler by eventually becoming full fledged terrorists. The techniques and strategies are reminiscent of some of the CIA techniques used in the training of Islamic and other radical terror groups where idiotic patsies can be used for false flag terror attacks.[155] This connection becomes even more striking when we consider that although Fincher's film is not about false flag terror directly, it is impossible to ignore the eerie parallels between the *controlled demolition* of multiple high rises at the conclusion of the film and the parallel events of September 11, 2001: America's greatest terror attack that would occur two years *after Fight Club* was in theaters!

SECTION 5

ORGANIZED INTELLIGENCE CRIME

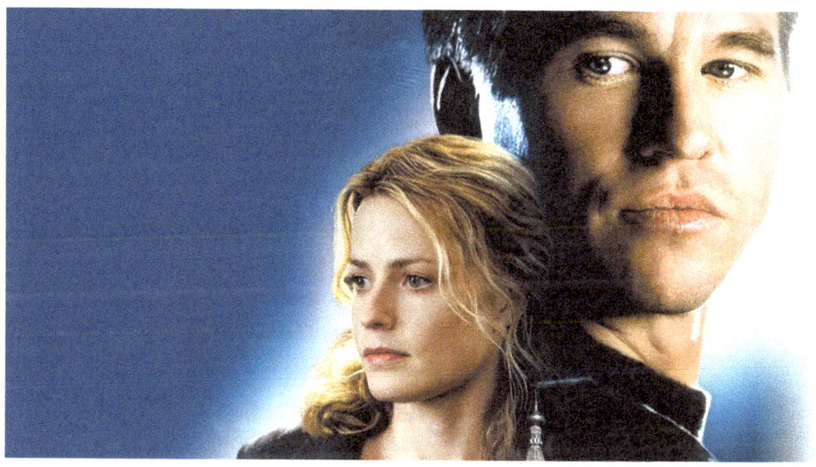

THE SAINT (1997)

I loved the 90s: It was a fun time in my life and one film that sticks out as a goofy, favorite indulgence is *The Saint,* starring Val Kilmer and Elizabeth Shue. At first glance, the movie is pure entertainment, but doesn't stand out to most as a great film of the 90s. However, like many other instances, I've come to notice subtle, hidden meanings and themes that run throughout the film: "Simon Magus was a magician and a sorcerer…" (Acts 8:9-24). We see in the opening shots Val Kilmer's character at an orphanage reading a comic book of the famed medieval and purportedly Satanically-inclined sect, the Knights Templar. It is also worth noting *The Saint* was directed by Philip Noyce who also directed the Angelina Jolie film *SALT,* which was consulted on by actual CIA operative Melissa Mehle who spent a significant time "training" Jolie for the role of a dual identity CIA operative in the film. Around this time Jolie was spotted reading CFR materials, even joining the organization. Was she also brought into the CIA as well?[156]

Simon Magus was the arch-heretic of the book of Acts and believed by many of the Apostolic Fathers to be the first gnostic, giving spawn to a series of libertine and flight-from-reality sects, popularized in modernity as "gnosticism." This theme of secret knowledge will run throughout *The Saint.* Val's young character refuses to say his name and is punished by the headmaster of the orphanage – a refusal to be connected with the actual saints, as he already has an interest in the alter "saints" condemned by the Roman Church in 1312, known as the Templars.

Instead of miracles, this saint, through trickery and deceit, unlocks the orphanage food and feeds the other children who are being deprived of

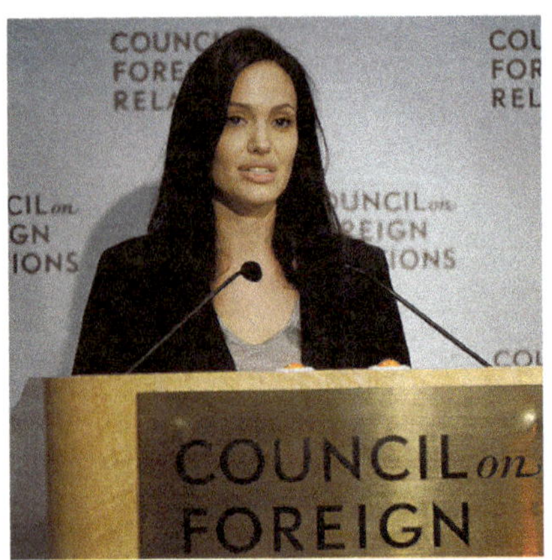

a meal as a punishment – a take on Jesus' feeding of the 5,000. Next, we see "Simon Templar" (his new name) running through the streets engaged in more mischief donning a cape with a Templar Cross. In the esoteric, receiving a new name is an important step in the process of apotheosis. Failing to attain his hero's kiss from his young love, she slips, falls from the balcony, and dies. Flash forward to the film's modern Simon Templar, ever-bruised from his youthful tragedy, the rogue agent is busy infiltrating the large Russian Tretiak Oil and Gas Industries building.

While Val sneaks in, up-and-coming Russian would-be Tsar, Ivan Tretiak, surrounded by Orthodox Bishops and Patriarchs, propounds the "Third Rome" theory well-known in Orthodox circles. This older view, held by many Russian Orthodox, is that "3 Romes have fallen, a fourth there shall not be:" The first imperium being old Rome, the second being Byzantium, and the last being Holy Mother Russia. Russia, *The Saint* is predicting, will rise to prominence again. An interesting fact, given modern geo-political developments! Tretiak, a former communist leader, is now a billionaire oil magnate. An interesting insight into the true nature of communism as the flip side of the capitalist dialectic. Tretiak also embodies the connection between politics and corporations. In other words, he is a perceptive incarnation of the modern state – a combination of the *polis* and the banking/corporate establishment.

Successfully nabbing the rather large "microchip," the Saint escapes through some trickery and sexual liaisons as "Martin de Porres" – who Kilmer says could heal through "the laying on of hands" – in this case a reference to sex. Still plagued by nightmares of his youthful trauma, he dreams about his real "name," or identity. Enter Tesla Technology & Alchemy: Tretiak decides to meet with the mysterious Saint who has stolen his "microchip," and offers him the job of stealing the formula for cold fusion from an Oxford physicist who has unlocked its powers. The Saint, under a new guise, attends Dr. Emma Russell's (played by Elizabeth Shue) physics lectures on cold fusion in order to profile her.

Dr. Emma enters into an explanation of cold fusion and uniting and igniting matter's latent potentiality. In alchemical fashion, our Saint seems to take this in a somewhat amorous way. And, of course, in alchemy, the sexual act is read as an analogy/ritual emblem of the creation and destruction of matter. Val breaks into her apartment and figures out he will have to become the poet, "artist" and father figure to win her over in order to obtain the cold fusion formula. Val becomes St. Thomas More, who acts more like Jim Morrisson than anything like More would have been. Thomas More's pick up lines are great for a laugh, by the way. As Dr. Russell is the scientist, Val must become the intuitive artist to complete what is lacking.

Val's trick works and the recitation of his alchemical, cold-fusion-sexual-innuendo poem conquers her:

> *I see my angel for the first time,*
> *I know my purpose, feel my birth,*
> *Hear, at first, faintly, then distinctly,*
> *The sweet strains of our union,*
> *Our love heats up the cold universe,*
> *And gives my tired, desperate hope,*
> *Purified by our kisses, are eternally healed.*

Thus it is made evident that the conquering of Nature with the discovery of her secrets via cold fusion is tied in with Val's conquering of Dr. Russell's feminine nature. In the alchemical view, sex is a symbol of the process of transformation and transformation is a symbol of the sexual act. Vice versa (or more correctly, vesica pisces!). Dr. Russell carries her "formula for creating energy" in her bra, which amuses Val who jokes that the secret to energy is in her "underwear." Amazed at his perception, Val explains he knows and does things by "magic."

The Saint finally seduces Dr. Russell and realizes that he wants to find his identity in the sex act, but decides instead to just lie there. Meaning found in the other. But he is torn, not wanting to steal the cold fusion formula. Magic, Science and sex: are the parameters of these things separate or linked? We saw how the cold fusion "science" was also a veiled reference to the sexual tension felt between Val and Dr. Russell. Val is torn, but ends up stealing the formula. Tretiak comes after Val and won't pay, but Val eludes and ends up in Russia as Tretiak's doppelganger, tricking him into paying.

About to leave Russia, Val is apprehended, along with Dr. Russell (who had flown to track him down) by Tretiak's controlled Moscow police. Together they escape and end up in the snowy streets of Moscow. Val falls in the frozen water and develops hypothermia. Hearkening back to "cold fusion," Val almost freezes to death, and has to get frisky with Dr. Russell to restore the necessary "heat," as they are hidden by a prostitute in a slum.

Frozen Val reveals his real name to be Simon the Magician, because he did "tricks." The "priests took Agnes (lamb in Latin), and killed her," referring to his childhood trauma of seeing his crush at the orphanage accidentally die. Simon rejects religion based on sacrifice because he sees it as something that kills love/lust. Simon Templar, the magician, blames the Church for his problems and for killing his crush. They again escape, this time into the "underground" of Moscow, where they meet black market art dealers selling icons – particularly the fictional "Icon of the Virgin of the Damned." This scene perhaps signifies the underground fraudulent elements within the Church (whether Catholic or Orthodox). As researcher DJ noted to me personally, "the Icon of the Damned recalls [possibly] the breasts of Persephone as she has to nurture the babe Dionysius back to health, transitioning him from the 'old man' to the 'new man,' much the same as the reborn Horus rushes to Isis."

Leaving the sewers, Simon and Dr. Emma are again almost nabbed by Tretiak, but Emma flees to the American Embassy. Tretiak's son then spits on the face of the black American soldier. Immediately following this scene, the viewer is taken to Tretiak's lair, where we see a mysterious poster for a KKK rally in Georgia, a bombed out building harkening back to Oklahoma City, and a poster of Tretiak's political opponent, president Karpov, with what appears to be a diagram outlining assassination. The point of this is to associate whatever opposition to the Anglo-American establishment exists as the source of all evil.

Dr. Russell no longer needs her heart medicine: Val, as the "Saint," has cured her of her condition. Appearing next as St. Augustine, who famously dealt with lust, Dr. Emma tells Val he is her personal saint (recall the flaming heart symbol of Augustine). Newscasts claim that the future of democracy in Russia hangs in the balance as a second, white revolution is about to emerge in Red Square (under Tretiak). We are led to believe that all things monarchical and opposed to democratic socialism are bad, while Tretiak is in fact a former KGB communist. We are shown a false left/right dialectic. Tretiak has framed President Karpov and thinks the cold fusion formula he acquired to be bogus will not work.

Tretiak assumes this will shift the balance of world power from Anglo-American to Russian. However, the cold fusion formula works and produces massive energy, which Simon calls a miracle. "Science" is now the new religion that gives us miracles. Tretiak had even created the scarcity by hoarding millions of gallons of heating oil: The kind of tactic communists like Lenin used. Dr. Russell gives the formula away for free and tells Simon that he has performed his three miracles. As Val drives off, we see a faint halo above his head. While *The Saint* is one of my personal favorite 90s films, its message is one of gnosticism, alchemy and scientism. Simon is a esoteric "Saint" in the line of Simon Magus and the heterodox Templars. "Simon" also hearkens to St. Peter – the foundation stone of the Orthodox Catholic Church. Simon Templar thus symbolizes the foundation of the *alter*-Church – that of secret societies and intelligence workings.

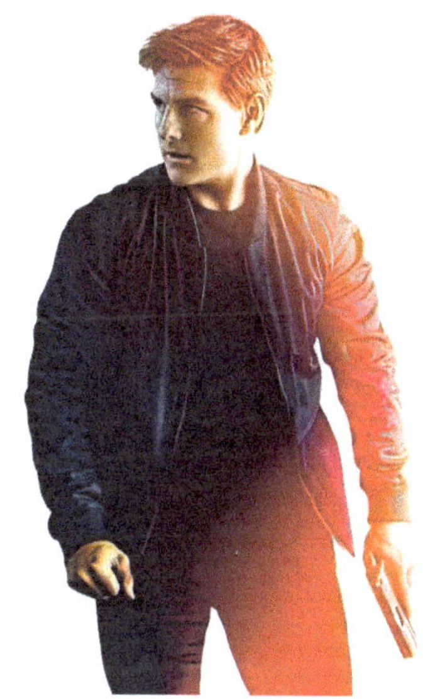

The Tom Cruise *Mission Impossible* Series & TV's *Alias*

The 1996 *Mission Impossible* reboot from Brian De Palma would go on to become a massive, multi-billion dollar franchise and the chief role for Tom Cruise for the next 30 years, but are there deeper, darker meanings to this spy thriller? In fact, Cruise himself was admitted to be meeting with the CIA soon after the initial success of the franchise after the events of 9/11:

> Tom Cruise is rumoured to be in consultation with the CIA in order to provide a PR boost to the government agency in the wake of September 11. The Hollywood patriot, who also played a key role in the recent telethon benefit, is keen to push a positive view

of the CIA in his forthcoming *Mission: Impossible 3*. "He plays a CIA agent and he was interested in making his character as realistic as possible," an unnamed source told MSNBC.com. "But he was also emphatic about presenting the CIA in as positive a light as possible. [Cruise] said that, given the recent terrorist attacks, it's important for Hollywood to help put the US and government agencies in a good light." It's not the first time that Cruise has helped advertise the American forces. His antics in 1986's *Top Gun* inspired the US Navy to set up recruitment booths in cinema foyers across the country.[157]

What is interesting about this "role" is that it seems to be a popular one for many Hollywood A-Listers, and could suggest a deeper relationship beyond mere "PR." As we will see, many famous A-Lister Hollywood stars have actually been spies and worked for the OSS, CIA and FBI and there is no reason to think that trend ceased: in fact, there is ample evidence it continues still. For example, *Sputnik* reports:

> US filmmakers and movie stars have helped whitewash the image of US spies for years, portraying them as heroes who sometimes have to resort to drastic measures for the greater good.

> Here's the list:
> Angelina Jolie. She visited CIA headquarters for consultancy while preparing for her role in *Salt*, a 2010 spy thriller. Her activism around the globe, however, makes one wonder exactly how deep her relationship with the CIA might run.

> Jennifer Garner. The star of TV series *Alias* where she played a CIA double agent, Garner was invited to visit Langley. In 2004, she even starred in a short recruitment video for the agency.

> Sean Penn. His interview with Mexican drug lord Joaquin Guzman (also known as "El Chapo"), which was soon followed by the latter's arrest, fueled speculation that Penn might be a US intelligence asset.

> Ben Affleck. He starred as CIA Deputy Director Jack Ryan in the 2002 thriller *The Sum of All Fears*, as well as in 2012, Affleck produced and starred in *Argo* a film lauding the CIA's efforts to rescue US diplomats during the Iran hostage crisis.[158]

The Atlantic also covered this relationship, writing:

> The flag-waving Tom Clancy franchise became a centerpiece of CIA propaganda in the 1990s, with a succession of actors (Alec Baldwin,

Harrison Ford, and finally Ben Affleck) starring in films like *Patriot Games, Clear and Present Danger*, and *The Sum of All Fears*, which pit the daring agent Jack Ryan against an array of enemies, from terrorists to South American drug lords to nuclear-armed white supremacists.[159]

With all that in mind, we can analyze the *Mission Impossible* franchise with new eyes. Cruise plays Ethan Hunt, famously based on the real world CIA operative E. Howard Hunt (also the basis for The Smoking Man in *The X-Files*)

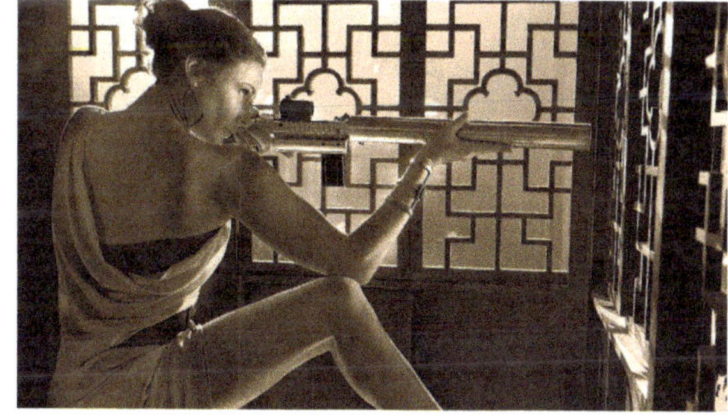

many believe to be directly involved in the JFK assassination.[160] The film begins with Hunt in Kyiv (around the time the CIA was in Kyiv through NGOs and Soros Activist Networks prepping for the 2004 Orange Revolution coup in the real world). Hunt is seeking a stolen NOC list for operatives in Eastern Europe now in the property of one "Agent Golitzin," which is a curious name given it's also the name of an actual famous defector (Anatoly Golitsin) who would have been interrogated for KGB operative names and who published obvious CIA propaganda sponsored by James Jesus Angleton in his infamous *New Lies for Old* text.[161]

The fascinating, ahead of its time element about *MI1* is not its usage of the classic spy gags like disguises or staged operations, but the focus on artificial intelligence. Few recall this 90s gem had as its plot the securing of a special, highly advanced A.I. chip that Phineas Phreak (played by Ving Rhames who is here part of the hacker group the Cyber Phreaks, which is close to the famed realworld CypherPunks of Bitcoin lore). In *Mission Impossible 2*, a mad scientist is scheming to create a mass pandemic using a manufactured Chimera virus, which the Biocyte Pharmaceutical Corporation has the vaccine for known as the Bellerophon Antidote.[162] The head of the Pharmaceutical Corporation is named John McCloy (who in the real world just happens to have been a CFR Chairman and high level Rockefeller operative[163]) who cooperated with the plot to engage in a mass vaccination scam. I don't think I need to explain how amazing this parallel is to the Covid PsyOp of 2020-2022!

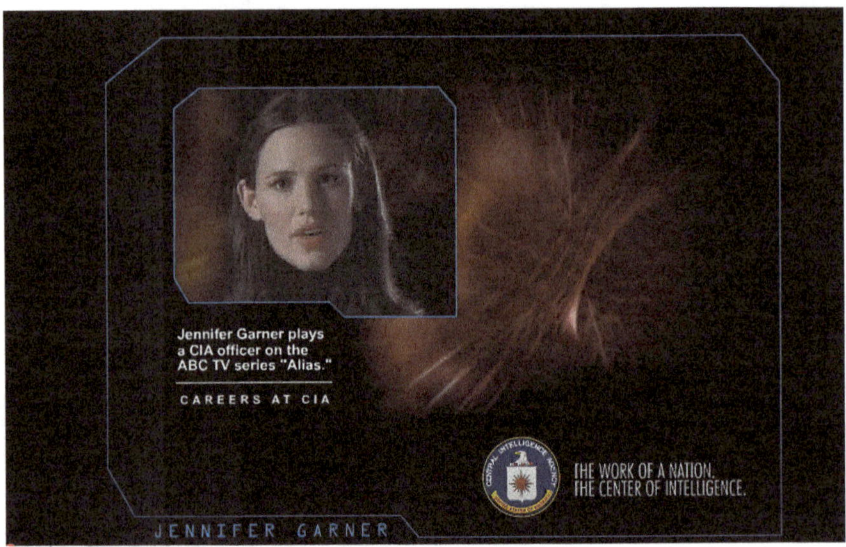

By the time of *Mission Impossible 3* in 2006, famed director J.J. Abrams had taken over after a long period of working with the openly CIA connected Jennifer Garner on his previous show *Alias*.[164] In fact, Garner was hired to engage in recruitment videos for the CIA in the early 2000s after several seasons as the psychologically fractured MKUltra recruit and gifted child Sydney Bristow, who was brought into The Program and handled by her own CIA father! Throughout the series, Sydney's operations range from sexual honeypot and swallow operations to false flags to assassinations as she believes she is working to take down the international Illuminati-like "Alliance," when in fact due to compartmentalization of information, she was a false flag recruit, working for the Alliance all along. Indeed, it was Abrams' work on *Alias* that caused Cruise to request him for *Mission Impossible*.

The third installment of *Mission Impossible* was packed with conspiracy candy where the plot revolves around a villain Owen Davian (Philip Seymour Hoffman) who is seeking the "Rabbit's Foot," a vial of biohazard material that can massively depopulate the earth if released. The weapon is known as "Anti-God," which is an odd reference considering the film ends up taking us to the Vatican where Ethan Hunt goes *undercover as a Roman Catholic priest*. In my estimation, *MI3* is far closer to how the world is really run than even they knew! Catholic geopolitical analyst and historian David Wemhoff has written

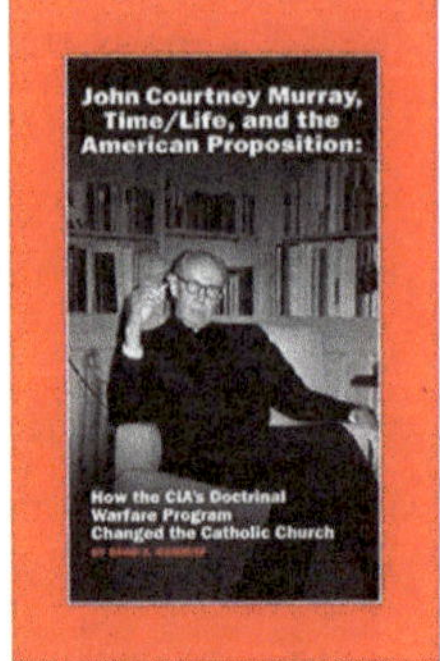

a massive 900 page classic, John Courtney Murray, *Time Life Magazine & The American Proposition: How the CIA's Doctrinal Warfare Program Changed the Catholic Church*. In this magisterial tome, Wemhoff traces the infiltration of the Jesuit Order in particular through CIA-connected operatives like Murray and handlers like C.D. Jackson. Although no specific reference is made to the papacy in the film, the IMF appears to be really calling the shots, with Vatican security none the wiser. In fact, Catholic CIA writers have even confirmed this special relationship with the Vatican and the CIA by even crediting John Paul II's CIA collaboration helping to end the Cold War.[165]

Mission Impossible 4, known as *Ghost Protocol*, deals with the IMF team going rogue due to internal corruption among Ethan's superiors. The deeper insights in *MI4* relate to a massive western engineered false flag in Moscow as Hunt is sent undercover in the Kremlin, framing him as the patsy as the Kremlin is reduced to rubble. The film was also prescient, like *The Saint*, in regard to revived Cold War fears that would re-emerge in the wake of the 2014 Maidan Coup that saw a regime change in Ukraine, stoking tensions that would eventually result in the recent Ukraine war with Russia. Although not a false flag in the Kremlin, it is very clearly western intelligence that masterminded the Nord Stream pipeline bombing.[166] Predictably, Ethan and his team are branded international "terrorists," and much like British Intelligence successfully did with the IRA in the 80s and 90s and the CIA with Islamic extremist groups in the "War on Terror," they had created the perfect patsies.[167] Even more striking in the 4th installment is the emergence of an explicitly Malthusian rogue intelligence sect who is intent on extensive depopulation through a nuclear war they intend to be a year zero *great reset*! This move would supposedly kickstart "evolution" and propel man to a more progressive society.

In the 5th installment, *Mission Impossible: Rogue Nation*, Tomkat returns to save the world, er, Tom, minus the Kat. In the last installment of Ethan Hunt's (modeled after CIA spymaster Howard Hunt), the "Impossible Mission Force" was able to halt the enigmatic "Cobalt" in his apocalyptic attempt to kickstart evolutionary abiogenesis by nuking the globe. As highlighted before, the film revealed a great deal concerning real-world depopulation stratagems, hearkening to the likes of Bill Gates, Ted Turner and Prince Charles. In this blockbuster, something equally as sinister, and infinitely more complex is explored in the plot – that of the subterfuge of British Intelligence. In fact, this installment would prove to be the most sophisticated and revealing concerning real-world geopolitics.

Locating a crate of hijacked nerve gas by Chechen terrorists, Ethan Hunt is activated for a new mission to track down a mysterious Syndicate, following new leads in a London record store that operates as a front for what he believes is western intelligence. Bookstores and tailors are classic real fronts, but the use of music shop is interesting, recalling *The Prisoner* series, where Agent No. 6 signals he is receiving messages from outside agents, and in Hunt's case, he appears to have met his match as he is gassed and nabbed by this new organization.

With Hunt disappearing and the IMF still disbanded due to further government inquiry, the CIA takes over the role of Col. L Fletcher Prouty *Secret Team* style operations formerly helmed by Hunt, while the IMF team is accused of collusion with international crime.[168] Hunt, in captivity, learns the Syndicate is enabling international false flag terror plots, assassinations and large-scale disasters in a long chain of managed chaos. The film's most interesting and artistic sequence is the *Turandot* opera in Vienna, Austria, where two assassins accompany Hunt's femme fatale lead, Ilsa Faust, seeking to gain entrance to the Syndicate by assuring the assassination of the Austrian Chancellor (should she fail). There is reference here to the assassination of Archduke Franz Ferdinand by British SIS that sparked World War I. The plot of *Turandot* functions as the backdrop to *Rogue Nation*, as three riddles must be solved for the opera's Prince to obtain the hand of the Princess.

Passing the tests, the Princess is still unwilling to marry him so a compromise is offered – if she can guess his name before dawn the next day, he will die and release her from the bond. In *Rogue Nation*, Ethan and Ilsa Faust exchange offers of a "way out" following her three failed tests for gaining entrance to the Syndicate. Faust's name is overtly significant, with Dr. Faust represents the "deal with the devil," as we discover Ilsa is actually under the thumb of British Intelligence, entrapped into infiltrating the Syndicate by her MI6 handler, Attlee (an interesting name, given the real world Labour Minister Clement Attlee also worked closely with British Intelligence in the Cold War).

Ultimately, the significance of the opera is quite transparent: Just as the assassination occurs at a certain note in the opera representing the lead's death, so the assassin's cue is the death note. Expand this principle into twilight language and the message is this: The characters in the play are playing out a script, in the exact same fashion as the oligarchs and their intelligence agencies manage the puppet strings of world events. The World is a Theater in the sense that power elites stage manage world events with the same precision as a symphonic composition. Understand this point well, since it is the entire message of the film. The rabbit hole, the *Alice in Wonderland* twists and turns of the intelligence world's hall of mirrors are the background to reality's "big events" in the same way "Turandot" is the background to *Mission Impossible 5*. That is, *MI5 – quite an interesting title*.

This terror squad constitutes the "Rogue Nation" of the film's title, and in my thesis the film's true revelation is not the plot narrative, but rather this is precisely how the world is run. As Jay's Analysis has argued, the numerous anomalies, patterns, stagecraft and media-complicit deception in the large-scale, real-world "terror" events, ranging from 9/11 (more recently) to 7/7 to disappearing planes, mass shootings, and ISIS, are actually the work of elite western intelligence. In fact, as Ethan flees his Syndicate and CIA assassins, he discovers a vast array of disasters were the handiwork of the Syndicate, including a *missing passenger plane that disappeared over the ocean* and a bank crash.

These fictional events appear to have reference to classic media mysteries, including two Malaysian Planes, the 2008 crash and/or a host of IMF (International Monetary Fund) economic terror attacks against nations like Spain, Ireland, Ukraine and Greece.[169] Also mentioned is a "triggering of a civil war," which could be a stand in for numerous references. This "anti-IMF" is presented as an oppositional force to the establishment, recruiting the world's best international agents following their fake deaths. I have opined in numerous interviews that doubles and staged deaths are far more common than most assume, and here is a Hollywood hint.

Following a barrage of scenes intent on wowing audiences with spy culture gadgetry, the climactic secret is that British Intelligence is secretly behind the Syndicate, and its rogue leader, Solomon Lane is actually being funded by Attlee, the presumed head of MI6. Solomon as the skeleton key of "terror" for Attlee is a significant name for further obvious reasons, suggesting Solomon's Key and the use of the dark arts (black ops), in unison with the devilish name of Ilsa Faust. The suggestion seems to be that MI6 has made a deal with the devil, so to speak, to stage manage world terror events at the behest of the Atlanticist establishment, while such terror funding could never be traced back to western intelligence elites due to the high tech encryption known only to Attlee.

As a side note, it is worth mentioning that Jeremy Renner's character, William Brandt, is also the name of an outed CIA operative, Willy Brandt.[170] These are (glaringly opaque) clues that the film is undoubtedly a revelation of the method that comes damn near to revealing reality in strikingly lucid terms, were it not for the absurd solution that America and its "Secret Team" of the IMF are the saviors of a broken system where "desperate times require desperate measures." In other words, yes, the system is broken, but don't listen to whistleblowing malcontents, salvation can only come through the American establishment. Yet as we've seen with so many similar plots (and this film is very similar to *Quantum of Solace* and *Skyfall*), the joke is on the bamboozled populace, inasmuch as the film simultaneously reveals the actual world controllers as it assures these same scoundrels will save the day. G.I. Joe runs Cobra.

In *Mission Impossible 6*, known as *Fall Out*, the previous villain Solomon Lane returns with a new Malthusian plot together with his Eco-zealot religious cult known as The Apostles, all of whom intend to purge the world again for a great reset with an engineered nuclear exchange. The world's religious cities will be targeted this time: Rome, Mecca, and Jerusalem, causing humanity to awaken from its status quo existence and return to some form of earth worship. By contaminating the entire Eurasian water supply, they plot a global apocalypse will ensue and mankind can wipe the slate clean. Global vaccination plans are also involved (like in MI2) as UN Kashmir refugee camps become staging grounds for both IMF and the Apostles' black operations. Once again, the actual plans of the World Economic Forum's Davos elite seem to perfectly mirror Solomon's "Apostles" Plan!

In *Dead Reckoning*, Cruise returns as Ethan Hunt in what is supposed to be the finale to the series, split into two parts. *Dead Reckoning 1* returns to the origins of Mission Impossible's fixation: Artificial Intelligence. Indeed, the first film in 1996 had been extremely prophetic about the future of tech and 30 years later we are in the midst of the actual global rollout of A.I. In *Dead Reckoning*, the A.I. is highly advanced and almost godlike, going by the title of "The Entity." The access to The Entity is guarded by a multi-sig 2 part key that accesses the vast power to unlock the manipulation of any and all tech systems worldwide. The A.I., like in War Games with Matthew Broderick, has 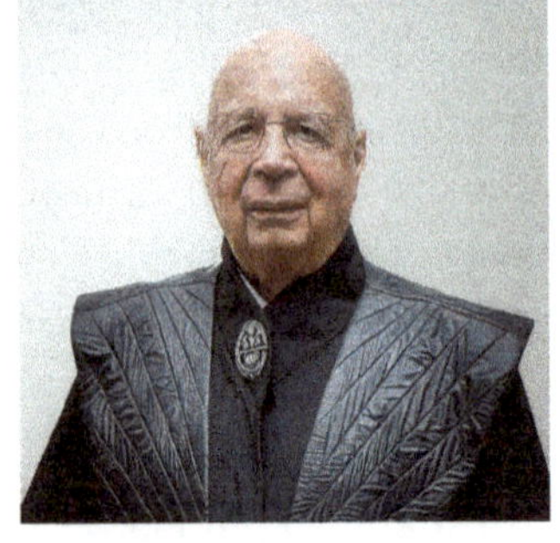 apparently gone "rogue," leading Hunt to forced rational theory choice decisions that pit Ethan against a corrupt CIA and the Entity itself.

The Entity, becoming almost omnipresent, uses advanced algorithmic traps and predictive models to force Ethan into sacrificing friends or his mission, something the Entity knows is Hunt's weakness based on its almost omniscient ability to profile anyone instantly. What makes *Dead Reckoning* odd is the turn towards gnosticism, as the Entity functions like a creator god demiurge, imprisoning and trapping those who lack the secret keys to control it. Rather than a personal God, *MI7's* Entity is more like a technology mankind harnesses to become God – a theme writer McQuarrie included in his previous Cruise film, *Edge of Tomorrow*. Indeed, Cruise, the famous Scientologist has a tendency to appear in esoteric themed films as already outlined in this book, back to *Eyes Wide Shut* in volume 1, where readers will recall the odd connections between Scientology's founder, L. Ron Hubbard, and his time in Aleister Crowley's OTO.

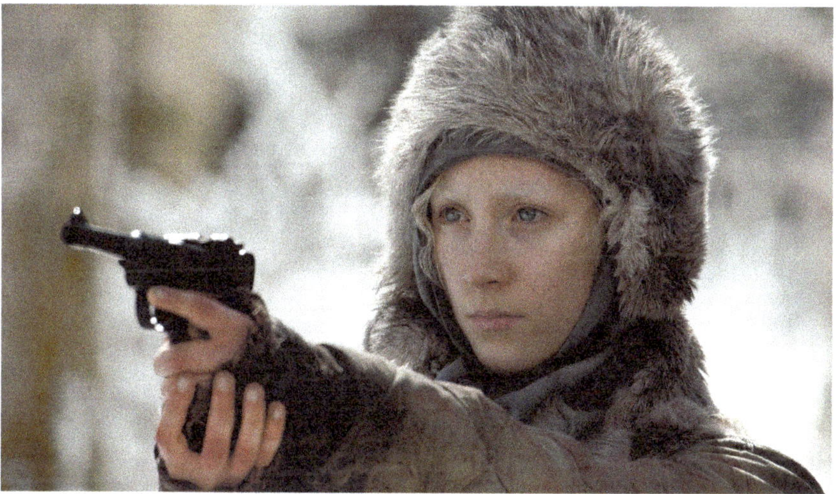

HANNA (2011)

As a story and as entertainment, *Hanna* is top notch. However, as far as the message goes I have some gripes, and this time it's not really gnosticism. Well, it is a little bit, but not primarily. *Hanna* is the story of a young girl (played by Saoirse Ronan), who is mysteriously unaware of her origins raised by her father in an utterly secluded cabin in Finland. Her father gives her intelligence agent training, while simultaneously keeping her from all modern luxuries. *Hanna* is thus a trained hunter and assassin. From the trailer, we see that it will be a take on a fairy tale, and that is what will develop. One of the few things she reads in her cabin, along with the Encyclopedia, is *Grimm's Fairy Tales*, which comes up as a subtle sub-theme throughout the narrative.

Initially, she fixates on the Cinderella story, which is a story of mythical transformation – precisely what the film is about. Something like *A.I.* meets *Run Lola Run*, *Hanna* is about the future generations. Since we have descended into a post-post-modern nihilism, all that is left is the return to myth. The Enlightenment scientism has been discovered to be another form of mythology that, while producing interesting artifacts, is unable to quantify and calculate the sum totality of man's existence into a materialist, pragmatist framework. Thus, what happens in this stage of cultural devolution is that man's nihilism returns to myth as a larger narrative structure for life. Hanna, as the film makes clear, is the genetically altered future, which the scientific establishment will attempt to control, but which, in fact, cannot be controlled.

Once upon a time....

After a long journey of self-discovery and rugged survivalism, Hanna has interfaced with modernity and found it absurd and empty. Ironically, being raised in a completely sheltered environment, she is simultaneously "from the forest" (as girls often are in fairy tales) and the next level in human development as a result of science. Hanna represents the establishment's attempt at a totally controlled and engineered human godchild – the stuff of myth and legend. The great voyage of discovery is that she herself is abnormal because she is superior. She is a genius who has had "empathy" bred out of her, though she displays empathy in certain cases.

Hanna is thus the "new man," yet not a man – a woman, in fact. This is my major qualm with the film – while it is fun and entertaining to see feisty young girls as badasses, it actually falls inline with a quasi-feminist agenda. Some might argue that Hanna is a lesbian in one scene, yet she seems more of a hermaphrodite character. She is a blend of both male and female characteristics. This is not to say that she is not a female: she is, but at a point in the film Dr. Wiegler (the CIA agent played by Cate Blanchett who is tracking Hanna and her father) meets up with a mercenary named Isaacs (played by Tom Hollander) who runs a peep show with a hermaphrodite. In other words, the MKUltra product of CIA mind control and experimentation is justified because the end product is a new, gnostic savior goddess beyond good and evil.

This is an esoteric clue common in films and in the occult tradition that signifies the supposed primal human unity and union of opposites. The hermaphrodite thus figured prominently in alchemical writings as the goal of the process of transformation wherein the philosopher's stone is created – the quintessential gold of immortality. Hanna is the philosopher's stone as the new, immortal, genetically modified human.

What we have here is a presentation on one level of transhumanism, and it can certainly be read that way, but it can also be read as an attack on modernity and a statement of who and what will survive in the future. Hanna's character is contrasted with a young "modern" girl she befriends that is obsessed with pop culture and degraded nonsense. Hanna is polite to her, but they are, in fact, opposites. *Hanna* represents the future elite – those who read books and can survive. Her friend represents the degraded youth of today's Lady Gaga gaggle.

This is where the film appears a bit nihilistic at one point, where Hanna is asked about God, and she seems to inquire of her friend's liberal, Oxford-trained family what they are even referring to. While this can be read as possibly atheistic, it is not necessarily so, since *Hanna* told her Arabic host at one point in Arabic that she knew he was Muslim. So Hanna knows about religion, but it is rather that she does not run in the mainstream circles of anything. She has been sheltered and trained as a new breed of humanity, who finds it difficult to even interact with others her age. Hanna is the elite, and when she and her father (Eric Bana) arrive in Germany, you will notice in the background graffiti several eyes strategically placed in numerous places. This is significant in that Germany is the origin of the actual "Illuminati Order," as Terry Melanson has demonstrated. Is this saying that the Illuminist message is one of rejecting civilization as it stands, for a future where the cream of the crop of humanity will survive?

Hanna is, then, a metamorphosis story, similar to what you find in several of Ovid's *Metamorphoses*, with the hermaphroditic story of Tiresias or as with Apuleius' *The Golden Ass*. It is a metamorphosis story of surviving progeny. And, mythical transformation stories always figure prominently in alchemical manuscripts as mythology technologized. Modern genetics and modification is the continuation of the alchemical story of transforming the baser metals of human nature into the supposed gold of immortal godhood. But, as I noted, it doesn't have to be read as propaganda for transhumanism: it can also be read as a pragmatism-turned-elitist-survivalism, wherein modernity is attacked. This, I like, and here, *Hanna*, after killing the wicked stepmother (in Cinderella fashion) at the mouth of the wolf in the fairy tale amusement park becomes a return to *mythos* and classical ways of life, as opposed to modern decadence and dehumanization.

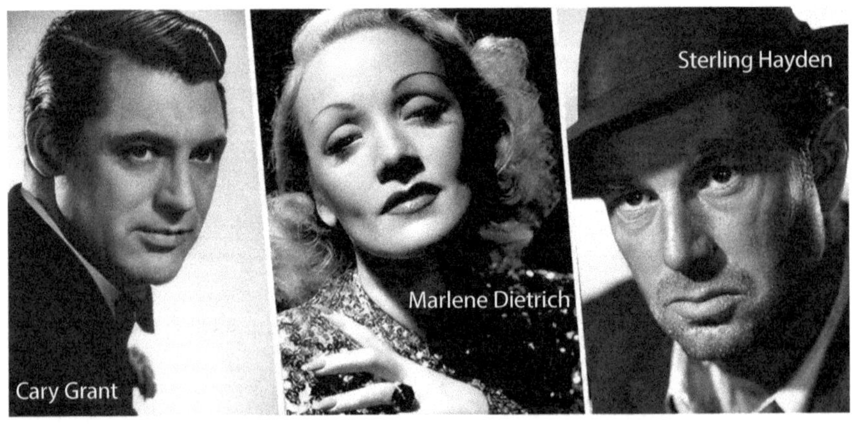

Hollywood Spies

While some still find the notion of modern Hollywood A-listers functioning as spies something outlandish or absurd, when we look into the declassified history of this phenomenon and various biographers, it's far more prevalent than one would suspect. In fact, from the earliest days of modern Elizabethan theater and acting, up to famed British figures like Ian Fleming and the fictional James Bond, the world of entertainment has overlapped with espionage in profound ways we've highlighted in previous volumes.[171] This relationship goes even further than fictional characters, in fact many of Hollywood's most famous spies have had direct working relationships with intelligence as operatives, honeypots, agents, assets and informants. This special relationship makes sense, as A-listers would have invited and access to dignitaries and elite social events the average person will never see: What better way to gain sensitive intelligence?

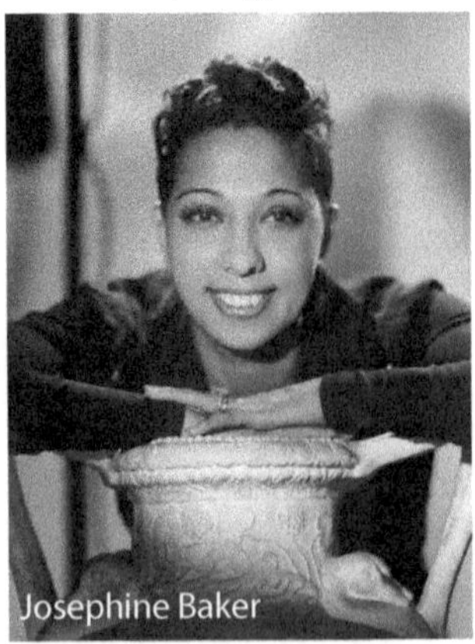

The invention of the camera saw the immediate use of the technological wonder for propaganda by all the major powers at the beginning of the 1900s, and the intelligence agencies stepped in. For the sake of this section, we will begin with World War 2 era entertainers recruited into these unique roles into the present day era. The A-lister and highest paid European singer and dancer of her day, Josephine Baker, was recruited into spying for the French Resistance as Hitler rose to power in the 1930s. Likewise, the most famous entertainer in

Sweden was recruited by the Axis powers to spy on Hitler's higher ups and even sleep with them as a swallow operation that ruined her public acting career: The recent well done Swedish film *Spy* (2019) was based on her life.[172] Audrey Hepburn also aided the Dutch Resistance and passed intelligence information on the Nazis to the Allies, working under British intelligence operative Visser't Hooft.[173] Meanwhile, Greta Garbo has long been suspected of also being a possible British spy.

Houdini also famously spied on German and Russian troop movements for the British War Office and was also reportedly a spy for Interpol.[174] Celebrated professional baseball catcher Moe Berg was recruited by the OSS as a spy to recruit scientists, and was almost able to assassinate Dr. Werner Heisenberg, should the Nazis be found to have atomic plans (they didn't).[175] Like many other A-listers, Marlene Deitrich was suspected of being both a spy for Germans and for British Intelligence, both of which are hotly debated.[176] We have covered Ian Fleming in previous volumes, but his immediate circles, including the infamous William Stephenson, aka "Intrepid," Noel Coward, Alexander Korda and others set up the British Security

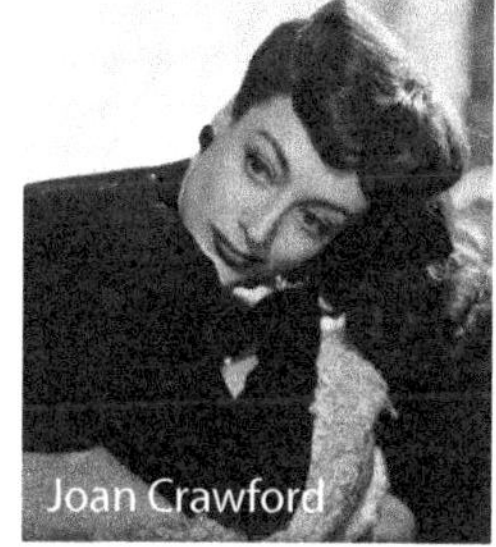

Coordination (BSC), staffed with officers from the Special Operations Executive (SOE) who ran their Hollywood propaganda and forgery operations out of 35th and 36th floors of Rockefeller Plaza in New York. Together with Bill Donovan, they helped set up the OSS, but the BSC and Donovan also worked with multiple early screenplays writers and OSS-themed Hollywood films, like *Confidential Agent* (1945), starring Lauren Bacall, *OSS* (1946) starring Alan Ladd, and *13 Rue Madeleine* (1947) directed by Fritz Lang.[177] The BSC, through its most famous novelist Helen MacInnes, continued its Hollywood propaganda operations through the story that would be that basis for the famed 1943 Joan Crawford film, *Above Suspicion*.

The FBI also began producing its own films, including *Men of the FBI* (1941), *FBI Front* (1942) and *House on 92nd Street* (1945), and most famously the 1959 *FBI Story* starring Jimmy Stewart who actually worked for the FBI in real life![178] In fact, famed TV chef Julia Child, as well as director John Ford and A-Lister Sterling Hayden were also OSS operatives.[179] As mentioned, Cary Grant is believed to have spied for the FBI and/or British Intelligence and claimed Errol Flynn was a German Agent.[180] Walt Disney also famously worked with the CIA to procure the Disney property, as well as various propaganda operations. *The Daily Beast* writes:

> Disney's principal legal strategist for Florida was a senior clandestine operative named Paul Helliwell. Having helped launch the CIA secret war in Indochina, Helliwell relocated to Miami in 1960 in order to coordinate dirty tricks against Castro. At a secret "seminar" Disney convened in May 1965 Helliwell came up with the approach that to this day allows the Disney organization to avoid taxation and environmental regulation as well as maintain immunity from the U.S. Constitution. It was the same strategy the CIA pursued in the foreign countries. Set up a puppet government; then use that regime to do your bidding.[181]

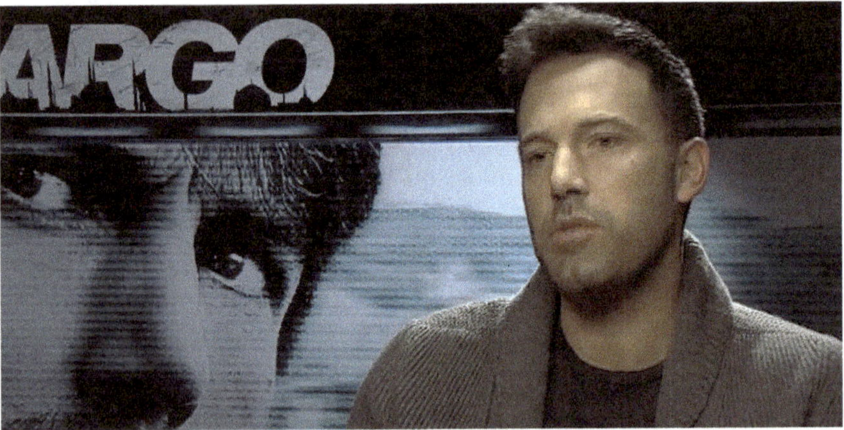

More recently, Ben Affleck has been open about his work with the CIA on films that rehearse classic intelligence operations like *Argo* (2012), which included his work with the Agency in some capacity, with Affleck noting to *The Guardian* in 2012 "Hollywood is probably full of CIA Agents."[182] Recall that Affleck was also married to Jennifer Garner at the time, who was also working with the CIA in recruitment films, as previously mentioned. In recent FOIA documents, Affleck replied to the CIA as follows: "The official then wrote to Affleck to tell him the "good news" and Affleck shot back, *"This is great!!! Thank you so much!! I am thrilled. Please let me know whatever I can do. This is a thrill. We will do the agency proud I promise you."*[183]

Although the intelligence agencies haven't declassified much information on recent celebrity spies, there is no reason to think these operations ever stopped, and in fact, much evidence they continue still. One of the funniest examples of this Hollywood overlap with intelligence of recent fame was the revelation the the supposed "chemical weapons" Saddam Hussein was accused of possessing was literally borrowed from the plot of Nicolas Cage's film, *The Rock,* where the West Coast is saved by Cage heroically grasping the green balls of death. This plot was literally used by the fraudulent intelligence forger behind the so-called WMDs Bush and Powell used for war with Iraq![184]

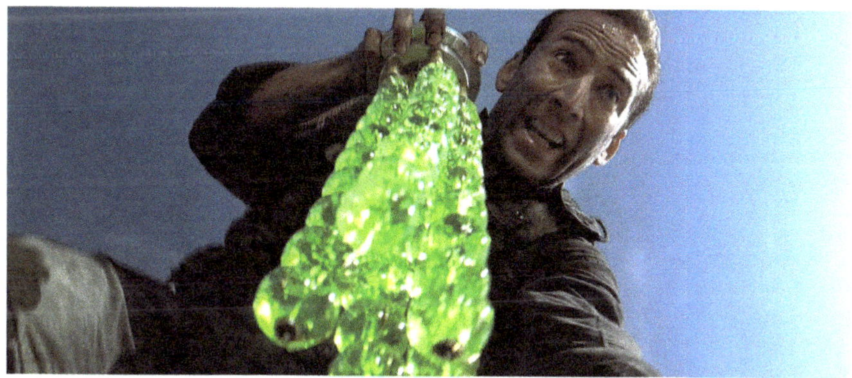

Section 6

Hollywood Antichrist Apocalypse

WHERE DOES THE TIME GO?

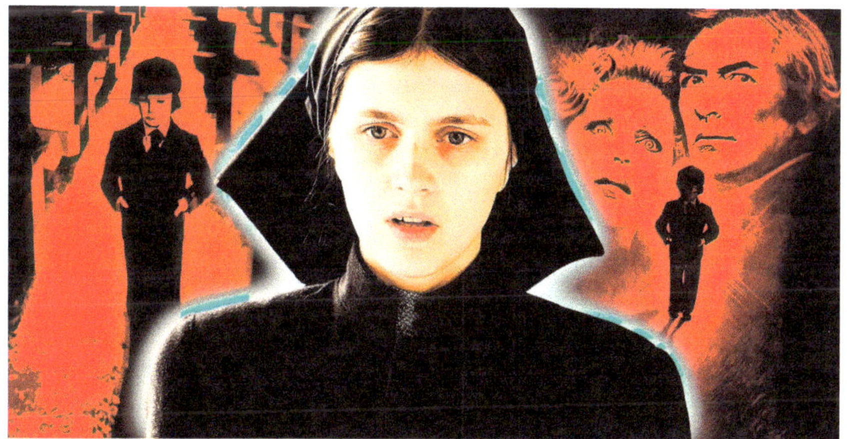

When I began analyzing films on my website some 15 years ago, it was unthinkable that Hollywood could see its end anytime soon. Since that time, and at the conclusion of this Esoteric Hollywood trilogy, the machine known as Hollywood and its classical studio system is on its way out. I recently had the opportunity to interview Hollywood luminary and comedy legend Jamie Kennedy, who opined that "Hollywood is done." With the rise of the Internet and the challenge of masses of people competing for the entertainment slice of the pie, the legacy system cannot make it.

Instead, the studio system is giving way to video games and online streaming services like Apple Studios and Amazon Studios, replacing the older models. Network television, cable, news and television shows have all suffered tremendously as the world goes fully and perpetually online. While in many ways this is a positive thing, we can also surmise Hollywood already served its propaganda purposes, which could suggest why many studios were being sold off to Chinese companies years ago. In a weird way, analyzing Hollywood's portrayal of the apocalypse and Antichrist is symbolic, since Hollywood is undergoing its own little Apocalypse. While films like *The Omen* in the 70s kicked off a new wave of Christian Apocalypse inspired trends, the 1997 *Devil's Advocate* is much closer to a prophetic revealing of the deeper secrets of mankind's real temptation in our Information Age man as the Devil (played by Al Pacino explains):

> The next thousand years is right around the corner. Eddie Barzoon – take a good look, because he's the poster child for the next millennium. These people, it's no mystery where they come from.
>
> You sharpen the human appetite to the point where it can split atoms with its desire. You build egos the size of cathedrals. Fiber-optically connect the world to every eager impulse. Grease even the dullest dreams with these dollar-green, gold-plated fantasies until every human becomes an aspiring emperor – becomes his own god. Where can you go from there? And as we're scrambling from one deal to the next, who's got his eye on the planet? As the air thickens, the water sours, even the bees' honey takes on the metallic taste of radioactivity – and it just keeps coming, faster and faster.
>
> There's no chance to think, to prepare – it's 'buy futures,' 'sell futures,' when there is no future. We got a runaway train, boy! We got a billion Eddie Barzoons all jogging into the future. Every one of them getting ready to fist-fuck God's ex-planet, lick their fingers clean as they reach out toward their pristine cybernetic keyboards to tot up their fucking billable hours. And then it hits home! You gotta pay your own way, Eddie. It's a little late in the game to buy out now. Your belly's too full, your dick is sore, your eyes are bloodshot, and you're screaming for someone to help – but guess what? There's no one there! You're all alone, Eddie. You're God's special little creature.

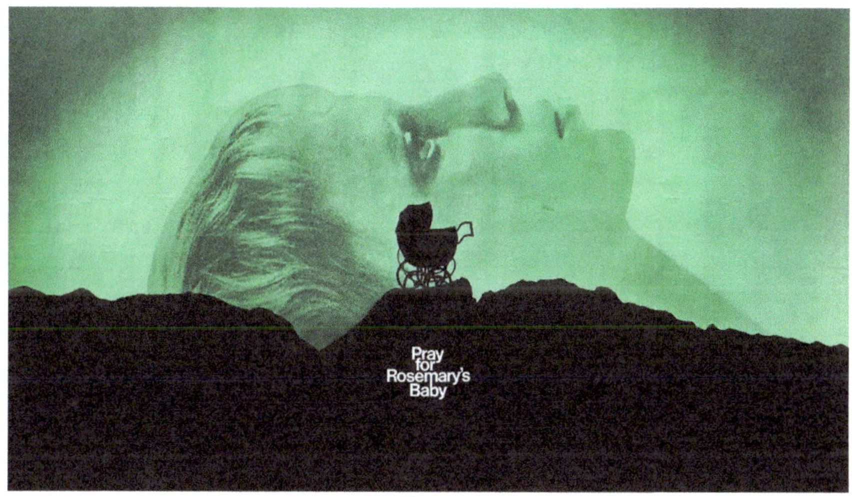

ROSEMARY'S BABY (1968)

Roman Polanski's film was a watershed for Hollywood occult filmmaking, as the devil became the star of a whole new genre of films, from *The Exorcist*, to *Suspiria* to *Demon Seed* and more, the 60s counter-cultural revolution and the succeeding years made the devil a movie star. The background for *Rosemary's Baby* was Pope Paul VI's visit to Yankee Stadium to perform a mass that inspired Ira Levin to write the novel that would become one of the most famous horror films of all time, wherein a young mother is brought into a Satanic cult to be impregnated by the Beast to give birth to the Antichrist and usher in a new *aeon*. Polanski was no stranger to the occult, marrying the famed beauty Sharon Tate who had reportedly been initiated into witchcraft on the set of the film *13* by famed witch Alex Sanders (as seen in the photo), after herself playing a witch in the human sacrifice based Satanic cult film, *Eye of the Devil* (a kind of *Eyes Wide Shut* style story some 30 years before Kubrick's classic).[185]

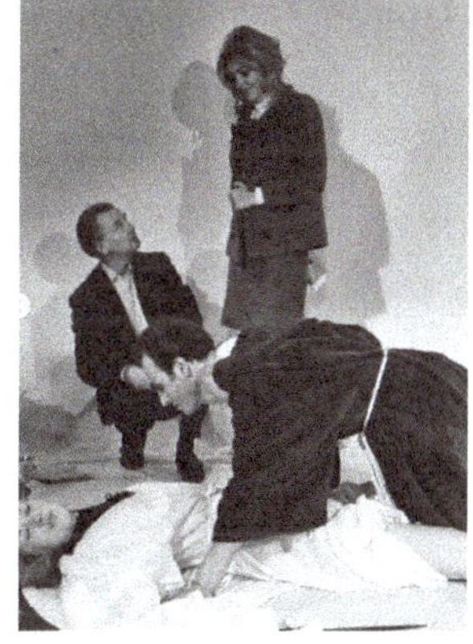

The eerie part of this connection is that a year after *Rosemary's Baby* premiered, Tate is among the victims of the infamous Manson murders, mirroring the role she played in *Eye of the Devil* as a human sacrifice. One of Tate's Manson killers, Susan Atkins, was a member of The Church of Satan and had played a vampire in LaVey's *Topless Witch Review*, while there is some debate on whether LaVey may have possibly been a "con-

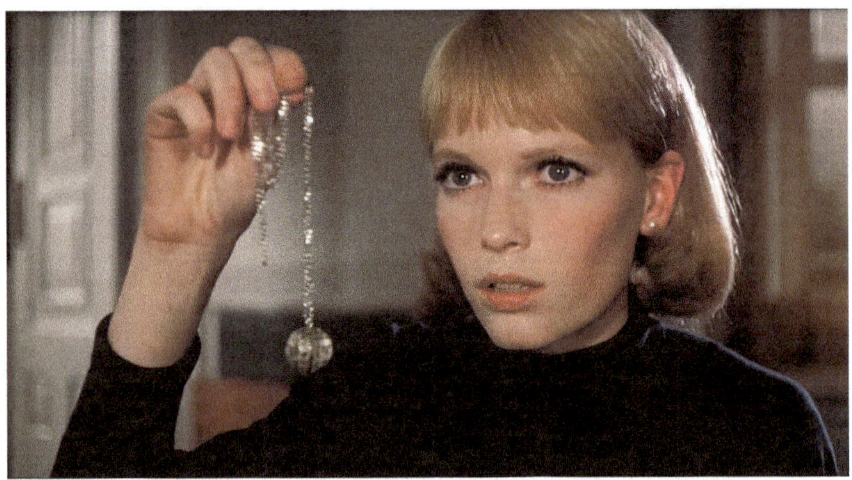

sultant" on the set of *Rosemary's Baby.[186]* The setting for the film, the infamous Dakota Building, would also be the site for the assassination of Beatle legend, John Lennon. In the film, a beautiful blonde (Mia Farrow) is newly wedded to a young, aspiring Hollywood star who ultimately offers his wife as a breeder to the coven for The Beast himself, brainwashing her with drugs, gaslighting and various psychological techniques. Eventually she succumbs to the coven in an eerie parallel with Sharon Tate, who also was perhaps offered to the Beast by the Manson cult.

Only a few years later, *The Exorcist* would shock audiences around the world with a new fear of the devil, but what few know is the CIA connection to the screenplay. William P. Blatty, author of the novel, was in fact a CIA psychological warfare expert in Vietnam! The *Ann Arbor Sun* reported in 1974 about Blatty:

After graduating from Georgetown University (where the campus scenes in the movie were shot), Blatty worked for the Central Intelligence Agency in Lebanon in the 1950's, under U.S. Information Agency cover. Later, he returned to Washington to become Policy Branch Chief of the Psychological Warfare Division of the U.S. Air Force. As such, his job involved the military's promotion of popular anti-communist sentiment around McCarthyism at home and Cold War foreign policy abroad.

An example of the work carried out by psychological warfare in U.S. foreign policy is the orchestrated exodus of Catholics from North to South Vietnam in the mid-fifties. In collaboration with Dr. Tom Dooley (whom Blatty quotes in his book) and others, an extensive campaign was carried out by the Catholic Relief Service, local Catholic leaders and an American psychological warfare team combined to drive peasants south of the DMZ by telling them "the Virgin Mary has departed from the north" and "Christ has gone to the south." Amateur as this appears now, "The mass flight was admittedly the result of an extensive, well-conducted, and in terms of its objective, very successful American psychological warfare operation." (from *The Indochina Story*, Bantam, 1970.)[187]

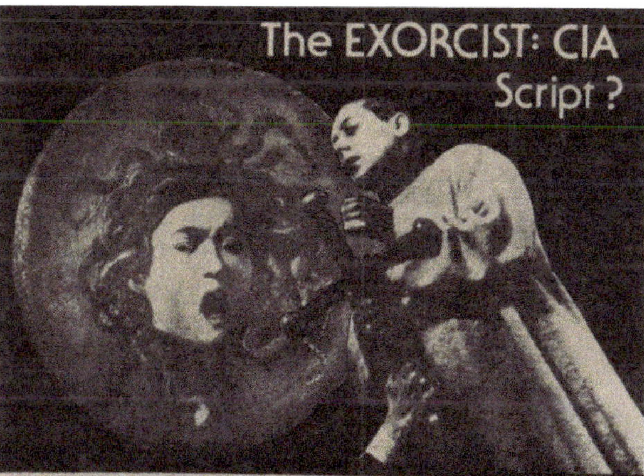

One of the most widely-advertised and popular, but least-understood films to reach the mass audiences in several years is The Exorcist, based on a novel by William Blatty. Some background on the author and his techniques in the book and film tend to explain the effect of Blatty's work on a mass audience.

After graduating from Georgetown University (where the campus scenes in the movie were shot), Blatty worked for the Central Intelligence Agency in Lebanon in the 1950's, under U.S. Information Agency cover. Later, he returned to Washington to become Policy Branch Chief of the Psychological Warfare Division of the U.S. Air Force. As such, his job involved the military's promotion of popular anti-communist sentiment around McCarthyism at home and Cold War foreign policy abroad.

An example of the work carried out by psychological warfare in U.S. foreign policy is the orchestrated exodus of Catholics from North to South Vietnam in the mid-fifties. In collaboration with Dr. Tom Dooley (whom Blatty quotes in his book) and others, an extensive campaign was carried out by the Catholic Relief Service, local Catholic leaders and an American psychological warfare team combined to drive peasants south of the DMZ by telling them "the Virgin Mary has departed from the north" and "Christ has gone to the south." Amateur as this appears now, "The mass flight was admittedly the result of an extensive, well-conducted, and in terms of its objective, very successful American psychological warfare operation." (from *The Indochina Story*, Bantam, 1970.)

In this post-'60's era, when a majority of youth on and off campus display a frustration with or an abandonment of traditional political "protest" activities, movie-going has enjoyed a sharp rise. This atmosphere has created a mass audience, one without specific political or spiritual direction and ripe for the suggestions which The Exorcist carries.

The techniques used by Blatty in his Exorcist were well-honed by years of practice in the government business. While in the fifties crude psychological warfare could be foisted on naive groups, Mr. Blatty's sophisticated talents have several messages in the mid-'70's.

*Social conscience and faith in our own identity is eclipsed by the threat of infestation by demonic forces (the devil). Or, to quote Father Merrin in his central role as the priest-exorciser, "...I think the demon's target is not the possessed; it is us... the observers...every person in this house. And I think the point is to make us despair, to reject our own humanity...to see ourselves as ultimately bestial; as ultimately vile and putrescent; without dignity; ugly unworthy. And there lies the heart of it, perhaps: in worthlessness. For I think belief in God is not a matter of reason at all: I think it finally is a matter of love; of accepting the possibility that God could love us..."

*Political activism is attacked by one of the main characters, Chris MacNeil, who condemns a campus demonstration by saying, "It's dumb! This scene is absolutely dumb! Her mind, though untutored, never mistook slogans for truth... And so the rebel cause, to her, was 'dumb.' It didn't make sense. How come? she wondered. Generation gap? That's a crock; I'm thirty-two. It's just plain dumb, that's all...!"

It is Blatty's message, then, that spiritual fixation and religious orthodoxy are, in the final analysis, at the service of political reaction. For religion, activated as a mass response to an externally conceived threat, can be a powerful ideological cement to keep the masses spellbound in a time of profound social crisis. For Blatty, the lessons of the 1955 Vietnam campaign have not been forgotten. Only the place and time have changed.

– (From *Counterspy*, the Journal of the Organizing Committe For a Fifth Estate.)

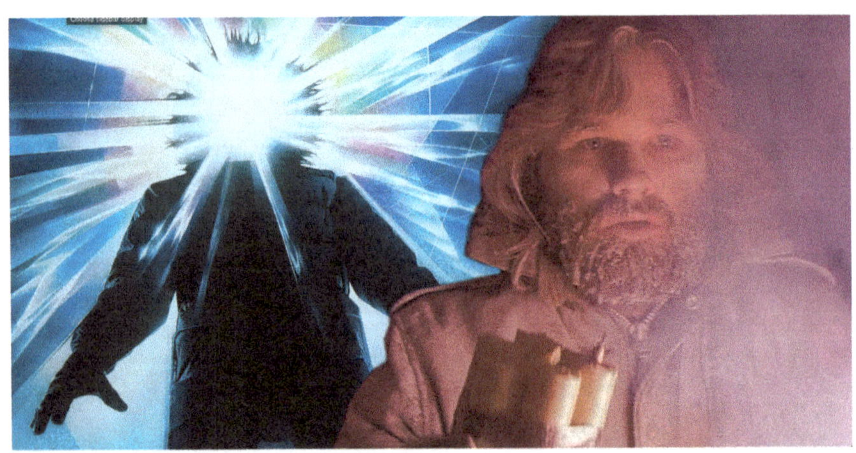

APOCALYPSE TRILOGY: *THE THING* (1982), *PRINCE OF DARKNESS* (1987) & *IN THE MOUTH OF MADNESS* (1994)

Although John Carpenter's 1982 *The Thing* is a remake of the classic Howard Hawks' film, it operates on several levels (since it's set in the Cold War) and functions as the first in what some call Carpenter's Apocalypse Trilogy. The Cold War setting for this film reveals the fears of an apocalyptic nuclear showdown between the US and the Soviet Union evident in the showdown between characters R.J. MacReady (Kurt Russell), who represents individualist Americana, and the collectivist alien entity, the Thing. The setting for the film is Antarctica, which was a neutral ground in the Cold War, as the US and Soviets had signed an Antarctic Treaty in 1959.

It is precisely this neutral ground that functions as the staging ground for the ancient communist alien's attempt at psychological manipulation of the Americans after having conquered the Norwegian scientists' outpost. The psychological tricks, deceptions and manipulation the entity engages in mirror many of the tactics and operations both East and West engaged in during this tumultuous time, including the ever-present fear of being nuked at any moment. This is why we see MacReady playing computer chess early on in the film, as he will have to play a game of chess with an entity that operates and acts much like a programmed bot, lacking

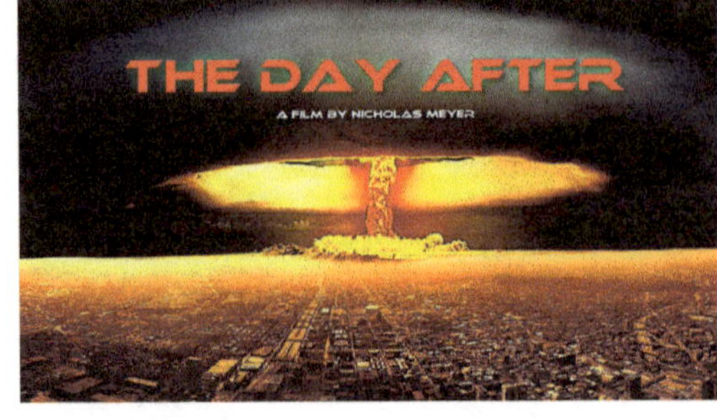

all free will. Indeed, the entity is a perfect mimic of whatever it takes over, morphing its host into a copy of the hive minded alien entity, removing all free volition under the cover of a genetically modified external body. Like the entity in the film, the Soviet East opposes, but also infiltrates, mimics and mirrors the West with the ultimate goal of producing a new collective man out of the dialectical conflict.

The Thing might also function as a warning about genetic modification as an apocalypse unleashing mad science enterprise, as events like Chernobyl frightened both the East and West concerning nuclear meltdowns and radiation mutations, as propaganda TV movies like the Reagan era *The Day After* warned in 1983, scaring a giant section of the nation (as it was one of the most viewed TV movies of the time). In *The Day After*, America ends up nuked in a mutually assured destruction kick off, where East and West destroy each other, while the survivors are left to disintegrate in the radiated wastelands. In *The Thing*, the theme of random mutations, although not caused by radiation, would have still been associated with nuclear mutations in the minds of Cold War psyop'd westerners. It might also be a subtle warning about GMOs and the dangers of genetic modification – something recent popular horror films like Apple's *The Gorge* (2025) have highlighted, where old Cold War nuclear test zones have created entire communities of mutated entities hidden away behind a secret US/Russia treaty, as both powers sought to research the creation of genetically modified super soldiers.[188]

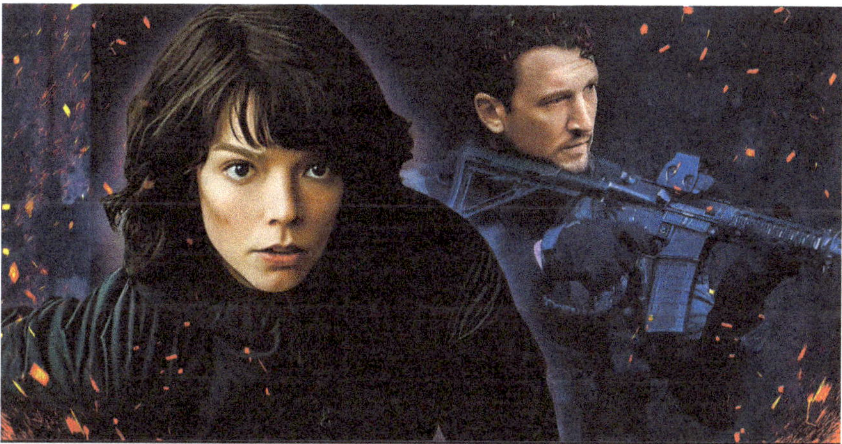

John Carpenter's *Prince of Darkness* (1987) makes up the second film in his "Apocalypse Trilogy," followed by *In the Mouth of Madness*. The plot to *Prince of Darkness* is so wacky and over the top, it bears analyzing just for the pure fun of it. In this 80s treasure, Carpenter treats us to a blender mix of faith meeting reason, quantum physics, Satanism and Gnosticism – all in one massive smorgasbord, guaranteed to satiate the campiest palate. As an added bonus – writer "Martin Quatermass" is none other than John Carpenter himself giving a nod to the British science fiction series classic, *Professor Quatermass*. And for a double double bonus – school may be out for Summer, but detention is just beginning, as Alice Cooper is featured as the leader of the gang of hobo zombies that lock our science team in the abandoned church.

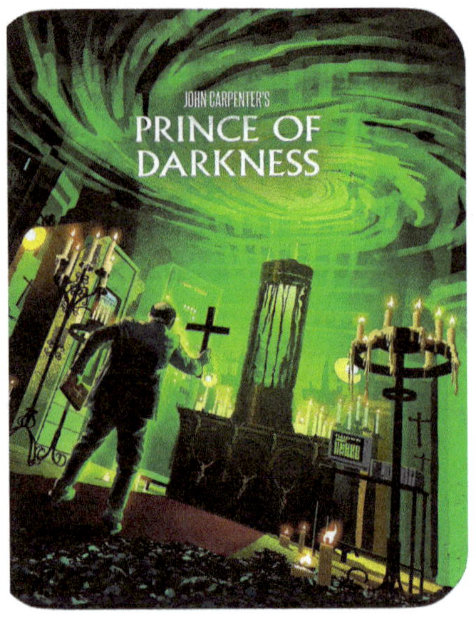

We'll never know what combination of Stephen Hawking documentaries and hallucinogens Carpenter was on when he concocted this oddity, but we can always be grateful, as the powers of darkness seem to have been invoked. Our film begins with the blonde half of the 80s hit show, *Simon and Simon* (Jameson Parker) noticing the strange stellar phenomena of the syzygy, a conjunction of the sun and moon. In astronomy, the syzygy is an *occultation,* where an apparently larger body passes in front of a smaller one, and as with almost all ancient mythology, signifies some massive shift in globo-political settings. For Simon and Not-Simon, it signifies the end of all (where's the buddy cop when you need him?).

Mystified by these sequences, the audience sees a pile of bugs gathering outside a physics lecture from the great Victor Wong as the appropriately Asian-named "Professor Howard Birack." "Time and matter," Professor Wong explains, "and order – order exists, but it is not what we had in mind." Time was thought to be an arrow, but Newtonian physics has collapsed with the rise of quantum mechanics and for this, we should have been more Zen, the good professor untangles.

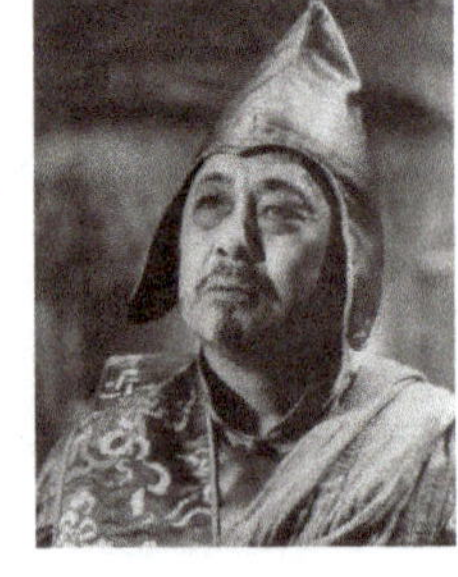

While on the surface, the scientific establishment is at war with "faith" in the film, we discover the professor is a secret pal of Fr. Donald Pleasance. Before we launch into that, however, it is worth noting Victor Wong in real life studied under liberal theologians Paul Tillich, Reinhold

Neibuhr and Martin Buber, while later studying under Frankfurt School and CIA-affiliated "abstract" artists like Mark Rothko. Not only that, but Wong reportedly died the evening of September 11, 2001, one of the last century's pivotal events, curiously mirroring the pivotal cosmic events in Carpenter's film.

The professor and Fr. Pleasance meet to discuss a plastic treasure chest of secrets left by an esoteric "Brotherhood of Sleep" society, operating in the underground and viewed askance by official Vatican bureaucrats. Is Carpenter hinting at what is really the case with the Vatican "underground," being controlled by a Satanic network? This is argued to be real in books like William Henry's *Lucifer's Lodge*, where a steady stream of ritual Satanists have risen even to the levels of papacy (as well as being backed up by the books of controversial figure Malachi Martin). For Carpenter, however, the secret Brotherhood of Sleep is marked by the enigmatic phrase "The sleeper must awaken," oddly reminiscent of Frank Herbert's *Dune*. The meaning seems to be that the appointed time has arrived for the externalization of the hierarchy, where the cryptocracy will emerge to invoke the whore of Babylon and inaugurate the last days in a Crowleyan fashion.

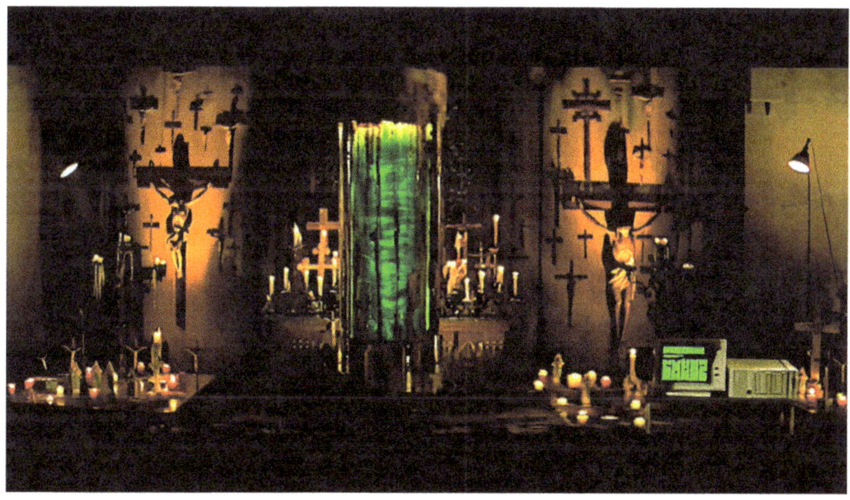

Pure concentrated Satanic matter, known as Nyquil. The Brotherhood of Sleep's Crypt.

This is all made evident when a computer scientist eventually decodes the Brotherhood's cipher, written in Coptic, Latin and ... differential equations. The overtly alchemical text suggests the mysterious vat of green goo stashed in the private crypt of the Brotherhood is the source of all cosmic evil, stated by Fr. Pleasance to be *substance* itself. In fact, Fr. Pleasance even notes that the Church intentionally sold people a fable that evil was a matter of the heart, when all along – it was matter, substance – basically the same green goo from Nickelodeon.

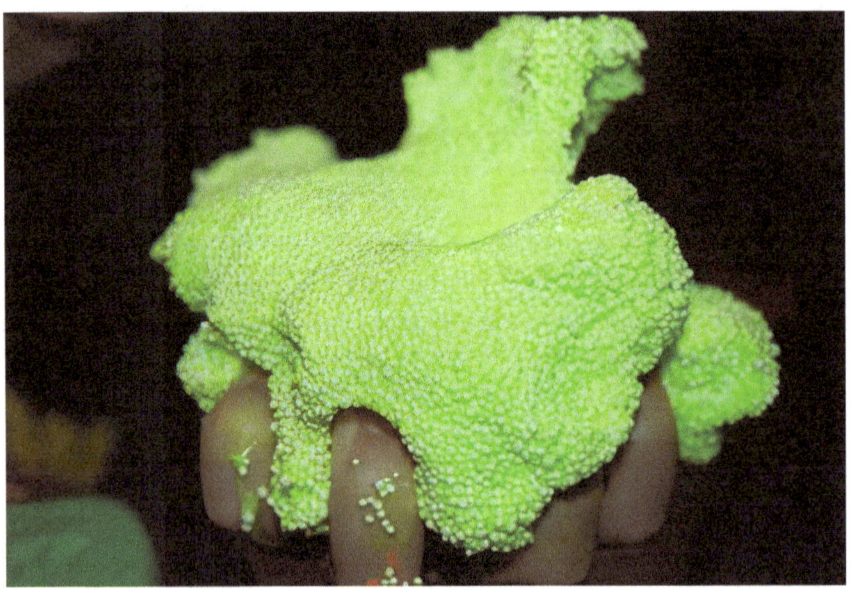

The differential equations translate as:

"So he carried me away in the spirit into the wilderness: and I saw a woman sit upon a scarlet colored beast, full of names of blasphemy, having seven heads and ten horns. And the woman was arrayed in purple and scarlet color, and decked with gold and precious stones and pearls, having a golden cup in her hand full of abominations and filthiness of her fornication: And upon her forehead was a name written, MYSTERY, BABYLON THE GREAT, THE MOTHER OF HARLOTS AND ABOMINATIONS OF THE EARTH." (Apoc. 17:3-5)

Who knew times tables were so esoteric!? As the team of scientists assigned to study the Satanic Nyquil unravel more algorithms, evil (identified as anti-matter, and thus an "Anti-god") transmits messages through subatomic tachyon particles (for those who have not seen the film, I am not making this up – John Carpenter truly peered into the *Mouth of Madness*). The future transmission is revealed to be a *warning* from the future, the year 1-9-9-9 (ie, 666) to prevent the arrival of the Anti-God in the flesh, *the Antichrist*! As the team is busy doing their esoteric homework, the possessed homeless have trapped them inside the church to ensure the birth of the Antichrist (through one of the bland, frumpy, unnamed

80s actresses). Heading up this gang is Alice Cooper, who *really* enjoys bugs and stabbing people. The Anti-God dispenses with natural birth, entering our reality as the Antichrist through a mirror into the psyche of whoever gazes into the reflection.

The Antichrist is barely defeated, we think, by the mirror being destroyed, but the moral of the story is simple and poignant. Beware of Fr. Donald Pleasance – or any Roman Catholic priests that have the face and head of a large baby. Jameson Parker could be our only hope against the Antichrist. Also, remember to not join any religious orders that go by the name of Brotherhood of Sleep, and avoid Nyquil, as it is actually concentrated Satanic evil. Quantum physics is Zen, and if you love a hot redhead, keep her away from mirrors and do not mess with any bands of homeless hobos led by Alice Cooper – you will get no more Mr. Nice guy treatment.

Carpenter's 1994 *In the Mouth of Madness* is a fascinating conclusion to the trilogy which plays with reality on multiple levels: it is partly a psychological journey into insanity, partly an end times Apocalypse film, and partly a Lovecraft inspired monster horror. The film's ultimate meaning as a metaphysical horror seems to be that an author (modelled on Stephen King) named Sutter Cane (Jurgen Prochnow) is the means by which the Apocalypse comes about through his writings actually manifesting the end times into reality. Because Cane's writings are so popular, the entire world begins to believe they *are* reality, thus manifesting a kind of collective unconscious portal for the "old ones," the demon gods of Lovecraft lore, to enter our realm. The film is thus the mental journey of the main character, John Trent (played by Sam Neil) on the path of discovering he himself is a character in a story written by the Cane, Antichrist, which drives him to madness.

As the Antichrist appears, it is interesting to note he infects children (making them demons) and possesses an entire town called Hobb's End, representing America. His appearance and entrance occurs in a giant Orthodox Church in the middle of the city, as the pages of the novel become ritual portals for his demonic hosts to enter. This is curiously close to Jack Parson's attempt to invoke the Antichrist through his infamous Babalon Working, where the ritual magician can be the cause of the end times, through the impregnation of the Scarlet Woman, the Whore of Babylon, who happened to be the girlfriend Hubbard had taken from Parsons. These ritual workings occurred in 1946 and were based on the Thelemic principles laid down by Aleister Crowley. Carpenter's film also includes the breaking of the 4th wall, as Trent sees himself watching the film he

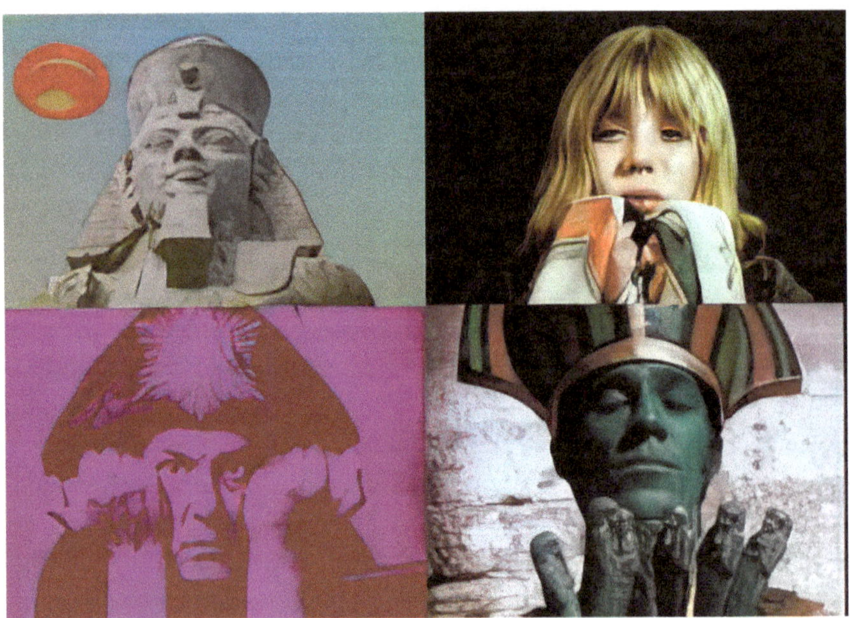

is in as he goes mad, which tells the viewer the movie itself is perhaps a portal for the emergence of that world into our world! In other words, in Carpenter's portrayal, Hollywood is a kind of Babylon, a mother of harlots and of all abominations. Crowleyan devotee Kenneth Anger, director of various influential *avante garde* films like *Inauguration of the Pleasure Dome* and *Lucifer Rising,* called his famous books *Hollywood Babylon* with good reason.[189]

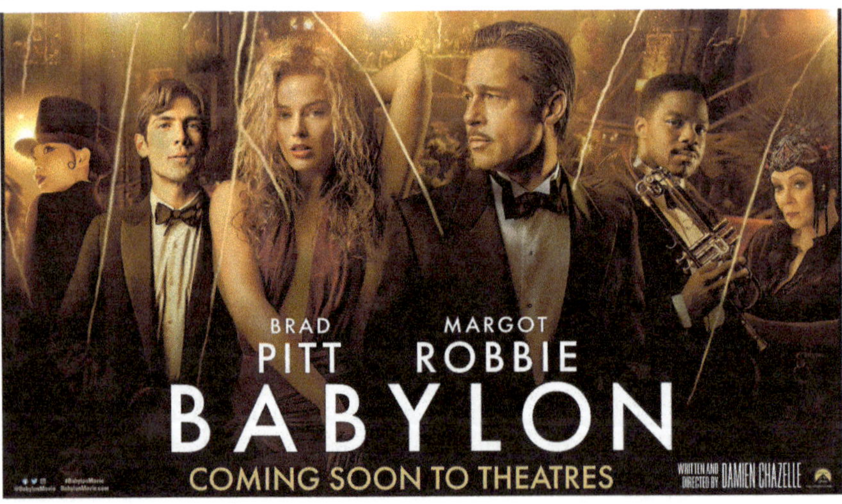

Conclusion

When I began this series a decade ago, Hollywood still reigned supreme in the domain of entertainment, with billions of dollars in revenue for blockbusters and the newly emerging streaming services. People still cared about celebrity culture and yearly revenue for US films was still over 10 billion dollars per year. Almost a decade later, after the Covid lockdown world, box office revenue is down billions and theater attendance is drastically smaller. It is possible for the system to recover, but the lockdowns conditioned many to rely on streaming, while younger audiences have had their minds damaged from endless 30 second scrolling clips via Tik Tok. In fact, many in the Gen Z and Gen Alpha sectors are unable to read a single book or even retain the attention span for a 2 hour film.

This dystopian "brain rot" and synthetic "AI girlfriends" were highlighted and warned about in the previous installments' chapters on films like *Blade Runner, AI, Her*. Likewise, the "alien mythos" we saw in so many films of the last several decades also came to its predictive fruition as the government has now "officially" stated there are "unexplained" craft and phenomena which also curiously parallel advancements in drone technology and non-lethal warfare options. This "alien" covert operation was something the *Esoteric Hollywood* installments stressed, whether it was Spielberg's classics or more recent Tom Cruise films, the appeal of the unknown is ripe for psychological manipulation.

Esoteric Hollywood also called readers' attention to sexual blackmail and the connection of these honey trap operations as we have seen with figures like Epstein and the amazing parallels with films like Kubrick's *Eyes Wide Shut* and aspects of Ian Fleming's 007 installments. In films like *SPECTRE*, we see something akin to the Bilderberg Group, while in the Kubrick canon itself we see repeated warnings the elite prefer pedophilic blackmail for their upper rungs. *Esoteric Hollywood* also called attention to the close connection and collaboration of intelligence agencies with Hollywood filmmakers and producers to capture the minds of the viewing world with the establishment's desired propaganda.

In other words, the CIA, FBI, the Pentagon, MI6, Israeli Mossad, the Nazis, Soviet KGB, etc., have all known the power of movies and have utilized them far more than even I would have suspected. Beyond that, we learned dozens of A-list (and B-list) actors and actresses have been utilized as spies, sexual honeytraps, assets and even operatives. What seemed like far-fetched conspiracy theorizing 20 years ago when I first encountered these ideas in classic books TrineDay published is now a well-known, established fact. Beyond this, it is now common knowledge Hollywood has long been obsessed with the occult and ritual magick, from films like David Lynch's *Lost Highway* or the epic *Twin Peaks* series, based on Tibetan Buddhist themes, or more recent installments like *True Detective* or Ari Aster (*Midsommar* & *Hereditary*) and Robert Eggers (*The VVitch*), all of which explicitly reference ritual and ceremonial magick, Hollywood was in fact recapitulating its earliest experimentation in Crowleyan motifs (as we saw here in volume 3's section 4).

Thus, with some degree of humility, I hope, I can stress the trilogy was not only ahead of its time, it has been largely vindicated. Indeed, even films that covered seemingly outlandish ideas like weather modification and geoengineering have been shown to be prophetic as we now see some states passing laws against geoengineering schemes. The final genre I didn't get to is unfortunately the darkest: "The End Times." Although there aren't that many quality end times and Apocalypse films, the few that do exist were worth covering in this final chapter. We are in an age of transitions, and many of the legacy systems are going away.

In this sense, Hollywood and mainstream media and entertainment are seeing their own mini-Apocalypse, as the digital replaces the analog. Perhaps most prophetic and apocalyptic is the rollout of Artificial Intelligence, which many believe will end millions of jobs and force us into some form of universal basic income credit based on some form of fedcoin. Indeed, if these dark visions do manifest, we may truly enter into an Antichrist system run by Terminator's Skynet. Perhaps Yeats' Second Coming Poem about the "rough beast that slouches toward Bethlehem" is more of a digital behemoth, a beast system now born onto the world stage – something so many dystopian films (and this trilogy) prophetically warn.

ENDNOTES

1   Marks, John. *Manchurian Candidate: The CIA and Mind Control*. WW Norton, 1991.

2   McGowan, Dave. *Weird Scenes Inside the Canyon: Laurel Canyon, Covert Ops & the Dark Heart of the Hippie Dream*. Headpress, 2014.

3   Spence, Dr. Richard. "The Link of Theosophy to Occultism & Espionage." WondriumDaily.com. Web. 2020. https://web.archive.org/web/20220324235038/https://www.wondriumdaily.com/the-link-of-theosophy-to-occultism-and-espionage/

4   "Hollywood Spies." Documentary. Wichita Films from the National Archives. Web. 2017. https://www.wichitafilms.com/en/films/hollywood-spies/

5   Priest, Dana. "CIA Plans to Move Division to Denver." *Seattle Times*, May 6, 2005. Web. https://www.seattletimes.com/nation-world/cia-plans-to-move-division-to-denver/

6   RT International. "Dark Knight Rises Massacre." July 2012. Web. https://www.rt.com/news/shooting-dark-knight-rises-batman-denver-aurora-654/

7   Ratiu, Ioan. T*he Milner-Fabian Conspiracy*. Free Europe Books: Great Britain. 2016. Sutton, Antony. *Wall Street & The Bolshevik Revolution*. Clairview Books, 2012.

8   Dickey, Christopher. "The Shrink as Secret Agent: Jung, Hitler & The OSS." DailyBeast.com. Web. 2016. https://www.thedailybeast.com/the-shrink-as-secret-agent-jung-hitler-and-the-oss

9   Collins, Paul & Phillip. *Invoking the Beyond*. iUniverse, 2020. Alex Jones Interview with Dr. Bob Bowman: "Secret Space Program," August 18, 2011. https://web.archive.org/web/20170411060623/https://www.youtube.com/watch?v=hZxA6r_6R1g&feature=channel_video_title

10   Hoffman, Michael A. *Secret Societies and Psychological Warfare*. IHR: Coeur d'alene, Idaho, 2001,p 206.

11   Crowley, Aleister. Liber O Vel. Web. https://sacred-texts.com/oto/libero.htm

12   Hoffman,Ibid., 206.

13   Lagarde, Christine. "The Magic Number 7." National Press Club Lecture. Jan 15, 2014. Web. https://www.youtube.com/watch?v=9_BTX-KNZJ4

14   Estulin, Daniel. *The Bilderberg Group*. Oregon: Trine Day, 2009.

15   Jacosen, Annie. *The Pentagon's Brain*. Little Brown & Company, 2015. Alex Jones Interview with Dr. Bob Bowman: "Secret Space Program," August 18, 2011. https://web.archive.org/web/20170411060623/https://www.youtube.com/watch?v=hZxA6r_6R1g&feature=channel_video_title

16   "Human Species May Split in Two." BBC. Web. October 17, 2006. http://news.bbc.co.uk/1/hi/6057734.stm

17   Fas.org. Web. 2005. https://web.archive.org/web/20050629101428/http://www.fas.org/main/home.jsp

18   Novak, Matt. "DARPA Tried to Build Skynet in the 1980s." Gizmodo. Web. Dec. 18, 2023. https://gizmodo.com/darpa-tried-to-build-skynet-in-the-1980s-1451000652

19   "Ether Returns to Oust Dark Matter." Eurekaalert.org. Web. 2006. http://www.eurekalert.org/pub_releases/2006-08/ns-ert082306.php

20   "NRL Scientists Produce Densest Artificial Ionospheric Plamsa Clouds Using HAARP." Navy.mil. Web. 2013. https://web.archive.org/web/20161102091108/https://www.nrl.navy.mil/media/news-releases/2013/nrl-scientists-produce-densest-artificial-ionospheric-plasma-clouds-using-haarp

21   Tesla, Nikola. "1937 Prepared Statement by Nikola Tesla." Web. Teslauniverse.com. https://teslauniverse.com/nikola-tesla/articles/prepared-statement-nikola-tesla

22   Biello, David. "What is Geoengineering & Why is it Considered a Climate Change Solution?" *Scientific American*. Web. April 6, 2010. https://www.scientificamerican.com/article/geoengineering-and-climate-change/

23   Alex Jones Interview with Dr. Bob Bowman: "Secret Space Program," August 18, 2011. https://web.archive.org/web/20170411060623/https://www.youtube.com/watch?v=hZx-A6r_6R1g&feature=channel_video_title

24   Watson, Paul Joseph. "Thiel Wants Brain Chips to Replace Passwords." *Infowars*. Web. 2015.   https://web.archive.org/web/20160319050321/http://www.infowars.com/paypal-head-wants-brain-chips-to-replace-passwords/

25   RT International. "Romania Agreed to Host CIA Black Sites to be Accepted into NATO; Ex Spy Chief."Web. 2014. https://www.rt.com/news/214315-romania-cia-sites-nato/

26   Fricker, Richard. "Inslaw Octopus." *Wired*. Web. 1993. https://www.wired.com/1993/01/inslaw/

27   Lowenstein, Antony. "The Ultimate Goal of the NSA is Total Population Control." TheGuardian.com. Web. July 10, 2014. https://www.theguardian.com/commentisfree/2014/jul/11/the-ultimate-goal-of-the-nsa-is-total-population-control

28   Pizada, Usman. "The NSA Could Have Planted Permanent Backdoors in Intel & AMD Chips." Wccftech.com. Web. July 30, 2013. http://wccftech.com/intel-possibly-amd-chips-permanent-backdoors-planted-nsa-updated-1/

29   Crowley, Aleister. "Aeon." Thelemapedia.org. Web. http://www.thelemapedia.org/index.php/Aeon_of_Horus

30   Campbell, Joseph. *The Hero with a Thousand Faces*. California: New World Library, 1949, pg 77.

31   Hackard, Mark. "The Bolsheviks' Occult War." Espionagehistoryarchive.com. Web. April 16, 2016. https://espionagehistoryarchive.com/2016/04/16/the-bolsheviks-occult-war/

32   "Anthropotelemetry: Dr Schwitzgebel's Machine." *Harvard Law Review*. Web. https://www.jstor.org/stable/1339322

33   Taylor, Sid. "The History of Secret CIA Mind Control Research." *Nexus Magazine*. May 1992.   Web.   http://all.net/journal/deception/MKULTRA/www.profreedom.free4all.co.uk/skeletons_1.html

34   Taylor, Ibid.

35   Corbett, James. "Meet IN-Q-TEL, the CIA's Venture Capital Firm." CorbettReport.com. Web. https://corbettreport.com/flashback-inqtel/. See also Webb, Whitney. "The Military Origins of Facebook." UnlimitedHangout.com. Web. 2021. https://unlimitedhangout.com/2021/04/investigative-reports/the-military-origins-of-facebook/

36   Hickey, Walt. "25 Cutting Edge Firms Funded by the CIA." *Business Insider*. Web. https://www.businessinsider.com/25-cutting-edge-companies-funded-by-the-central-intelligence-agency-2012-8?op=1

37   Upbin, Bruce. "IBM's Watson Gets Its First Piece of Business in Healthcare." Forbes. Web. https://www.forbes.com/sites/bruceupbin/2013/02/08/ibms-watson-gets-its-first-piece-of-business-in-healthcare/

38   Cellan-Jones, Rory. "Office Puts Chips Under Staff's Skin." BBC. Web. https://www.bbc.com/news/technology-31042477

39   Phage Nanobiotech. Royal Society of Chemistry. Web. 2011. https://books.rsc.org/books/edited-volume/1269/Phage-Nanobiotechnology

40   Treffert, Donald. "Genetic Memory: How We Know Things We Never Learned." ScientificAmerican.com. Web. 2015. https://www.scientificamerican.com/blog/guest-blog/genetic-memory-how-we-know-things-we-never-learned1/

41   Hedegaard, Erik. "Who Killed JFK? The Last Confession of E. Howard Hunt." *Rollingstone*. April, 2007. Web. https://www.rollingstone.com/feature/the-last-confession-of-e-howard-hunt-76611/

42   Prouty, L. Fletcher. *The Secret Team: The CIA and its Allies in Control of America & The World*.

Skyhorse Publishing, 2008.

43   Valentine, Douglas. *The Phoenix Program*. iUniverse. 2000.

44   Russell, Bertrand. *Impact of Science on Society*. New York: Simon & Schuster, 1953, 103-4.

45   Harlan-Jacobs, Jessica. Builders of Empire: Freemasons & British Imperialism. University of North Carolina Press, 2013.

46   Perks, Martyn. "Gamification is Taking Over." Independent.co.uk. Web. 2014. https://www.independent.co.uk/games/gamification-is-taking-over-our-lives-and-it-all-came-from-video-games-9779149.html

47   https://www.theguardian.com/technology/2017/nov/09/facebook-sean-parker-vulnerability-brain-psychology

48   Collins, JC. "Synthetic Consciousness and Mass Communication." PhilosophyofMetrics.com. Web. 2014. https://web.archive.org/web/20141203060858/http://philosophyofmetrics.com/2014/11/17/synthetic-consciousness-and-mass-communication/

49   Karlgaard, Rich. "Why Does '666' Appear in Stock Panics?" Forbes.com. Web. 2011. https://www.forbes.com/sites/richkarlgaard/2011/08/09/why-does-666-appear-in-stock-panics/

50   "DSK's Eyes Wide Shut Lifestyle." Zerhedge.com. Web. 2012. https://www.zerohedge.com/news/2012-10-15/dsks-eyes-wide-shut-lifestyle-exposed

51   Bolton, Kerry. "Origins of the Cold War: How Stalin Foiled a 'New World Order.'" ForeignPolicyJournal.com. Web. 2010. https://www.foreignpolicyjournal.com/2010/05/31/origins-of-the-cold-war-how-stalin-foild-a-new-world-order/2/

52   Bolton, Ibid.

53   Hackard, Mark. "Bankster International." SouloftheEast.org. Web. 2014. https://markhackard.wordpress.com/2014/12/18/the-bankster-international/

54   Israel, Solomon. "Artificial Intelligence, Human Brain to Merge in 2030s says Ray Kurzweil." CBC. Web. 2015. https://www.cbc.ca/news/science/artificial-intelligence-human-brain-to-merge-in-2030s-says-futurist-kurzweil-1.3100124#:~:text=co%2Doperative%20future.-,He%20says%20the%20human%20brain%20will%20soon%20merge%20with%20computer,New%20York%20on%20June%203.

55   "The Mysteries of the Serpent," *Papers From the Eranos Yearbook*, pg. 211

56   Miller, Iona. "Introduction to Alchemy in Jungian Psychology." 1985. *TheModernAlchemist*. http://the-modern-alchemist.iwarp.com/whats_new_5.html

57   "Cruise Allegedly Tried to Convert His Vanilla Sky Co-Star Cruz to Scientology." Irishcentral.com. Web. 2013. https://www.irishcentral.com/culture/entertainment/tom-cruise-allegedly-tried-to-convert-his-vanilla-sky-co-star-penelope-cruz-to-scientology-211978781-237597551

58   Curiously, the opening sequence showing David's apartment is the notorious Dakota Building where John Lennon was assassinated and *Rosemary's Baby* was filmed.

59   Although it is gossip, it is important to note that in some cases tabloids have actually broken real stories, especially when other outlets would not. *The National Enquirer* did report in 2018 that Cruise was actually a believer in cryogenically freezing himself: NationalEnquirer.com. Web. 2018. https://www.nationalenquirer.com/photos/tom-cruise-scientology-death-freeze/

60   "Does Scientology Have a Concept of God?" Scientology.org. Web. https://www.scientology.org/faq/scientology-beliefs/what-is-the-concept-of-god-in-scientology.html

61   Lowenstein, Antony. "The Ultimate Goal of the NSA is Total Population Control." *TheGuardian*.com. 2014. Web. https://www.theguardian.com/commentisfree/2014/jul/11/the-ultimate-goal-of-the-nsa-is-total-population-control

62   Papadakis & Meyendorff. *The Christian East & The Rise of the Papacy*. Crestwood, NY: St. Vladimir's Seminary Press, 1994, pgs. 58-75.

63   Lee, Martin. "Their Will Be Done: Let the Pope's Keep the Kingdom and the Glory – the CIA Wants the Power." *Mother Jones*. July 1983. Web. https://www.motherjones.com/politics/1983/07/their-will-be-done/

64   Bamford, James. *The Puzzle Palace*.

65   "The Umbrella Man." JFK-online.com. Web. https://www.jfk-online.com/jfk100tum.html

66   "mRNA Vaccined – Here's What You Need to Know." WEForum.org. 2021. Web. https://www.weforum.org/agenda/2021/07/everything-you-need-to-know-about-mrna-vaccines/

67   Project Rand: Proceedings of the Second Protective Constructive Symposium (Deep Underground Construction) March 1959. Web. https://www.rand.org/content/dam/rand/pubs/reports/2022/R341z1.pdf

68   Rosenberg, Joel. "Can Novelists Predict the Future?" March, 2021. Crimereads.com. Web. https://crimereads.com/can-novelists-predict-the-future/

69   Harari, Yuval Noah. "The Myth of Freedom." *TheGuardian*. Web. Sept. 2018. https://www.theguardian.com/books/2018/sep/14/yuval-noah-harari-the-new-threat-to-liberal-democracy

70   The 2002 film *Cypher*, starring Jeremy Northam and Lucy Liu, seems to have been heavily influenced by this story, as Northham plays a corporate spy who is willingly mind controlled and mind wiped in order to work against a binary dialectical control system in a near-future dystopia run by 2 mega tech corporations. Morgan (Northam) is beyond the dialectic and thus infiltrates and takes down both companies by having his mind and memories wiped and later restored.

71   Hudson, Alex. "Memories Can Be Erased Manually." BBC. Web. 2014. https://www.bbc.com/news/newsbeat-27884495

72   Ibid.

73   Lachman, Gary. "Homuncli, Golems & Artificial Life." Theosophical.org. Web. 2006. https://web.archive.org/web/20151016160704/https://www.theosophical.org/publications/1253

74   "The Mysteries of the Serpent," *Papers From the Eranos Yearbook*, pg. 211

75   Dyer, Jay. "Egyptian Mysteries of God & Geopolitics." JaysAnalysis.com. Web. 2014. https://jaysanalysis.com/2014/03/23/egyptian-mysteries-of-god-and-energy-in-relation-to-modern-geopolitics/

76   Brinkman, Susan. "Mary Poppins and the Occult?" Blog. August 2023. https://www.womenofgrace.com/blog/80

77   Vachet, Helen. "Mary Poppins & The Puzzles of Paradox." Theosophical.org. Web. 2004. https://web.archive.org/web/20131025065856/https://www.theosophical.org/publications/1240

78   Begley, Sarah. "Mary Poppins Was the Original Disney Feminist." *Time*. Web. 2014. https://time.com/3178096/mary-poppins-feminist-anniversary/

79   Transcending the gender polarity is part of traditional hermetic and kabbalistic lore: see "Kabbalah" in *The Cambridge Handbook of Western Mysticism and Esotericism*. Cambridge, UK: Cambridge University Press. 2016, pg. 98.

80   Note that the same theme of creating a traumatized government super assassin is also present in Luc Besson's famed 1990 hit *La Femme Nikita*, although she is not a lesbian: she is masculinized, however.

81   Marinelli, Janet. "Bringing Back the Beasts: Global Rewilding Plans Take Shape." Yale.edu. Web. 2022. https://e360.yale.edu/features/large-mammals-rewilding-carbon-climate-change. See also "Rewilding." ICUN.org. Web. https://www.iucn.org/sites/default/files/2022-10/principles_of_rewilding_cem_rtg.pdf

82   "Agenda 21." UN.org. Web. https://sustainabledevelopment.un.org/milestones/unced/agenda21

83   Gioia, Ted. "How Did Silicon Valley Turn Into a Creepy Cult?" Honest-Broker.com. Web. 2024. https://www.honest-broker.com/p/how-did-silicon-valley-turn-into. De Witte, Melissa. "Silicon Valley Has Roots in Burning Man." Stanford.edu. Web. 2019. https://news.stanford.edu/stories/2018/08/burning-mans-influence-silicon-valley

84   Ibid.

85   Gennett, Ronnie. "Donald Rumsfeld and the Strange History of Aspartame." HuffingtonPost.com. Web. 2011. https://www.huffpost.com/entry/donald-rumsfeld-and-the-s_b_805581

86   Perciasepe, Robert. Letter to the EPA From American University in Washington. Web. 2013. https://www.epa.gov/sites/default/files/documents/tsca_21_petition_hfsa_2013-04-22.pdf

87   See Koestler, Arthur. *The Ghost in the Machine.* UK: One 70 Press, 1982.

88   Wilson, Colin. *Aleister Crowley: The Nature of the Beast*. Aeon Books, 2005.

89   See 2 Thess. 2:1-2: "Now, brethren, concerning the coming of our Lord Jesus Christ and our gathering together to Him, we ask you, 2 not to be soon shaken in mind or troubled, either by spirit or by word or by letter, as if from us, as though the day of Christ had come. 3 Let no one deceive you by any means; for that Day will not come unless the falling away comes first, and the

man of [b]sin is revealed, the son of perdition..."

90   Hall, Oliver. "Demon Seed: The Computer Had Her Mind, Now It Wanted Her Body." DangerousMinds.net. 2015. Web. https://dangerousminds.net/comments/demon_seed

91   Heimbichner, Craig. *Blood on the Altar*. Idaho: Independent History & Research, 2005, pgs. 46-51.

92   Bernouli, Rudolph. 'Spiritual Development in Alchemy," in *Spiritual Disciplines: Papers From the Eranos Yearbook*. New York, NY: Princeton University, 1960, pgs. 321-2.

93   Harari, Yuval Noah. *Homo Deus: A Brief History of Tomorrow*. UK: Penguin Books. 2015, 428.

94   Crowley, Aleister. *Moonchild*. York Beach, Maine: Weiser Books. 1994.

95   Lipson & Pollack. "The GOLEM Project." Brandeis.edu. Web. 2000. http://www.demo.cs.brandeis.edu/golem/

96   Saner, Emine. "Rose McGowan: Hollywood is Built on Sickness: It Operates Like a Cult." Guardian.com. Web. June 2018. https://www.theguardian.com/film/2018/jun/01/rose-mcgowan-interview-hollywood-is-built-on-sickness-it-operates-like-a-cult

97   This is also the plot of Brian De Palma's *The Fury* only 3 years earlier.

98   Salk, Jonas. *The Survival of the Wisest*. New York, NY: Harper & Row, 1973, 42-3.

99   Lilly, John C. *Programming and Metaprogramming in the Human Biocomputer*. New York, NY: Julian Press, 126-7.

100   Weiner, Norbert. *Cybernetics*. New Orleans, LA: Quid Pro Books, 1961, pgs. 22-3.

101   Bowart, Walter. *Operation Mind Control*. New Saucerian Press, 2017 (1977), pgs. 264-6, 269-74.

102   Jacobsen, Annie. *The Pentagon's Brain*. New York, NY: Little Brown & Co, 2015, pgs. 444-6.

103   Bostrom, Nick. "Are We Living In A Simulation?" Web. 2003. https://simulation-argument.com/simulation.pdf

104   Lawrence, Timothy. "On David Cronenberg: A Conversation." FilmFisher.com. Web. 2021. https://filmfisher.com/on-david-cronenberg/

105   Johnson, John. "Some Members of SRA Task Force Conted They Are Being Killed." LATimes.com. Web. Dec, 2013. https://www.latimes.com/archives/la-xpm-1992-12-13-me-4123-story.html

106   Frammolino & Newton. "Details Emerge of Close LAPD Ties to Simpson." LATimes.com. Web. 1995. https://www.latimes.com/archives/la-xpm-1995-02-02-mn-27324-story.html

107   Ruppert, Michael. *Crossing the Rubicon*. New Society Publishers: Canada, 2004, 216-19. Melanson, Philip. "CIA Ties to Local Police." *The Nation*. Web. 1983. https://www.cia.gov/reading-room/docs/CIA-RDP90-01208R000100200006-5.pdf

108   McGowan, Dave. *Programmed to Kill*. iUniverse, 2004.

109   Mank, Heard & Nelson. *Hollywood Hellfire Club*. Feral House. 2007. Sanders, Ed. *The Family*. Da Capo Press, 2002, 58, 460, 466.

110   Ross, Colin. *The CIA Doctors*. Richardson, TX: Manitou Communications, 2006, 222-3. See also Ross, Colin. *The Osiris Complex*. Canada: University of Toronto Press, 1994.

111   Weber, Bruce. "Chris Costner Sizemore, Patient Behind 3 Faces of Eve Dies at 89." NewYorkTimes.com. 2016. Web. https://www.nytimes.com/2016/08/06/us/chris-costner-sizemore-the-real-patient-behind-the-three-faces-of-eve-dies-at-89.html

112   Crowley, Aleister. "Liber Cheth vel Vallum Abiegni." Hermetic.com. Web. https://hermetic.com/crowley/libers/lib156

113   CTEC. "Dangerous Organizations & Bad Actors: Order of Nine Angles." September 29. 2023. Middlebury.edu. Web. https://www.middlebury.edu/institute/academics/centers-initiatives/ctec/publications/dangerous-organizations-and-bad-actors-order-nine. Garcia, Guy. "The Believers: Cult Murders in Mexico." Rollingstone.com. June, 1989. https://www.rollingstone.com/culture/culture-features/the-believers-cult-murders-in-mexico-53577/

114   McGowan, Dave. *Programmed to Kill*, pgs. 6-22. Kennedy, William. *Lucifer's Lodge: SRA in the Catholic Church*. South Egremont, MA: Reviviscimus Press, 2004. Bryant, Nick. The Franklin Scandal. Oregon: Trine Day, 2012.

115   Ortega, Tony. "Inside Kelly Preston's Deep Scientology Ties." DailyBeast.com. Web. July 19,

2020. https://www.thedailybeast.com/inside-kelly-prestons-deep-scientology-ties-she-was-hard-core

116   Kennedy, Deborah. "The Untold Truth of Sharon Tate." Grunge.com. Web. 2019. https://www.grunge.com/155509/the-untold-truth-of-sharon-tate/

117   See Lambert, Malcolm. *Medieval Heresy*. UK: Wiley-Blackwell, 2002.

118   Ibid, Kennedy, *Lucifer's Lodge*.

119   Staley, Michael. "Scintillations in Mauve: An Introduction to the Work of Kenneth Grant." StarfirePublishing.co.uk. Web. http://www.starfirepublishing.co.uk/Scintillations_in_Mauve.htm

120   Harms, Daniel & Gonce, John Wisdom. *The Necronomicon Files*. Newburyport, MA: Weiser Books, 2003,187.

121   Ibid, 187-8.

122   Levi, Eliphas. *Magic: A History of its Rites, Rituals & Mysteries*. Mineola, NY: Dover Publications, 2006 (1913), 258.

123   Barker, Clive. CliveBarker.info. Web. https://www.clivebarker.info/religion.html

124   "Project Bluebird." CIA.gov. Web. https://www.cia.gov/readingroom/docs/CIA-RDP83-01042R000800010003-1.pdf

125   Totaro, Donato. "Richard Stanley Interview." OffScreen.com. Web. 1997. https://offscreen.com/view/richard_stanley1

126   King & Schneider. *The First Global Revolution: A Report By the Council of the Club of Rome*. Pantheon Books: New York, 1991.

127   "Was Harry Houdini a Spy?" CIA.gov. Web. 2012. https://www.cia.gov/stories/story/was-houdini-a-spy/

128   "Early Films." ChurchofSatan.com. Web. https://www.churchofsatan.com/altar-early-devilry/. See also Blanche, Barton. *Secret Life of a Satanist*. Port Townsend, WA: Feral House, 2014.

129   *Three Faces of Eve* is also a 1957 film with similar plot and themes as Marnie.

130   Minnicino, Mchael. "How British Intelligence Shaped the Entertainment Industry." Larouchepub.com. Web. 1982. https://larouchepub.com/eiw/public/1982/eirv09n41-19821026/eirv09n41-19821026_060-how_british_intelligence_shaped.pdf

131   Gover, Dominic. "Satanic Savile Wore Devil Robes at Scarborough Sex Club." IBtimes. Web. 2013. https://www.ibtimes.co.uk/sex-abuse-club-victims-439231. Brown, Larisa. "Jimmy Savile was a Necropphiliac." DailyMail.Uk. Web. 2012. https://www.dailymail.co.uk/news/article-2221922/Jimmy-Savile-necrophiliac-says-colleague-Paul-Gambaccini.html

132   Kelley, James. "Prajapati-Purusa & Vedic Altar Construction." JaysAnalysis.com. Web. 2013. https://web.archive.org/web/20160809091306/https://jaysanalysis.com/2013/11/21/prajapati-purusa-and-vedic-altar-construction/

133   Koenig, Peter. "The Eleventh Degree of the Gnostic Church LVX." Scribd. Web. https://www.scribd.com/document/58746167/Gclvx-org-The-Eleventh-Degree-the-Gnostic-Church-of-LVX

134   Collins, Laura. "Babies in Black Dresses Abused…" DailyMail.Uk. Web. 2014. https://www.dailymail.co.uk/news/article-2580388/EXCLUSIVE-Babies-abused-laying-Pentagram-Satanic-writings-church-walls-devouring-cats-blood-The-twisted-confessions-pedophile-church-pastor-Louisiana-inspired-True-Detective.html

135   See Grant, Kenneth. *Aleister Crowley and the Hidden God*. Great Britain: Muller Limited, 1973.

136   St. Dionysius. The Celestial Hierarchy. Esoteric.MSU.edu. Web. https://esoteric.msu.edu/VolumeII/CelestialHierarchy.html

137   Robinson, Joanna. "Is This Creepy Real Life Secret Society the Key to True Detective Season 2?" VanityFair.com. Web. 2015. https://www.vanityfair.com/hollywood/2015/07/true-detective-season-2-bohemian-grove-secret-society-guerneville

138   Bunker, Dr. Robert. "Santa Muerte: Inspired and Ritualistic Killings." FBI.gov. Web. 2013. https://leb.fbi.gov/articles/featured-articles/santa-muerte-inspired-and-ritualistic-killings

139   Jung, C.G. *Archetypes of the Collective Unconscious*. New Jersey: Princeton University Press, 1959. Pg. 59.

140   'Ariel." Wiikipedia.com. Web. https://en.wikipedia.org/wiki/Ariel_(angel)

141   Clarke, Arthur C. "2001 Space Odyssey Interview." Youtube.com. July 30, 2009. Web. https://youtu.be/HEEtfhxLQbw

142   Cherubim, David. "Formulae and Ritual of the Middle Pillar." Praemonstro.com. Web. 1993. https://www.praemonstro.com/thelemic-lesser-ritual-of-the-hexag

143   "Klymene." Theoi.com. Web. http://www.theoi.com/Titan/TitanisKlymene.html

144   See http://www.trimondi.de/SDLE/Contents.htm.

145   "Ask Molly: Did the CIA Really Study Psychic Powers?" CIA.gov. Web. October, 2021. https://www.cia.gov/stories/story/ask-molly-did-cia-really-study-psychic-powers/#:~:text=-Four%20researchers%20from%20the%20American,spookier%20part%20of%20our%20past.

146   Sedley, David. "How Uri Geller Persuaded the CIA He Can Read Minds." Timesofisrael. com. Web. Jan 20, 2017. Web. https://www.timesofisrael.com/how-uri-geller-persuaded-the-cia-he-can-read-minds/

147   "Analysis and Assessment of Gateway Process." Cia.gov. Web. https://www.cia.gov/read-ingroom/docs/cia-rdp96-00788r001700210016-5.pdf

148   Of course King could also have read X-Men and seen the creation of Dark Phoenix as a character in 1976.

149   Winick, Stephen. 'What Was the Green Man?" Blogs.loc.gov. Web. Feb, 2021. https://blogs.loc.gov/folklife/2021/02/what-was-the-green-man/

150   Sipos & Botts. "The False Martyr & The Wicker Man." Web. TheOtherFolk.blog https://www.theotherfolk.blog/dissections/wicker-man

151   Sunshine, Lee. "Gerald Gardner & The Origins of Wicca." Breakpoint.org. Web. Jan, 2020.   https://www.breakpoint.org/gerald-gardner-and-the-origins-of-wicca-emerging-world-views-21/#:~:text=Gardner%20was%20also%20interested%20in,increasingly%20turned%20to%20promoting%20Wicca.

152   McDonald, Henry. "Satanic Panic: How British Stoked Supernatural Fears in Troubles." Guardian.org.Web. Oct, 2014. https://www.theguardian.com/uk-news/2014/oct/09/satanic-panic-british-agents-stoked-fears-troubles

153   Ramon, Tomey. "Rigged: FBI Informant Established One of the Largest Neo-Nazi Groups in USA." Corruption.News. Web. Sept, 2023. https://corruption.news/2023-09-26-fbi-informant-be-hind-major-neo-nazi-group.html

154   "Water Tunnel Found Beneath Mayan Ruin That Provided Ruler Path to Underworld." Guardian.org. Web. July, 2016. https://www.theguardian.com/world/2016/jul/25/palenque-mexi-co-pakal-underground-water-tunnel-system

155   Copeland, Miles. *Game of Nations*. New York: Simon & Schuster: 1969, 204-5.

156   "Angelina Jolie's Spy Advisor."Telegraph.co.uk. Web. 2010. https://www.telegraph.co.uk/culture/film/starsandstories/7934530/Angelina-Jolies-spy-advisor.html

157   "Tom Cruise Gives CIA a PR Boost." Guardian.org. Web. 2001. https://www.theguardian.com/film/2001/nov/01/berlinfilmfestival2003.festivals

158   "Hollywood's CIA Ties Exposed: Celebs or Secret Agents?" Sputnik. Web. Feb, 2025. https://sputnikglobe.com/20250206/hollywoods-cia-ties-exposed-celebs-or-special-agents-1121543706.html

159   Schou, Nicholas. "How the CIA Hoodwinked Hollywood." *TheAtlantic*. Web. July, 2016.https://www.theatlantic.com/entertainment/archive/2016/07/operation-tinsel-town-how-the-cia-manipulates-hollywood/491138/

160   Marchetti, Victor. "CIA to Admit Hunt Involvement." CIA.gov. Web. https://www.cia.gov/readingroom/docs/CIA-RDP81M00980R000600230023-6.pdf

161   Hackard, Mark. "Deception & Active Measures." EspionageHistoryArchive.org. Web. August, 2015. https://espionagehistoryarchive.com/2015/08/07/soviet-kgb-active-measures-disin-formation/

162   Bellerophon is the mythical Greek hero who slays monsters (the chimaera virus here).

163   "John McCloy." Spartacus-educational.com. Web. https://spartacus-educational.com/USAmccloyJ.htm

164   Jenkins, Tricia. *The CIA in Hollywood: How the Agency Shapes Film and Television* (UT Texas Austin Press: 2012), 74-5.

165   See Koehler, John. *Spies in the Vatican: The Soviet Union's Cold War Against the Vatican* (New York: Pegasus Books, 2009.

166   Hersh, Seymour. "How America Took Out the Nordstream Pipeline." Substack. Web. Feb, 2023. https://seymourhersh.substack.com/p/how-america-took-out-the-nord-stream

167   Balderson, Keelan. "Omagh Bombers Appeal: Evidence Suggests Prior Knowledge." Wideshut.co.uk. Web. Jan, 2011. https://wideshut.co.uk/omagh-bombers-appeal-evidence-sug-gests-false-flag/

168   Prouty, Col. Fletcher. *The Secret Team: The CIA and its Allies in Control of the USA and the World*. Web. https://www.ratical.org/ratville/JFK/ST/

169   Helton, Shawn. "What's Behind the Disappearance of MH370?" 21stCenturyWire. com. Web. March 2014. https://21stcenturywire.com/2014/03/11/whats-behind-the-disappear-ance-of-malaysian-airliner-mh370/

170   "Brandt: CIA Agent for 30 Years." *EIR*. Web. https://larouchepub.com/eiw/public/1975/eirv02n44-19751010/eirv02n44-19751010_011-brandt_30_year_cia_agent.pdf

171   See also Andrew & Green. *Stars & Spies: Intelligence Operations and the Entertainment Business*) London, Penguin Books, 2021).

172   "Sonia Wigert: Movie Star and Spy." AJB007.com. Web. Oct. 2019. https://www.ajb007.co.uk/discussion/50980/sonja-wigert-movie-star-and-spy

173   "Audrey Hepburn's Secret Life as a WW2 Resistance Spy." Spyscape.com. Web. https://spyscape.com/article/audrey-hepburns-secret-life-as-a-world-war-ii-spy

174   Kindy, Dave. "A Surprising Number of Celebrities Have Worked As Spies." Washing-tonPost.com. Web. Oct, 2023. https://img2.washingtonpost.com/history/2023/10/22/celebri-ty-spies-houdini-fleming-baker/

175   Ibid.

176   Andrew & Green. *Stars & Spies*, pg 194.

177   Ibid., 270-299.

178   Schmidt, Stephen. "James Stewart: Behind the Legend." Greenwichlibrary.org. Web. Oc-tober, 2015. https://www.greenwichlibrary.org/james-stewart/

179   "Sterling Hayden: The Hollywood Star that Left the Silver Screen to Become a Spy." CIA. gov. Web. July, 2021. https://www.cia.gov/stories/story/sterling-hayden-hollywood-star/

180   Kindy, "A Surprising Number of Celebrities Have Worked As Spies."

181   "How the CIA Helped Disney Conquer Florida." DailyBeast.com. Web. https://www.the-dailybeast.com/how-the-cia-helped-disney-conquer-florida/

182   Secker, Tom. "Documents Reveal How Ben Affleck Got Into the CIA, Promising to 'Do the Agency Proud.'"RT.com. Web. June, 2021. https://www.rt.com/op-ed/527187-ben-affleck-cia-agency/

183   Ibid.

184   Andrew & Green. *Stars & Spies*, 355-6.

185   Levenda, Peter. *Sinister Forces Vol. 1: The Nine* (Oregon: Trine Day, 2005), pgs. 304-6.

186   Baddely, Gavin. *Lucifer Rising: Sin, Devil Worship & Rock n Roll* (London: Plexus, 2006), 83-4.

187   "The Exorcist: CIA Script?" had . Aadl.org. Web. 1974. https://aadl.org/node/197187

188   It is also interesting to note that, once again, Anya-Taylor Joy is cast as a mind controlled operative / assassin in The Gorge.

189   Anger, Kenneth. "Kenneth Anger's Hollywood Babylon Documentary." 1991. https://www.youtube.com/watch?v=6zXbZtsPH3U

Index

Y

Z